# The Accountant
# as Business Advisor

# THE ACCOUNTANT
# AS BUSINESS ADVISOR

WILLIAM K. GROLLMAN, Editor

A Ronald Press Publication

**JOHN WILEY & SONS**

New York · Chichester · Brisbane · Toronto · Singapore

This publication is designed to provide accurate and
authoritative information in regard to the subject
matter covered. It is sold with the understanding that
the publisher is not engaged in rendering legal, accounting,
or other professional service. If legal advice or other
expert assistance is required, the services of a competent
professional person should be sought. *From a Declaration
of Principles jointly adopted by a Committee of the
American Bar Association and a Committee of Publishers.*

**Library of Congress Cataloging in Publication Data:**
Main entry under title:

The Accountant as business advisor.
    "A Ronald Press publication."
    1. Managerial accounting.  2. Accountants.
3. Business consultants.  I. Grollman, William K.,
1942–
HF5635.A198  1986      658.1'511       85-29449
ISBN 0-471-80255-7

Printed in the United States of America

10 9 8 7 6 5 4 3 2 1

# PREFACE

When I began my career in public accounting 20 years ago, the environment was vastly different from that of today. By almost any standard, public accounting was and is a noble profession. However, the metamorphosis that has taken place over the past 20 years is quite startling.

I had always believed that technical competence was the hallmark for success in any given profession. The emphasis in public accounting, however, has shifted toward marketing of professional services, affecting other professions in a similar manner. It is no longer sufficient to be merely "an excellent accountant." Firms now openly compete with each other for clients and professional talent, they advertise their wares in the mass media, they compete aggressively on the basis of fees, and they offer an increasing range of services that were virtually non-existent 20 years ago.

In order to compete fairly and aggressively, public accountants today must expand their services so that they are not just "excellent accountants" but are also trusted business advisors. This book covers many of the areas that public accountants are involved in today: financing the business, cash management, cost reduction techniques, fixed asset management, systems automation, taxes, business insurance, mergers and acquisitions, government regulation, employee and executive benefits, personal financial planning, and training. There are many other areas that we could have included, such as inventory control, energy management, strategic planning, and so on. This book is not intended to be an exhaustive study, but merely to cover some of the most important areas in which accountants serve as advisors.

My career has given me a unique perspective from which to edit this book. As Partner and National Director of an international public accounting firm for 11 years, I had the opportunity to observe first-hand some of the changes as they took place. In the public accounting sector, I have worked with firms ranging in size from one of the largest "Big Eight" firms to a medium-sized firm and on down to a smaller firm. Five years ago, I co-founded a firm that provides video-based educational services to all segments of the accounting and auditing industry. It is in this latter role of entrepreneur that I have had the opportunity to observe similar trends taking place in the internal auditing and management accounting fields. It is clear that both internal auditors and management accountants are becoming business advisors within their organizations, as is emphasized in Chapters 2 and 3 of this book.

In recognition of the trend toward business advisors, I feel that there is a need for a publication of this type and have assembled a broad spectrum of experts in their respective fields to help make this become a reality.

Not all accountants will identify with each of the chapters in this book. Some subjects may be more suited to a particular field of accounting than others. Similarly, what is basic information to one accountant may be more advanced information to another. Nevertheless, each accountant who recognizes his or her changing role will find several chapters of interest in this book. This publication will not provide all of the answers; one would need a separate book for each area to even approach that goal. However, I believe that this work will serve as a useful starting point for those accountants who seek to improve their competence as business advisors.

William K. Grollman

*New York, New York*
*April 1986*

# ACKNOWLEDGMENTS

I am indebted to many individuals for their help and assistance. Much of this help has been cumulative, rather than related to the narrow confines of this book. First, and above all, I wish to thank my mentor throughout my career, Dr. Emanuel Saxe, Dean Emeritus, Bernard Baruch College of the City University of New York. Manny is a gentleman and a scholar, and very few individuals deserve that accolade. He has been a trusted advisor, a source of motivation to excellence, an exemplar of ethical standards, and a good friend. I will be forever indebted to this great man.

The contributors to this book are leaders in their respective fields. I am thankful to each one and to them collectively as the true source of knowledge in this publication. Many of the contributors found the task of writing quite considerable in view of their normal work demands, but all saw fit to honor their commitments.

Richard Lynch, my acquisitions editor at John Wiley, directly encouraged me to write this book. Dick is a real professional, an unflappable optimist, and an individual with great initiative. His outstanding work qualities, as well as his keen sense of humor, helped get this author through many difficult moments.

Expert typing and handling of details by Tami LaRock and Laura Hayward also contributed in great measure to the completion of this book. Finally, I am grateful to the highly capable John Wiley staff, including Jeff Brown (who succeeded Dick Lynch), Sheck Cho, and Kathleen Kelly. It is a true pleasure to work with the Wiley team.

W.K.G.

# CONTENTS

# ABOUT THE EDITOR

**William K. Grollman** is Robert M. Schaeberle Professor of Accounting at Pace University, and President of the Center for Video Education, Inc., a leading producer of video-based education for accountants and auditors. He is a nationally known educator, author, and speaker. He has authored *Accounting Theory CPA Review Course,* National Protape Institute; *Inventory Observation and Valuation,* with Jack Fingerhut, Center for Video Education, Inc.; and *Professional Ethics,* with Ernest Pavlock, Center for Video Education Inc. In addition, he has written numerous articles for professional journals as well as several custom CVE courses for accountants, insurance companies, and securities firms. Previously, he was partner and National Director of Continuing Professional Education for Seidman & Seidman from 1970–1981. He served as Chairman of the AICPA National CPE Conference for Firms in 1978 and Co-Chairman in 1979. He began his career as an auditor with Coopers & Lybrand and consultant to Chase Manhattan Bank.

# CONTRIBUTORS

**Howard C. Alper** is President of Audit-Rate, Inc., insurance cost reduction consultants in Chicago. A CPCU and ARM, he has published numerous professional articles and has led seminars in insurance for accounting firms and the Illinois CPA Foundation.

**Raymond J. Beninato** is President of Raben Capital Growth Corp. He is both a CLU and CFP and is a member of the board of directors, Iona Insurance Institute. He speaks frequently to professional groups and is a member of the Westchester Estate Planning Council.

**Robert W. Colby** is consultant to CPA firms on practice management and quality control. A CPA, he resides in Fort Meyers, Fla. and is also author of *Auditing Practice Manual* (Warren, Gorham & Lamont).

**Kenneth O. Cole** is President of Cole International Consultants, Inc., a Marietta, GA firm which specializes in all phases of data processing and communications consulting. He was formerly National Director of Management Advisory Services for Seidman & Seidman.

**Donald Keller** is Professor in Managerial Accounting and Tax at California State University-Chico. A DBA, he was formerly Director of Technical Services for the National Association of Accountants.

**Alfred M. King** is managing Director of Professional Services for the National Association of Accountants, Montvale, NJ. He is Technical Advisor to the International Federation of Accountants and a former Regent of the Institute of Management Accountants. A CMA and MBA, he is a frequent author and speaker.

**Philip Kropatkin** is a former Assistant Inspector General for Auditing at the U.S. Department of Health and Human Services, is the author of *Audit Logic: A Guide to Successful Audits* (Wiley, 1984) and co-author with Richard P. Kusserow of *Management Principles for Asset Protection: Understanding the Criminal Equation* (Wiley, in press). He has served with and acted as advisor to many federal and state agencies, local governments, professional societies, and a number of private clients.

**Leon I. Lipner** is Associate Professor of Accounting and Taxation, Adelphi University, Garden City, NY, and Partner, Lipner, Jankowitz, Gordon & Co., Great Neck, NY. He is a CPA and MBA.

**George S. Miller** was the accountant, financial advisor and sales director for a corporation in Pittsburgh, PA before joining Center for Video Education, Inc. as Corporate Sales Director.

**Patricia S. Miller** is an educational design specialist at Center for Video Education, Inc. An MBA, she was previously a senior financial analyst with Gulf Oil Corporation.

**Joseph M. Morris** is Corporate Controller of Scientific Software-Intercomp, Inc. in Denver, CO. Mr. Morris is the author of *Acquisitions, Divestitures, and Corporate Joint Ventures* (Wiley, 1984).

**Richard M. Morris, III** is President of R.M. Morris and Associates, Inc., Dayton, OH, through which he serves as consultant to international audit departments. Both a CIA and CBA, he is a frequent author and public speaker.

**Felix Pomeranz** is Distinguished Lecturer and Director of the Center for Accounting, Auditing, and Tax Studies, Florida International University, Miami, FL. Mr. Pomeranz is the author of four textbooks including *Managing Capital Budgets* (Wiley, 1984); he has also written more than 100 articles, many of them at the leading edge of audit technology. He recently retired as a senior partner of Coopers & Lybrand; in addition, he directed the systems program of Westvaco Corporation, and the Management Auditing Program of American-Standard.

**Patrick L. Romano** is Director of Research, National Association of Accountants, Montvale, NJ. Previously, he was Controller and Vice President-Treasurer of Potters Industries, Inc. and Chief Financial Officer for Holmes Protection Inc. He is a frequent author and speaker, and is both a CMA and CPA.

**Donald Walsh** is Vice President and Manager of Community Development for Bank of America in San Francisco. In this capacity, he is involved in a variety of programs: financing for small businesses, housing for low-income families, volunteer community work, programs for bank employees, and a minority vendor program. Mr. Walsh is an MBA.

# The Accountant
# as Business Advisor

# PART 1

# Tools for Finding Problems and Opportunities

# CHAPTER 1

# THE INDEPENDENT PUBLIC ACCOUNTANT AS CONSULTANT AND ADVISOR

## Robert W. Colby

## EVOLUTION OF THE INDEPENDENT PUBLIC ACCOUNTANT AS CONSULTANT AND ADVISOR

In varying degrees, independent public accountants (certified public accountants, public accountants, and other noncertified individuals practicing public accounting)[1] have always served their clients in a capacity of consultant and advisor. Such activities historically have focused on areas of a client's operations that are directly or indirectly related to the accounting function, with which the CPA is obviously most familiar. Examples of such areas include accounting systems, inventory control systems, electronic data processing, tax and estate planning, budgeting, and financial control and reporting systems. It is common for clients to request advice from their accountants concerning specific, planned courses of action. Typical inquiries include:

Should our new business operate as a partnership or a corporation?

What sources of financing are available to us and can you assist us in obtaining the capital we need?

What information will prospective lenders require and can you help us to prepare it?

Should we purchase or lease the new equipment we require?

How can we provide for continuity of the business in the event of the death of one of the owners?

What steps should we take before year-end to minimize our tax liabilities?

---

[1] For our purposes we will use the terms *certified public accountant* (CPA), *public accountant*, and *independent public accountant* interchangeably when referring to those practicing public accounting.

Clients typically consider their accountants to be their principal source of guidance on matters such as these for several reasons. One, most of the matters are either tax-related or accounting-related, so they are clearly within the accountant's realm of expertise. Two, the in-depth knowledge of the client's finances and operations possessed by the accountant provides an excellent basis for rendering sound advice on such matters. Third, the client not only has confidence in the accountant's technical competence but, very important, in his or her independence and objectivity.

The CPA's reputation for independence and objectivity emanates primarily from their traditional role as auditors of historical financial statements prepared by their clients. In recent years, the so-called attest function has been expanded to include engagements to report on matters and forms of information other than financial statements, including financial forecasts and projections, results of statistical surveys, market feasibility studies, computer software performance, systems of internal accounting control, union election results, contract costs, and so forth.

The expansion of the CPA's attest function has induced the American Institute of Certified Public Acountants (AICPA) to propose a new set of professional standards called *attestation standards*. These new standards would apply to those engagements in which an AICPA member expresses a conclusion in writing with respect to the reliability of an assertion that is the responsibility of one party where another (third) party relies, or reasonably might be expected to rely, on the conclusion, as is the case in an engagement to audit or review a client's financial statements. Although the attestation standards would not apply to tax and management advisory services (MAS) performed by AICPA members, they are mentioned here to emphasize the ever-changing and expanding role of the CPA in our society caused, in large part, by the very high regard in which the accountant is held by the general public and business community.

Several recent studies have shown that the accountant is considered to be the business executive's most trusted advisor, particularly in the small-business environment. For example, in the study "Meeting the Needs of Private Companies" sponsored and published in 1983 by Peat, Marwick, Mitchell & Company, the results indicated that "the external accountant is the primary business advisor." In eight of 10 areas of need of advice (e.g., internal accounting controls, compliance with government regulations, cash management, planning, raising capital, etc.) the external accountant was rated higher in terms of serving the need than any other professional group, such as attorneys or bankers.

Similar results were obtained in a 1983 study conducted for Chemical Bank ("Small Business Speaks: The Chemical Bank Report"). Over half of the entrepreneurs who participated in the study stated that when they have to make a business decision, they are most likely to turn first to their accountant. The six ways in which the entrepreneurs surveyed believe the accountant is most helpful are:

1.   Analysis of financial statements
2.   Tax planning
3.   Helping to understand the business' performance
4.   Advice on systems for better management information
5.   Locating equity financing
6.   Structuring loans

The study results also indicate that the most important characteristics in choosing an accountant are the entrepreneur's personal trust and confidence in the individual. Recommendations of friends or associates were also considered to be important factors in the selection process. Such studies serve to highlight the unique position of the CPA and the many opportunities that are available to him or her to expand the scope of consulting services.

## SCOPE OF CONSULTING SERVICES

There can be a fine line between acting as a buisness advisor to a client and undertaking a full-fledged consulting engagement. In fact, many areas in which an accountant functions as a business advisor later become consulting engagements. The distinction is more clear-cut in larger firms in which separate departments perform MAS work. However, even in these firms audit partners will serve as business advisors and call in MAS experts as needed. Consulting involves providing professional or expert advice. It encompasses a myriad of activities engaged in by various professional disciplines, including law, medicine, engineering, and accounting. The more narrow term *management consulting* is widely used to describe the endeavor of helping to solve the management and operating problems of businesses and other organizations. There is no clear-cut or authoritative definition of what management consulting does or does not entail, however, although several professional organizations in the consulting field have developed and promulgated definitions. For example, the Association of Consulting Management Engineers (ACME), in its advertising brochure, defines management consulting as follows:

> Management consulting is the professional service performed by specially trained and experienced persons in helping managers identify and solve managerial and operating problems of the various institutions of our society; in recommending

practical solutions to these problems; and helping to implement them when necessary. This professional service focuses on improving the managerial, operating, and economic performance of these institutions.

The foregoing definition certainly applies to many of the types of consulting services rendered by accountants. In fact, in recent years some of the major CPA firms have begun to identify themselves as "certified public accountants and management consultants" or use similar descriptions that emphasize their consulting capabilities. The consulting activities of some of the major CPA firms are so extensive that according to *Consultant News*, five of the top 10, and nine of the top 30 consulting firms in the United States are CPA firms. Annual growth rates for consulting services currently being experienced by the major CPA firms typically range from 15 to 25 percent, and there have been several recent instances where these firms have acquired substantial management consulting firms.

Although various terms are used to describe management consulting services rendered by CPA firms (e.g., general business consulting, management information consulting, and systems consulting), these services are most often referred to as *MAS*. The AICPA, in its Statement on Standards for Management Advisory Services (SSMAS) No. 1, defines MAS as "the management consulting function of providing advice and technical assistance where the primary purpose is to help the client improve the use of its capabilities and resources to achieve its objectives." SSMAS No. 1 further states that MAS activities may involve:

**a.** Counseling management in its analysis, planning, organizing, operating, and controlling functions.

**b.** Conducting special studies, preparing recommendations, proposing plans and programs, and providing advice and technical assistance in their implementation.

**c.** Reviewing and suggesting improvement of policies, procedures, systems, methods, and organization relationships.

**d.** Introducing new ideas, concepts, and methods to management.

Generally, MAS activities are directed toward the achievement of one or more of the broad objectives of the client's management, such as improving profitability, improving information systems, improving organizational effectiveness and efficiency, or evaluating plans or projections. Examples of specific types of assistance that the CPA may render to help management achieve such objectives include:

Improving profitability

    Design of budgeting and cost control systems

Analyses of production costs and operating expenses

Design of inventory and production control systems

Improving information systems

Evaluation of electronic data processing requirements (hardware and software)

Design of cash management reporting systems

Design of cost accounting systems

Improving organizational effectiveness and efficiency

Performance of operational audits

Evaluation of organizational structure and human resource requirements

Development of compensation programs

Evaluating plans or projections

Assist with development of strategic plans and short- and long-range projections and forecasts

Perform merger or acquisition and financial feasibility studies

Assist in structuring of financing arrangements

Many of these types of projects are discussed in depth in the remaining chapters of this book.

## APPLICABLE PROFESSIONAL STANDARDS AND SOURCES OF GUIDANCE

Members of the AICPA are rquired to adhere to the "general standards" contained in Rule 201 of the AICPA Rules of Conduct when performing any type of services for the public, including MAS. These standards are:

*Professional competence*. A member shall undertake only those engagements which he or his firm can reasonably expect to complete with professional competence.

*Due professional care*. A member shall exercise due professional care in the performance of an engagement.

*Planning and supervision*. A member shall adequately plan and supervise an engagement.

*Sufficient relevant data*. A member shall obtain sufficient relevant data to afford a reasonable basis for conclusions or recommendations in relation to an engagement.

*Forecasts*. A member shall not permit his name to be used in conjunction with any forecast of future transactions in a manner that may lead to the belief that the member vouches for the achievability of the forecast.

The standard relating to professional competence has some interesting implications with respect to the MAS area. For example, considering the broad range of possible MAS activities and projects discussed earlier in this chapter, is it possible for an accountant to possess the necessary competence to undertake any and all MAS engagements? Obviously not.

An accountant who is not computer-literate would be ill-advised to undertake an engagement to design and install a computerized accounting system for a client. However, an accountant need not be a computer expert to properly undertake such an engagement provided he or she (1) utilizes staff personnel (e.g., computer specialists) or outside consultants who are experts in the computer field and (2) has the ability to supervise and evaluate the quality of work performed by such individuals.

Interpretation 1 of Rule 201 states: "competence relates both to knowledge of the profession's standards, techniques and the technical subject matter involved, and to the capability to exercise sound judgment in applying such knowledge to each engagement." In other words, know when to call for help. If competent help is not available, the proper course of action is to suggest to the client that someone else be engaged to perform the services.

It has become a common practice, particularly among smaller accounting firms, to engage other firms or individuals to perform MAS engagements that require specialized technical knowledge on a subcontract basis. This type of arrangement is usually fair and mutually beneficial to all parties involved. Such arrangements enable a small firm to offer a broader range of services without investing in the hiring and training of specialists in various fields.

The CPA should, of course, carefullly investigate and evaluate the professional qualifications and reputation of prospective subcontractors prior to their engagement. It is also important to have good communications between the three parties to the arrangement during all phases of the engagement. Such communications might include planning memoranda, engagement progress reports, and preissuance reviews of any written reports to the client.

It has been the author's experience that CPAs are sometimes not as diligent in conforming with the general standards relating to planning, supervising, and obtaining sufficient relevant data in the conduct of MAS engagements as they are in the conduct of audit engagements. To illustrate, auditors are usually proficient in the documentation (generally in the form of a set of working papers) of every step or procedure planned and performed during the course of an audit engagement. There is also good documentation of the evidence examined that supports the conclusions reached, as well as evidence that work performed by assistants was reviewed by supervisory personnel (e.g., initials of reviewers and/ or completed review checklists). These disciplines are not always applied in the case of MAS engagements, perhaps because of inadequate training of non-CPA,

MAS specialists in the techniques of documentation of work performed and review of such work, or because the firm has not established its own policies and procedures for the conduct of MAS engagements, including those relating to planning, supervision, and review.

In 1982, the AICPA initiated a new series of authoritative (i.e., enforceable under Rules 201 and 204 of the AICPA Rules of Conduct) statements, SSMAS. The purposes of these statements, which are prepared and issued by the Management Advisory Services Executive Committee of the AICPA, are to provide guidance to enable members to comply with the general standards previously discussed and to establish (under Rule 204) other standards deemed appropriate for MAS. Rule 204 stipulates that:

> A member shall comply with other technical standards promulgated by bodies designated by Council to establish such standards, and departures therefrom must be justified by those who do not follow them.

Accordingly, any AICPA member involved in providing MAS to the public should be aware of, and conform with, the provisions of SSMASs, of which three have been issued to date. The complete text of these pronouncements is included in *AICPA Professional Standards*, Vol. 1, MS § 11.01–31.15 (AICPA, New York, 1985). The major provisions of the pronouncements are summarized here.

### SSMAS No. 1, "Definitions and Standards for MAS Practice"

MAS may range from a response to an inquiry to an extensive project. MAS are categorized as either MAS consultations or MAS engagements, for which professional practices will be different.

Definition of MAS (stated earlier in this chapter)

Definition of MAS engagement:

> That form of MAS in which an analytical approach and process is applied in a study or project. It typically involves more than an incidental effort devoted to some combination of activities relating to determination of client objectives, fact-finding, opportunity or problem definition, evaluation of alternatives, formulation of proposed action, communication of results, implementation, and follow-up.

Definition of MAS consultation:

> That form of MAS based mostly, if not entirely, on existing personal knowledge about the client, the circumstances, the technical matters involved, and the mutual intent of the parties. It generally involves advice or information given by a practitioner in a short time frame. Usually, information is received through discussions

with the client and, by mutual agreement, is accepted by the practitioner as represented. The nature of an MAS consultation and the basis for the practitioner's response are generally communicated to the client orally. The practitioner's response may be definitive when existing personal knowledge is deemed adequate; otherwise, it may be qualified, in which case limitations are stated. A qualified response often reflects cost, time, scope, or other limitations imposed by the client's specific circumstances.

### Definition of MAS practitioner:

Any Institute member in the practice of public accounting while engaged in the performance of an MAS service for a client, or any other individual who is carrying out MAS for a client on behalf of any Institute member.

General standards contained in Rule 201 (which were stated earlier) apply to both MAS engagements and MAS consultations.

### Technical standards for MAS engagements:

*Role of MAS practitioner*. In performing an MAS engagement, an MAS practitioner should not assume the role of management or take any positions that might impair the MAS practitioner's objectivity.

*Understanding with client*. An oral or written understanding should be reached with the client concerning the nature, scope, and limitations of the MAS engagement to be performed.

*Client benefit*. Since the potential benefits to be derived by the client are a major consideration in MAS engagements, such potential benefits should be viewed objectively and the client should be notified of reservations regarding them. In offering and providing MAS engagements, results should not be explicitly or implicitly guaranteed. When estimates of quantifiable results are presented, they should be clearly identified as estimates and the support for such estimates should be disclosed.

*Communications of results*. Significant information pertinent to the results of an MAS engagement, together with any limitations, qualifications, or reservations needed to assist the client in making its decision, should be communicated to the client orally or in writing.

### SSMAS No. 2, "MAS Engagements":

Professional competence to perform MAS engagements includes ability to (1) identify and define client needs, (2) select and supervise staff, (3) apply an analytical approach and process, (4) apply knowledge of the technical subject matter under consideration, (5) communicate recommendations effectively, and (6) assist in implementing recommendations, when required.

In deciding whether to undertake an MAS engagement, the MAS practitioner should carefully assess the combined abilities, education, and experience of the individuals who will participate in the engagement, including his or her staff, client personnel, and any persons engaged by him or her (e.g., outside specialists).

MAS engagements normally include a documented understanding with the client, either in the form of an accepted proposal letter, engagement letter, contract, or a file memorandum to document an oral understanding. Key elements of such an understanding would include:

Engagement objectives

Nature of services

Engagement scope

Roles, responsibilities, and relationships of all parties involved

Planned approach, major tasks and activities, and methods to be used

Work schedule

Manner in which engagement status and results are to be communicated

Fee arrangements

The understanding should be modified if circumstances require a significant change in the nature, scope, or limitations of services to be provided.

Before commencing an MAS engagement, the MAS practitioner should obtain an understanding of the possible tangible and/or intangible benefits that the client wishes to achieve. Results should not be guaranteed either explicitly or implicitly, and any reservations the MAS practitioner may have concerning the achievability of anticipated benefits should be communicated to the client. Any quantified potential benefits should be described as estimates, and the support for such estimates should be disclosed. Subsequent changes in estimated costs or benefits should be reported to the client.

An MAS engagement should be planned and supervised in a manner that provides reasonable assurance that it is conducted in accordance with (1) the understanding with the client, (2) SSMASs, and (3) the AICPA Rules of Conduct.

Key elements of engagement planning and supervision include (1) adequate staffing, (2) development of a detailed engagement plan, (3) proper supervision, and (4) an apporpriate level of documentation of work performed.

Sufficient relevant data should be obtained (by interview, observation, review of client documents, research, computation, and analysis) as needed to analyze the courses of action that might be considered and to support conclusions and recommendations. The nature and quantity of information required is a judgment determination considering (1) the objectives, nature, and scope of the engagement, (2) cost/benefit factors, (3) intended use of engagement results, and (4) related engagement circumstances. The source, reliability, and completeness of data obtained, as well as any limitations thereof, should be considered in forming and reviewing conclusions and recommendations.

The MAS practitioner's role is that of an objective advisor. The MAS practitioner should not assume the role of management. The roles and responsibilities of all parties should be clearly defined in the understanding with the client. The engagement should be structured to enable management to make necessary decisions or authorize courses of action, and to review and approve findings, conclusions, and recommendations.

Principal findings, conclusions, recommendations, or other results of an MAS engagement, including major facts and assumptions on which results are based, as well as any limitations, reservations, or other qualifications, should be communicated to the client either in writing or orally, depending on such factors as:

Understanding with the client

Extent of prior, interim communications

Intended use, significance, and sensitivity of results

Need for a formal record

Interim communication of results, particularly in lengthy or complex engagements is desirable. If final or interim reports are not in writing, a file memorandum outlining the results should be considered.

**SSMAS No. 3, "MAS Consultations":**

The nature of MAS consultations is such that they may:

Occur concurrently with the performance of other services for a client (e.g., audit, review, or compilation of financial statements, tax services, MAS engagements)

Constitute the only or major type of service performed for a client

Entail advice concerning a single matter or continuing consultations on various matters

Occur in a casual manner or setting

Entail specific written inquiries or responses

The basis for MAS consultations is usually the MAS practitioner's existing knowledge of the technical matters in question and those aspects of the client's financial, business, and perhaps, personal, affairs to which the inquiry applies. The client relies on the adivce given based on implicit and explicit understandings with the MAS practitioner. Examples of MAS consultations include advice in the form of specific recommendations, guidance on a suggested course of action, limited analysis of alternative courses of action, and limited technical research on a specific matter.

Due professional care in the context of MAS consultations includes making sure that advice furnished is clearly communicated, and that the advice and the manner in which it is given do not generate unwarranted reliance thereon. Planning steps in MAS consultations will usually be completed in a mental process that considers (1) The MAS practitioner's understanding of the inquiry and nature of service requested, (2) his or her knowledge of the client and subject matter of the inquiry, and (3) the steps to be taken to respond to the inquiry. If staff is used, the extent of supervision required will depend on their qualifications and experience.

When information furnished by the client in connection with an MAS consultation is not verified, corroborated, or reviewed by the MAS practitioner, as is often the case, the client should be informed that the advice given is dependent on the accuracy and completeness of the information. If the MAS practitioner decides that sufficient relevant information has not been obtained, he or she should consider whether his or her response should be qualified or withheld pending further study and analysis.

Technical standards for MAS consultations are identical to those stated earlier for MAS engagements, except for substitution of the term *consultation* for *engagement*.

The MAS practitioner should seek to minimize the possibility of the client concluding that he or she has assumed responsibility for making management decisions, guaranteed any benefits the client seeks, or that his or her advice is predicated on full consideration of all relevant information.

Because most aspects of MAS consultations involve oral communications, the MAS practitioner should take reasonable steps to avoid possible misunderstandings. In some cases it may be appropriate to communicate significant matters in writing.

The application of these standards in practice should not cause undue difficulty for the MAS practitioner except, perhaps, in the case of very small MAS engagements (e.g., an engagement to assist in the selection and installation of a microcomputer). The advantage of having such standards, and having them be enforceable under a professional code of conduct, is the protection and assurance of quality the standards provide to clients, who might otherwise select non-CPAs to serve their needs for consultation and advice. Conforming with the standards, which are generally based on good common sense and business practice, also protects the CPA, who is typically held to a higher standard of performance in the eyes of the general public in his or her endeavors than non-CPAs who offer consulting services to the public.

Consultations and MAS engagements are certainly not performed in a risk-free, or even a low-risk, environment. There have been many significant cases of litigation based on client dissatisfaction with the results obtained from consultants, including CPAs. The prudent MAS practitioner will consider the general and technical MAS standards promulgated by the AICPA to constitute the minimum requirements and develop good quality controls over its MAS practice, particularly in the areas of planning, supervision, and review, consultation, and professional development.

Subsequent chapters of this book examine in detail the process and steps involved in acting as an advisor in specific areas (e.g., cash management, cost reduction, inventory management, fixed asset management, systems automation). The AICPA publishes several series of practice aids in the MAS area that are also very valuable sources of guidance for MAS practitioners, particularly for those involved in serving smaller clients. The following publications are currently available:

**MAS Technical Consulting Practice Aids Series**

*No. 1 EDP Engagement Systems Planning and General Design*

*No. 2 Financial Model Preparation*

*No. 3 Financial Ratio Analysis*

*No. 4 EDP Engagement: Software Package Evaluation and Selection*

*No. 5 EDP Engagement: Assisting Clients in Software Contract Negotiations*

*No. 6 Assisting Clients in the Selection of Dedicated Word Processing Systems*

**MAS Small Business Consulting Practice Aids Series**

*No. 1 Assisting Small Business Clients in Obtaining Funds*

*No. 2 Identifying Client Problems: A Diagnostic Review Technique*

*No. 3 Assisting Clients in Maximizing Profits: A Diagnostic Approach*

*No. 4 Effective Inventory Management for Small Manufacturing Clients*

*No. 5 Assisting Clients in Determining Pricing for Manufactured Products*

**MAS Practice Administration Aids Series**

*No. 1 Developing an MAS Engagement Control Program*

Other AICPA publications of particular interest to MAS practitioners include MAS special reports on:

*Operational Audit Engagements* (1982)

*Operational Review of the EDP Function* (1978)

*Energy Conservation Studies Including Energy Audits* (1977)

*Environmental Cost/Benefit Studies* (1977)

*Introduction to Microcomputer Processing Capabilities* (1984)

*Benefits and Applicability of Local Area Networks* (1985)

All of the aforementioned AICPA publications are available through its order department.

The amount of resource materials, including literature and continuing professional education programs relating to MAS that is currently available to the accountant is limited compared with the wealth of materials available relating to the accounting, auditing, and tax practice areas. Nevertheless, the public accountant who desires to expand his or her knowledge and level of expertise in MAS-related topics to better serve clients' needs does have access to enough material to make a healthy start in achieving such a goal.

# IDENTIFYING CLIENTS' NEEDS FOR MAS

Virtually every business and organization has a need for MAS. The accountant's challenge is to make the most of this opportunity, and the starting point is to identify the specific needs of client organizations. The designation of this starting point is predicated on the author's beliefs that (1) most public accounting practitioners could improve services (i.e., increase their value) to clients if they would take more initiative in trying to help the clients to manage their operations and (2) the greatest potential for practice development and growth lies in the practitioner's existing client base. This does not mean that achieving growth through continual acquisition of new clients is not necessary or important, but it does mean that it is more important to serve existing clients properly, which, in turn, normally will lead to acquisition of additional clients as a result of the referral process.

The small- and medium-size entities that constitute the bulk of a local or regional accounting firm's clientele probably provide the greatest opportunities in the MAS area. The owner/managers of these entities require a great deal of advice, counsel, and assistance. A 1982 special report published in *Inc*. [B. W. Ketchum, Jr., "You and Your Accountant (How to evaluate the relationship betrween you and your company's most trusted adviser)"] includes the following statements that are pertinent to this discussion:

> If all you're getting out of your accountant is tax returns and financial statements, if your accountant thinks only as an auditor and not as an adviser, then a switch probably makes sense.

Small companies should evaluate their accountants at least once a year to identify anything that may justify a change. The business may simply have outgrown the accountant's capabilities. Is your accountant, for example, keeping pace with your company's needs for more sophisticated advice on matters such as data processing, inflation management, new cost controls, and benefit packages? If your accountant has a thorough knowledge of your business and continues to serve as a sounding board for top management, then there is little merit in making a change.

Your accountant should be someone you can trust, someone who understands how your business operates, and someone who is willing to listen and respond with ideas. When you find a public accountant who fits that description, chances are you've found your best professional adviser.

In today's extremely competitive environment, a CPA can ill afford to not take such advice being given to owner/managers of small businesses very seriously. In fact, his or her very survival as a "going practice" may depend on responding to the current trend to become "more of an advisor and less of an accountant." If audits are to become a "commodity," as many observers of the accounting profession contend, and if "tax simplification" should ever become a reality, and if microcomputer technology continues to reduce the need for outside accounting assistance, what will become of the nonconsultant accountant?

Various approaches or techniques might be employed to help identify a client's need for MAS, some of which are very easy to use and others of which require higher levels of sophistication and expertise. It is important to understand that the accountant cannot rely on, or wait for, a client to identify such needs, even though clients will sometimes make specific inquiries concerning MAS matters.

The accountant must take the initiative for several reasons. First, the client may not realize that a particular operating problem exists, perhaps because of a lack of expertise in certain aspects of the business (e.g., very few owner/managers are experts in manufacturing, marketing, and finance). And even if the client realizes that a problem exists (e.g., declining gross profit or working capital deficiency), he or she may not understand the causes of the problem, or may improperly identify what is actually a symptom as a problem (e.g., declining sales may be symptomatic of sales-employee dissatisfaction with compensation methods).

Second, the client's perception of his or her accountant may be that the accountant lacks the requisite acumen to deal with the problem (i.e., only understands numbers and taxes) and thus will not express any concern about the problem and may go elsewhere for help.

Third, the accountant's cumulative experience in working with a multitude of client organizations coupled with his or her intimate and in-depth understanding of the particular client's operations. This understanding, gained as a result of serving as its auditor or accountant, places him or her in the special position of being able to identify areas of operations that might be improved with which the owner/manager may be unaware.

The foundation for the employment of any approach or technique for identifying potential needs for MAS, certain of which are discussed briefly in this chapter, is a proper, overall attitude toward client service. Critical elements of this attitude, which must be shared by the accountant and all of his or her associates in practice, include:

Genuine care and concern for the well-being of the client

Desire to contribute to (and benefit from) the client's success

An entrepreneur's perspective (much broader than that of the "pure accountant")

Desire to initiate actions

Inquisitiveness ("Why do you do it this way?")

Imaginativeness ("I have an idea for you to consider")

Diagnostic approach to financial analysis and problem-solving

Discipline and a sense of urgency ("We must write the management letter immediately")

## MANAGEMENT LETTER

Probably the finest vehicle available to the accountant for demonstrating the type of overall attitude toward client service described earlier is the so-called management letter, or letter of recommendations for improvement in internal control and operations. This form of communication usually emanates from (i.e., is a by-product of) engagements to audit, review, or compile the client's financial statements. Such letters are not required under professional standards applicable to such types of engagements. In an audit engagement, however, any material weaknesses in internal accounting control that come to the attention of the auditor must be reported to senior management and the board of directors either orally or in writing. The purposes of management letters are to:

1.  Make recommendations for improving the client's:
    a.  System of internal accounting control
    b.  Accounting methods and procedures
    c.  Management practices
    d.  Income tax situation (i.e., ways to reduce or defer tax liabilities)

2.  Help ensure that constructive services are rendered to clients

3.  Improve and cement relationships with clients through effective communications

4.  Identify areas where the CPA might provide additional services to the client (e.g., MAS, tax, personal financial planning)

Clients are likely to place a higher value on well-written management letters containing substantive observations and recommendations than on the auditor's report and financial statements submitted by the accounting firm. By the time this information is submitted it is usually "old news," and it may be perceived by the client as being of a perfunctory or compliance nature (e.g., to meet the requirements of a loan agreement).

It has been the author's personal experience in "sitting on the other side of the fence" as a board member of organizations which engage CPA firms, that top management is most anxious to receive management letters because they constitute a form of report card and commentary on how well management is meeting its responsibilities, particularly in such areas as safeguarding of assets and maximizing return on investment. Unfortunately, many CPA firms are lax in meeting their stated goal of providing high-quality, timely management letters, usually because of time or fee restraints. Such laxity often occurs even within the largest CPA firms, according to the results of recent informal inquiries of partners of such firms made by the author. Perhaps, in the current marketing-oriented practice environment, greater emphasis on the practice development potential of management letters can lead to improved discipline and performance in this area of a firm's practice.

A common deficiency in management letters is that they often portray an accountant's perspective of the business instead of an entrepreneur's perspective. As a result, the letters are perceived by top management (or the owner/manager) to be of limited value. For example, a letter whose content is restricted to subject matter such as internal control procedures for bank and petty cash accounts, the need to segregate incompatible control functions (which a small business may find impossible to do), or the need to prenumber various types of documents certainly reflects an accountant's perspective of the client's business. The letter provides no "bottom-line" oriented advice that would spark an owner/manager's interest.

One possible approach to presenting management letters that are more meaningful to an owner/manager (or senior management of a larger entity) is to prepare two letters. The first letter is addressed to the owner/manager or president and addresses the more substantive and entrepreneur-oriented findings and recommendations (e.g., profit planning, cash management systems, inventory valuation methods, receivable collection methods, organizational structure, executive compensation plans). The second letter is addressed to the controller or chief accountant and addresses matters of an administrative or accounting nature (a copy should be forwarded to the owner/manager or president for information purposes). The purpose of two separate letters is, of course, to avoid the coverage of mundane matters in letters addressed to senior management personnel.

The quality and effectiveness of management letters will depend on the observations made by all members of the audit (or compilation or review) team during the course of the engagement. By maintaining the attitude toward client service described in this chapter, both partners and staff should be able to develop meaningful suggestions. It is good practice to write a "management letter point" as soon as an idea for possible inclusion in the letter is identified. Such points should identify the general subject matter (e.g., inventory controls or cost controls) and describe (1) the existing weakness or condition, including the possible consequences of not implementing the recommendation, (2) whether the weakness is considered material, and (3) the recommended new or revised procedure or management action. It is advisable for the person who suggests the point to draft the complete proposed wording for that suggestion to reduce preparation time and to facilitate issuing the letter on a timely basis. Limiting working papers used to accumulate the points to one suggestion per page will aid in organizing and writing the draft of the letter.

Many suggestions that are appropriate for inclusion in a management letter are identified during the early stages of an engagement (e.g., most suggestions relating to internal accounting control), including during preliminary fieldwork, if performed. It is somemtimes advisable to issue an interim management letter in such circumstances, especially if there will be a significant lapse of time until the engagement is completed. This course of action is especially prudent if weaknesses noted could result in losses to the client, if not remedied. Any material weaknesses must be reported promptly. Suggestions regarding tax-planning considerations that are raised during preliminary fieldwork should also be reported promptly so that recommended actions may be taken by the client prior to year-end, if appropriate.

The following additional guidelines for preparation of management letters are adapted with permission from R. W. Colby, *Auditing Practice Manual* (Warren, Gorham & Lamont, 210 South Street, Boston, Mass. 02111, 1985, pp. 21-9–21-10):

1. Good organization of a management letter will greatly enhance its effectiveness. Plan the organization of each letter to suit the particular client. Consider using graphs or tables to illustrate potential financial effects of recommendations.

2. When preparing a management letter, bear in mind that the individuals receiving it will be owners or senior officers of the client. They will expect the letter to be concise and well-organized, and to deal with matters that are significant. They will be interested in the reasons or causes underlying the comments and recommendations that are made.

3. Improve the effectiveness of management letters by including comments concerning operations and ideas to improve efficiency and/or reduce costs; that is, they should contain useful information from the business-person's perspective. The auditor obtains a large amount of information about the client's business in performing an audit engagement; therefore, he or she is in a good position to offer constructive suggestions regarding operations, financial planning, and ideas for improving efficiency, as well as to comment on opportunities to improve internal accounting controls.

4. Consider the practicability of possible recommendations. The client should not be expected to adopt an idea that is obviously too expensive to consider, or to reorganize its system solely for the purpose of helping the auditor to find things more easily. However, the auditor is required to communicate all material weaknesses in internal accounting control, even those where management believes corrective action is not practicable. If management believes corrective action is not practicable in the circumstances, indicate this in the management letter and summarize the weaknesses.

5. Provide a clear, concise description of the controls to be strengthened, the tax practices to be considered, or inefficiencies to be corrected. Review comments carefully and avoid the use of technical jargon where it would not be readily understood by the layperson. Do not generalize by using phrases such as "accounting records are inadequate." Attempt to express recommendations in positive terms.

6. Review any previous correspondence with the client with respect to internal accounting control, tax considerations, or improvement in efficiency. If no action has been taken on previous recommendations, determine the reasons; however, continue to make recommendations if there is definite need for steps to be taken. Take care not to fall into a stereotype pattern of reporting to the client by merely duplicating the prior year's letter.

7. Review the nature and volume of adjusting journal entries to determine whether such entries are indicative of internal accounting control weaknesses for which management letter comments might be appropriate.

8. Obtain the input of reviewers and other firm personnel (e.g., MAS and tax specialists) involved in serving the client.

Two types of review are pertinent to management letters: Internal review and external review. The internal review consists of a reading and editing of the letter by the partner responsible for the audit (or compilation or review) engagement, as well as MAS and tax specialists, as appropriate. When it is ascertained that the content of the letter is thorough, factual, and technically correct, a conference for appropriate firm and client personnel to discuss the draft of the letter should be arranged. The purposes of this conference are to explain the findings and recommendations and to listen and respond to the client's reactions to the recommendations. It may be appropriate to add statements concerning client reactions (e.g., concurrence or lack thereof) to the letter.

To maximize the practice development benefits of management letters, the accountant should not be bashful about expressing (both in the letter and during the conference) interest in, and capabilities to, assist in implementing the recommendations. Wording such as the following might be effective:

> Our management advisory services personnel have had considerable experience in designing and installing computerized inventory control systems for certain businesses such as yours. We would welcome the opportunity to explore with you various ways in which we can provide valuable assistance in the implementation of this recommendation.

There should also be a follow-up (visit or telephone call) within a short time following the issuance of the letter to ascertain the steps being taken by the client to implement the recommendations, whether or not the accountant is to be involved in the process.

The use of some sort of checklist approach to identify clients' needs for MAS may be fruitful in certain situations—for example, for new accounting and audit clients. Under this form of diagnostic approach, staff personnel assigned to the engagement are asked to give explicit attention to the client's needs by addressing and responding to a set of questions contained in a "client service questionnaire" or "checklist of possible management letter points." Examples of typical questions include:

> Does client prepare annual operating budgets?
>
> Has client developed a long-range financial plan and forecast?
>
> Does management receive the information it needs to monitor operations on a timely basis?
>
> Are reports prepared for management
>
> > Accurate?
> >
> > Well-organized, clear, and concise?

Prepared in an economical and timely manner?

Designed to meet the specific needs of various levels of management?

Are controls over credit-granting functions adequate?

Is the average collection period for receivables in line with industry norms?

Is there adequate information regarding gross profit margins by product, product line, territory, and so on?

Is the purchasing function centralized to the maximum extent possible?

Does the client have a production control system for scheduling, routing, dispatching, and expediting production in an efficient and orderly manner?

Is a suitable and reliable cost accounting system in operation?

Are all accounting and related systems computerized, as appropriate, and are such systems adequate and functioning properly?

Is the client sufficiently capitalized and are present methods of financing appropriate and economical?

Are compensation methods, including fringe benefits, well-designed and comprehensive?

A "no" response to any of these illustrative questions, if properly followed up, can lead to either an MAS engagement or consultation.

A less rigid approach to accomplishing the same objective of diagnosing a client's MAS needs is to request staff personnel assigned to an audit (or compilation or review) engagement to specify three to six of the client's most critical MAS needs at the conclusion of the engagement. A step might be included in the general work program or review checklist used by a firm to force the discipline required to bring such information to the surface. Certain types of procedures applied during an audit or review engagement, particularly analytical review procedures, can provide very valuable information to serve as a basis for diagnosing operational problems (e.g., declining profit margins, decreases in working capital, low turnover rates for receivables or inventories, and decreases in production statistics).

Coverage of the topic of identifying clients' needs for MAS would be incomplete if it did not at least mention the concept of "operational auditing" (also referred to as diagnostic review, management auditing, expanded-scope auditing, or systems auditing). Recently CPAs have begun to provide this type of service, which is commonly performed by internal auditors in large organizations. An operational audit might be considered as strictly a diagnostic tool or an actual MAS engagement, depending on the particular circumstances. The following definition of operational auditing is contained in the Report of the Special Committee on Operational and Management Auditing, "Operational Audit Engagements," AICPA (New York, 1982, p.2):

An operational audit engagement is a distinct form of management advisory service that may also have some of the characteristics of a financial audit engagement. It involves a systematic review of an organization's activities, or of a stipulated segment of them, in relation to specified objectives. The purposes of the engagement may be (a) to assess performance, (b) to identify opportunities for improvement, and (c) to develop recommendations for improvement or further action.

The performance of an operational audit obviously requires more knowledge and experience than the preparation of a management letter, particularly if it involves such nonaccounting functions as marketing and production. However, it is certainly feasible for an accountant to acquire the requisite competence (or use outside specialists) to provide such a service to clients. Some good sources of guidance in this area (in addition to the AICPA publication cited earlier) are D. L. Flesher and S. Siewart, *Independent Auditor's Guide to Operational Auditing* (Wiley, New York, 1982), and J. D. Willson and S. J. Root, *Internal Auditing Manual* (New York, Warren Gorham & Lamont, 1983). The accountant who desires to expand capabilities and competence in the MAS area should consider operational auditing as one of the areas offering excellent potential for significant practice growth and development.

# DEVELOPING AND EXPANDING MAS CAPABILITIES

This chapter has explored the expanding role and services of the accountant and how he or she might identify clients' need for additional services. The challenge faced by the accountant is how to fulfill clients' needs for MAS, recognizing that it is not possible for the CPA to be all things to all people. In other words, there are limitations on the range of skills and expertise that any one person, or small group of persons (e.g., a local accounting firm) can be expected to possess.

It is a formidable challenge merely to keep abreast of new developments in the accounting, auditing, and tax areas, as well as additional areas such as computer technology, organizational development, personnel management, production control, and so forth. The larger the firm becomes, of course, the better able it is to meet the diverse MAS needs of clients because it is able to employ and train specialists in many different disciplines. But even the largest CPA firms tend to develop certain specialties for which they become well-known, usually based on specialized-industry knowledge (e.g., banking, health care, hospitality, governmental units, and real estate). Therefore it makes sense for the accountant (or his or her firm) to develop realistic goals and plans for expanding MAS capabilities on a long-term basis.

Specific goals and plans should be based on a thorough assessment of the accountant's (1) present capabilities, (2) perception of present clients' needs for MAS, (3) desire to enter new market areas, and (4) achievability of expansion goals and plans considering available resources and market conditions and limitations. This assessment process may involve such steps as the following:

1. Inventory MAS skills already acquired and evaluate present level of expertise (i.e., high, medium, or low).

2. Identify and describe significant MAS engagements and consultations performed during past few years (perhaps by category—e.g., general business consulting, electronic data processing, accounting systems, business planning).

3. Aggregate identified or perceived client needs (present and future) by type (and, if feasible, size) of project. This information may be difficult to develop, but might be accumulated by interviewing partners and staff, reviewing recent management letters, and employing the need-identification techniques discussed earlier in this chapter. The perceived needs of prospective clients within the community should also be addressed.

4. Evaluate the gaps between present capabilities and aggregate client needs and identify two or three of the most significant ones.

5. Consider possible actions required to fill the gaps. Possibilities include additional continuing professional education, hiring of personnel who are experienced in the specialized areas, and engaging specialists on a consulting or subcontract basis.

6. Design a detailed plan and timetable to achieve identified goals for expansion of service capabilities considering such factors as personnel requirements, amount of investment needed, and marketing approach and methods.

The essence of this approach is to focus on client needs and how to fulfill them, which, of course, is one of the accountant's primary obligations, and to attempt to carve out a niche (or a few of them) in the market for MAS.

As previously discussed, the modern CPA has little choice but to take the steps necessary to expand his or her capabilities in the rapidly emerging area of MAS to assure that he or she continues to be the clients' most trusted business advisor.

# CHAPTER 2

# THE MANAGEMENT ACCOUNTANT AS CONSULTANT AND ADVISOR

**Alfred M. King**

## RESPONSIBILITIES OF THE MANAGEMENT ACCOUNTANT

Management accountants have recently gained an important role in management. Rather than just accumulating and reporting responsibility for *interpreting* operating results, *measuring* performance, and *forecasting* the future. In the final analysis, they are involved in overall business strategy. No other functional area, whether it be marketing, engineering, or production has such an intimate grasp of the overall business. This arises because business activities are always measured and reported in dollars and it is the management accountant who deals with dollars.

**PLANNING.**   A company must be managed in terms of overall objectives, both long- and short-term. For example, as business becomes more complex, capital must be raised to finance expansion; new product lines are added while old ones are phased out. In the shorter run, management thinks in terms of specific operating plans. The management accountant usually coordinates the entire planning process. Most large- and medium-sized firms have both a formal operating plan or budget for the current year and longer-term 5-year plans. Most firms, in addition to the annual profit planning exercise, prepare and revise forecasts periodically throughout the year, adjusting the operating plan to take account of ever changing business conditions. The management accountant also prepares, at a minimum, the monthly financial statements which compare actual performance with the plan.

Business plans usually start with a sales forecast, consisting of two estimates — unit volume and anticipated selling prices. Coordinated production plans are then developed, taking into consideration planned increases or decreases in inventories. These anticipated production levels are then broken down into planned human resource levels, and priced out for current wages and salaries plus any budgeted wage increases. The final step in the budget or planning process involves a forecast of balance sheet levels for receivables, inventories, and capital expenditures. The net impact on cash can then be calculated, which results in determining how much additional funds must be raised from external sources or what cash is available for dividends, reinvestment, or potential acquisitions.

Although the overall policy and philosophy of management must come from the top *down*, most companies successfully build the budget *up* from lower levels of management through to a consolidated companywide plan. Assuring consistency among plans and methods requires complete involvement by the budget planner or management accountant. Thus the individual who has overall responsibility for the corporate budget has an unparalleled view, not only of how the company operates today, but what is planned for the future. Any budget, to be meaningful, must take into consideration all anticipated changes. Such changes have to be identified, analyzed, priced out, and integrated into existing operating plans.

With respect to the terms of reference of this book, the management accountant acts as a consultant and advisor in the planning process by assuring that coherent plans are made. For example, the forecast level of production must tie in with the anticipated sales level. An optimistic sales manager may want to set out a *target* for salespersons — which may be above the amount of sales actually planned. If production plans are adjusted upward to provide sufficient product to meet this unrealistic sales goal, the company may end the year with too much unsold inventory. Mediating between the sales and production departments is one of the accountant's responsibilities, although in case of an unresolvable conflict, a higher level of management may have to become involved. However, identifying conflicts, and bringing them out into the open, is the management accountant's responsibility.

EVALUATION.    Businesses and businesspersons keep score. For the business, the final scorecard is the annual profit and loss report, as reported to shareholders in terms of earnings per share. Dividends can only be paid out of earnings. Shareholders, as well as management, are interested in increasing earnings. Evaluating performance at lower levels of management, must be done by measuring individual results in terms of the responsibilities of each position.

For example, a division may purchase raw materials or intermediate goods from a sister division and sell the finished product to still another division, perhaps for export. How can the performance of each division manager be measured when there is interdependence? Pricing policies for intracompany sales have to take account of a number of factors such as taxes, capital investment base, and competitive market conditions. What if purchases by division B from division A are less than planned? How should the performance of division A be evaluated if the drop in division A's volume was outside its own control?

It is the management accountant's job to provide guidelines for evaluating performance and handling intracompany pricing and volume situations. Reliance on rigid formulas or unrealistic performance measurements can produce poor results and, at worst, demotivate managers. There is no single "best" method of evaluating management performance, so the management accountant must understand the pros and cons of each approach and recommend the best solution for each situation.

A critical factor in the success of any management accountant is to determine the right method of keeping score, to develop the rules and then see they are applied fairly and uniformly. For virtually every executive, the salary level, bonus, and perhaps promotion itself results from how well each individual is judged to have done his or her job. If the measurement system focuses on the proper success factors, the company and the individual executive will have goals in common. A poorly designed evaluation and performance measurement system— one that focuses on items other than the critical factor—will encourage inappropriate behavior. Executives will be motivated to take actions that will improve the reported score for the individual or the division, but *not* optimize profits and performance for the company and its shareholders.

**CONTROLLING.** There is great confusion throughout American industry over the use of the terms *controller* and *control*, especially when related to management accountants. Taken literally, the company controller would have to be the firm's chief executive officer (CEO). Looked at another way, the CEO has the final responsibility for controlling what a company does and evaluating how well it is performing. The use of the term *controller*, to refer to the functions of the accountant or financial manager, is both a benefit and, at times, a detriment.

Each functional manager, obviously, has to control his or her own area. For example, consider the inventory production scheduler. In large measure this person "controls" raw materials, work-in-process, and finished goods inventory levels, usually performing the function in accordance with rules and guidelines set forth by corporate management. These rules probably take into consideration financial constraints. The corporate or division controller does not personally manage the inventory on a day-to-day basis. Or take the sales manager, who hires, trains, motivates, and "controls" the work effort of the company's sales force. The corporate or division controller does not act as a "super" sales manager. Similar analyses govern throughout all functional areas of a business operation. The term *controller*, therefore, should be used in a slightly different manner.

In this chapter, we use the term *controlling* corporate performance to indicate that the management accountant has the responsibility for assuring the integrity of all financial information, and then seeing that proper feedback is given to responsible managers for corrective action, as and when necessary.

**JUDGMENT.**   Many commentators have made the point that accounting is an art, not a science. Judgement and discretion are required; rules cannot be applied rigidly. Because of both the complexity of business and the need to develop interim measures of performance, financial statements (which are the principal means of controlling a firm's operations), involve a lot of judgment. Will present levels of finished goods inventories be sold at the anticipated price? Can accounts receivable be collected 98 cents on the dollars, or will significant allowances have to be given? What kind of warranty obligation is a company going to experience over the next year on products recently sold? These and hundreds, if not thousands, of similar questions must be answered before financial statements can be drafted, and even then individuals usually will arrive at different answers.

Because of the amount of judgment involved in developing financial reports, it is perfectly possible (and happens more often than outsiders might imagine) for a company unit to report optimistically—even when things are not going well. If a plant manager is going to be judged on the ability to meet a production and shipping schedule, quarter-by-quarter or month-by-month, then determining the proper cutoffs for month-end shipments is critical. Should overtime be worked the last weekend of the month? Which shipments should count as last month's and which properly belong in next month's? Answers to these and similar questions involve not only the plant manager, but all of the management staff, including the plant controller.

**INVOLVEMENT VERSUS SCOREKEEPING.**   Should the controller be involved in the day-to-day decision process, and then also be responsible for reporting results? Or should the management accountant be an outside scorekeeper, an umpire, and not be involved in the business decisions? Most organizations, and most management accountants choose to be involved, personally and professionally, in the key business decisions. But this can put a strain on the integrity of the management accountant who is later called on to develop the raw data from which the month-end or quarter-end financial statements are drawn.

Bias may be impossible to avoid, but the professional management accountant has an obligation to himself or herself—and to top management—as well as the outside shareholder, to report accurately. Bad news and bad results will ultimately become clear to everyone; in the short run, misleadingly optimistic information can be developed and often "justified." Proper control of an operation can only be maintained if the reported numbers reflect "reality." In some ways the internal audit function is designed to assure the integrity of the numbers and to make certain that controls developed are being applied properly. But no firm can afford enough auditors for them always to be on the spot, looking over management's shoulder every minute. So the ultimate ethical behavior of a management accountant ends up being a personal responsibility.

Another aspect of "controlling" is making sure that, when bad or unforeseen results are experienced, corrective management action is initiated. Again, the management accountant does not have the responsibility and cannot undertake, for example, to dismiss an unproductive salesperson; that properly is the responsibility of the sales manager. But once it is determined that a particular salesperson is not meeting the goals, and is unlikely to, the management accountant has the responsibility to consult and advise the sales manager that the costs of keeping the wrong person on the job are excessive, and that profits are being affected adversely. Similarly, if inventories rise because of an error in estimating sales deliveries, the management accountant cannot nor should not unilaterally order a reduction in factory production leading to staff layoffs; the impact of *not* taking such corrective action should be brought to the attention of those responsible.

In short, an effective management accountant not only is reporting on what is happening, but is providing options and alternatives for management decisions.

**ACCOUNTABILITY.**    This is one area where the management accountant has primary responsibility. With regard to responsibility for corporate assets, he or she has a greater role than that of just consultant or advisor. The owners of the business look to management to make sure that all assets are used for the purpose for which they were required, that asset values are maintained, and resources expended in accordance with corporate policies. In most organizations, then, in order to accomplish these objectives, the management accountant usually takes the lead in developing systems of internal control.

The 1977 adoption by Congress of the Foreign Corrupt Practices Act (FCPA) institutionalized, and gave the force of law to, what had been previously the practice on the part of most businesses. Good records must be maintained, and asset inventories must be taken periodically and compared with the underlying records. Any discrepancies must be analyzed and reconciled. Access to corporate assets must be limited to those who have a business purpose. Following the adoption of FCPA, many companies strengthened the internal control function, adopted much more formal procedures, and then tested the reliability of the controls, using both internal staff and outside independent public accountants.

Cash, receivables, inventories, and fixed assets represent the bulk of funds appearing on most balance sheets. Expenditures of corporate resources to increase assets in any area, often referred to as capital expenditure control, represents another major area of responsibility for the management accountant. Most companies have developed procedures to evaluate and choose among competing requests for capital. The independence of the management accountant is invaluable in assessing such competing proposals.

Perhaps because they cannot be measured as accurately, other "assets" such as research and development results, corporate distribution systems, and human resources all represent values for which controls should be developed and maintained, even if the corresponding numbers do not appear on the basic financial statements.

**EXTERNAL REPORTING.**    The final end product of most accounting systems is the preparation and distribution of periodic financial statements, often referred to as the P&L and balance sheet, together with the related statement of the source and application of working capital or funds flows. In any particular industry, the format for external publicly disclosed financial statements is well developed.

Creativity is usually not encouraged in the preparation of external financials. The basic underlying numbers, from which the external reports were generated, also represent the raw material from which internal financial statements are prepared. And it is in the latter area, as we have seen, that management accountants can provide a real service to management.

Proper measures of budget performance, cost control through standard cost systems, and responsibility accounting to evaluate profit centers all require imagination and initiative. The fact that the same set of financial data is used to develop both the external audited reports and the internal management reports is the underlying challenge for the management accountant. External reports have to be prepared at least quarterly. The data that goes into such reports must also be molded to provide useful management information for running the business on a daily, weekly, and monthly basis.

The rules under which external financial reports are prepared, often referred to as GAAP (Generally Accepted Accounting Principles), are presently developed by the Financial Accounting Standards Board (FASB) and the Securities and Exchange Commission. These rules are continually being modified; for example, the FASB has required companies to capitalize interest expense as part of long-term construction projects, whereas many companies previously had chosen to write off all interest each year as an expense.

Questions arise as to whether the requirements for external reporting, which are "nonnegotiable," should be applied to internal management reporting. Companies can, for internal purposes, charge off interest as an expense. Different companies choose differently; the important thing is that a choice must be made, adhered to, and, when necessary, explained to all levels of management affected by the decision.

Although the subject of taxes is outside the scope of this chapter, choices involving the application of alternate accounting methods face the management accountant. Firms often use one method of depreciation for financial reporting and a different one for taxes. This involves multiple record keeping, which is relatively straightforward. The length of time over which assets are depreciated is also subject to judgment. Prior to the accelerated cost recovery system, asset lives sometimes were chosen to optimize tax consequences and then applied to financial statements whether they "fit" or not. Today, explicit judgment of asset lives is required for internal reports. Companies can use last-in, first-out inventory accounting to minimize taxes but choose to control inventories internally on first-in, first-out basis, making working paper adjustments at the end of the year.

As tax and book accounting get farther apart, it becomes harder for the management accountant to communicate to others in management just what is going on. In developing transfer prices for international transactions, efforts are often made to minimize taxes and custom duties and to optimize currency flows. In this circumstance, financial considerations may well dictate business decisions even at the expense of understandable internal management reporting. So, in the tax area, many observers feel that the tax tail sometimes ends up wagging the business dog. The management accountant must often make difficult choices involving trade-offs between useful information to management and optimizing the "real" tax, currency, and financial results. One solution is to "keep two (three or four) sets of books." But this approach adds complexity and also makes it difficult to determine real corporate priorities.

# THE MANAGEMENT ACCOUNTANT'S RESPONSIBILITIES IN PLANNING

**SETTING ATTAINABLE GOALS.**    In some ways the planning and budgeting function represents the single greatest contribution that the management accountant can perform. His or her advice and role as a consultant and facilitator is critical to the successful implementation of an effective budgeting system. And the critical element of a successful budgeting system is the setting of attainable goals. There are two schools of thought on the budgeting process. One is often referred to the top-down approach, whereas the other, on a parallel basis, is referred to as the bottoms-up approach. Books have been written that justify and recommend each of these approaches. It is beyond the scope of this chapter to discuss specific budgeting techniques. Suffice it to say that either approach, handled consistently, will produce workable results.

Whether budgeting starts from the top of the organization or is built up from the bottom, subject to continuing review at each higher level, the end product *should* be the same. A profit plan or budget for the year should be developed which represents what the company is most likely to do if things work out as anticipated. A budget should *not* be an unattainable wish, which can only occur if 101 separate things happen to come together. Similarly, the budget should not be so easy to attain that no one has to work very hard to achieve the goals.

Many companies solve the budget by using a flexible budgeting approach. Under this concept a targeted level of sales and production is planned. The buildup of the cost elements (e.g., in the production area) consists of anticipated levels of fixed expense—those that will go on irrespective of short-term volume changes during the year—and variable costs, defined as those that *should* fluctuate with changes in volume. A good, flexible budgeting system will encompass not only direct and indirect labor and material changes, but those elements of supervision and other overhead expenses which management should control if projected targets are to be reached. Also, elements of the working capital equation should be built into the budget system so that anticipated levels of receivables and inventory will be forecast, depending on sales and production targets.

Studies have shown that if management is working against a budget which it feels cannot be met, the budget becomes a negative motivating factor. Making executive compensation a function of attaining budget goals multiplies the pressure for making budgets easy to attain. On the other hand, if executive compensation is *not* attuned to meeting budget goals, the budget will be considered an exercise in "numbers," the preserve solely of the accountant.

Thus a fine line has to be drawn between unrealistically tight budgets that cannot be met, and loose budgets which can be met. The latter do not provide a degree of "stretch," and can unfairly reward executives. This is a major challenge to management accountants.

While on the subject of setting attainable goals, a point should be made here that it is possible to implement a system of sales, quotas, or goals for individual sales territories and/or products and product lines which is independent of the budget and forecast system. It is feasible to run a sales quota system for compensating the sales force that parallels, but is not identical with, the corporate or division profit plan. Many management accountants would recommend this approach, as opposed to developing a sales budget for the company, which is considered a motivating tool for the sales force, but may not be totally realistic in terms of the organization actually achieving such levels.

If the basic economic forecast suggests that the company may be level next year, and the company's own sales growth is likely to be no more than 5 percent, the company may still set sales quotas for individual territories averaging a 10 percent increase. The sales staff can be told that results in excess of quota will result in additional sales compensation. Some of the top salespersons undoubtedly will exceed such goals, whereas others may find it difficult to equal last year's results.

Forecasting a 10 percent sales increase for the company and including this as a part of the budget puts unrealistic production and working capital requirements into play. On the other hand, failing to stretch the salespersons' efforts may unfairly enrich them and not motivate them to provide maximum sales effort. Balancing the corporate goals with functional goals in the production and marketing areas requires the highest performance, including skilled interpersonal relationships, that the management accountant can bring to bear.

**DEVELOPING PLANNING SYSTEMS.**    The first few times that an organization undertakes a formal budgeting and planning process, there is relatively little involvement other than from the accounting staff. The goal in any organization should be for the total organization to be committed to the planning process. The role of the management accountant should ultimately be to monitor the system and consolidate the results for top management review and approval.

Almost every observer suggests that the best way to develop involvement is through participation in setting the organization's goals. A critical factor is that each segment should be measured, and only those things for which the unit manager has responsibility and over which the manager exercises control should be budgeted. This means, for example, that a plant manager is held accountable for meeting cost targets at the level of production dictated by actual or planned sales. A plant manager, with no sales responsibility, should not be measured on sales performance or profit generated from sales. A 15 percent drop in sales volume, when a company has only a 10 percent gross operating profit margin, might well turn a budgeted profit into an actual loss. If, however, the plant manager has been able to control direct and indirect manufacturing expenses in line with predetermined standards, he or she might have done an outstanding job and should be compensated for that work.

The other side of the same equation is when actual sales may exceed planned levels by, say, 15 percent. The much higher gross profit, in the absence of good planning, might appear to provide opportunities for sizable executive bonuses. But if expenses had risen disproportionately, what should have been a 20 percent increase in profits on the 15 percent increase in volume, may turn out to be a 12 percent increase in profits—which may be poor executive performance.

Another way that a planning system should recognize organizational responsibilities involves allocations of corporate or divisional overhead charges. Many managers want to see the "profitability" of particular plants, product lines, or sales territories. There is a feeling, perhaps justified, that for the shareholders to receive dividends out of profits, *all* corporate and divisional overhead expenses have to be absorbed. From this a conclusion is drawn that such overhead costs should be "charged back" to individual plants, product lines, and sales territories both to be "fair" and in order to measure profitability. This concept, when applied in practice, quickly leads to the concept of "relevant costs."

If management wishes to measure the relative profitability of product line *A* and product line *B*, or is competing for government contracts where overhead costs *must* be allocated, then overhead cost allocations usually are desirable. But if the purpose of the numbers is to measure individual executive performance, then charging the plant manager with corporate research and development or corporate advertising expenses does not motivate the plant manager to control indirect plant labor. The plant manager should be responsible for the latter and has virtually no influence on levels of the former.

The management accountant should be very sensitive to requests for allocating corporate charges. The intended use of the allocations should be clearly specified and the appropriate measures of performance developed in advance. If everyone understands the purpose of the allocations and is measured on the same basis, little harm can come.

What is often perceived as unfair, however, is for an organizational unit to be charged with a corporate allocation that is higher than planned—and then be measured on the basis of the "bottom line." The manager would feel, correctly, that there was no input in the decision to increase company advertising expenses and the unit should not suffer adversely. Of course, if the decision to increase advertising made sense to the company as a whole, where does that advertising charge belong? Someone has to take the responsibility for the decision. The answer is that whoever is responsible for the level of advertising should have the increased advertising charge appear only on his or her profit and loss report.

**MONITORING PERFORMANCE.**   No profit plan or budget can be static. Even in a period as short as a quarter, business conditions change—customers' needs vary, competitors make unexpected moves, new products are delayed, and so forth. A company that put together an annual profit plan and then relied solely on that to control ongoing operations, would be at best myopic.

Revisions must be made periodically. Some companies prepare a new forecast month-by-month for the balance of the quarter, and on a quarterly basis for the balance of the year, whereas others forecast only on a quarterly basis. The frequency of the formal forecasting process is not as important as having companies review actual results and project forward on the basis of the latest known assumptions.

Equally important as comparing actual results with the profit plan is to compare the current actual results with the most recent forecast. This may appear to be rather complex, inasmuch as actual results for each month, and on a year-to-date basis, will be compared with the most recent forecast *and* profit plan. But this is the only way of instilling in the minds of those involved the importance of both the original profit plan, which many feel should be fixed for the year, and the forecast, which should be revised as often as needed.

**INTERPRETING THE EFFECTS OF PLANNED TRANSACTIONS.**    It is vital that financial reports not be sent to various levels of management without a written set of comments. The value of a set of financial statements is almost always enhanced by interpretation, and the responsibility for interpretation rests with the management accountant. There are interrelationships which should be understood by the accountant and explained by him or her to management. As a simple case, advertising expenditures may be over budget, but if this resulted in higher than anticipated sales, simply commenting on the over-budget position and expenses, without relating the effect on sales and gross profit margins, would be worthless. However, other kinds of relationships among manufacturing volume, inventory levels, and customer service may not be so easy to determine. The management accountant must work closely with all functional areas of management to identify what caused actual results and provide a reasonable interpretation.

As a general rule, the top management of any organization, and even more important, the management accountant, should know what the financial results for a period are *before* the financial statements are drawn off and published. Unexpected surprises are a system of poor control, poor communication, or both. Similarly, if there are no surprises, it means that the management accountant knows what should happen because he or she understands the underlying business. And, in the latter case, the financial statements then can be treated as a reflection of the business itself. Financial reports by themselves are unimportant. To the extent they convey information for better management decisions they are going to be worth the resources required. In the final analysis, the information is primary—and the financials represent only the best available medium. Pictures and words, however, will make the numbers infinitely more useful.

# Trends in Management Accounting and Control

Two major factors seem to be at work in the economy, and these factors will have a beneficial impact on the responsibility and role of the management accountant. Business is becoming more complex. The effect of government regulations, taxes, narrowing of GAAP, combined with changing economic forces such as inflation/deflation, the role of the dollar in world trade, and the increasing interdependence of countries, all make business decisions far more complex and difficult than they were previously.

In addition, we have the added impact of computers, primarily personal or microcomputers. Accountants now have access to desk-top computing power which 20 years ago was limited to centralized data processing departments. The impact is only beginning to be realized. In many organizations the management accountant has taken the lead in the firm's use of personal computers. Utilizing some of the advanced financial modeling and spreadsheet packages which have become available for personal computers, the management accountant can capture many of the variables referred to previously, assign quantitative values, and manipulate a series of "what-if" equations.

Let us now look at the impact of business complexity and computers in two key business areas and see how the management accountant can cope with these. First we will look at inventories and changes in production control techniques. Second, we will look at the impact on new products, marketing strategies, and responsiveness of the firm to the market itself.

**INVENTORIES AND PRODUCTION CONTROL.**   The efforts of U.S. industry to emulate the Japanese have been written about and reported in many forums. Whether there is a Japanese "secret," or whether the management techniques used by the Japanese can be developed and applied in the United States, may not yet be fully established. But there is little doubt that if American industry is to remain competitive, more automation must be applied, and production control systems must be better integrated. As this happens, the direct labor content of most production will decrease still further.

Present cost accounting and management control systems in most factories have been developed on the assumption that overhead expense items can be accumulated and related to direct labor. These assumptions will no longer be appropriate. Companies will be unable to function with overhead or burden rates of 1000 percent and total absorbed direct labor costs of $50 or $60 per hour, even up to $100 per hour. In point of fact, cost accounting techniques will have to change to reflect the substitution of capital for labor. Productivity can no longer be measured in terms of labor, but will have to be calculated and reported on a total factor basis, including labor, overhead, material content, and capital assets employed. This may well be the number one challenge facing management accountants in the 1990s.

As production techniques change, so will production control. Long lead times will have to be reduced so that companies can be more responsive to the market. The introduction of quicker turnaround in production techniques will allow inventories to be reduced and, at the same time, allow companies to provide faster delivery and higher on-time delivery to customers.

Many companies have tried to integrate their cost accounting and production control systems. This has been very successful in a few cases and a total failure in others. Over the next few years, one of the major challenges facing the management accountant will be integration of production control and cost accounting into one comprehensive system.

Perhaps microcomputers, in an integrated environment, will allow each functional area to control its own destiny and, at the same time, provide data input to other users. It is beyond the scope of this chapter to forecast the future or suggest how accounting and production can be more closely integrated. There can be no doubt though, that successful companies will accomplish this. Those firms that are unsuccessful will be at a terrible competitive disadvantage.

**MARKETING RESPONSIVENESS.**   Many analysts suggest that the most successful firms, those given an excellent rating, are customer oriented or marketing oriented. The best managed firms consider users' needs rather than emphasizing the needs of the producers. Traditionally, there has been a significant conflict between marketing management and financial management. It may be a stereotype, but financial managers view "salespeople" as "big spenders," whereas the salespeople view accountants as "bean counters." As with every stereotype there is undoubtedly an element of truth to both viewpoints.

In the last part of the twentieth century, companies cannot afford the luxury of a "we" and "they" approach between finance and marketing. Financial managers must work closely with marketing personnel. Convincing marketing of the benefit of good cost accounting and budgeting information, showing how it can help to meet the ultimate profit goal of any organization, is a challenge to the management accountant. The management accountant must show that producing a product or service at a price which generates a profit for the shareholders is critical.

As business becomes more complex, the rate of new product introduction accelerates. Pricing decisions, sourcing decisions, and information about product line profitability will have to be developed and communicated much more quickly. Perhaps the importance placed on a "five-year plan" will diminish, and more emphasis will have to be placed on the short-term profit plan and forecast. If a company is in a situation where half or two-thirds of the products being sold now were not on the market five years ago, and that rate of change can be projected into the future, it means that determining a five-year plan may be just wishful thinking. But, more important, good *current* management accounting data has to be provided quickly and accurately, on a short-term basis, to help management make critical marketing decisions, decisions that will now be made far more frequently and with a shorter lead time than in the past.

At present, the impact of microcomputers has not actually been felt by marketing staffs. The initial round of programs available on microcomputers appeared to be more relevant to the needs of the accountant. As the costs of computing power decrease and sophistication of programs increases, the availability of programs that can make sales projections, test alternate pricing strategies, and analyze market research data will undoubtedly make marketing departments more numbers oriented.

A critical factor which the Management Accountant will have to keep abreast of is that any company should maintain only one basic accounting system. Just as it is crucial for the production control system to tie into the cost accounting system, so should the sales reporting system be used both to prepare financial statements and for special analyses by marketing.

## SUMMARY

If the management accountant can accomplish all of the tasks set forth in this chapter, he or she will be a vital part of the management team. In addition to being a consultant and advisor, the management accountant will, in fact, ultimately be part of management. And, for most accountants, this is the ultimate goal.

# CHAPTER 3

# THE INTERNAL AUDITOR AS AN INTERNAL MANAGEMENT CONSULTANT

## Richard M. Morris III

## INTRODUCTION

Internal auditing is defined by the Institute of Internal Auditors as

> An independent appraisal function established within an organization to examine and evaluate its activities as a service to the organization. The objective of internal auditing is to assist members of the organization in the effective discharge of their responsibilities. To this end, internal auditing furnishes them with analyses, appraisals, recommendations, counsel, and information concerning the activities reviewed.
>
> The members of the organization assisted by internal auditing include those in management and the board of directors. Internal auditors owe a responsibility to both, providing them with information about the adequacy and effectiveness of the organization's system of internal control and the quality of performance. The information furnished to each may differ in format and detail, depending upon the requirements and requests of management and the board.[1]

An internal auditor assists management and the board of directors by reviewing the system of internal control which management has designed and implemented within the organization. The internal auditing department's mission statement is often expanded to include a review of the operations, facilities, and organizational structure to determine the compliance with management's operational policies and procedures. This operational auditing perspective allows an internal

---

[1] *Standards for the Professional Practice of Internal Auditing*, Altamonte Springs, FL, Institute of Internal Auditors, 1978, p. 1.

auditor to provide additional information to assist management in its understanding of the organization and its ability to manage it effectively. This assistance is not from the perspective of an internal consultant, but an extension of the auditing philosophy utilized within the department.

**INDEPENDENCE CONSIDERATIONS.**    The independence of an internal auditor could be challenged if an auditor functioned as an internal consultant and was then required to audit the same function or activity within a short period of time. This conflict has been recognized within the public accounting profession and has resulted in the development of the various management advisory service functions or departments.

This approach may be utilized within an internal auditing department by a revision of the departmental charter and by a memorandum from senior management or the board of directors, requesting a specific study or analysis. It is important that operating personnel understand that a consulting review is not an audit and that the information developed during the course of the analysis will not be included in an audit report.

Internal auditors are able to assist management (i.e., function as business advisors) because of their training, experience, and independent perspective. This chapter will describe how an organization may utilize this experience without compromising the traditional roles, objectives, and independence of the internal auditing department.

# Defining the Internal Auditing Department[2]

The internal auditing department is organized and defined under delegated authority of the organization's board of directors. Within this framework, the director of internal auditing reports on an administrative basis to a senior operating officer and on a functional basis to the chairman of the audit committee or the full board of directors. Exhibit 3.1 outlines the primary sources of external influence upon the definition and development of an internal auditing department. However, the definition of specific influences and requirements is dependent upon the service or product which the organization is providing and its particular industry structure. The same developmental model and structure would also be appropriate if the internal auditing department was in a government or not-for-profit environment.

---

[2] Material in this section has been adapted from *Defining the Internal Audit Function*, an unpublished manuscript by Richard M. Morris III, Spring Valley, Ohio, 1984.

**EXHIBIT 3.1.    Sources of External Influence on Development of Internal Auditing Department.**

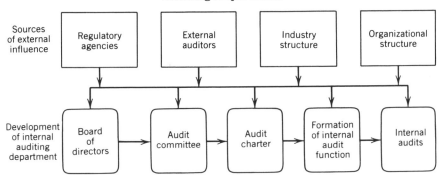

The four primary structural influences that act on an internal audit department may be summarized as:

1. **Regulatory agencies.**   Any national, international, regional, or local governmental or authoritative body that may influence the organizational structure, staffing, reporting requirements, or operational activities of the firm or department.

2. **External auditors.**   Any organization that has the right, privilege, or statutory requirements to audit or review any or all of the organization's operations, documents, procedures, or records. This would include representatives of regulatory agencies, public accounting firms, auditors from a partnership or joint venture operation.

3. **Industry structure.**   The primary industry structure in which the organization is functioning. This would include such influences as legislative constraints, centralized or decentralized operations, competition, environmental influences, labor supply, and requirements.

4. **Organizational structure and corporate culture.**   The unique organizational structure, training requirements, staffing, and corporate philosophy of the specific organization.

These four elements influence the organization, its structure and philosophy. They have a specific and often direct influence on the board of directors and senior management, and either a direct or indirect impact on the internal auditing department.

## Board and Audit Committee Influence

The board of directors is responsible for the activities and functions of the organization. Board members are typically classified as inside or outside directors, with the distinction being the current or past employment of an individual member. Senior officers of the organization who also serve on the board of directors are considered as an inside member because of their dual responsibilities. An outside director is not closely associated with the day-to-day operations and decision-making of the organization. It is these board members who are members of the audit committee, compensation committee, and perhaps the long-range planning committee.

The audit committee is responsible for establishing the tone and effectiveness of the audit activities within the organization. The specific accountabilities of the committee are defined by the full board, although there is a legislative and judicial history of what is traditionally expected of this committee. Under delegated authority, the audit committee meets with and reviews the activities, reports, and recommendations of the internal auditing department, the external auditors, and any regulatory agencies that may review the organization. The audit committee is also accountable for reviewing, and either approving or referring to the full board for discussion and approval, the appointment of the independent public accounting firm, the director of internal auditing, the departmental charter, the annual audit program, departmental budget, and so forth.

## INTERNAL AUDITING DEPARTMENT CHARTER

The internal auditing department's charter defines the accountabilities and authority of the function, with the specific elements and language dependent on the structure and philosophy of the individual organization. The tone and philosophy are broadly defined by the audit committee and approved by the full board of directors, and may range from a limited compliance review to a comprehensive audit program.

Research has shown that five common elements may be identified in many internal auditing department charters.[3] These are:

1.  **The introduction.** The initial section which defines the nature and purpose of the internal auditing function within the organization.

---

[3] Richard M. Morris III, *Developing a Charter for the Internal Audit Function*, Altamonte Springs, FL, Institute of Internal Auditors, 1983.

2.  **The role of the function.**    The overall perspective of the internal auditing department within the organization. The specific placement of the function within the organizational structure is often identified in this section.

3.  **Authorizations and responsibilities.**    The specific definition of the authorization of the function (as compared with specific individuals) to records, personnel, and properties during the course of an audit or review. A statement is often included indicating that the auditor will exercise due care over the records and information of the function being reviewed, but that the auditor has no direct managerial or decision-making responsibilities over the function or operations being reviewed.

4.  **Definitions of audit scope.**    A general definition of scope and audit approaches or a specific listing of activities for which the internal auditing department is or is not accountable. The audit philosophy of the organization is often summarized in this section.

5.  **Reporting accountability.**    Defines the specific type, format, and distribution of the reports that are to be issued by the department. This section may also restate the reporting responsibilities of the director of internal auditing and may also outline the requirements for a written response from the auditee.

## COMPONENTS OF AUDIT ACTIVITY

Within the requirements of the charter, the structure of the internal auditing department is developed and an audit program designed and put into place. Exhibit 3.2 illustrates the relationships of the four traditional components of an audit activity. These are:

1.  **Financial.**    The traditional balance sheet verification and attestation process.

2.  **Compliance.**    The review of the organization and its activities for compliance with regulatory and statutory requirements and adherence to the policies and procedures as defined by the board of directors and senior management.

3.  **Operational.**    An expanded scope audit in which the activities, policies, procedures, and operations of the organization are reviewed for effectiveness and consistency. The objective is to review a function or activity as a whole and, if applicable, make recommendations for the operating manager's consideration.

**EXHIBIT 3.2.   Audit Framework**

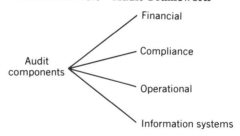

4.   **Information systems.**   The review of the information system, often computerized, utilized by the organization for completeness, security, and internal control as well as from a technical effectiveness perspective.

The audit program is designed by the director of internal auditing and approved by the audit committee to utilize these four methodologies to accomplish the departmental mission. Any significant modification of this program would require prior approval to ensure that appropriate resources were available and that the revised audit scope was consistent with the overall needs of the organization.

The definition of the internal audit department's activities (or scope) within an organization is included in the departmental charter. The specific function or activity reviewed during the course of an audit is defined in the departmental work papers and summarized in the audit report. This definition of parameters or audit coverage ensures that the auditee, management, and the board of directors know what was reviewed during an audit. This also states that the audit was defined or limited to the listed activities and that other activities in the same function may not have been reviewed.

It is perhaps more important that the auditee and management know what was not reviewed in the event of a question or problem at a later date. This will ensure that any corrective responses taken by management are restricted to the specific activities reviewed by the auditor.

Within a traditional audit environment, the internal auditor reviews an activity or function to determine the degree or level of compliance with a predefined criterion or standard. This standard is documented in the organization's policy and procedure manuals and in other defined sources (i.e., industry standards, and legal or accounting requirements). After an audit is completed, a formal written report is prepared and issued which (1) states that the activity is or is not in compliance with the predefined standards and (2) if appropriate (or required), recommends that management correct the exceptions noted during the review.

The structure and requirements of an audit report may be outlined in the charter or subsequent memorandums from senior management. A reporting format, however, is also dependent on the scope and operating philosophy of the internal auditing department. If the department concentrates on financial and compliance reviews, the corrective measures to be taken by operating management are fairly self-evident. The expanded scope of an operational or information systems audit normally allows an auditor the opportunity to make additional recommendations to correct the findings.

Within the constraints outlined in the departmental charter or supplemental documents, operating managers may or may not be required to follow these recommendations (unless a legal problem is involved). The audit function is primarily concerned that appropriate corrective measures are taken by the operating managers.

**THE INTERNAL AUDITOR AS AN INTERNAL MANAGEMENT CONSULTANT.** The utilization of the internal auditing department as an internal consulting function is not a new concept in today's business environment. However, the extent of this utilization was not readily apparent until a 1983 survey by the Institute of Internal Auditors (IIA). With a question response of 1579 internal auditing departments, 39.9 percent indicated that they were responsible for internal management consulting activities within their organization. The level of activities ranged from 34.5 percent of the larger firms (more than 10 internal auditors) to a high of 43.5 percent for smaller firms with three or less internal auditors. The high level of activity in the smaller firms is not surprising because of the active personal management participation and limited resources (both financial and staff) within a smaller organization.

Nine nonauditing activities were included in the survey responses, which indicates that the scope of internal auditing activities is expanding within many organizations. It would be interesting to review the specific charters and/or supplemental management directives for these departments to determine the extent and/or restrictions of these consulting activities.

Exhibit 3.3 lists nine nonauditing activities and Exhibit 3.4 summarizes the responses for internal management consulting by primary standard industrial classifications. Even with the number of respondents who acknowledged responsibilities for internal management consulting, it is important to note the number of internal auditing departments that are not accountable for outside nonauditing operations or activities. Forty-five percent of the larger departments and 35 percent of all sampled functions indicated that nonauditing activities are beyond their charter and scope.

Although these activities may represent a growth potential for an individual department or function, the defined or perceived need within an organization

**EXHIBIT 3.3.** What Nonauditing Operations or Activities Is Your Internal Auditing Department Responsible For?[a]

| | Departmental Size[b] | | | |
|---|---|---|---|---|
| Activity | Small | Medium | Large | Total |
| Developing financial systems | 14.8 | 7.4 | 3.5 | 8.9 |
| Installing financial systems | 4.8 | 1.6 | 1.1 | 2.6 |
| Developing operation systems | 18.2 | 7.8 | 3.7 | 10.3 |
| Installing operation systems | 6.5 | 2.9 | 0.9 | 3.6 |
| Developing controls for financial systems | 33.5 | 26.7 | 17.8 | 26.5 |
| Developing controls for operation systems | 31.2 | 24.1 | 15.6 | 24.2 |
| Policy and procedure development | 39.0 | 25.2 | 15.0 | 27.2 |
| Bank reconciliations | 9.3 | 6.5 | 8.0 | 8.0 |
| Internal management consulting | 43.4 | 40.8 | 34.5 | 39.9 |
| None | 25.9 | 35.9 | 45.1 | 35.0 |
| Other | 12.7 | 9.4 | 9.5 | 10.6 |
| Sample size | 567 | 551 | 461 | 1579 |

[a] Any number of categories could be checked by the respondent.

[b] Department size: Small—three or less internal auditors; Medium—four to nine internal auditors; Large—more than 10 internal auditors.

Adapted from White, Kenneth R., and James A. Xander, *Survey of Internal Auditing: Trends and Practices,* Institute of Internal Auditors, Altamonte Springs, FL., 1984, Table 5, p. 13.


**EXHIBIT 3.4.** Internal Auditing Departments Indicating Responsibility for Internal Management Consulting by Industrial Classification

| Industrial Classification | Number | Sample Size |
|---|---|---|
| Banking | 85 | 273 |
| Government | 79 | 162 |
| Insurance | 52 | 124 |
| Utilities | 31 | 86 |
| General manufacturing | 30 | 88 |
| Education | 30 | 81 |
| Heavy industry | 114 | 296 |
| Trade | 87 | 204 |
| Service | 144 | 324 |
| Total | 652 | 1638 |

Adapted from White, Kenneth R., and James A. Xander, *Survey of Internal Auditing: Trends and Practices,* Institute of Internal Auditors, Altamonte Springs, FL., 1984, Table 5, p. 59.

may not be present or desirable. This may especially be true in larger organizations, in which an internal management consulting activity is already formalized and/or handled by another activity or function.

## INDUSTRY ANALYSIS

Exhibit 3.4 summarizes the responses by industrial classification for those departments which indicated that one of their nonauditing responsibilities within their organization is internal management consulting. The published data did not include a size classification, and the totals are different than in Exhibit 3.3 because of incomplete data that did not allow the researchers to classify all responses by industrial code.

The number of banking organizations that acknowledged responsibility for internal management consulting is surprising. The Statement of Principle and Standards for Internal Auditing in the Banking Industry, published in 1977 by the Bank Administration Institute, includes several elements which provide for an activity of this nature. The first Organization Standard states that "The organization shall have an internal audit function responsible for evaluating the adequacy, effectiveness and efficiency of its systems of control and the quality of ongoing operations."

This same language is repeated in the second Communication Standard and in the third Performance Standard. It would therefore appear that bank internal audit departments which also subscribe to these professional standards would already include internal management consulting within their standard scope of activities. Thus these activities may be considered as "normal or routine," which would indicate the low number of positive responses to the IIA questionnaire.

In many organizations the concept of evaluating the adequacy, effectiveness, and efficiency of ongoing operations may imply an adaptation of industrial engineering techniques. These skills are becoming more common in internal auditing departments, but are also utilized elsewhere within the organization. Therefore it is probable that some organizations have not expanded their basic scope into the area of operational efficiency because of the presence of an industrial engineering or methods section elsewhere within the organizational structure.

Because of the specialized skills required to conduct a technical review of this nature, the number of internal auditing departments that approach a review of this type is probably limited. This is especially true if one considers the implicit and explicit organizational and "political" impacts which a study of this type has on an organization. An internal auditing department must be aware of how the function is perceived within the organization. An extensive or technical analysis of the efficiency of operations may have an adverse impact on the overall effectiveness of the department. This concern does not, however, limit the responsibility of the function to evaluate the effectiveness and efficiency of the internal controls system, which management has designed and implemented within the organization.

**THE INTERNAL AUDITING PERSPECTIVE.**    The internal auditing department is a staff function, and an auditor has no authority or responsibility for the daily operating decisions of the organization. This exclusion from the formal decision-making process ensures that any recommendations which an auditor makes during or subsequent to an audit will be reviewed by the operating manager responsible for implementing any corrective actions.

The auditor is able to approach a review with a different perspective than a manager who must often react to a situation in a short period of time, often with incomplete information. An auditor is able to devote adequate time to the collection and analysis of information, as an audit may be compared with a snapshot of a function at one point (e.g., eight A.M. Monday, the 21). The period of time that is reviewed during the audit is defined in the scope paragraph of the completed audit report.

An auditor is often accused of reviewing a function with knowledge of what occurred subsequent to a manager's decision. The potential to second guess a decision made with incomplete information or under time or operating constraints is one which any manager faces, and an auditor is no exception. An auditor is not reviewing a decision to issue a grade or to determine if a decision was right or wrong, however, but for compliance with defined corporate policies and procedures.

A function is reviewed as an individual operating entity and as an element of the complete organization. This dual evaluation is important, whether the analysis is from a financial or operational audit perspective. In a financial analysis, the primary criteria are the function's compliance with both standard accounting and the organization's accounting policies and practices. An operational analysis is for compliance with the organization's operating policies and procedures.

This dual perspective is important, because a procedural change in one function may have an impact on the operations or profitability of another function within the organization. This impact may offset any financial or operational gains that were obtained by making the initial change. Management is also accountable for reviewing all recommendations from this overall organizational perspective prior to implementing any corrective actions.

An auditor also approaches a function or activity from several additional perspectives. These include:

1. **A top-down management perspective.**   The analysis of a situation, problem, or objective for its effect on the entire organizational structure, as well as on the function or activity being reviewed.

2. **Analyzing the function as it exists, not as it should exist.**   An expansion of the top-down perspective. To analyze an activity or function effectively, the reviewer must determine what is actually occurring and the way in which it is occurring. This information will subsequently be compared with management's predefined standards for the function.

3. **As of a specific point in time.**   The primary advantage of an outside review of a function or activity. Events, transactions, and activities can be frozen and analyzed apart from the time constraints and emotion of a dynamic function.

4. **For compliance with predefined standards, criteria, and procedures.** From the information obtained in activities 2 and 3, a comparison may now be made with the predefined policies and procedures of the organization.

5. **With no authority to change operations or practices within the function.**   An auditor does not have the authority to install or change a process or procedure. Auditors are change agents in that they can only recommend that practices and procedures be reviewed by management and, if appropriate, revisions made in the operating procedures.

6. **Without a predefined criteria of a specific finding or recommendation to be developed from the analysis.**   The independence and perspective of auditors ensures that they are open and will review all aspects of an activity or function prior to developing and presenting their findings and recommendations to management.

7. **Analyzing the function and not the personnel in the function.**   An auditor reviews and evaluates the activities of the function and the function's compliance with the predefined organizational policies and procedures. This review does not include an analysis or evaluation of the individual employees within an activity or function. This is management's responsibility, and must be done on a continuous basis—not just at one point in time.

    To these attributes, an internal auditor adds experience, formal education and training, and professional expertise and practice. These tools and techniques provide an auditor with an approach and the ability to relate a specific activity to the organization as well as the organization's needs and requirements of the activity.

An auditor's perspective is a valuable resource for an organization and should be effectively utilized. However, management must decide whether these skills should be utilized within an auditing perspective or within the expanded scope of an internal consulting function. The goals and expectations of an individual auditor must also be reconciled within the departmental definition.

It is possible that an individual auditor may not wish, or may not have the additional professional and personal skills to facilitate an effective transition between the requirements of the two positions within the function. It is important that these needs be identified and, as much as possible, met within the definition of the departmental scope and objectives. Additional training, new personnel, and perhaps the formation of a separate internal consulting function may be alternatives that have to be explored by the organization.

**COMPLIANCE WITH CORPORATE POLICIES AND PROCEDURES.**    Policies and procedures are defined by senior management and provide the criteria for the daily and long-term operations of an organization. These are documented and distributed to help ensure that the organization is moving in an organized and consistent manner toward accomplishing the desired goals and objectives.

These procedures also provide a criterion from which the activities of a function may be measured and evaluated. This review against a defined standard assists management in evaluating the effectiveness of an activity as well as the individuals employed within the activity. Additionally, a benchmark has been defined from which management can evaluate the quality of the product produced or the services provided.

Senior management must review these policies and procedures on a regular basis to ensure that they are accomplishing their intended objectives. If the structure, goals, or operations of the organization change, new policies and procedures must be prepared and distributed within the operating functions. Operating management must then review their functions and revise their activities to comply with the new procedures. It is their responsibility to see that the activities completed within their functions are in compliance with the newly defined procedures.

An auditor must be knowledgeable of the organization's written policies and procedures prior to conducting an audit or review. These procedures provide a "standard" from which the actual activities of a function may be compared. As part of an audit analysis, a determination may be made as to the effectiveness of the documented procedures in accomplishing the defined goals and objectives.

If the activities conducted within a function differ from the defined procedures, the auditor documents the procedures being utilized and determines the reason for the difference. If the deviations are significant, the auditor may include a statement in the audit report and recommend that the predefined standards be utilized by the function.

It is important to remember that the report prepared by the auditor states that a deviation from the defined policies and procedures has been noted. If a recommendation is included in the report, it normally states that the operating manager revise the procedures utilized within the function to bring them into compliance with the predefined organization procedures. It is not within the scope of internal audit departments to accept a deviation from defined practices. An internal auditor may agree that the modified procedures are as effective (or more effective) than the defined procedures. As a staff function, however, an auditor does not have the operating authority to accept or approve the modified procedures.

In the written response to the audit report, the operating manager has several alternatives. These are:

Agree to comply with the predefined policies and procedures

Request a variance from the practices

Request that the organization's procedures be changed to incorporate the approach utilized in their function

Members of senior management review the audit report and the responses and determine what course of action would be appropriate for the specific activities and functions. The operating manager is accountable for implementing and monitoring any procedural changes in the function.

Even if the charter and scope of the internal audit function included an operational auditing perspective, the same approach would be followed. Organizational placement of the internal audit department as a staff function does not provide for line operating authority or responsibility. The authority to revise operating practices and procedures is an accountability of senior management and its implementation is delegated to the line operating managers.

If an internal auditor is acting in an internal consulting capacity, it is still from the capacity of a staff advisor or consultant. After reviewing the activity or function, recommendations may be made to operating or senior management for review and possible implementation. Because these recommendations were not developed during the course of an audit, their "political" impact would not be as threatening to operating management. This may result in more recommendations of changes in policy and procedures being accepted and implemented within the organization.

This acceptance of change may be viewed as a positive element by an internal auditor functioning in a consulting role. Operating personnel and managers are not as defensive towards ideas and comments proposed during the course of a consulting review. As a result, it might be possible to gain an easier acceptance and implementation of a recommendation through this "informal" approach. The acceptance and implementation of an effective system of policies, procedures, and internal controls is one of an auditor's concerns, and this is one way in which that objective may be accomplished.

**INTERACTING WITH OTHER CORPORATE GROUPS.**    It has been said that people cry when the auditors arrive and celebrate when they leave. It is this impression of an auditor's roles, objectives, and impact that has and will continue to create obstacles for the profession. The extent of these objectives is dependent on the professional abilities of the individual auditor, as well as the support which the function receives from senior and operating management. This obstacle may often be attributed to the perception of an auditor being a "cop on the beat" or a reviewer issuing grades on the function and its employees. This, plus the inconvenience to an auditee's operations during the course of an audit, may contribute to a stressful situation on both sides.

However, for an effective internal auditing function, both auditing and operating management must increase their efforts to reduce this stress. The use of more formal (and informal) discussion between operating departments and the internal auditing department can assist in reducing these negative images and concepts. These discussions, and understanding of the department's operations and personnel, assist in obtaining a more effective review and acceptance of the audit findings and recommendations.

The expansion of audit scope to include operational reviews has also assisted in increasing the interaction and cooperation between operating departments in the internal auditing function. This expansion of departmental scope allows an auditor to review the complete organization, and not to concentrate solely on the verification and attestation of the financial statements. From this overall perspective of the organization, auditors are able to review the work flow throughout the organization and assist management in obtaining a more effective operation.

An auditor is not an efficiency expert (in the negative sense of the term) but a employee with an awareness of the organization's overall objectives, operating constraints, organizational structure, and control environment. Therefore in some organizations it was a logical expansion of the internal auditing department's charter to encompass the perspective of an internal consultant within their activities. This formal acknowledgment of a previously informal role helped to increase the positive interaction between the auditing department and the operating departments of the organization.

Within this internal consulting perspective, an auditor would be able to assist management as a member of a special project or review team. This would include such assignments as the initial design, development, and implementation of information systems, security reviews, organizational restructuring, mergers, acquisitions, and so forth.

The inclusion of an auditor on these special project teams would enable a preliminary review of internal control considerations prior to completion of the project. This assists in increasing management and departmental cooperation, because revisions may be suggested or made during the course of the project and prior to completing a formal audit. From a cost and time perspective, this approach is even more important. An auditor would less likely be faced with having to request modifications to an information systems program or new product or service subsequent to its introduction or installation.

## AUDIT REQUESTS OR RECOMMENDATIONS

An audit request or recommendation at this time would be to correct any significant internal control weaknesses which were noted in the initial audit of the project. The costs in time and money of making procedural revisions or control modifications during the development stages of a program are less than if the entire project had to be delayed (or perhaps abandoned) while the changes were made. If requests for audit and control changes were made after the project was completed, installed, and ready for operational introduction, it is not unlikely that the recommended modifications would be delayed until additional enhancements were also requested by the users of the application or product.

The delay of implementing recommended audit changes within an information system or production system may create difficulties for the auditing department and the respective operating manager or department. The manager is accountable for the functioning of the system or practice, yet the audit function is accountable for reviewing these systems to ensure that an effective system of internal controls has been designed, installed, and utilized.

An operating manager may assume the accountability and risk for not implementing recommended or other appropriate corrective measures within an activity or function. If the director of internal auditing is not in agreement with this decision and is unable to convince the operating manager of the need for the changes, a request for assistance may have to be made to senior management. If, in the opinion of the director of internal auditing, senior management's actions do not satisfactorily resolve the issue, a series of meetings between all parties will be necessary to discuss the identified exposure, recommended courses of action, and the specific action taken (or not taken) to resolve the issue.

Most disputes of this nature are resolved at this stage of activity. However, there may be isolated instances in which the director of internal auditing is not satisfied with the course of action taken by senior management. It then becomes the auditor's responsibility to convince management of the need for different or more effective procedures to be utilized. If differences of opinion still exist, the only available course of action might be to the audit committee. However, there would have to be significant differences of professional opinion to request that the audit committee make a determination as to the need and extent of appropriate procedures to be introduced. This could result in "political problems" within the organizational structure.

There may also be the possibility of an ineffective procedure, practice, or information being utilized within an activity or function. Or, an ineffective or potentially dangerous product or service may be produced and distributed to the organization's customer base. This may or may not result in an exposure (either financial or public-relations oriented) to the organization. If the potential exposure is great enough, however, the issue will have to be defined and resolved within the organization in a reasonable period of time.

This is one significant advantage to the utilization of an internal auditing function as a source of internal consultants within the organization. When an operating manager requests assistance from an internal auditor—either formally by a written request or informally during conversation—the internal auditing director can be assured that the objective of increased cooperation, or pehaps coordination of efforts, within the organization is being realized.

**EVALUATING INTERNAL AUDITING PERFORMANCE.** The evaluation of the performance (or lack thereof) of an individual, department, function, or activity is dependent on several factors. These are:

1. A predefined standard of expectations or objectives
2. A predefined review format and process
3. A predefined and published schedule of review dates
4. Consistent internal documentation standards

The evaluation of the internal auditing function would be in conformance with the standards which have been defined for the department. The review would be conducted by senior management and would be similar to a review of any other function or department within the organization.

The definition of criteria for the internal auditing department would be based on the departmental charter which was prepared by the board of directors. Additionally, the annual audit schedule, staff training and development program, and departmental budget and expense analysis prepared by the director of internal auditing, would provide criteria for the evaluation.

If the charter of the auditing department was expanded to include, or if the board had specifically requested the use of the internal auditing department staff as internal consultants, the time spent in this capacity must be included in the evaluation process. The criteria for the evaluation of these efforts could be based on several factors, which could include:

1. Percentage of time spent consulting versus auditing
2. The type and function of the consulting reviews conducted
3. A number of consulting assignments which were requested by operating management versus those requested by senior management or the board of directors
4. A determination (based on predefined criteria) of the effectiveness of the consulting assignments in assisting the organization in accomplishing its stated objectives. However, it is important that senior management and, perhaps more important the director of internal auditing, remember the primary objective of the internal auditing department: that of providing management with an independent appraisal of their organization to assist management in its operation and control of that organization. The internal auditing department is not an element of the managing segment of management, but of the control segment.

## THE NEXT STEP

The use of the internal auditing function as an internal consulting group requires that several specific issues be reviewed and an organizational policy statement be prepared and distributed within the organization. Issues that must be addressed would include:

Who can request consulting assistance from the department?

What priority will these consulting requests carry within the scheduling criteria of the auditing department?

How will the consulting assignments be scheduled and by whom?

Who is responsible for reviewing and controlling the time and cost estimates and budgets?

How will the costs of these assignments be determined and who is responsible for their payment?

Who is responsible for selecting the auditor who will complete the assignment and what selection criteria will be used?

How will the consulting assignments affect the departmental audit schedule?

Who will receive copies of the report prepared after the consulting assignment?

What is the auditor's responsibility or liability for recommendations included in the written report?

If work papers are prepared during the review, are they considered as part of the audit department files or is a separate file developed?

As the scope of the internal auditing function expanded into operational and information systems audits, the function was able to provide more assistance to the organization and management. The assistance which was provided expanded, but the recommendations were within an audit perspective.

Management is in a position in which it can more effectively utilize the skills and knowledge of the auditor and the internal auditing function. An auditor's approach to the organization is based on experience, training, orientation, and knowledge of the overall organizational structure and philosophy. It is this knowledge and experience that enables an auditor to provide additional assistance to management, if the departmental charter and organizational structure are appropriately defined to allow this role.

To function effectively within a formalized internal consulting role, the audit department charter will have to be revised by the board of directors and a specific memorandum of understanding issued for each consulting review. The director of internal auditing must ensure that the auditee is aware of this change in assignments, because a consulting assignment is concerned with reviewing the existing structure and making specific recommendations for modification. Once this is accomplished, however, the assistance which an internal auditor can provide to an organization and its management can be effectively increased.

# PART 2

# Specific Techniques

# CHAPTER 4

# FINANCING THE BUSINESS

## Don Walsh

Business owners and managers often turn to their accountants for advice and assistance in obtaining financing. The accountant may be asked to answer several questions on an informal basis or to provide extensive help in evaluating sources of financing and in preparing a loan proposal. This is particularly true with respect to smaller businesses.

Through lack of financial understanding and planning, business owners may obtain the wrong type of financing, over- or underestimate the amount of financing needed, fail to synchronize their funding with their needs, or underestimate the real cost of money.

This chapter provides information to help accountants steer clients toward the type of financing appropriate for their business. It discusses basic financing situations, provides an overview of debt and equity financing, and outlines information often requested by lenders and investors.

## BASIC FINANCING SITUATIONS

**BUSINESS START-UP.** Different types of businesses require different amounts of capital to get started. Facilities and equipment must be bought or rented, inventory purchased, and enough cash left over to run the business until the business's income can support its operations.

By turning a detailed business plan into a capital expenditures budget and profit and loss and cash flow projections, the new business owner can estimate how much capital will be needed. If the individual can put up all the necessary

---

This chapter is adapted from "Financing Small Business," *Small Business Reporter* (copyright Bank of America NT&SA, 1983).

cash, he or she will hold all the equity (ownership) in the business and begin debt free. Usually, however, the capital expenditures budget shows a need for more funds, or the profit and loss and cash flow projections forecast an inability to meet expenses.

To supplement inadequate start-up capital, the entrepreneur can sell equity or incur long-term debt. If shares of equity are sold, the capital is not repaid, but the investor takes an ownership interest in the business's assets and receives a portion of the business's profits, either in the form of dividends or through appreciation of shares. Long-term debt must be paid with interest, but normally gives the lender no ownership control.

Borrowing money at the outset can drain off a new firm's needed income into debt payment. Therefore the entrepreneur should plot out a second set of financial projections incorporating the loan's effects. A projected profit and loss statement should show the firm's ability to pay loan interest as an expense and to repay loan principal from net profit. The cash flow projection should prove the firm's ability to repay the total amount owed (principal and interest) with enough left over to support current operations.

Equity financing does not burden the business with loan repayments and interest charges, but it does utimately reduce the owner's share of the business's profits.

**WORKING CAPITAL SHORTAGE.**    Creeping expenses, a slowdown in sales or customer payments, or rapid growth may create a shortage of working capital that can financially squeeze the company.

The typical solution is an infusion of *medium- to long-term credit*, but the businessperson should understand that borrowing money is not always the answer to correcting a working capital shortage. New or additional debt should be assumed only if the cash flow projections indicate that the funds will generate sufficient profits to pay the debt.

A cash budget detailing expected cash flow might have uncovered the trend before financing was needed and allowed the company to consider several alternative solutions to improve liquidity. To maintain control of working capital, cash budgeting should be an ongoing process.

**SEASONAL PEAK.**    Businesses that operate on a seasonal sales cycle often rely on *short-term credit*. They borrow at the beginning of their production-sales cycle and repay the loan when receivables or inventory are converted to cash.

A new business should use a cash flow projection to determine the amount of money needed to meet projected inventory increases. Once the business is established in its cycle, the entrepreneur can estimate the amount of capital needed and then match the repayment term of the loan to the company's sales cycle.

**NEW EQUIPMENT AND FACILITIES.**    When businesses need money to replace or add equipment or facilities, they usually turn to sources of *long-term credit*. (Leasing is another option discussed later in this chapter.) Profit and loss projections should show that the new equipment or space will eventually pay for itself by cutting expenses, improving efficiency, or increasing sales. Loan repayment funds will come out of the business's cash flow; so the projections must reveal an adequate monthly surplus.

**SHARP, SUSTAINED GROWTH.**    When orders pour in, the expanding business may need money to move into larger quarters, add personnel, increase production, and expand the product line. When a business experiences this kind of rapid growth, it may use several types of financing concurrently, including *equity investments*, *long-term credit*, and a *line of credit* that expands along with the firm.

A line of credit allows the entrepreneur to borrow up to a certain amount of money within a defined period, usually up to one year. The entrepreneur pays interest only on the amount actually borrowed. However, a loan commitment fee may be required on the entire commitment or on the unused portion of the credit.

During rapid growth, an experienced company may face almost as many new situations as a new company. A detailed business plan should be used to clarify and control the process: Profit and loss and cash flow projections will show the amount of financing required and when it will be needed; projections will indicate the company's ability to pay its debts. Balance sheets should be prepared periodically to see how the company's net worth is being affected by all the changes.

# SELECTING THE TYPE OF FINANCING

When choosing a type of financing to fit a particular situation, the business owner must also consider the *debt-to-equity ratio*—the mix of debt dollars to ownership dollars. Generally speaking, the greater the percentage of ownership dollars, the more solid the business.

When a heavily capitalized company—one with a high proportion of equity to debt—needs money, it should seek debt dollars. For one thing, lenders are usually responsive to such a solid company. And by not taking on any more equity investments, the firm does not dilute the profits of its present investors. On the other hand, a highly leveraged firm—one with a high proportion of debt to equity—is usually advised to increase its ownership capital if it needs additional funds. Additional loans would increase the burdens of the heavily indebted company, lessening its chances for survival.

What is the ideal debt/equity ratio for a business to maintain? There is no "proper" ratio for all businesses at all times. Most financiers rely on *Annual Statement Studies*, published by the Robert Morris Associates, for median debt/equity and other ratios that are recorded by industry. These median debt/equity ratios vary greatly between industries and, according to the Robert Morris Associates, even these medians represent a wide range of difference. Bankers usually look for a debt-to-equity ratio that is consistent with the industry average for the particular business.

The basic difference among financing sources is the amount of risk each is willing to take in granting a loan or making an investment. Sources that specialize in high-risk projects usually expect the greatest return in profits or charge the highest interest on their loans. More conservative sources expect and receive less. Various sources of both equity and debt financing are listed in the "Small Business Financing Guide" near the end of this chapter.

# BOOTSTRAP FINANCING

Bootstrap financing means using the company's internal ability to generate capital. By stretching trade credit, turning fixed assets and receivables into ready cash, and cutting expenses, some businesses can operate with minimal or no outside help and avoid difficulties later on. In addition, lenders and investors look favorably on stringent business management that maximizes internal sources of funds, and they may be more inclined to provide funds if outside financing is needed in the future.

**TRADE CREDIT.**   By circulating trade credit through the business, hard-working managers can keep a company alive even when cash is short. Although a bank loan would accomplish a similar feat, banks sometimes consider the new firm a poor credit risk because it has not had a chance to establish a trade record. Also, beginning businesses may not be able to bear the added burden of loan repayments. Consequently, suppliers may often be the major source of short-term credit for new businesses.

Of course, suppliers also are affected by general economic conditions, and they may be forced to restrict trade credit policies when money is tight. Usually, however, suppliers will extend interest-free credit for up to 30 days—once the business has established a satisfactory payment record. Business owners sell the goods and collect sales before payments are due, then pay the bills out of the proceeds.

To establish and maintain good supplier relations, initial orders should be paid on delivery and all credit references promptly supplied. Major suppliers might appreciate a copy of the business plan, and it never hurts to keep them informed of business developments. If payments cannot be met, alerting the suppliers before the account becomes overdue can prevent animosity and credit curtailment.

**CUSTOMERS.**   When customers furnish a company's raw materials or pay for the work in installments as it is completed, they are, in effect, financing the business. A building contractor, for example, avoids some expenses when the customer provides the building materials. Similarly, the interior decorator who requires progress payments receives "financing" from the customer as each stage of the work is finished.

In some industries, when the business fills a highly specialized need, the owner may demand partial or total prepayment or payment on delivery. In addition, it is not uncommon to request a deposit with the order for custom sales. Also, a new business may decide to limit sales to cash or credit card purchases to avoid the expense of maintaining an accounts receivable system.

**REAL ESTATE.**   Pride of ownership can mean business failure if too much working capital is tied up in real estate or other fixed assets. Most business owners avoid large real estate investments by renting or leasing their facilities. Those companies that own buildings or land can turn their equity into cash by mortgaging their property to banks, commercial finance companies, savings and loan associations, or insurance companies.

*Real estate loans on commercial or industrial property* usually are written for not more than 75 percent of the appraised value. Repayment in regular installments (normally monthly) is amortized over 10 to 25 years: Payments completely pay off principal and interest by the end of the loan term. In certain cases, the loan term may be for a shorter period than the amortized payments schedule with the loan culminating in a bulk or "balloon" payment at the end of the repayment period. The borrower can either pay off the remaining balance or, if the lender is willing, refinance.

*A second mortgage* may be written on the owner's remaining equity in already mortgaged property, providing an additional way of obtaining cash. Interest rates on the first mortgage remain unchanged, while the entrepreneur repays the second mortgage at currently prevailing rates—customarily higher than first mortgage rates.

If the value of already mortgaged property has increased, *refinancing* may be possible. Through refinancing, a new mortgage is written based on the current value of the property. The owner receives the cash difference between the old and new mortgage loans. To justify refinancing, the owner must use this cash to generate business profits that will more than compensate for continued mortgage payments at new (and probably higher) interest rates. The business person should deal only with reputable mortgage lenders and explore all types of mortgages offered. In addition to a mortgage on business property, a *residential mortgage* on one's residence can sometimes be used to provide business financing.

**EQUIPMENT.**   If the business owner spends too much money buying equipment, the company may find itself without enough working capital to keep the business running. By using an *equipment loan* instead, the owner retains working capital to generate profits. Lenders generally finance 60 to 80 percent of the equipment's value. The balance represents the borrower's down payment on a new purchase or the amount of equity that the business retains in its own used equipment. The loan is repaid in monthly installments over one to five years or the term of the equipment's usable life. Later, if the company needs extra cash, already-owned equipment can be used to secure a loan. Generally, the bank finances 70 to 80 percent of the equipment's appraised value. Again, the loan is repaid in monthly installments over one to five years or the term of the equipment's usable life, whichever is less. In certain cases, seasonal payments may be available.

*Equipment leasing* is another way to avoid frozen capital. Everything from food processing machines to office furniture can be leased from banks, commercial finance companies, or numerous leasing companies. Equipment lease payments may eventually total more than the purchase price of the equipment. By feeding money back into the business instead of investing it in furniture or other fixed assets, however, the owner may receive more than the difference in profits. When the lessor retains the tax benefits of ownership, the lease rate to the customer usually is reduced. In this case, lease payments may even total less than equipment loan payments.

A business that already owns equipment can arrange a *sale and leaseback agreement*. The company sells its equipment to the bank, finance company, or leasing firm at a price near the equipment's current market value. The lessor then becomes the owner and leases the equipment back to the original owner, who continues to use it for the remainder of its usable life.

**STRINGENT MANAGEMENT.**   Bootstrap financing begins and ends with alert, tightfisted management. The owner should analyze recent business history to see how the business came to need financing. Profit and loss statements should first be scrutinized to see where expenses can be cut:

> What salaries are too high? Salaries are perhaps the single most troublesome expense to control. The business owner must be prepared to limit his or her personal earnings while the business is struggling to attain financial security.

How do the company's costs of goods and other expenses compare with other companies' in the industry?

Why are utility bills so high?

Are supplies being wasted?

How do actual expenses compare with budgeted expenses?

Only the individual business owner knows where the fat can best be trimmed from the organization. In addition to controlling expenses, the owner should look for ways to increase profits, sell surplus inventory or assets, and embark on an aggressive receivables collection program. If financial problems become severe or recur frequently, however, an outside business consultant may be able to help set the company on the road to profitability.

# EQUITY FINANCING

Equity financing necessitates dividing business ownership among investors who contribute capital but who may or may not participate in running the business. When one person capitalizes a business using only his or her assets (and possibly loan dollars), the firm is legally called a *sole proprietorship*. The individual is the sole owner, or equity investor, and that one owner is responsible for all the business's debts.

If two or more people form a *partnership*, equity investments can be added to the company's assets, with or without the partners' sharing business management and liabilities. General partners may have almost any management and profit-sharing arrangement; however, each partner is liable for the business's debts. Limited partners contribute capital without necessarily incurring management responsibilities and are generally liable only to the extent of their investment in the business.

A *corporation* may be preferable to a partnership—whether there are few or many investors—because of its tax benefits and limitation of legal liability. Generally, corporate stockholders are not liable for claims against the corporation beyond the amount of their original investment. Creditors have claim only against the assets of the corporation, although officers may be personally liable in some cases. A privately held corporation ordinarily consists of a limited number of stockholders, whereas a publicly held corporation offers its stock to the public at large through national stock exchanges or "over the counter."

Most small businesses use equity financing in a limited way. Whether the businesses are partnerships or corporations, additional equity usually comes from nonprofessional investors: friends, relatives, employees, customers, or industry colleagues. Professional investors—the venture capitalists and government-funded small business investment corporations—do sometimes invest in "small" businesses. However, they are looking for companies that will grow into major regional or national concerns, returning healthy profits to their stockholders.

Generally, it is advisable to prepare a written agreement for both professional and nonprofessional investors that documents the conditions of the investment. The agreement should detail the investment amount, terms, and risks involved. The entrepreneur should consult an attorney before taking on any equity investors to ensure compliance with state and federal regulations.

If a corporation is formed, the following investment vehicles are commonly used:

*Common stock* represents shares of ownership in a company and provides maximum potential return on investment for the company's founders and other investors. Should the corporation fail, all creditors and other investors are repaid before holders of common stock.

*Preferred stock* gives its holders a prior claim on the repayment over holders of common stock should the business fail. Holders of preferred stock are limited to fixed dividends and usually do not have voting privileges. Because preferred stock offers a smaller potential return than common stock, convertible preferred stock may be used so that shareholders can exchange preferred for common when the company's future looks bright.

*Convertible debentures* are long-term debt, all or a portion of which may be converted into common stock instead of being paid.

*Debt with warrants* is similar to the convertible debenture but allows the creditor/investor to purchase a specified amount of stock at a set price, even after the business has paid the debt but before the expiration of the warrant.

Because debentures and debt with warrants are both debt, they must be paid before holders of common and preferred stock are reimbursed. An attorney, accountant, or investment banker can provide a more detailed description of these investment tools. An accountant or banker also can help the entrepreneur determine which vehicles to offer and what stock prices would be fair.

**NONPROFESSIONAL INVESTORS.** Before considering professional investors, business owners should contact anyone who might contribute out of goodwill and a little faith. Relatives, co-workers, suppliers, and customers of the business are all traditional sources of capital. However, financial experts warn owners to keep family and social relationships separate from business decisions and to document loan transactions (as they would with professional investors) to avoid potential difficulties in the future.

Other nonprofessional investors can be recruited from the ranks of the wealthy who often are interested in investment opportunities as a tax shelter. Other accountants or a knowledgeable banker, insurance broker, stockbroker, or investment banker can provide sources.

**VENTURE CAPITALISTS.**    Venture capital makes available investment dollars for new, relatively unproven enterprises. Such money never has been easy to obtain because venture capital firms are in the business of investing money to make money. These concerns do not make charitable contributions; they gamble that a business will return their investment not only with interest, but with a large profit.

Many venture capital firms are affiliated with banks, other financial institutions, insurance companies, and large corporations. Other venture capital firms are owned by individuals, wealthy families, and private groups of investors. A few firms are publicly owned. Investment minimums range from $50,000 for some of the smaller firms to $500,000, which the larger firms require to justify their investment of time. Investment ceilings, however, are almost unlimited. The most heavily capitalized firms specify no ceiling and have invested several million dollars in a single business. The small venture capitalists achieve the same result by syndicating or sharing the investment among several firms. Venture capitalists usually have definite preferences concerning location, type, and size of business, and its stage of development. Venture capital directories (see "Sources of Further Information," at the end of this chapter) can help the entrepreneur find appropriate investors.

Most venture capitalists purchase common or convertible preferred stock rather than burden the fledgling enterprise with interest payments on debt or debentures. Because there is no limit on the amount of stock that they may purchase, investors could own more than 50 percent of the business. Although venture capitalists generally choose to sit on the board of directors and offer management and technical advice, they usually are not interested in running the daily business operations, unless the business's survival is at stake.

Although venture capital implies risk, some investors are more cautious than others. Generally, investors expect a projected return on investment that is proportionate to the risks involved. The risks and return on an investment decrease as the company grows. Although getting in on the ground floor, or "seed financing," is the most profitable, it is also the riskiest investment. Few ventures capitalists will become involved at this stage, because the company is usually no more than an idea or a prototype without any solid management organization or production-sales plan.

Once a business organization and plan is developed and the company is ready to start up, a larger number of venture capitalists will be attracted to promising deals. In the first-round financing stage, the risks are lessened, but stock prices remain attractively low.

More conservative venture capitalists prefer to invest when the risks and rewards decrease still further in second- and third-round growth financing. Others hold back until the company is ready for "bridge financing" to tide it over until a merger or public offering ends its small business life and launches it into the next stage of corporate growth.

A company's business plan serves as the primary analytical tool for venture capitalists. In analyzing such a plan, these investors focus on three basic features:

1. **Management capability.**   Sophisticated investors emphasize that no matter how good the product is, the quality and experience of the management makes or breaks the company.

2. **A better product.**   Investors are looking for a competitive advantage—product or service innovations that will elevate the new company above healthy competition in the field. A new idea, backed by market surveys and competition analysis, is a tempting lure for investors.

3. **Growth industry**.   Investors look for businesses in industries that are growing at a much faster rate than the gross national product.

If the venture capitalist has no interest in a proposal, a "no" answer will come in a matter of days. But if investors decide to consider the proposal seriously, a decision may take up to a few months; full processing of the deal may stretch over another several months.

**SMALL BUSINESS INVESTMENT COMPANIES AND MINORITY ENTERPRISE SMALL BUSINESS INVESTMENT COMPANIES.**   Historically, private venture capital firms never have been able to fill small businesses' capital needs, and minority-owned small businesses have had a particularly hard time attracting investors. In 1958, the federal government acted to improve conditions by authorizing *small business investment companies* (SBICs) —privately owned capital firms eligible for federal loans to invest in or loan to small businesses.

In 1969, the U.S. Small Business Administration (SBA), in cooperation with the U.S. Department of Commerce, created *Minority Enterpise Small Business*

*Investment Companies* (MESBICs or 301(d) licensees) to serve only those small businesses that were at least 51 percent owned by socially or economically disadvantaged Americans.

Both SBICs and MESBICs are licensed and regulated by the federal government under the SBA. They must be privately capitalized with at least $500,000; then they are eligible for $3 to $4 in SBA funding for every dollar of private capital. Most SBICs and MESBICs are owned by small groups of individuals. A few are publicly owned, and corporations and financial institutions own the rest.

Usually SBIC and MESBIC investments are smaller than those of their larger, privately funded counterparts. By federal regulations, MESBICs may spend up to 30 percent of their private capital on a single investment, and SBICs may spend only 20 percent of their private capital on each client. (They may also extend debt financing within these same limitations. Both SBICs and MESBICs may assist only those small businesses that have net worth of less than $6 million and an average net income after taxes of $2 million or less for the latest two years.

Like privately funded venture capitalists, SBICs and MESBICs may specify preferences in investment type, dollar amount, location, and industry. The *Directory of Operating Small Business Investment Companies*, published by the SBA, lists each company and its preferences.

These investment companies normally purchase common and preferred stock or limited partnership interests in their clients' small businesses. Because companies must pay interest on funds received from the SBA, however, they often prefer income-generating debentures or loans with warrants to straight equity investments. The majority of these investment companies prefer financing expanding businesses rather than those just starting out, and they look for an annually compounded return at least 20 percent on an investment. Generally, SBICs and MESBICs expect to divest themselves of their interest in a business within five to seven years.

Like any other venture capitalist, SBICs and MESBICs scrutinize the business plan. Basically they are looking for growth potential in a healthy industry, sound management, and a proven track record.

## DEBT FINANCING

Debt financing is available from a variety of sources, including both commercial and government lenders. In addition to familiar types of business loans, there are special loan vehicles geared to businesses with special needs and problems.

The discerning credit shopper will quickly learn that commercial lenders—

those who operate for a profit—consider risk an important factor when setting loan charges. Lenders who cater to rock-solid businesses generally have lower loan interest rates than lenders who specialize in newer or less predictable concerns and must charge accordingly.

Government lenders often charge the lowest interest rates. These government agencies operate to aid small business rather than to make a profit, and their limited funds are always in great demand. The borrower must shop around, first locate the type of loan that best fits the business's need, and then find the source that will make the loan for the desired amount and duration. Ideally, the borrower should also check for the most advantageous interest rates, although small business borrowers often do not have many choices.

**BANKS.**    Commercial banks, the center of the lending market, are by far the most visible lenders, making the greatest number and variety of loans. Generally, however, banks are considered conservative lenders. Although they accept collateral for business loans, this security is considered merely "secondary support": Loan approval rests on a business owner's repayment ability as indicated by the firm's profitability, its management expertise, and the entrepreneur's personal record.

**Short-Term Loans.**    Granted for less than a year, short-term loans are a primary source of funds for a business's day-to-day financial needs. All types of companies use such loans to take advantage of supplier discounts, boost inventory, or increase production for seasonal sales peaks. Short-term loans usually are self-liquidating—that is, repaid when the receivables or inventory financed are converted to cash.

The *commercial loan*, repaid in a lump sum after three to six months, is the basic short-term vehicle. It is normally unsecured (made without any specific collateral), although the bank relies on the firm's financial statement to determine whether the borrower is creditworthy and will draw on the business's assets should the business fail to meet the loan terms. Stocks and bonds, a time certificate of deposit (TCD), the cash value of life insurance, or a personal guarantee may be accepted as support of the borrower's ability to repay the loan.

If the loan exceeds a specified amount, usually about $100,000, some banks require that the borrower maintain a cash reserve in a bank account. The size of this reserve or "compensating balance" will depend on several variables; in some cases, this balance may be a combination of 10 percent of the credit committed plus 10 percent of the credit in use. Most banks, however, will accept fees or additional interest as a substitute for compensating balances.

When a major part of a company's working capital is tied up in unpaid accounts, or when more credit is needed than the bank will extend in an unsecured loan, *accounts receivable financing* may be the answer. Receivables financing gives the company a cash injection that grows along with its sales, yet protects the banker with an asset that can be readily liquidated.

An accounts receivable loan turns unpaid invoices into ready cash: The bank advances up to 80 percent of the eligible receivables' value as ordered goods are shipped or work is completed. Generally, banks do not finance receivables that are more than 60 days past due or more than 90 days from invoice date. The borrower grants a security interest in the receivables to the bank as collateral for the loan. The borrower sends customers' payments to the bank, and the bank credits the loan with the agreed-on percentage and deposits the remainder in the borrower's account. Receivables loans form a *revolving line of credit* in which funds are continually advanced, repaid, and readvanced. Interest is paid only on the outstanding loan balance. The receivables line is usually contracted for a year, reviewed by the lender and, if approved, renewed for an additional year.

*Inventory financing* or a *commodities loan*—a second type of revolving credit—is secured by the raw materials, work in progress, or finished goods that constitute the firm's inventory. Because inventory is less easily liquidated than receivables, banks usually advance only up to 50 percent of the inventory's value. Inventory financing is very effectively combined with receivables financing to build inventory for peak selling seasons. The inventory loan is paid off by receivables advances, which in turn are repaid when the accounts are collected.

An established borrower of known profitability may qualify for an *unsecured line of credit*. Banks usually extend a line of credit for one year, promising to loan the borrower up to a certain amount. Like a receivables or inventory line, the unsecured line is usually revolving; that is, the business can repeatedly borrow, repay, and borrow again all or part of the credit available.

**Medium- and Long-Term Loans.** Extended for more than a year, medium- or long-term loans are used for business start-ups, purchase of facilities and equipment, construction, real estate improvements, or for added working capital. Term loans are repaid monthly or quarterly from cash flow.

*Unsecured term loans* are usually granted only to firms with profit histories and whose current or projected financial data demonstrate that cash flow will be sufficient to repay the loan. If a term loan is extended for a new business start-up, most banks require the entrepreneur to contribute at least 50 percent of the venture's cost. The term loan usually requires a written loan agreement which, among other things, limits the company's other debts, dividends, and principals' salaries. In addition, the agreement may set a percentage of company profits that must be used to accelerate repayment of the loan. Violation of this agreement constitutes a default. Sometimes a compensating balance is also required.

Term loans may be supported by personal guarantees, stocks and bonds, and TCDs or, sometimes, partially secured by equipment. Medium- or long-term loans that are fully secured by equipment or real estate are separate loan vehicles.

*Equipment Loans* can enable a business to purchase new or used equipment or provide funding for the company that cannot qualify for unsecured credit. With an unsecured term loan a business could cover 100 percent of its equipment costs, but most banks limit their equipment loans to 60 to 80 percent of the equipment's value. The loan is usually repaid monthly over one to five years or the length of the equipment's usable life.

*Real estate financing*, or a commercial or industrial mortgage, is offered by most banks. The commercial mortgage is usually made for up to 75 percent of the property value and amortized over a set period—usually from 10 to 25 years. Banks also provide residential mortgages and real estate refinancing.

*Equipment leasing* has become a financing tool for more and more banks. They generally write equipment leases for a minimum of three years, stretching up to 80 percent of the equipment's useful economic life—possibly as long as 15 years. As equipment lessors, banks may offer comparatively low lease rates by retaining the investment tax credit and depreciation on the leased equipment.

**Specialized Credit Vehicles.**    To serve retailers of expensive items such as cars, boats, and mobile homes, some banks have developed specialized credit vehicles.

In *flooring*, the bank finances the retailer's purchase of big ticket items and holds a security interest until the merchandise is sold and the loan is paid off. The bank collects monthly interest on the amount advanced, and the retailer repays principal as each item is sold. A flooring line may be renewed annually.

*Indirect collection financing* is used to help retailers sell big ticket items on an installment basis. As in accounts receivable financing, installment sales contracts are turned into ready cash when the bank advances up to 80 percent of their value as the item is sold. The borrower grants a security interest in these contracts as collateral for the loan. This line of credit is handled in the same manner as an accounts receivable line of credit.

**Bank Loan Criteria.**    Generally, bankers require the most information from first-time borrowers. Unsecured loans require more proof of repayment ability than secured loans, and the loan package usually becomes more detailed as the size of the loan or its term is increased. Bankers view a loan package with three main criteria in mind.

They look for *borrowers with experience* in the business they propose to enter. Like investors, bankers view management as their "security" in making a loan.

They check *personal credit records*. Most lending officers advise applicants to establish credit through local stores or credit cards before seeking a bank loan.

Bankers investigate the business's *ability to repay the loan*. Depending on the type of financing requested, the banker will pay particular attention to different aspects of the business.

When a bank considers a short-term loan, it studies the firm's liquidity—its working capital available to meet short-term debt. If a firm's current working capital situation is strong, inventory turns swiftly, and accounts are collected on time, the business will be a good prospect for short-term credit.

Receivables or inventory merit special attention when a company applies for a loan secured by one of these assets. Receivables more than 60 days past due are generally not accepted as security. Lenders also avoid large concentrations of receivables in a few accounts. Sloppy bookkeeping is enough to discourage some lending officers. On inventory loans, bankers look for rapid turnover and prefer goods with established market values; perishable or fad items are avoided.

When considering intermediate- or long-term loans, lending officers search for proof of business profitability. Therefore for equipment loans, equipment leasing, real estate loans, and especially the high-risk unsecured term loans, bankers require long-term profit and loss and cash flow projections to document the business's ability to pay off the debt, as well as some historical profit and loss information which would indicate that projections are realistic. Projections should be explained and backed up with facts. Lending officers compare projections with published industry standards and, therefore, quickly notice overestimated earnings or underestimated costs.

Borrowers should strive to establish and maintain relationships with their bankers. The business owner who avoids the banker until he or she needs money may find that a loan is harder to get because the lender is unfamiliar with the history of the business.

**Interest Rates.**    Interest rates have been a major concern of business owners during recent years. Many borrowers (and potential borrowers) may question why some types of loans carry higher interest rates than others, why certain borrowers pay higher or lower interest for the same loan and, finally, why some interest rates remain stable for long periods, whereas others fluctuate with the prime rate.

The key to understanding the pricing of loans is the realization that banks price their products as any other business does: Banks must allow enough margin to cover their cost of "goods," operating expenses, and business risks and still leave a profit.

**Cost of funds.**    Because the bank obtains money from various depositors to make its loans, the interest rate on each loan reflects the amount that the bank itself must pay to attract deposits. Interest rates on short-term loans fluctuate according to the interest paid on short-term deposits, which in turn depends on conditions in the money market—the supply of and demand for short-term funds. The best barometer of interest rates on all short-term business borrowings is the prime rate, the interest rate that an individual bank charges for short-term loans to large, creditworthy business customers. Small businesses usually are unable to qualify for the prime rate; generally they pay one to four points above prime. By watching the rate's movement in the daily newspaper, the small business owner can get some idea of the interest expense the company would incur.

Banks make fixed-rate long-term loans from a pool of long-term funds—those that remain with the bank for more than one year. Consequently, the interest rates charged on fixed-rate long-term loans do not fluctuate in the same way as the prime rate or the day-to-day changes in the money market. The primary factors in long-term rates are the current inflation rate and the market's expectations of the future inflation rate.

Banks and other lenders also make adjustable-rate loans in which the lender can increase or decrease the interest rate at specified intervals to keep pace with current market conditions. Lenders determine changes in the interest rate based on movements in an interest rate index that is independent of their control, such as the monthly average of six-month U.S. Treasury Bills.

**Operating Costs.**    To the cost of funds, the bank must add the specific time and labor costs required to administer each loan. A short-term commercial loan, for example, costs less to arrange than the more formal term loan with complex terms and conditions.

**Risk of Loan Loss.**    The bank's final consideration is the amount of risk inherent in lending a specific amount of money to a specific borrower for a specific period of time. Loans to more established and stable businesses carry less risk than loans made to new or less stable enterprises. As a borrower requests money for longer periods, the risk of failure and the interest rate increased together. Unsecured loans entail greater risks and therefore may command higher interest rates than secured loans.

Ultimately, the interest charged on any loan will reflect the bank's effort to measure the preceding variables and add a margin for profit. Although all banks generally work with the same factors in pricing their loans, interest rates will vary because of competition.

Processing time varies widely depending upon the bank, the type and size of loan, and the reputation and preparedness of the borrower. Some lending officers advise business owners, even when they have prepared all the necessary loan documentation, to solicit funds one or two months before the business will need them.

Generally, unsecured loans—and loans secured by liquid collateral such as time deposits—require the least amount of processing time. Loans secured by accounts receivable or inventory may require several weeks to complete necessary auditing and filing procedures. Equipment financing may take several days or weeks to arrange, whereas a real estate mortgage might entail one to two months of work.

**COMMERCIAL FINANCE COMPANIES.** New or quickly expanding small businesses sometimes are denied bank loans because of their limited track records, high degree of debt, or large financing needs. Even long-established businesses may find themselves in similiar situations. They may be denied bank financing because of business reversals, or they simply may be in need of more money than their bankers are willing to lend.

These businesses can turn to commercial finance companies for many of the same loans banks offer. Finance company loans sometimes exceed the net worth of the borrower—a situation that is undesirable to most banks, which consider a low debt-to-net-worth ratio as one index of business stability and acceptable risk. Commercial financiers, like banks, are concerned with a company's ability to repay the loan; however, they are more willing to rely on the quality of a firm's collateral rather than its track record or the profits forecast in its financial projections.

Accounts receivable financing is the most popular financing company tool because receivables are the most easily liquidated security. But if a company's need surpasses its outstanding accounts, an inventory loan is usually added to expand the line of credit. Commercial finance companies use these two vehicles in essentially the same way that banks do. Finance companies also provide two- to five-year term loans secured by new equipment or already-owned equipment. Some commercial finance companies will even permit borrowers to assign their equity in already-owned equipment in lieu of cash down payments on equipment purchase.

Longer-term loans—extending up to 10 years—may be secured by commercial or industrial real estate. Not all finance companies make commercial mortgages, but those that do typically provide refinancing and second mortgages as well. Partially or totally unsecured long-term loans are the newest addition to the finance company spectrum. Some companies now make these two- to 10-year loans based on a banklike assessment of the borrower's profitability rather than collateral.

Other commercial finance company vehicles include equipment leasing and factoring—the outright purchase of accounts receivable. Finance companies parallel banks in their equipment leasing methods. They often transact equipment sale and leasebacks, however, which many banks avoid. When commercial finance companies engage in factoring, they normally follow the methods described in the next section.

Although commercial finance companies assess a business's financial statements, tax returns, credit references, and management history, they will not require the extensive financial projections requested for unsecured lending. Instead, accounts receivable and inventory are examined following bank criteria. Equipment and real estate are privately appraised.

Because commercial finance companies specialize in higher risks than banks and often borrow some of their funds from banks, their interest rates on all loans usually run above banks' stated rates. If the borrower has supplied all the pertinent information and has been properly audited, most finance companies will make or deny a loan within two days to a few weeks.

**FACTORS.**    A factor is a business that purchases outright the accounts receivable of another business and assumes responsibility for credit evaluations and collections. Through factoring, the business is essentially paid cash on delivery while its customers get the credit terms they require. Factors' cash advances can help a business expand, build seasonal inventory, finance an acquisition, or generate cash to buy out partners.

Unlike accounts receivable financing, factoring is not a loan. The factor purchases accounts receivable for their value, usually advancing 60 to 80 percent of their worth when the company ships the goods and remitting the remainder—less the factor's fees and interest charges—when customers pay. After checking the credit of each account, the factor purchases receivables "without recourse," meaning that the factor will absorb any bad debt losses. The factor may withhold from the reserve only when an account will not pay for faulty merchandise the company refuses to replace.

Because the factor buys receivables without recourse, it assumes the entire risk should the account fail to pay. Although factoring has traditionally been used in the garment industry by eminently "bankable" companies, some clients are struggling enterprises rejected by other financiers. To compensate for these risks, factors charge a one to two percent fee for each invoice plus interest on their advance. The total fee is usually above both bank and commercial finance company rates for receivables financing.

Factors do not require extensive loan documentation because they are less concerned with debt-to-net-worth ratios or business profitability. Instead, they look for:

The basic honesty of the business owner

The credit reliability of the client's customers

Diversified receivables without heavy concentration of debt in one or two accounts

The ability and willingness of the client company to honor warranties, service merchandise, and handle customer complaints

When the factor receives the client's personal and business financial statements and credit references and is satisfied that there are no outstanding liens against the client, processing of a factoring request can be accomplished in as little as 24 hours.

**LIFE INSURANCE COMPANIES.** A whole life insurance policy (not a term policy) can double as business cash when the business owner borrows on his or her policy. This is a standard loan for most life insurance companies. Along with such policy loans, life insurance companies also offer commercial mortgages for customers and noncustomers alike. Some insurers even provide unsecured term loans to certain selected businesses.

The *policy loan* can be used for any business or personal need. It usually takes two years for a policy to accumulate sufficient cash value; then the insured may borrow up to 95 percent of the cash value of the policy for an indefinite period. Interest is charged yearly but can be deferred indefinitely so long as the borrower continues to pay the insurance premiums. The borrower should realize, however, that the loan drains the dollar worth of the insurance policy. Should the life insurance be needed, the coverage will be reduced by the amount borrowed under the policy.

Insurers make *mortgage loans* on properties worth at least $500,000. Mortgage loans from life insurance companies generally are made available through branch offices or independent loan correspondents, such as mortgage bankers. The mortgage banker, in return for a loan servicing fee, acts as an intermediary between businesses seeking mortgage financing and insurance companies interested in investing funds in mortgages. Insurers normally advance 75 percent of the property's appraised value. To keep monthly mortgage payments minimal, insurers often schedule loan payments over 25 to 30 years with a bulk or balloon payment due after 10 to 15 years.

Mortgage loans imply a slightly greater risk, and insurers' mortgage rates may be limited by state usury laws. In states without usury laws, insurers' rates correspond to bank mortgage rates. When making a mortgage loan, insurance companies consider the value of the real estate before the borrower's personal or business financial capability. All buildings are independently appraised; cost estimates and analyses must be submitted for loans on proposed structures. After the value of the real estate has been determined, the insurer/lender examines the business's credit rating and the owner's financial statements and comparable personal data for the previous three to five years.

*Unsecured term loans* from insurance companies are relatively hard to obtain, because borrowers must qualify under guidelines established by the National Association of Insurance Commissioners (NAIC). Insurers make unsecured term loans primarily to businesses with histories of profit for at least five years. Loans usually begin at $500,000 and are paid back periodically over 10 to 15 years.

Unsecured term loans are usually moderately risky, but NAIC regulations effectively limit the insurers' risks by admitting only blue-ribbon companies. These unsecured term loans generally carry interest rates higher than short-term bank rates, reflecting their longer term, the current inflation rate, and the market's expectation of the future interest rate. The loan request requires detailed documentation similar to the sample loan package outlined on pages 88–89.

Loan processing time varies with the particular life insurance company in question, but a policy loan usually can be advanced within two weeks. Both the mortgage loan and the term loan can take from one to three months to obtain.

**CONSUMER FINANCE COMPANIES.**    When other sources of debt financing have turned their backs, many small businesses have been launched on personal loans. Consumer finance companies provide personal loans up to and exceeding $25,000 for any personal need—including financing a small business. Loans below $5000 to $10,000 are often secured by personal property or "consumer durables": cars, boats, or collections of personal items. Monthly payments are scheduled over a set period, varying between six months and 10 years.

A loan exceeding $10,000 usually is known as a "homeowner's loan" or home equity loan, because it is traditionally secured by a second mortgage on the home. Homeowner's loans are paid back in monthly installments, usually over five to 10 years. Individual states determine maximum loan amounts. However, some companies set their own loan ceilings below the maximum allowed by the state.

Some personal finance companies offer unsecured or "signature" loans in addition to their secured lending. These loans are made to customers with established credit references. The loan ceiling varies greatly among individual finance companies, and repayment may extend over periods from one to five years. Because personal finance companies often serve those who are denied bank credit, they are high-risk lenders and their interest rates may be somewhat higher than bank rates for similar loans.

Consumer finance companies base their loans on the personal creditworthiness of the applicant. They request that the applicant supply current credit and financial information. If the borrower's business is the source of income for loan repayment, business financial information will be requested to demonstrate repayment ability. Processing usually takes from three days to two weeks.

**SAVINGS AND LOAN ASSOCIATIONS.**    Savings and loan associations specialize in real estate financing. Both state and federally chartered savings and loan associations make loans on commercial and industrial property and personal residences. The commercial and industrial mortgage is a fairly standard tool. Savings and loans make mortgages for as little as $50,000, advancing up to 75 percent of the property's value and spreading the loan amortization over periods of up to 25 years. Interest rates vary with the mortgage market at levels competitive with banks, commercial finance companies, and life insurance companies.

Savings and loans offer mortgage loans for customers and noncustomers alike. They usually do their own appraisals, looking for marketable real estate of a general nature in a good location. Savings and loan associations, like banks, tend to avoid some very specialized types of manufacturing buildings. They analyze borrowers' personal and business financial statements, relying on a business's profitability to repay the mortgage. Two to eight weeks are needed to approve the savings and loan mortgage, depending on the individual company as well as the complexity of the particular property.

Passage of the Garn-St. Germain Depository Institutions Act of 1982 allows federally chartered savings and loan associations to invest portions of their assets in commercial and industrial loans not secured by real property. Many states have enacted similar legislation for their state chartered associations. Although savings and loan associations are now able to expand their services to include many of the financial products and services once available only from commercial banks, the majority continue to specialize in real estate financing.

**SMALL BUSINESS ADMINISTRATION.**    The U.S. SBA, established as a federal agency by the Congress in 1953, guarantees intermediate- and long-term bank loans to small businesses and makes a limited number of direct loans to small businesses.

In order to be eligible for any assistance, an enterprise must fit SBA criteria for small business. Under current definitions, small businesses include:

Retailers with gross annual sales of less than $2 million to $7.5 million (depending on the industry)

Wholesalers with gross annual sales of less than $9.5 million to $22 million (depending on the industry)

General construction firms with gross annual sales under $9.5 million (a $5 million ceiling applies to some special trade construction firms)

Manufacturers who employ a maximum of 250 to 1500 workers (again, depending on the industry)

Service businesses, transportation concerns, farms, and agricultural enterprises each have their own specific size standards.

The federally funded SBA either makes direct loans or guarantees loans through several programs. Commercial banks, savings and loan associations, and some nonbank lenders can make SBA-guaranteed loans.

*Direct loans* generally are limited to $150,000. The SBA cannot consider a direct loan request if funds are available from a bank or other lending source. The applicant's loan request must have been declined by at least one bank— two in a city with a population greater than 200,000—before the SBA will consider a direct loan. Funding for direct loans is often limited. Generally, about 90 percent of the SBAs transactions are loan guarantees.

The *7a loan guarantee* may be made for up to $500,000 or 90 percent of the loan, whichever is less. The SBA and the lender require the borrower to put up a "reasonable amount" of the project's cost, depending on the loan request and borrower's ability to repay the loan. (Members of economically or socially disadvantaged groups may qualify for reduced collateral requirements.) Fixed assets, real estate, and inventory are taken as security. The loan is usually limited to seven years for working-capital financing, 10 years for purchasing fixed assets, and 25 years for construction.

*Seasonal lines of credit* guarantee loans to finance a seasonal increase in business activity. Amounts are similar to those under 7a. Although a business may have other SBA loans outstanding, only one seasonal loan can be outstanding at any one time. Seasonal lines of credit are not revolving; each loan must be repaid within 12 months and be followed by an out-of-debt period of at least 30 days. Seasonal loans, secured by inventory and accounts receivable, are paid as assets are liquidated. Credit can be used only for labor and materials, and the client must show sufficient working capital to cover expenses. Prior to the termination date, the bank and/or the SBA will review the contract, at which time the line of credit may be reduced or extended.

*Export revolving lines of credit* guarantee lines of credit extended by lenders to small businesses engaged in exporting. Amounts are similar to those in the 7a loan guarantee program. Funds may be used for labor and materials and to penetrate or develop foreign markets; they may not be used to pay existing obligations or to purchase fixed assets. Borrowers must have been in business (not necessarily in exporting) for at least 12 months prior to filing an application. The term of the loan is based on the borrower's business cycle, but may not exceed 18 months.

*Contract loan guarantees* assist contractors and subcontractors in construction, manufacturing, and service industries. Each loan covers labor and materials for one contract and is for the short term (usually 12 months, although sometimes for up to 18 months on larger contracts). Ceilings and rates are similar to those under 7a.

*Guarantees to small general contractors* cover new or rehabilitated residential or commercial structures for resale. Financing, only for expenses on a single project, cannot be used for land purchases and is secured by a first lien on land and building or buildings. These loans are repayable 36 months after construction has been completed.

*Disaster recovery loans* assist businesses that have suffered either physical damage or economic injury from a natural disaster. To qualify, a business must be located in a region officially declared a disaster by the President, Secretary of Agriculture, or Administrator of the SBA. Physical disaster loans (other than home loans) are restricted to 85 percent of verifiable loss up to a maximum of $500,000. Economic injury loans have higher ceilings. Both types of loans generally carry lower than market interest rates. Disaster loans are extended for up to 30 years, and repayment usually begins five months from the date of the loan.

The *energy loan program* assists small businesses that develop, manufacture, sell, install, or service specific solar energy and energy-saving devices. Applicants must indicate projected and actual energy savings and number of jobs created by the business. Direct loans are made for up to $150,000, and loan guarantees for up to $500,000. Terms may be extended up to 25 years.

The *handicapped assistance loan program* makes low interest loans and guarantees to public or private nonprofit organizations operating in the interest of handicapped individuals. Businesses owned by handicapped individuals may also qualify for financing through this program. Guaranteed loans are limited to $350,000 with a maximum term of 15 years. Direct loans are made for up to $100,000.

Because the SBA serves businesses not bankable without its guarantee, clients are obviously intermediate risks. They may be undercapitalized, lack sufficient collateral, and have a minimal track record or imperfect operating history. Or, they may require a repayment period that is longer than lenders may be willing to extend in order to accommodate projected cash flow. To curb its lending risks, the SBA sets modest loan ceilings and offers clients free management assistance. Interest rates on its guaranteed loans cannot exceed maximums set by the SBA. The interest on hard-to-get direct loans normally is slightly below comparable bank rates.

The SBAs loan documentation requirements generally are more complex than banks' snd closely resemble the sample loan package shown later in this chapter. Applications for SBA loan guarantees are first reviewed by the lender and, if approved, passed to the SBA. Like banks, the SBA must first be convinced that a business can repay the loan from profits. Consequently, the SBA is interested in profitability ratios and business projections. But unlike commercial lenders, the SBA will sometimes ignore a losing track record if the business shows signs of improvement leading to a healthy future. The SBA also will make loans for longer maturities than bank loans and accept borrowers whose collateral does not support the full value of the loan.

Processing time for term loan guarantees normally takes two to three weeks after receiving approval from the lender. Because seasonal line-of-credit applicants are typically established customers, the SBA often can process these guarantees in less time. Direct loans may require several months' processing time, if funds are available.

In an effort to reduce paperwork and streamline the delivery of financial services to small businesses, the SBA initiated the Certified Lenders Program (CLP) in 1979. Under the CLP, the lender performs an initial credit analysis of applications and then forwards them to the SBA for final approval. Under the newer Preferred Lenders Program (PLP), credit authority is more fully delegated to the lender. Preferred lenders make final approvals on loan requests and then report them to the SBA, which guarantees up to 75 percent of the borrowed amount. The loans under PLP are guaranteed for a minimum of $100,000 and a maximum of $500,000. Interest rates are negotiable between borrower and lender. Preferred lenders can normally process loan requests in a matter of days.

**SMALL BUSINESS INVESTMENT COMPANIES AND MINORITY ENTERPRISE SMALL BUSINESS INVESTMENT COMPANIES.** In addition to their equity investments, most SBICs and MESBICs make long-term loans and loan guarantees. Loans or investment dollar maximums are based on their private capital—equal to 30 percent of the MESBICs private capitalization or 20 percent of the SBICs private funds.

Minimum loan maturities are two and one-half years for MESBICs and five years for SBICs. Almost all loans are subordinated to other creditors; that is, other creditors would have a prior claim on repayment. Loans generally are made for five to seven years, though they may be extended for as long as 20 years. The loans are primarily for business expansion, not for short-term, working-capital needs.

Most investment companies prefer to lend to established companies or finance acquisitions and mergers. They usually do not lend more than the net worth of the business, and they encourage participation by other lenders such as banks. Because loan interest can burden struggling companies, many SBICs and MESBICs defer loan amortization for the first three years or until the borrower can begin repaying both interest and principal in monthly installments without straining.

The business plan is the key to both loans and investments. SBICs and MESBICs analyze these plans closely, usually lending to the most surefire enterprises and acquiring equity in the riskier ventures. SBIC and MESBIC interest rates depend on long-term market conditions or the limit established by usury laws in the state involved. Processing time for loans equals that for equity investments: a few weeks to several months for an answer.

**LOCAL DEVELOPMENT COMPANIES AND CERTIFIED DEVELOPMENT COMPANIES.**  Small business contributes to the economic well-being of a community by providing jobs, broadening the local tax base, and upgrading neighborhoods. To assist small business on the grass-roots level, the federal government encourages community residents to form local development companies (LDCs) under the SBAs 502 loan program and certified development companies (CDCs) under the SBAs 503 loan program. Organized and capitalized by at least 25 local residents as either for-profit or nonprofit corporations, LCDs and CDCs solicit private sector and government funds to provide long-term financing to small businesses. Development companies are often organized and supported by city and county government as part of the Neighborhood Business Revitalization Program. Both LDCs and CDCs tend to limit their activities to a single community or metropolitan region, although CDCs are authorized to function on a statewide basis.

Development companies have become popular methods of attracting or retaining job-creating industries in areas where considerable tax breaks or other inducements are not available. Through either of these programs, a growing small business may satisfy its plant requirements without tying up working capital in fixed investments for real estate, improvements, and major equipment. With SBA and bank loans added to their own funds, development companies build, buy, or rehabilitate structures and purchase machinery and equipment.

Clients' monthly lease or mortgage payments are geared to repay bank and development company loans over a period of up to 25 years. At the end of a lease agreement, small business may have the option of renewing the lease or purchasing the facilities at their current market value or for a nominal sum (such as $1), depending on the development company's profit status.

A development company usually supplies only 10 percent of a project's cost. Often, the small business client will supply all or part of this investment. (Some communities make low interest funds available for this portion of the cost.) Through SBA-guaranteed bank loans, LDCs arrange for the balance of financing. Financing for CDCs is arranged through bank loans and the sale of SBA-guaranteed debentures. Participation of the SBA through either program is limited to $500,000 per project and may not exceed 50 percent of project's total cost.

Both LDCs and CDCs can finance all of a company's facilities, but neither can supply working capital or fund the purchase of inventory, supplies, or freestanding equipment. They can, however, sometimes arrange companion loans from banks and other sources.

**Development Company Loan Risk/Return.**    Relatively high-risk ventures can be aided through a development company because the development company, not the small business, is the actual loan recipient. Through development company assistance and companion loans, a small business can set up shop or expand existing facilities with relatively little private capital. If an enterprise fails, the development company can bring in another tenant who continues to repay the loan; in this way the banks and the SBA stand a good chance of repayment.

Loans guaranteed by the SBA are made at the funding bank's interest rate, subject to any limits set by the SBA. The interest rates on SBA-guaranteed debentures are set by the Federal Financing Bank. Many development companies are nonprofit organizations and therefore charge minimal interest rates for their percentage of funds. Development companies that operate for a profit charge rates near bank standards. Both LDCs and CDCs also may charge small service fees.

In addition to packaging and processing loans, CDCs are required by law to provide free professional legal and accounting services to their small business clients. Some LDCs offer similar services, although they're not required to do so.

A small business that applies for LDC or CDC assistance is evaluated by the development company, the SBA, and the lending institution. Development companies require a standard loan package and look for businesses with product potential, management capability and, preferably, a proven track record. Prospective clients should have enough of their capital to support business growth.

A development company can usually process a financing request within 30 to 60 days. A business owner interested in development company assistance should contact the local SBA office.

**ECONOMIC DEVELOPMENT ADMINISTRATION.** The Economic Development Administration (EDA) of the U.S. Department of Commerce is authorized to provide direct loans and loan guarantees to businesses in areas of high unemployment or low family income. Business development assistance provided by EDA is designed to upgrade an area economically by creating or retaining permanent, well-paying jobs for local residents. To qualify for assistance, a business must be located in an EDA redevelopment area, the financial assistance provided must be of direct benefit to the local residents, and the venture must not provide excess capacity for the particular industry in that area.

There is no loan ceiling on EDA financial assistance programs; however, loans must generally be for $500,000 or more and must not be obtainable through any other government agency. Direct fixed-asset loans may not exceed 65 percent of the total cost of land, buildings, machinery, and equipment for industrial or commercial enterprises. Depending on the availability of funds and the nature of the project, the EDA may limit its loan to less than 65 percent of these costs. Direct working-capital loans may be in the full amount required. Fixed-asset loans and loan guarantees may be extended up to 25 years. Working-capital loans and loan guarantees are generally limited to a term of five years.

All projects must be adequately supported by investment capital. At least 15 percent of total costs for projects financed by direct fixed-asset loans must be in the form of equity or a subordinated loan. And one-third of this amount usually must be supplied by the state or nongovernmental community or area organization, although in certain cases this requirement may be waived. Generally, an applicant should obtain the advice of area experts on a proposed project before submitting application for assistance. Applications for projects costing less than $1 million need sufficient background information to support the technical and economic feasibility of the project. Projects costing more than $1 million will require an economic feasibility study by a qualified independent consultant.

Financial specialists from EDA are available at regional offices to assist in planning the project and preparing the application. Because of the complexity of the factors involved, processing of EDA applications generally takes at least six months.

**FARMERS HOME ADMINISTRATION.** The U.S. Department of Agriculture, through the Farmers Home Administration (FmHA), guarantees term loans to nonfarming business in rural areas; that is, localities with populations below

50,000 not adjacent to a city where densities exceed 100 persons per square mile. The FmHA does not make direct loans but will guarantee up to 90 percent of a bank loan to qualifying rural applicants. Unlike the SBA, the FmHA sets no loan guarantee ceilings. It guarantees 30-year loans for real estate acquisition, 15-year loans for financing fixed assets, and seven-year loans for increasing working capital. Collateral requirements are set by the participating bank.

The FmHA will guarantee loans to business owners with good business histories who can supply as little as 10 percent of their capital needs, but the agency requires a "considerably greater" equity investment in most cases. Guaranteed loan rates are negotiated between the borrower and the lender.

The FmHA requires the same extensive loan documentation as the SBA. But, because the FmHA tries to increase rural prosperity by expanding business activity, it additionally requires a detailed description of jobs to be created and the impact they would have on the overall employment in the area.

Each loan application is analyzed to determine the borrower's ability to repay the loan. Priorities are given to businesses in open country or in towns with populations below 25,000. Business expansions are preferred to relocations. The FmHA looks for projects that will save existing jobs, improve an existing business or industry, or create jobs. Business owners who are military veterans are given priority over other applicants. Processing time varies according to the complexity of the assistance sought.

## THE BUSINESS PLAN

The business plan describes a company's past and current operations, then demonstrates how the desired investment or loan will further the company's goals and reward the prospective investor. In the search for equity financing, the business owner presents a plan that will be almost the sole basis for the investor's decision. Therefore the plan submitted—to private investors, venture capitalists, SBICs, and MESBICs—should closely adhere to the sample business plan shown in Exhibit 4.1.

**EXHIBIT 4.1.  Sample Business Plan Outline**

---

  I. Cover Letter
    A.  Dollar amount requested
    B.  Terms and timing
    C.  Type and price of securities
  II. Summary
    A.  Business description
        1.  Name

**EXHIBIT 4.1.** (*continued*)

  2. Location and plant description
  3. Product
  4. Market and competition
  5. Management expertise
 B. Business goals
 C. Summary of financial needs and application of funds
 D. Earnings projections and potential return to investors

III. Market Analysis
 A. Description of total market
 B. Industry trends
 C. Target market
 D. Competition

IV. Products or Services
 A. Description of product line
 B. Proprietary position: patents, copyrights, and legal and technical considerations
 C. Comparison to competitors' products

V. Manufacturing Process (if applicable)
 A. Materials
 B. Source of supply
 C. Production methods

VI. Marketing Strategy
 A. Overall strategy
 B. Pricing policy
 C. Methods of selling, distributing, and servicing products

VII. Management Plan
 A. Form of business organization
 B. Board of directors composition
 C. Officers: organization chart and responsibilities
 D. Résumés of key personnel
 E. Staffing plan/number of employees
 F. Facilities plan/planned capital improvements
 G. Operating plan/schedule of upcoming work for next one to two years

VIII. Financial Data
 A. Financial statements (five years to present)
 B. Five-year financial projections (first year by quarters; remaining years annually)
  1. Profit and loss statements
  2. Balance sheets
  3. Cash flow charts
  4. Capital expenditure estimates
 C. Explanation of projections
 D. Key business ratios
 E. Explanation of use and effect of new funds
 F. Potential return to investors; comparison to average return in the industry as a whole

Although it may be advisable in many cases for the business owner to seek professional help in preparing the business plan, he or she should be familiar with every detail of the plan. The entrepreneur's knowledge and understanding of the plan will be an important factor to analysts and loan officers who evaluate the firm's management.

## THE LOAN PACKAGE

The outline of a complete loan package in Exhibit 4.2 illustrates the type of detailed presentation sometimes required by lenders such as banks and the SBA. However, this degree of detail is often unnecessary for businesses already known to the lender. Many debt sources never require such complete documentation. Instead, they seek the particular information described in previous sections of this chapter.

The sample loan documentation on the following pages demonstrates an acceptable rendition of only the major parts of a loan package. It does not represent the complete loan package outlined in Exhibit 4.2, and it adheres to the business buy-out format rather than the forms for business start-up or expansion. Because the business described in the loan package operates on a cash basis, no provision is made for an accounts receivable system. This particular example involves a hypothetical SBA-guaranteed bank loan, but does not include any SBA loan forms.

### EXHIBIT 4.2.   Sample Loan Package Outline

---

I. Summary
  A.  Nature of business
  B.  Amount and purpose of loan
  C.  Repayment terms
  D.  Equity share of borrower (debt/equity ratio after loan)
  E.  Security or collateral (listed with market value estimates and quotes on cost of equipment to be purchased with the loan proceeds)

II. Personal information (on all corporate officers, directors, and any individuals owning 20 percent or more of the business)
  A.  Education, work history, and business experience
  B.  Credit references
  C.  Income tax statements (last three years)
  D.  Financial statement (not over 60 days old)

III. Firm information (whichever is applicable below —A, B, or C)
  A.  New business
      1.  Business plan (see outline of business plan on pages 86–87)
      2.  Life and casualty insurance coverage

**EXHIBIT 4.2.** (*continued*)

    3. Lease agreement

    4. Partnership, corporation, or franchise papers, if applicable

  B. Business acquisition (buyout)

    1. Information on acquisition

      a. Business history (include seller's name, reasons for sale)

      b. Current balance sheet (not over 60 days old)

      c. Current profit and loss statements (preferably less than 60 days old)

      d. Business's federal income tax returns (past three to five years)

      e. Cash flow statements for last year

      f. Copy of sales agreement with breakdown of inventory, fixtures, equipment, licenses, goodwill, and other costs

      g. Description and dates of permits already acquired

      h. Lease agreement

    2. Business plan

    3. Life and casualty insurance

    4. Partnership, corporation, or franchise papers, if applicable

  C. Existing business expansion

    1. Information on existing business

      a. Business history

      b. Current balance sheet (not more than 60 days old)

      c. Current profit and loss statements (not more than 60 days old)

      d. Cash flow statements for past year

      e. Federal income tax returns for past three to five years.

      f. Lease agreement and permit data

    2. Business plan

    3. Life and casualty insurance

    4. Partnership, corporation, or franchise papers, if applicable

IV. Projections

  A. Profit and loss projection (monthly, for one year) and explanation of projections

  B. Cash flow projection (monthly, for one year) and explanation of projections

  C. Projected balance sheet (one year after loan) and explanation of projections

## Summary of Loan Application

| | |
|---|---|
| Applicant | Mr. Gene K. Cho and Mrs. Betty S. Cho (husband and wife) <br> 555 Seaside Avenue <br> San Francisco, CA 94112 <br> (415) 201-0613 |
| Business | Rainbow Liquors <br> 5775 Ocean Avenue <br> San Francisco, CA 94112 <br> (415) 201-6789 |
| Type of business | Retail liquor store |
| Size of business | Annual sales have been about $200,000; meets the SBA definition of small business. |
| Method of acquisition | Buyout |
| Ownership | Husband and wife partnership |
| Availability of funds from net worth outside of business | Mr. and Mrs. Cho are injecting $20,000 from the sale of their previous business. In addition, they will use their station wagon in the business. They will maintain $2000 for personal emergencies. Their home will provide the collateral for the loan. The Chos have no other assets that can be contributed to the business. Thus they meet SBA requirements on outside net worth. |
| | The Chos are members of an economically disadvantaged group and qualify for reduced collateral requirements under the SBA 7a loan guarantee program. |

## Loan Request

| | |
|---|---|
| Amount | $60,000 |
| Terms | Eight years with no prepayment penalty. First payment due four months after date of note. |
| Interest rate | Current SBA rate |
| Debt/equity ratio | $60,000/$20,000 = $^3/_1$ |
| Collateral | 1. Security interest under California UCC-1 on all business assets<br>2. Personal guarantees of Mr. and Mrs. Cho<br>3. Second deed of trust on home<br>4. SBA guarantee |
| Guarantee fee | Borrowers to reimburse bank for SBA guarantee fee of 1 percent of amount guaranteed, or $540. |
| Other conditions | 1. Borrowers will assign life insurance in the amount of the loan and keep it in force during the term of the loan<br>2. Borrowers will maintain hazard insurance with loss payable endorsement in the amount and type required by lender<br>3. Borrowers will provide annual financial statements to lender |
| Purpose of loan | The loan, together with the applicants' equity, will enable Mr. and Mrs. Cho to purchase the liquor store, buy new equipment and fixtures, make improvements, and provide working capital. |

The complete financial plan and specific use of loan funds is shown on the following page.

| Use of Funds | Source of Funds | | |
| --- | --- | --- | --- |
| | Loans | Equity | Total |
| Purchase of business | | | |
| Inventory | $28,000 | $ 0 | $28,000 |
| Liquor license | 10,000 | 0 | 10,000 |
| Fixtures and equipment | 2,500 | 0 | 2,500 |
| Goodwill, convenant | | | |
| not to compete | 0 | 17,500 | 17,500 |
| Subtotal | $40,500 | $17,500 | $58,000 |
| Closing costs | 0 | 1,200 | 1,200 |
| Deposits | 0 | 1,300 | 1,300 |
| Working capital | 4,500 | 0 | 4,500 |
| New equipment, fixtures, leasehold improvements | 15,000 | 0 | 15,000 |
| Subtotal | $19,500 | 2,500 | $22,000 |
| | | | |
| TOTAL | $60,000 | $20,000 | $80,000 |

New equipment includes new refrigeration ($4000); fixtures include new shelving and displays ($7000); leasehold improvements include painting and floor covering ($4000). Price quotes from suppliers and contractors are included in the documents section.

Loan repayment   The loan will be repaid from the business's cash flow. The projections of sales, expenses, and cash flow indicate that there is sufficient earning power to provide adequate loan coverage.

| Cash Sources | 10/1/83–9/30/84 |
| --- | --- |
| Earnings | $20,735 |
| Depreciation | 3,000 |
| | $23,735 |

| Cash Uses | |
| --- | --- |
| Loan Principal* | $ 5,108 |
| Owners' Draw | 14,000 |
| Income Taxes | 1,000 |
| | $20,108 |

*Interest portion of loan payments was included as an expense before net earnings.

The cash coverage is 1.2 ($23,735/$20,108) and is adequate to assure repayment of the loan. Owners' draw is, of course, subordinate to loan payment. As the business grows, the cash coverage will become even stronger.

**Break-even analysis**

The break-even analysis shows that the sales projections, upon which payment ability is calculated, are reasonable.

$$\frac{\text{Fixed expense and loan principal payments (\$35,143)}}{1.00 - \text{variable cost as a percentage of sales (.76)}} = \begin{array}{c}\text{Break-even sales}\\ \$146,429\end{array}$$

The sales level needed to break even on this basis is $146,429 or 70 percent of projection ($208,000). This provides ample leeway for meeting fixed obligations.

**Analysis of purchase price**

Evaluation of the purchase price using the SBA formula indicates the price is reasonable. The purchase price is analyzed in two components: the tangible assets and goodwill, which includes the noncompetition convenant. The tangible assets to be purchased include:

| | |
|---|---:|
| Inventory | $28,000 |
| Equipment and fixtures (book values) | 2,500 |
| Liquor license | 10,000 |
| Assessment of value for goodwill: | $40,500 |

Average annual profits for the past three years ($15,283) less owner's salary ($7000) and earning power of tangible assets (based on SBA factor of 7 percent multiplied by $40,500) = $5448. Three years average earning power ($5448) multiplied by three gives a value to goodwill of $16,344, compared to $17,500 in the sales price.

The conclusion is that the sales price is reasonable based on the $58,000, compared to $56,844 by the formula.

| | |
|---|---|
| Name | Gene K. Cho |
| Address | 555 Seaside Avenue<br>San Francisco, CA 94112 |
| Phone | (415) 201-0613 |
| Personal | Born: February 23, 1940<br>Married, two children<br>U.S. citizen |
| Education | Lincoln University<br>San Francisco, CA<br>MBA, 1970 |
| | San Francisco State University<br>San Francisco, CA<br>B.A. in Business Administration, 1965 |
| Employment and<br>Business Experience | 1975-present<br>Dandy Wig Company<br>Daly City, CA<br>Owner-Manager |
| | Mr. Cho established and built this business himself. The company imported wigs from the Far East and sold them wholesale and retail. Mr. Cho established reliable supply lines and developed the distribution system for the West Coast. |
| | 1970–1975<br>Bank of America<br>San Francisco, CA<br>Data Processing Supervisor |
| | 1965–1969<br>East Wind Trading Company<br>San Francisco, CA<br>Salesman |
| | Duties included establishing and servicing sales accounts. Also was successful in developing new markets for new products imported by the company. |
| Personal Credit<br>References | Bank of America<br>Ocean Avenue Branch |

|                          | San Francisco, CA |
|--------------------------|-------------------|
|                          | Savings Account: 0123-45678<br>Checking Account: 1234-56789 |
|                          | Golden East Savings and Loan<br>5546 Seaside Avenue<br>San Francisco, CA |
|                          | Auto Loan No. 05532-05523<br>Home Loan No. 308-055921 |
| Personal Credit<br>References | Bank of America<br>Ocean Avenue Branch<br>San Francisco, CA |
|                          | Savings Account: 0123-45678<br>Checking Account: 1234-56789 |
|                          | Golden East Savings and Loan<br>5546 Seaside Avenue<br>San Francisco, CA |
|                          | Auto Loan No. 05532-05523<br>Home Loan No. 308-055921 |

## Résumé

| | |
|---|---|
| Name | Betty S. Cho |
| Address | 555 Seaside Avenue<br>San Francisco, CA 94112 |
| Phone | (415) 201-0613 |
| Personal | Born: October 1, 1947<br>Married, two children<br>U.S. citizen |
| Education | San Francisco State University<br>San Francisco, CA<br>B.A. in Political Science, 1969 |
| Employment and<br>Business Experience | 1974–present<br>Orient Importing Company<br>San Francisco, CA<br>Part-time office assistant<br><br>Duties included handling purchase orders and billings and bookkeeping.<br><br>1969–1972<br>San Francisco Chamber of Commerce<br>San Francisco, CA<br>Assistant Office Manager<br><br>Duties included supervising clerical staff and preparing reports for Chamber of Commerce officials. |
| Personal Credit<br>References | Bank of America<br>Ocean Avenue Branch<br>San Francisco, CA<br><br>Savings Account: 0123-45678<br>Checking Account: 1234-56789<br><br>Golden East Savings and Loan<br>5546 Seaside Avenue<br>San Francisco, CA<br><br>Auto Loan No. 05532-05523<br>Home Loan No. 308-055921 |

## Personal Financial Statement
## As of August 1, 1983

*Assets*

| | |
|---|---:|
| Cash on hand and in checking accounts | $ 625 |
| Savings accounts | 22,000 |
| U.S. government bonds | 0 |
| Accounts and notes receivable | 0 |
| Life insurance cash value | 0 |
| Other stocks and bonds | 0 |
| Real estate | 50,000 |
| Automobile | 4,500 |
| Other personal property | 14,000 |
| Other assets | 0 |
| TOTAL ASSETS | $91,125 |

*Liabilities*

| | |
|---|---:|
| Accounts payable | $ 840 |
| Notes payable to banks | 0 |
| Notes payable to others | 0 |
| Installment account (auto) | 1,820 |
| Installment account (other) | 317 |
| Loans on life insurance | 0 |
| Mortgages on real estate | 28,247 |
| Unpaid taxes | 0 |
| Other liabilities | 0 |
| TOTAL LIABILITIES | $31,224 |
| NET WORTH | $59,901 |

## Business Plan

| | |
|---|---|
| Name and Address of Business | Rainbow Liquors<br>5775 Ocean Avenue<br>San Francisco, CA 94112<br>(415) 201-6789 |
| History of Business | The business was established in 1940 by the current owner's husband, Carl Costello. Mr. Costello died three years ago, and since then Mrs. Costello has managed the business alone. She has not been in good health, nor has she had much interest in the business since her husband passed away. She has curtailed the hours of operation and often leaves the employees unsupervised. Sales have fallen from $235,000 to $180,000 in the past three and one-half years. Gross profit margins have been erratic, and no capital improvements have been made in years. |
| Plan of Operation Under New Owners | Mr. and Mrs. Cho have been customers of Rainbow Liquors for a number of years, as they have lived in this neighborhood since 1974. Mr. Cho believes that a younger and more vigorous management can make this well-established business begin to grow and prosper again. |
| Sales Plan | 1. Extend business hours (currently 10 A.M. to 7 P.M.) to 9 A.M. to 9 P.M.; extend business days (currently six days) to seven days a week.<br>2. Refurbish the store to make it more attractive and modern.<br>3. Expand the product line by adding cold sandwiches, magazines, and more wines.<br>4. Increase advertising, using the local weekly shopping edition and occasional neighborhood leafleting.<br>5. Improve point of purchase displays and do more in-store promotions. |
| Cost Reduction | Mr. Cho's plan to reduce costs is to:<br>1. Restore the gross profit margin. Cost of sales has fluctuated in the past three and one-half years, and profit margins have fallen to a |

current low of 13.5 percent. Compared to an industry average of 25 percent, there is great room for improvement. Strict control over inventory and pricing should make the business profitable again very quickly and restore the gross margin to an appropriate level.

2. Reduce payroll costs. The store presently employs three full-time workers as cashiers and clerks, with Mrs. Costello attending irregularly. Mr. and Mrs. Cho will both work in the store and will hire one full-time employee. They will add part-time and more full-time help as sales grow. At present, however, they can reduce payroll costs by about $17,000 a year.

| | |
|---|---|
| **Plan of Operation Under New Owners** | Mr. and Mrs. Cho have been customers of Rainbow Liquors for a number of years, as they have lived in this neighborhood since 1974. Mr. Cho believes that a younger and more vigorous management can make this well-established business begin to grow and prosper again. |
| **Sales Plan** | 1. Extend business hours (currently 10 A.M. to 7 P.M.) to 9 A.M. to 9 P.M.; extend business days (currently six days) to seven days a week.<br>2. Refurbish the store to make it more attractive and modern.<br>3. Expand the product line by adding cold sandwiches, magazines, and more wines.<br>4. Increase advertising, using the local weekly shopping edition and occasional neighborhood leafleting.<br>5. Improve point of purchase displays and do more in-store promotions. |
| **Cost Reduction** | Mr. Cho's plan to reduce costs is to:<br>1. Restore the gross profit margin. Cost of sales has fluctuated in the past three and one-half years, and profit margins have fallen to a current low of 13.5 percent. Compared to an |

*(continued)*

industry average of 25 percent, there is great room for improvement. Strict control over inventory and pricing should make the business profitable again very quickly and restore the gross margin to an appropriate level.

2. Reduce payroll costs. The store presently employs three full-time workers as cashiers and clerks, with Mrs. Costello attending irregularly. Mr. and Mrs. Cho will both work in the store and will hire one full-time employee. They will add part-time and more full-time help as sales grow. At present, however, they can reduce payroll costs by about $17,000 a year.

Market Potential

The growth potential is considerable. Ocean Avenue is a neighborhood shopping district for the adjoining residential area of moderate-income families. It is accessible by public and private transportation. The market area for this study has been defined as one square mile. Using the census data for the nine census tracts that fall into this radium, there was a total population of 47,347 in 1980. The average annual per capital spending in liquor stores for the entire city is $75. This would yield a potential market of $3.5 million for this one-square-mile area. Clearly, there is sufficient potential for Rainbow Liquors to expand, not only to reach the $235,000 sales level the store once had, but also to exceed it.

There are seven other liquor stores in the Ocean Avenue shopping district. Only two are of a size comparable to Rainbow Liquors. The other stores are old and quite small. With the planned improvements, Rainbow Liquors can expect to draw some of the market from these stores.

Managerial Capacity

Mr. and Mrs. Cho have substantial business and managerial background to operate this business successfully. Mr. Cho has a BA and an MBA in business administration and has shown he can run a prosperous business. Mrs. Cho has valuable retail skills from her work experience and is capable of doing the recordkeeping and bookkeeping so essential to good management.

In addition, Mrs. Costello has agreed to stay on for a short period to ease the transition and introduce the Chos to suppliers and regular customers.

**Rainbow Liquors**
**Projected Profit and Loss Statement**
**Prepared August 1, 1983**

| MLR | 1983 | | | 1984 | | | | | | | | | Total | % |
|---|---|---|---|---|---|---|---|---|---|---|---|---|---|---|
| | Oct. | Nov. | Dec. | Jan. | Feb. | Mar. | Apr. | May | June | July | Aug. | Sept. | | |
| Net sales | 15,000 | 16,000 | 19,000 | 17,000 | 16,000 | 17,000 | 17,000 | 17,000 | 18,000 | 18,000 | 19,000 | 19,000 | 208,000 | 100 |
| Less Cost of Sales | 12,000 | 12,480 | 14,250 | 12,750 | 12,000 | 12,750 | 12,750 | 12,750 | 13,500 | 13,500 | 14,250 | 14,250 | 157,230 | 76 |
| Gross Profit | 3,000 | 3,520 | 4,750 | 4,250 | 4,000 | 4,250 | 4,250 | 4,250 | 4,500 | 4,500 | 4,750 | 4,750 | 50,770 | 24 |
| Expenses | | | | | | | | | | | | | | |
| Salaries | 600 | 600 | 600 | 600 | 600 | 600 | 600 | 600 | 600 | 600 | 600 | 600 | 7,200 | 3.5 |
| Payroll Taxes | 60 | 60 | 60 | 60 | 60 | 60 | 60 | 60 | 60 | 60 | 60 | 60 | 720 | .3 |
| Alarm Service | 30 | 30 | 30 | 30 | 30 | 30 | 30 | 30 | 30 | 30 | 30 | 30 | 360 | .1 |
| Advertising | 80 | 80 | 80 | 80 | 80 | 80 | 80 | 80 | 80 | 80 | 80 | 80 | 960 | .5 |
| Delivery | 20 | 20 | 20 | 20 | 20 | 20 | 20 | 20 | 20 | 20 | 20 | 20 | 240 | .0 |
| Bad Debts | 20 | 20 | 20 | 20 | 20 | 20 | 20 | 20 | 20 | 20 | 20 | 20 | 240 | .0 |
| Dues and Subscriptions | 10 | 10 | 10 | 10 | 10 | 10 | 10 | 10 | 10 | 10 | 10 | 10 | 120 | .0 |
| Laundry and | 10 | 10 | 10 | 10 | 10 | 10 | 10 | 10 | 10 | 10 | 10 | 10 | 120 | .0 |

| Item | | | | | | | | | | | | | Total | % |
|---|---|---|---|---|---|---|---|---|---|---|---|---|---|---|
| Linen | 100 | 100 | 100 | 100 | 100 | 100 | 100 | 100 | 100 | 100 | 100 | 100 | 1200 | .6 |
| Legal and Accounting | 100 | 100 | 100 | 100 | 100 | 100 | 100 | 100 | 100 | 100 | 100 | 100 | 1200 | .6 |
| Office Expenses | 10 | 10 | 10 | 10 | 10 | 10 | 10 | 10 | 10 | 10 | 10 | 10 | 120 | .0 |
| Repairs and Maintenance | 50 | 50 | 50 | 50 | 50 | 50 | 50 | 50 | 50 | 50 | 50 | 50 | 600 | .3 |
| Supplies | 35 | 35 | 35 | 35 | 35 | 35 | 35 | 35 | 35 | 35 | 35 | 35 | 420 | .2 |
| Telephone | 35 | 35 | 35 | 35 | 35 | 35 | 35 | 35 | 35 | 35 | 35 | 35 | 420 | .2 |
| Utilities | 100 | 100 | 100 | 100 | 100 | 100 | 100 | 100 | 100 | 100 | 100 | 100 | 1,200 | .6 |
| Miscellaneous | 50 | 50 | 50 | 50 | 50 | 50 | 50 | 50 | 50 | 50 | 50 | 50 | 600 | .3 |
| Depreciation | 250 | 250 | 250 | 250 | 250 | 250 | 250 | 250 | 250 | 250 | 250 | 250 | 3,000 | 1.4 |
| Insurance | 100 | 100 | 100 | 100 | 100 | 100 | 100 | 100 | 100 | 100 | 100 | 100 | 1,200 | .6 |
| Rent | 300 | 300 | 300 | 300 | 300 | 300 | 300 | 300 | 300 | 300 | 300 | 300 | 3,600 | 1.7 |
| Taxes and Licenses | 150 | 150 | 150 | 150 | 150 | 150 | 150 | 150 | 150 | 150 | 150 | 150 | 1,800 | .9 |
| Interest | 512 | 509 | 506 | 502 | 499 | 495 | 491 | 488 | 484 | 480 | 476 | 473 | 5,915 | 2.8 |
| Total Expenses | 2,522 | 2,519 | 2,516 | 2,512 | 2,509 | 2,505 | 2,501 | 2,498 | 2,494 | 2,490 | 2,486 | 2,483 | 30,035 | 14.0 |
| Net Profit (Loss) | 478 | 1,001 | 2,234 | 1,738 | 1,491 | 1,745 | 1,749 | 1,752 | 2,006 | 2,010 | 2,264 | 2,267 | 20,735 | 10.0 |

# Explanation of Projected Profit and Loss Statement

**Gross Sales.** Sales are expected to have a seasonal variation as well as a growth component. With the changes planned in operations, sales are expected to return to the level of a year ago.

**Cost of Sales.** Cost of sales is expected to improve gradually until it reaches a standard 75 percent.

**Gross Profit.** (Also called Gross Margin.) This is the difference between sales and cost of sales.

**Expenses.** Operating expenses are itemized below.

**Salaries.** The Cho's plan to hire one full-time employee during their first year of operation. As sales increase, they can add staff as needed. Both Mr. and Mrs. Cho will work in the store; their wages are shown as owners' draw on the cash flow.

**Payroll Taxes.** Estimated at 10 percent of payroll to cover employers' share of FICA, unemployment insurance, and workers' compensation.

**Alarm Service.** Burglar alarm service is contracted at $30 per month.

**Advertising.** The Cho's plan to increase the advertising budget from $50 to $80 per month.

**Delivery.** A modest sum is allocated for business travel.

**Bad Debts.** For direct write-offs of bad checks. Based on the store's historical experience.

**Dues and Subscriptions.** A small amount is set aside for subscriptions to trade journals and memberships in trade associations.

**Laundry and Linen.** Smocks for clerks and restroom towels.

**Legal and Accounting.** Mr. Cho will use the accountant who serviced his previous business. The rate provides for financial statements and an annual income tax return.

**Office Expense.** For office supplies such as stationery and postage.

**Repairs and Maintenance.** For conservative purposes, this estimate is slightly higher than historical averages of $40 per month. It is more likely that this expense will be reduced, because a number of capital improvements will be made at the outset.

**Supplies.** Mainly for paper bags; estimated sightly higher than historical average of $30 per month due to inflation.

**Phone.** A $35 per month budget provides for some increase due to inflation.

**Utilities.**   Gas and electricity estimated at $100 per month based on historical experience, allowance for longer hours, and inflation.

**Miscellaneous.**   For contingencies and miscellaneous items.

**Depreciation.**   $17,500 of fixed assets, such as equipment, shelving, leasehold improvements; fixtures are depreciated over five years on a straight-line basis for about $3000 per year. This rate provides for a remaining salvage of $2500 at the end of the five-year period.

**Insurance.**   Fire and liability insurance at current rate.

**Rent.**   Based on the lease agreement.

**Taxes and Licenses.**   Includes business license tax.

**Interest.**   Interest on requested loan of $60,000 amortized over eight years at interest rate of 10.25 percent.

**Total Expenses.**   Sum of the above expenses.

**Net Profit.**   (Also called Net Income.) Difference between total expenses and gross profits. Net profit is about 10 percent of sales and is comparable to the historical experience two years ago when adjusted for a reduced payroll.

# Rainbow Liquors
## Projected Balance Sheet
### Current Status (after purchase of business) versus One Year Later

| Assets | Oct 1, 1983 | Oct 1, 1984 |
|---|---|---|
| *Current Assets* | | |
| Cash on Hand and in Bank | 4,500 | 8,127 |
| Accounts Receivable | 0 | 0 |
| Inventory | 28,000 | 28,000 |
| Total Current Assets | 32,500 | 36,127 |
| *Fixed Assets* | | |
| Fixtures and Equipment | 17,500 | 17,500 |
| Less Depreciation | 0 | (3,000) |
| Net Fixed Assets | 17,500 | 14,500 |
| *Other Assets* | | |
| Liquor License | 10,000 | 10,000 |
| Goodwill | 17,500 | 17,500 |
| Deposits | 1,300 | 1,300 |
| Total Fixed Assets | 46,300 | 43,300 |
| TOTAL ASSETS | 78,800 | 79,427 |

| Liabilities | Oct 1, 1983 | Oct 1, 1984 |
|---|---|---|
| SBA Loan (Current) | 5,108 | 5,657 |
| SBA Loan (Long-term) | 54,892 | 49,235 |
| Total Liabilities | 60,000 | 54,892 |
| Equity (Beginning) | 20,000 | 20,000 |
| Plus Earnings (Preoperating) | (1,200) | (1,200) |
| (Operating) | 0 | 20,735 |
| Less Draws | 0 | (15,000) |
| Ending Equity (Net Worth) | 18,800 | 24,535 |
| TOTAL LIABILITIES AND EQUITY | 78,800 | 79,427 |

## Explanation of Projected Balance Sheet

**Assets.**   Current and fixed.

**Cash on Hand and in Bank.**   Taken from projected cash flow statements.

**Accounts Receivable.**   Borrowers do not plan to extend trade credit.

**Inventory.**   Initial inventory level of $28,000 is expected to be purchased and is more than sufficient to support first year's expected sales level.

**Current Assets.**   Sum of cash and inventory.

**Fixed Assets.**   Detailed below.

**Fixtures, Equipment, and Improvements.**   includes $2500 worth of equipment purchased with the business and $15,000 worth of new expenditures.

**Depreciation.**   Amount taken from projected profit and loss statement.

**Net Fixed Assets.**   Difference between original cost and depreciation of equipment, fixtures, and improvements.

**Liquor License.**   Purchased as part of the business.

**Goodwill.**   Included as part of the business purchase price.

**Deposits.**   For rent, utilities, and sales taxes.

**Total Assets.**   Sum of current and fixed assets.

**Liabilities.**   Current and long-term liabilities.

**Current Liabilities.**   Current portion of loan requested.

**Long-term Liabilities.**   Sum of current and long-term liabilities.

**Beginning Equity.**   Includes $20,000 initial cash injection.

**Earnings.**   Preoperating loss of $1200 closing costs incurred at time of loan; at end of one year of operation, earnings are taken from projected profit and loss statement.

**Draws.**   Owners' draws for salaries and taxes are deducted from equity.

**Ending Equity.**   Beginning equity plus profits and less owners' draws equals ending equity.

**Total Liabilities and Equity.**   Sum of total liabilities and ending equity equals total assets.

## Small Business Financing Guide

| Use of Funds | Type of Money | Source | Financing Vehicle |
|---|---|---|---|
| *Business Start-up* | Equity | Nonprofessional investor | Partnership formation |
| | | | Stock issue |
| | | Venture capitalist | Stock issue |
| | | SBIC-MESBIC | Convertible debentures |
| | | | Debt with warrants |
| | Long-term debt | Bank | Term loan (limited) |
| | | Savings and loan association | Unsecured term loan |
| | | | Equipment loan |
| | | | Equipment leasing |
| | | | Real estate loan |
| | | SBIC-MESBIC | Term loan (limited) |
| | | | Unsecured term loan |
| | | | Equipment loan |
| | | | Equipment leasing |
| | | Commercial finance company | Equipment loan |
| | | | Equipment leasing |
| | | | Real estate loan |
| | | Life insurance company | Policy loan |
| | | | Real estate loan |
| | | Leasing company | Equipment leasing |
| | | Consumer finance company | Personal property term loan |
| | | Small Business Administration | Term loan guarantee |
| | | Certified or local development company | Facilities/ Equipment Financing |
| | | Farmers Home Administration | Term loan guarantee |
| *Working Capital* | Long-term debt | Bank | Unsecured term loan |
| | | Savings and loan association | Equipment loan |
| | | | Real estate loan |

## Small Business Financing Guide

| Use of Funds | Type of Money | Source | Financing Vehicle |
|---|---|---|---|
| | | Commercial finance company | Equipment loan |
| | | | Real estate loan |
| | | Life insurance company | Policy loan |
| | | | Real estate loan |
| | | | Unsecured term loan (limited) |
| | | Consumer finance company | Personal property term loan |
| | | Small Business Administration | Term loan guarantee |
| | | SBIC-MESBIC | |
| | | Farmers Home Administration | |
| | | Term loan guarantee | |
| *Seasonal Peak* | Short-term debt and Line of Credit | Supplier | Trade credit |
| | | Bank | Commercial loan |
| | | Saving and loan association | Accounts receivable association |
| | | | Inventory financing |
| | | | Flooring |
| | | | Indirect collection financing |
| | | | Unsecured line of credit |
| | | Commercial finance company | Accounts receivable financing |
| | | | Inventory financing |
| | | | Factoring |
| | | Factor | Factoring |
| | | Life insurance company | Policy loan |
| | | Consumer finance company | Personal property loan |

(*continued*)

## Small Business Financing Guide

| Use of Funds | Type of Money | Source | Financing Vehicle |
|---|---|---|---|
| | | Small Business Administration | Line of credit guarantee (limited) |
| *Equipment* | Long-term debt | SBIC-MESBIC | Term loan |
| *or* | | Bank | Equipment loan |
| *Facilities* | | Commercial finance company | Equipment leasing |
| *Acquisition* | | Savings & loan association | Real estate loan |
| | | Life insurance company | Policy loan |
| | | | Unsecured loan (limited) |
| | | | Real estate loan |
| | | Consumer finance company | Personal property term loan |
| | | Leasing company | Equipment leasing |
| | | Small Business Administration | Term loan guarantee |
| | | Certified or local development company | Facilities/ equipment financing |
| *Sharp,* | Equity | Nonprofessional | Partnership formation |
| *Sustained* | | | Stock issue |
| *Growth* | | Venture capitalist | Stock issue |
| | | SBIC-MESBIC | Convertible debentures |
| | | | Debt with warrants |
| | Long-term debt | SBIC-MESBIC | Term loan |
| | | Bank | Unsecured term loan |
| | | Savings and loan association | Equipment loan |
| | | | Equipment leasing |
| | | | Real estate loan |
| | | Commercial finance company | Equipment leasing |
| | | | Real estate loan |

## Small Business Financing Guide

| Use of Funds | Type of Money | Source | Financing Vehicle |
|---|---|---|---|
| | | Life insurance company | Unsecured term loan |
| | | | Policy loan |
| | | | Real estate loan |
| | | Consumer finance company | Personal property loan |
| | | Leasing company | Equipment leasing |
| | | Small Business Administration | Term loan guarantee |
| | | Certified or local development company | Facilities/ equipment financing |
| | | Farmers Home Term loan Administration | guarantee |
| | Line of credit | Supplier | Trade credit |
| | | Bank | Unsecured line of credit |
| | | Savings and loan association | Accounts receivable financing |
| | | | Inventory financing |
| | | | Flooring |
| | | | Indirect collection financing |
| | | Commercial finance company | Accounts receivable financing |
| | | | Inventory financing |
| | | | Factoring |
| | | Factor | Factoring |
| | | Small Business Administration | Line of credit guarantee (limited) |

Rainbow Liquors
Projected Cash Flow

| MLR | Preoperating | 1983 | | | 1984 | | | | | | | | | Total |
|---|---|---|---|---|---|---|---|---|---|---|---|---|---|---|
| | | Oct. | Nov. | Dec. | Jan. | Feb. | Mar. | Apr. | May | June | July | Aug. | Sept. | |
| Cash Sources | | | | | | | | | | | | | | |
| Equity | 20,000 | | | | | | | | | | | | | 20,000 |
| Loan | 60,000 | | | | | | | | | | | | | 60,000 |
| Net Profit | 0 | 478 | 1,001 | 2,234 | 1,738 | 1,491 | 1,745 | 1,749 | 1,752 | 2,006 | 2,010 | 2,264 | 2,267 | 20,735 |
| Depreciation | 0 | 250 | 250 | 250 | 250 | 250 | 250 | 250 | 250 | 250 | 250 | 250 | 250 | 3,000 |
| Total | 80,000 | 728 | 1,251 | 2,484 | 1,988 | 1,741 | 1,995 | 1,999 | 2,002 | 2,256 | 2,260 | 2,514 | 2,517 | 103,735 |
| Disbursements | | | | | | | | | | | | | | |
| Purchase of Business | 58,000 | | | | | | | | | | | | | 58,000 |
| Closing Costs | 1,200 | | | | | | | | | | | | | 1,200 |
| Improvements and equipment | 15,000 | | | | | | | | | | | | | 15,000 |
| Deposits | 1,300 | | | | | | | | | | | | | 1,300 |
| Loan Payments (Principal) | 0 | 406 | 410 | 413 | 416 | 420 | 424 | 427 | 431 | 434 | 439 | 442 | 446 | 5,108 |
| Owners' Draw | 0 | 1,000 | 1,000 | 1,200 | 1,200 | 1,200 | 1,200 | 1,200 | 1,200 | 1,200 | 1,200 | 1,200 | 1,200 | 14,000 |
| Income Taxes | 0 | | | | | | | 1,000 | | | | | | 1,000 |
| Total | 75,500 | 1,406 | 1,410 | 1,613 | 1,616 | 1,620 | 1,624 | 2,627 | 1,631 | 1,634 | 1,639 | 1,642 | 1,646 | 95,608 |
| Net Cash Flow | 4,500 | (678) | (159) | 871 | 372 | 121 | 371 | (628) | 371 | 622 | 621 | 872 | 871 | 8,127 |
| Cumulative Cash Flow | 4,500 | 3,822 | 3,663 | 4,534 | 4,906 | 5,027 | 5,398 | 4,770 | 5,141 | 5,763 | 6,384 | 7,256 | 8,127 | |

## Explanation of Projected Cash Flow

**Cash Sources.** Sources of cash detailed below.

**Equity.** The borrowers will inject $20,000 of cash into the business.

**Loan.** The requested loan will provide $60,000 of initial cash.

**Net Profit.** Net profit after expenses is a source of cash and is taken from line 26 of income and expense projection.

**Depreciation.** Depreciation was deducted as an expense before net profit. Because it is a noncash expense, it is added back here as a cash source.

**Total Sources.** The sum of items from cash sources through loan injection.

**Disbursements.** Detailed below.

**Purchase of Business.** The sales agreement calls for a purchase price of $58,000 including inventory.

**Closing Costs.** Escrow costs are estimated to be $1200 and are treated as a preoperating expense.

**Improvements and Equipment.** A capital outlay of $15,000 is expected at the beginning for new equipment, fixtures, and improvements.

**Deposits.** Deposits for rent, sales taxes, and utilities are estimated at $1300.

**Loan Payments.** Principal portion of loan payments, based on eight-year amortization of $60,000 loan at 10.25 percent interest.

**Owners' Draw.** Expected to fluctuate with state of the business and growth. Draw of $1000 per month for Mr. and Mrs. Cho is reasonable in the early months. As earnings grow, draws can be expected to increase, subject to their subordination to debt service.

**Income Taxes.** Income taxes for 1983 are due in April of 1984, and $1000 has been projected for this purpose.

**Total Disbursements.** The sum of items from purchase price to income taxes.

**Net Cash Flow.** Monthly cash flow is the difference between total cash sources and total disbursements.

**Cumulative Cash Flow.** Sum of the monthly cash flows cumulated month by month. The business ends with a healthy cash surplus of more than $8000.

# GLOSSARY

AMORTIZE   To pay a debt gradually through scheduled periodic payments; the process of writing off against expenses the cost of an intangible asset over the period of its economic usefulness.

APPRECIATION   The increase in property value over time.

BALLOON PAYMENT   The final bulk payment that retires a loan when minimal previous payments have not fully amortized it.

CAPITAL   Net worth of the individual or business; also, the excess of total assets over total liabilities; the funds used to start or *capitalize* a business.

CASH FLOW   (1) Cash generated from business operations; (2) net income after tax plus noncash expenses such as depreciation.

CASH (FLOW) POSITION   The presence or absence of surplus cash for recycling into business operations (sometimes known as "positive" or "negative" cash flow).

COLLATERAL (SECURITY)   Personal or real property possessions that the borrower assigns to the lender to help ensure debt payment. If the borrower does not repay the loan, the lender may take ownership of the collateral.

CURRENT ASSETS   Cash or such assets as accounts receivable and inventory that are readily converted to cash during the normal operation of a business cycle, usually within one year.

CURRENT LIABILITIES   Debts due within a year, including payments on long-term loans and any anticipated payables such as taxes.

DEBENTURES   The written evidence of a debt, usually issued by a corporation.

DEPRECIATION   The process of writing off against expenses the decrease in value of a fixed asset over its useful life.

EQUITY   (1) The difference between the value of an asset or business and what is owed on it; (2) the money—equity dollars or investment—that purchases ownership.

FIXED ASSETS   Permanent business properties such as land, buildings, machinery, and equipment that are *not* resold or converted to cash in normal business operations.

LEVERAGE   (1) The extent to which a business is financed by debt; (2) boosting a business's profit potential by injecting debt capital.

LIQUIDITY   The degree to which individual or business assets are in cash form or can quickly be converted to cash.

LIQUIDATE   To convert noncash assets into cash.

NET WORKING CAPITAL   The excess of current assets over current liabilities, or the pool of resources readily available for normal business operations.

TERM LOAN   A loan repaid in periodic payments over a period of more than one year.

USURY LAW   Ceilings set on loan interest rates by individual states, with exemptions for some competitive commercial lenders. (California's current usury limit exempts state and national banks, savings and loan associations, credit unions, industrial loan companies, pawnbrokers, personal property brokers, and agricultural cooperatives and licensed real estate brokers when the loan is secured by a lien on real property.)

# SOURCES OF FURTHER INFORMATION

## GOVERNMENT AGENCIES AND PUBLICATIONS
Where no specific publications are listed, contact the relevant agency for available information.

Economic Development
  Administration
U.S. Department of Commerce,
  Room 7800B
Washington, D.C. 20230
(202) 377-5081

Farmers Home Administration
U.S. Department of Agriculture,
  Room 5014 South Building
Washington, D.C. 20250
(202) 447-7967

Internal Revenue Service
Washington, D.C. 20224
(202) 566-5000

Minority Business Development
  Agency
U.S. Department of Commerce,
  Room 5053
Washington, DC 20230
(202) 377-2414
*Guide to Federal Assistance
  Programs for Minority Business
  Development Enterprises MBDA
  Funded Organizations Directory*
  (Biannual)

Small Business Administration
1441 L Street, N.W.
Washington, D.C. 20416
(202) 653-6385
(800) 433-7212

District Offices:
350 South Figueroa Street,
  Suite 600

Los Angeles, California 90071
(213) 688-2956

211 Main Street, 4th Floor
San Francisco, California 94105
(415) 974-0649
*Directory of Operating Small
  Business Investment Companies*
  (Annual)

U.S. Government Printing Office
Superintendent of Documents
Washington, D.C. 20402
(202) 783-3238
*Monthly Catalogue of United
  States Government Publications*

Department of Economic and
  Business Development
Office of Small Business
  Development
1030 13th Street, Suite 200
Sacramento, CA 95814
(916) 445-6545

*A Guide to Starting a Business,
  Buying a Business, Financing a
  Business*

## TRADE ASSOCIATIONS AND PUBLICATIONS

American Association of Minority
  Enterprise
Small Business Investment
  Companies
915 15th Street, N.W.

Washington, D.C. 20005
(202) 347-8600

National Association of Small
  Business
Investment Companies
618 Washington Building
Washington, D.C. 20005
(202) 638-3411
*Venture Capital, Where to Find It*

National Small Business Association
1604 K Street, N.W.
Washington, D.C. 20006
(202) 296-7400

National Venture Capital
  Association
1225 19th Street, N.W.
Suite 750
Washington, D.C. 20036
(202) 659-5756

Western Association of Venture
  Capitalists
3000 Sand Hill Road
Building 2, Suite 260
Menlo Park, CA 94025
(415) 854-1322
*Directory of Members* (Annual)

## PERIODICAL

*Venture Capital*
Capital Publishing Corporation
P.O. Box 348
Wellesly Hills, MA 02181

## BOOKS

Hayes, Rick Stephen,
*Business Loans: A Guide to Money
  Sources and How to Approach*

*Them Successfully,* Boston, MA,
CBI Publishing, 1980.

Simmons, James G.,
*Creative Business Financing,*
  Englewood Cliffs, N.J.
Prentice-Hall, 1982.

Welsh, John A. and Jerry F. White,
*The Entrepreneur's Master
  Planning Guide*
Englewood Cliffs, N. J.
Prentice-Hall, 1983.

Rao, Dileep,
*Handbook of Business Finance &
  Capital Sources,*Minneapolis, MN
InterFinance Corporation, 1982.

*Guide to Venture Capital Sources,*
  Seventh ed., Wellesley Hills, MA,
  Capital Publishing Corp. 1983.

Osgood, William R.,
*How to Plan and Finance Your
  Business,* Boston, CBI Publishing,
  1980.

Gumpert, David E. and Jeffrey A.
  Timmons,
*The Insider's Guide to Small
  Business Resources,* Garden City,
  NY, Doubleday, 1982.

Deloitte, Haskins & Sells,
*Raising Venture Capital,* New York,
  1982.

Mancuso, Joseph R.,
*Small Business Survival Guide,*
  Englewood Cliffs, NJ, Prentice-
  Hall, 1980.

Dible, Donald M.,
*Up Your Own Organization,*
  Reston, VA, Reston Press, 1982.

# CHAPTER 5

# CASH MANAGEMENT

## Patrick L. Romano

## INTRODUCTION

Prolonged high interest rates, volatile money markets, high U.S. government budget deficits, unfavorable export trade balances, and the bankruptcies of government securities dealers all tend to mirror the concern of the financial press and general populace with affairs financial. Popular business magazines with titles focused on investing, cash flow, money, and real estate exacerbate this theme. Yet, although this most recent economic history would have you believe the new discovery of money, the accountant, controller, and cash manager have been intimately involved, all along, in managing this asset called "cash." The paths taken by these financial managers, have been several; namely, to make sure the firm:

1. Does not run short of cash
2. Neither has too great an amount on hand so that it will cause a loss of earnings nor too small an amount so that liquidity is jeopardized and banking relationships strained
3. Obtain a return or yield on this excess cash not invested in the business

The focus of the financial manager has been, until this most recent decade, on internal matters. Refine the short-term cash forecasting techniques and then apply efforts in those areas, such as receivables, payables, inventories, prepaid expenses, and such, that contribute increased cash flow to the firm. The concern was with working capital items—the financial manager had great influence and control over these areas. Improve the systems and procedures for purchasing, billing, collecting receivables, and paying invoices in accordance with industry norms and thus improve internal cash management.

In this last decade, however, a multitude of cash management products have been developed and refined at an ever increasing pace by almost all the commerical banks and newer cash management product firms. This arsenal of tools available to the financial manager, when combined with his or her internal systems management skills, has greatly improved the performance of the firm's treasury department.

The purpose of this chapter is to examine those techniques, both internal and external, that contribute increasing profits to the firm. We will review those collection techniques that improve the inflow of funds to the firm and those disbursing methods that retain the use of funds as long as possible. We will cover the investment of funds in short-term money market instruments, as well as the cash management process the cash manager employs in obtaining and reporting on the firm's cash position and cash balance, on a daily basis.

# COLLECTION: IMPROVING FLOW OF FUNDS INTO THE BUSINESS

**INTERNAL PROCEDURES.**    Internal procedures are utilized to provide for a speedup of cash flows into the firm. On the collection side this would involve receivables and the associated functions of credit, billing, and collection. Additionally, inventory management techniques will be employed that reduce the inventory investment required to finance each dollar of sales. Reduce inventories and working capital is reduced and funds are freed for investment in other areas of the business.

*Improved billing procedures,* is clearly one of the simplest ways to increase cash flow. By accelerating the invoice preparation process, to comply with a billing standard, the customer is provided with an invoice immediately after the shipment. A delayed billing will mean a delay in the receipt of cash. Invoice errors also work against the firm, because the customer will use the incorrect invoice to delay payment.

Billing standards are important tools in this process. Exhibit 5.1. illustrates a firm that has fallen behind its standard, requiring 1.2 days to process an invoice when only one day has been established as the requirement. Periodic review and monitoring is required to contain slippage.

**Improved Credit Policies.**    Credit policies establish the expectations of payment in terms of time frames and the means of payment such as check, credit card, cash, and discounts offered. The formalization of these expectations into credit policy is a management responsibility, whereas implementation of the

**EXHIBIT 5.1.    Example of Billing Standard**

Target: One day for completion of the billing function.
(Ship one day and bill by the end of the next.)

| Invoice Prepared and Mailed | Aggregate Value of Invoices | Value Times Number of Days |
|---|---|---|
| Same day as shipment | $ 89,000 | $ -0- |
| One day after shipment | 117,000 | 117,000 |
| Two days after shipment | 40,000 | 80,000 |
| Three days after shipment | 30,000 | 90,000 |
| Four days after shipment | 11,000 | 44,000 |
| Five days after shipment | 4,000 | 20,000 |
| | $291,000 | $351,000 |

$$\frac{\$351,000}{291,000} = 1.2 \text{ days}$$

policy lies with the credit or receivables manager. Letting the credit manager develop as well as implement these policies is tantamount to abdication by management of its responsibilities.

**Improved Collection Procedures.**    A formalized procedure to remind the customer of past due payments accompanied by a request for payment is a must in collecting the unpaid account. Additionally, control devices such as the aged accounts receivable schedule, and collection period or days outstanding ratios, are employed. A careful monitoring will indicate the current trend—either toward slower or faster collections. Efforts can then be initiated to contain the company's investment in receivables. Lockboxes, which will be discussed later, are helpful in intercepting mailed remittances, and accelerating the collection of receivables.

**Inventory Investment Reduction.**    Inventory control systems and techniques such as ABC, reorder point (ROP), economic order quantity (EOQ), and materials requirements planning (MRP) are employed to achieve a minimum but adequate investment in inventory to support each sales dollar. The financial manager who takes time to learn these techniques can then be helpful in promoting a stategy for the freeing of cash from this investment. This manager can then convert "frozen assets" into liquid cash and earn interest income or reduce interest expense.

## EXTERNAL PROCEDURES

**Collection Systems.**   The objective of the modern cash manager, when studying the system of collecting payments from customers, is to obtain payment as soon as possible, concentrate funds in a line bank, and then apply those funds to working capital needs. To be effective, this collection system should reduce— to some minimum acceptable level—the time the money is unavailable for use, after the customer remits payment. This time is referred to as float.

Basically, in this system there are two types of float—mail float (the time for collection) and availability float (the time for availability of deposits). A third float, sometimes downplayed, is a function of the efficiency of both the corporation and the bank in the processing of remittances (processing float). Mail float is a function of the efficiency of the postal system to collect, process, and deliver mail from a customer to the offices of a firm. Establishing a collection system using the mail requires examination of the time funds will be idle in the postal system. Clearing float is the time required to collect funds deposited in the corporation's banks. This is normally set by the Federal Reserve system as stated availability. Factors to consider are:

1. The banks that customer checks are drawn upon
2. The availability granted by the bank of deposit

Processing float, from the corporate point of view, is the time it takes to process a check and deposit it into its bank deposit account. From the bank's point of view it means getting checks deposited into the clearing stream as quickly as possible.

Thus the ideal system for the collection of receivables payments is that system which will reduce mail, availability, and processing float to some minimum level within the operational boundaries of the firm.

**Methods and Systems Used.**   The remainder of this section will cover those systems, methods, and mediums for transfers of cash that reduce collection float and improve the flow of funds into the business. They are:

1. The lockbox system
2. Preauthorized payment systems
3. Cash concentration methods
4. Mediums for transfers of cash
   a. Depository transfer checks

**b.** Wire transfers

**c.** Automated clearinghouse (ACH) transfers

**THE LOCKBOX SYSTEM.** The most fundamental and widely used cash management system for receivables collection is the lockbox system. This system is used where the corporate unit is receiving payments by mail from its customers. The corporate unit is defined as a firm, division of a firm, or wholly owned subsidiary of a firm. Of prime importance is the fact that the corporate unit is directing its customers to remit payments to their offices by mail.

In a typical nonlockbox collection system, the following events take place:

1. Customers mail payments to the offices of the corporate unit (mail float).
2. The firm separates the payment from the returned invoice document, prepares, and deposits the checks at the bank (processing float).
3. The deposited checks clear back to the drawee bank and become collected funds (clearing float).

A lockbox system replaces the corporate unit with the lockbox bank as the initial recipient of payments (see Exhibit 5.2).

The lockbox functions in the following manner:

1. Customers continue to mail payments to the coprorate unit, only the address is changed to the post office box rented by your bank in the name of the firm (mail float).
2. The lockbox bank will receive the mail directed to the post office box, separate the invoice document from the checks, deposit the funds in the firm's account, and return all invoice material to the corporate unit (processing float).
3. Deposited checks clear back to the drawee bank and become collected funds (clearing float).

Although the sequence of events is not altered, the time frame is considerably shortened. Mail float is reduced because remittances are intercepted in the postal system. The lockbox bank, through repeated and continuous depositing during the evening and early morning hours, will process a greater quantity of checks than that received by the firm, and sort and package them by the early morning hours. Clearing float is thus reduced and better availability will then be passed on to the customers (see Exhibit 5.3).

## EXHIBIT 5.2.    Lockbox Banking

Without Lockbox

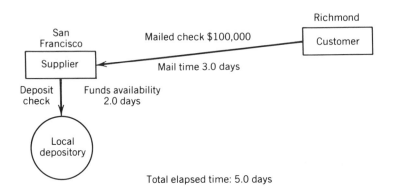

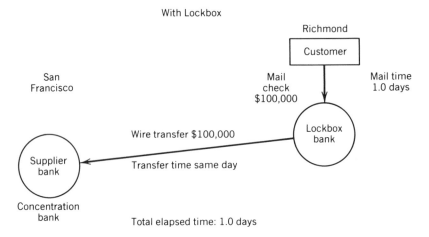

Earnings on available funds at 10%
$100M × 4 days × .10 = $109.59 gross earnings


To summarize, lockbox banking is a process by which the bank intercepts and deposits sales remittances mailed to its corporate customers with the use of special rental post office boxes (special to the extent that the bank is authorized to collect corporate mail). Establishing a lockbox collection system will reduce the total float associated with a given nonlockbox system, eliminate the need for a large clerical staff to prepare receipts for deposit, and speed the collection of receivables. Reducing funds "in transit time" enables the corporation to increase its earnings on funds not formerly available to it or to reduce short-

**EXHIBIT 5.3.   Example of Lockbox System**

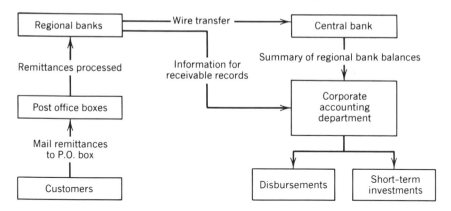

term borrowings and total annual interest expense. Although their advantages are many for lockbox systems, some of the disadvantages indicated are:

1.   Company accounting entries may be delayed by one or two days.
2.   It is more difficult to process special items such as the control of payments on delinquent accounts.

**Lockbox Cost/Benefit Analysis.**   The principal factors that must be considered when weighing the costs versus the benefits for a lockbox system are:

1.   The reduction in total float days—mail, availability, and processing float
2.   Lockbox expense—processing, maintenance, entries, and such
3.   Sales volume, daily, monthly, and annual
4.   The average face value of checks received (the larger the better)
5.   The corporate money ultilization rate—the cost to borrow or alternately to invest funds—for the corporation

Lockbox systems are most frequently designed for companies with small volumes of large dollar items—frequently referred to as the wholesale lockbox plan. Large checks increase the receipts level sufficiently for the benefits to overcome the high costs associated with lockbox systems (see Exhibit 5.4).

**Optimization of Corporate Lockbox Locations.**   Cash management oriented banks have developed elaborate optimization models with regularly scheduled updates on mail time surveys, sometimes available free of charge to potential or new corporate customers. A popular model, offered by many banks, is the

# EXHIBIT 5.4. Lockbox Cost/Benefit Analysis

## A. Lockbox Fees

Monthly:

| | |
|---|---|
| DDA Account Maintenance | $17.50 per month |
| Lockbox Maintenance | 60.00 per month |
| Local Telephone Call Simple (optional) | $60.00 |
| Daily: | $77.50 to $137.50 |
| Corporate Credit Entry ($2.25 × 21 days) | $47.25 |

Per Item:

| | |
|---|---|
| Manual Wholesale | $ .28 |
| Check Deposited (Average) | .07 |
| Total | $ .35 |

Variable:

| | |
|---|---|
| Postage (Cost + 20%) | $20.00 (est. per month) |

## B. Break-Even Analysis

Example

100 items per month
>  basic wholesale plan
>  1 day float saving
>  interest rate 10%
>  no telephone calls

| Service | Unit Price | Monthly Volume | Total Fee |
|---|---|---|---|
| DDA Maintenance | $17.50 | 1 | $17.50 |
| LBX Maintenance | 60.00 | 1 | 60.00 |
| Wholesale Plan | .28 | 100 | 28.00 |
| Checks Deposited | .07 (avg.) | 100 | 7.00 |
| Credit Entries | 2.25 | 21 | 47.25 |
| Telephone Call | 60.00 | N/A | 0– |
| Postage | | | 10.00 (est) |
| Total Monthly Cost | | | $169.75 |
| | | | × 12 |
| | | Annual Fee | $2,037.00 |

Daily Sales Required:

1 Day Saved × 10% × Daily Net Sales = $2,037 Cost
  (1)  (10%)  (x)                   = $2,037
           x                        = $20,370

Annual Sales Required:
  $20,370 × 250 = $5,092,000

lockbox location model. The objective of this model is to determine the optimum number of lockbox locations after the lockbox decision has been made, based on economic factors. The following are the principal model factors cited in these studies. They are:

1. Monthly receipts by state
2. Cost of capital (funds rate)
3. Receiving city—city where receipts are currently sent (depository vendor city)
4. Average bank clearing time—average availability
5. Special city considerations—permits use of a specialized city
6. Matrix of mail times between Federal Reserve cities, updated.

After the lockbox location decision is made, the firm must plan to review the model factors, especially for changes in mail times and clearing time, on a periodic basis. This review should be completed every year or at least every two years. Because the factor times and amounts change, so to do the costs and benefits.

**Lockbox Processing Systems.**   Customers concerned with the documentation received from the lockbox bank should be aware that banks have developed several basic systems for processing lockbox items, each providing information differently to the corporate customer. Costs can differ significantly, depending on the specific information requirements of the customer. The primary systems are as follows:

1. **Envelope System.**   Usually manually processed, its purpose is to provide the corporate customer with the amount recorded on the original envelope and the invoice for record-keeping purposes.
2. **Photocopy System.**   To provide the corporate customer with a copy of its check plus invoice and original envelope. This plan differs little from the envelope system but does provide additional corporate documentation. Both of these plans are recommended for low processing volumes with larger dollar amounts involved (wholesale plans).
3. **Data Transmission System.**   In this plan the bank separates and processes remittances in an automated mode using high speed check encoding and optical character recognition (OCR) processing equipment with the purpose of developing a magnetic tape. The magnetic tape inputs directly to the corporate accounts receivable system. This system is used with higher volume processing (thousands of smaller check items) under retail lockbox plans.

**Preauthorized Payment Systems.** Another useful technique for expediting the flow of remittance dollars is the preauthorized transaction. This service is particularly beneficial in situations where recurring bills are regular and do not vary in amount—for example, insurance premiums, mortgage payments, and installment loan payments. The preauthorized payment system automatically transfers funds from customer personal bank accounts into a company account on predetermined dates. This can be done through either a preauthorized check (paper based) or an electronic debit (preauthorized debit) to the customer's checking account.

To implement the process the customer is required to sign an authorizing agreement with the supplier company that will allow checks or an electronic debit to be drawn or charged against the personal account. The banks, receiving parties to the transaction, are notified by the supplier company. The supplier company provides the bank with a magnetic tape containing a list of the customers, their account numbers, and payment amounts. The bank will then produce a magnetic ink character recognition (MICR)-encoded paper check or an electronic transfer for each account. The payments will be totaled and credited to the supplier company account on the date the company specifies. A company using preauthorized payment systems will find:

1. Funds are available sooner, because mail and processing float is eliminated.

2. That payment processing costs are reduced (reduced personnel), because less manual labor is required.

3. Enhanced predictability of cash flows, because the company knows the exact information on availability. Although the benefit to the customer is less apparent, the customer does save time and cost by no longer having to organize and total invoices, or prepare, authorize, and mail checks. However, the customer loses mail, clearing, and processing float, which in part is made up by the supplier, providing additional days of credit or larger discounts for participating in the system.

**Cash Concentration Methods.** For a firm with multiple collection locations and/or the need to maintain accounts receivable information at each location, a concentration system is needed in order to gain effective control over a company's cash pool. The deposit concentration system is designed to provide rapid collection, deposit, and transfer of customer remittances from decentralized receiving locations, whether from banks or company operational facilities (lockbox processing services by local banks or corporate sales offices), into a central cash pool.

Mobilizing the transfer of deposits in multiple local bank accounts to a central cash concentration account gains earlier availability of funds for investment or other activities at the concentration bank. The chief components of these systems, are:

1. Local bank depositories
2. Concentration bank
3. Data collection and transmission of deposit amounts
4. Means used for the transfers of cash from local banks to the concentration bank are:
   a. Depository transfer checks
   b. Wire transfers
   c. ACH transfers

Tracing the remittance flows from the initial receiving points to the end point concentration bank involves the following activities:

1. Remittances are collected by sales offices and/or lockbox banks and deposited in local banks.
2. Deposit information is transmitted to the corporate cash department and/ or a network service (third-party vendors) such as First Data Resources, National Data Corp., GEISCO, ADP, and others, who in turn report the information both to the concentration bank and corporate cash department.
3. Funds are then moved from the local depository to the regional concentration bank through the use of:
   a. Depository transfer checks and/or
   b. ACH initiated transactions
4. Large dollar fund amounts are then transferred through the use of wire transfers from the regional concentration banks to the main concentration bank. From this concentrated pool, the corporate cash manager initiates the decision to invest, pay down, and transfer funds.

When regional concentration banks are not used—only local depositories and a main concentration bank account—expensive wire transfers are not required. Instead, inexpensive depository transfer checks (DTCs) and ACH initiated transactions are employed.

To summarize, the benefits derived by using cash concentration methods are as follows:

1. Rapid concentration of widely dispersed deposits converted into usable funds
2. Almost perfect predictability of funds flows and availability
3. Timely management information reflecting decentralized decision making
4. Greater audit control over local managers and local deposits
5. Simpler reporting procedures for local managers

**Depository Transfer Checks.**   A paper-based method for transferring funds, DTCs are utilized in concentration and lockbox systems in moving funds from local banks to a concentration bank. By definition a DTC is a nonnegotiable instrument made payable only to the company itself, generally requiring no signature. It is an unsigned check drawn on a corporation's account at one bank and payable to the corporation at a concentration bank. DTCs are nonnegotiable, preprinted checks that need only the date and amount filled in. This instrument is an inexpensive medium used for moving funds from one bank location to another.

When used with automated deposit reporting systems, the following process is observed (see Exhibit 5.5):

1. Amounts deposited daily in the local depository are reported to a central data collection system (a nationwide data processing network operated by a bank or independent service bureau).
2. The data service company then transmits data collected from all the local banks to a concentration bank, at a specified time each day.
3. The concentration bank automatically prepares a DTC, and deposits the DTC for collection the same day. The collection process is completed when the DTC is presented to the local depository bank. Converting DTC deposits into collected funds depends on the concentration bank availability schedule for these items, whereas funds deposited locally (usually there is overnight clearance of local checks) can be withdrawn the next day on presentation of the DTCs in the regular check collection process.

**Wire Transfers.**   Through the use of either the Fed Wire or Bank Wire System, transfers made by wire constitute the fastest means of moving locally collected cash or deposit information to a corporation's concentration account. Funds are

**EXHIBIT 5.5.    Graphic Representation of Automated Deposit Reporting System. (Reprinted with the Permission of First Data Resources, Inc.)**

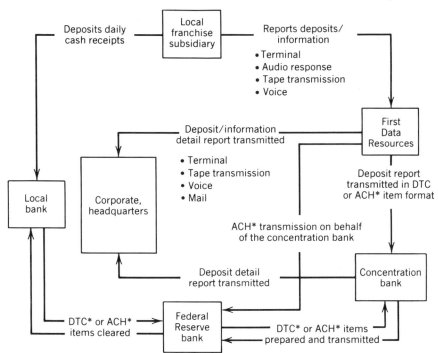

*Note: DTC = Depository Transfer Check
       ACH = Automated Clearing House

considered collected on receipt of the wire transfer and are immediately available for use. Further, the use of the wire transfer service allows a company quickly to calculate its daily cash position, and so reduce or eliminate excess borrowings. The clerical workload of the home office is also decreased. A wire transfer system generally requires regular transfers of large amounts to be economical. The fees charged on both end points limit transfers to $25,000 and above to overcome the cost impact of these transfers.

**Automated Clearinghouse.**    Utilized in preauthorized payment and cash concentration systems, ACH transfers are becoming more popular as a medium for fund transfers. Relatively inexpensive and providing one-day availability, ACH transactions will continue to increase as cash managers employ them in additional applications.

The ACH is a computerized clearing facility that effects the paperless exchange of funds between banks, using an electronic medium. The participants in ACH transactions are:

1. The Automated Clearinghouse Association
2. The Federal Reserve, the operator of the local ACH Facilities
3. Depository institutions, members of ACH, and
4. The corporations and customers

Because the settlement of all ACH transactions takes place predictably on the day after the initiation of the transaction, many advantages accrue to this network, namely:

1. Invoicing float is gone—there are no bills to prepare
2. Mail float is eliminated—mail is not used
3. Processing float is trimmed—there are no invoices to reconcile, checks to process
4. Clearing float is reduced to only one-day availability nationwide
5. Handling expense is lessened—an ACH transaction is less costly than a preauthorized check deposit

Financial managers not using ACH applications should consider setting up pilot programs in order to become familiar with their function. Because banking appears to be heading to an all-electronic environment, electronic systems should become a vital part of the cash manager's arsenal of tools.

## DISBURSING: RETAINING USE OF FUNDS AS LONG AS POSSIBLE

**INTERNAL PROCEDURES.**   To retain the use of funds as long as possible is simply to employ procedures that slow the outflow of cash from the company. Internal procedures, employed on the disbursement side, to accomplish this objective would involve the centralization of the payables function. When coupled with external techniques (which will be discussed later), funds outflow delay is maximized.

**Centralization of Payables.**   When possible, the centralization of payables is probably the most effective way of controlling cash outflow. The financial manager can evaluate the timing of payments coming due for the entire firm and schedule payments accordingly. By taking the optimal economic time in settlement of obligations, penalties associated with early payment are avoided. For example, a firm that pays $1½ million a month to vendors 10 days early is giving up $50,000 a year at a 10 percent opportunity cost. This would be especially important when paying larger invoices.

Other advantages stemming from the centralization of payables are:

1.  More efficient and effective monitoring of bank balances and current float position
2.  Timely payments to vendors, not only on due dates, but in accordance with industry payment standards
3.  Imposing a firm-wide cash discount policy—taking discounts only when the interest cost of foregoing the cash discount is less than the corporate borrowing rate

With reference to this latter point, managerial prudence dictates foregoing the discount on invoices providing only ½ percent 10, net 30 days terms (9.05 percent annual interest rate for postponing payment 20 days) when the cost of borrowing, for example, is 10 percent.

## EXTERNAL PROCEDURES

**Disbursement Systems.**   The objective of the modern cash manager, when studying the firm's disbursement system, is to optimize the method of paying suppliers in order to utilize the float of the system to the best interest of the firm. As in collection, there are several types of float:

1.  **Mail float**—the amount of time that a disbursement check remains out of the banking system, in transit through the postal system
2.  **Processing float**—the amount of time the check will be delayed in internal processing by the receiving corporation
3.  **Transit or clearing float**—the most important element of any disbursement system is the actual time a check is in transit from point of deposit to posting to the corporate account at the disbursement bank.

As stated earlier, banks will grant availability on deposited items based on several factors:

1.  The availability granted through the Federal Reserve bank in the specific district
2.  The improved availability through a direct send program

In some cases, this differs considerably from the stated availability schedules of the Federal Reserve. It is obvious in the paper-based check system that, although the depositing bank will grant availability of funds in accordance with the Federal Reserve bank in its district, or earlier, the actual physical handling of the checks in the clearing process may take considerably longer, especially due to weather, transportation failures, out-of-the-way distant locations, and so on. The ideal system for disbursements, therefore, is that system which optimizes the effectiveness of the corporation in its disbursement planning—to generate float from disbursements—taking advantage of the inefficiencies in the existing or planned clearing systems.

**Decelerated Bill Payment Systems.**    This refers to those systems used to slow the outflow of cash from the firm. The principal concepts employed are:

1.  Obvious procedures
2.  Playing the float, meaning disbursement float—the sum of the outstanding corporate checks not presented to the bank at any one time.

Procedures associated with the term *playing the float* (to be discussed later) are:

1.  Zero balance accounts
2.  Controlled disbursement accounts
3.  Remote and criss-cross disbursements
4.  Payable through drafts

**Obvious Procedures.**    Although some of these procedures may not have been employed by financial managers, the outcomes from their description are easily discernible. They are as follows (see Exhibit 5.6):

1.  Sending a check to corporate headquarters instead of the lockbox address (delay plus consternation)
2.  Holding payments for one or two days after postmarked, because cash discounts are based on the postmark. For example, if checks are postmarked on Friday and mailed Monday, the firm obviously will obtain the weekend float. However, note that the post office has been strict with companies on this point—insisting that the postmarked date and the date placed in the mail system are identical. Loss of metered mail privileges might result.
3.  Mailing from remote/distant post office stations with limited service and/or requiring multiple handling or connections for delivery

**EXHIBIT 5.6.   Procedures Applied to Increase Corporate Float Funds**

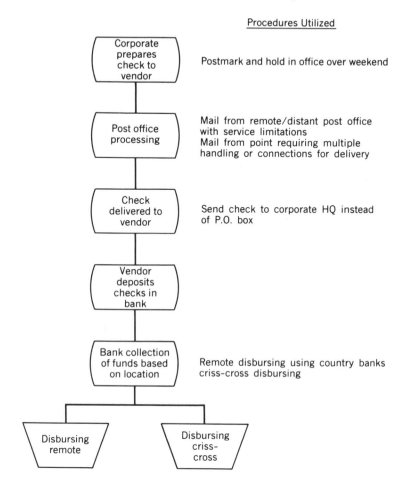

4. Paying bills from the bank furthest from the payee
5. Using country banks (those not in Federal Reserve cities) for all disbursements (delivery schedules are sometimes infrequent)

**Playing the Float.**   The objectives sought in "riding the float" are twofold:

1. By slowing cash outflows, float dollar balances are created, providing a source of funds at no cost (in lieu of borrowing). These funds are then invested in short-term investments providing additional income, increased productivity of cash and enhanced effectiveness of the cash function.

2. Tracking disbursements through central bank accounts and not through the company books while only maintaining balances sufficent to cover bank services and daily transactions. The books in many cases will reflect negative cash balances. The absolute difference between the cash book balances and the bank collected balances reflect the dollar value of investment float. This is illustrated in the section of this chapter entitled "Cash Position Information."

**Zero Balance Accounts.**   As part of the arsenal of external procedures utilized by companies, zero balance accounts (ZBAs) are effective in eliminating unproductive balances in disbursing accounts and extending disbursement float. They are designed for corporate customers that write a substantial number of checks each month and are concerned about control of disbursements. In the early 1980s ZBAs came into being to permit centralized control of cash while allowing division disbursing authority. Through this system, a company's authorized disbursing agents write checks drawn on their individual accounts—all located within the same bank. These accounts contain no funds, hence the term *zero balance*. By definition, ZBAs are special disbursement accounts having a "zero" dollar balance on which checks are written. As checks are presented to a ZBA account for payment (causing a negative balance), funds are automatically transferred from a central account (concentration account) to the ZBA account (see Exhibit 5.7).

All receipts are deposited in the general corporate (or concentration) account, not divisional ZBA accounts. Checks written on ZBAs clear through normal banking channels. Each day, as the checks are presented for payment, a debit balance builds in the ZBA. At the close of business, a credit is made to the ZBA equal to the day's debit (bringing the balance back to zero) and a corresponding debit is applied to the corporate concentration (control account).

These functions are computerized to assure accurate and timely posting of data. Typically, information about disbursements from each ZBA in the system is transmitted together with control account balance information to corporate headquarters each morning. This enables the corporate cash manager to make daily investment or funds allocation decisions. Separate statements and reconciliation reports are available for each account in the system.

The benefits of zero balance accounts are worth noting:

1. Centralized cash control, but decentralized disbursement.

   a. By disbursing checks from outlying plants, sales offices, and warehouse, the firm maintains disbursement autonomy at each of the above locations.

**EXHIBIT 5.7.   Zero Balance Account System**

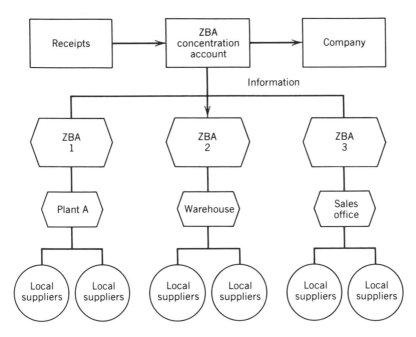

b.  Elimination of imprest accounts or balances at outlying banks. By not having funds idle at these locations, all funds become available to compensate for credit and services, or for corporate investment.

c.  Disbursement float is often extended, thus further increasing the corporate cash pool. Using local accounts, checks paid by divisions to local vendors tend to clear quickly. The same checks, when drawn on a more distant concentration bank, will tend to clear less rapidly, and thus gain float extension.

**Controlled Disbursement Account.**   Like the ZBA account the controlled disbursement account is effective in eliminating unproductive balances in these accounts and somewhat effective in extending disbursement float. The key reason, however, for use of this account is for disbursement control—the cash manager knows early in the morning the dollar amount of checks that will be paid later the same day—so that he or she can then determine the firm's cash balances and make timely investments in the money market. By definition, a controlled disbursement account is a form of zero balance account, located outside an organization's geographic area, that is funded through wire transfer from a master account after the bank informs the cash manager which checks have been presented for collection. It is an improvement over the old system, which told the cash manager tomorrow what was taken out of the company's account today. It is a specialized cash management service designed specifically for corporate customers with significant cash flows. This system identifies all checks presented against designated corporate accounts clearing through the Federal Reserve system and direct send transit-clearing relationships by 11:00 A.M., local time (See Exhibit 5.8).

To control the flow of items on these corporate accounts, your bank must delete a branch from its availability schedule for late cash letter clearings as well as the local clearinghouse. As a result, all checks drawn on accounts in the deleted branch must come either through the morning Federal Reserve cash letter or the bank's early direct send letters. Checks not presented any day are held over for the next day, thus effectively gaining float extension. This is why controlled disbursement accounts are maintained at branches or affiliates of large banks. Incidentally, some West Coast banks use East Coast affiliates for their controlled disbursement system.

To summarize, controlled disbursement systems are valuable, because they provide balance control, inform the firm in the morning exactly what checks will clear that day, minimize idle funds, and provide some float extension as

**EXHIBIT 5.8.   Controlled Disbursement Account System**

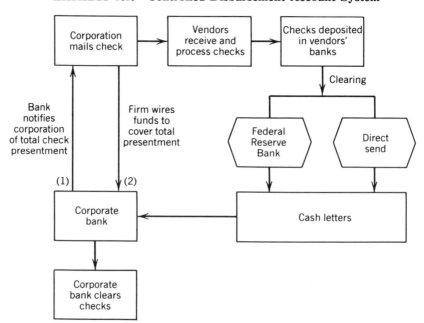

noted previously. Although new operating procedures imposed by the Federal Reserve, such as the Uniform Noon Presentment Program in 1983 and its High Dollar Groups Sort Program in 1984, have made it more difficult for cash managers to maintain precise disbursement control, new strategies continue to be divised by the banks and cash managers to overcome these obstacles. These new Federal Reserve procedures which provide for later check presentments have been effective in dramatically reducing the Federal Reserve float. As a result of this impact, the cash manager should reassess the effectiveness of the existing disbursement bank network to determine the bank's commitment to this market and to help keep the float on their side.

**Remote and Criss-Cross Disbursing.**    Both of these methods are designed to extend the disbursement float period for the firm. Remote disbursing involves drawing checks on distant country banks, not situated in Federal Reserve cities or served by regional check processing centers. Although Federal Reserve clearance time is two days maximum, issuing checks on small country banks that do not enjoy frequent delivery schedules delays physical check presentation by at least a day. The approach used by some firms is to study the current selection of banks with which they have accounts and optimize the float by allocating checking activity among them.

Criss-cross disbursing involves paying West Coast vendors by East Coast banks, paying East Coast vendors by West Coast banks, and so on. Although the Federal Reserve has clamped down on remote disbursing and has dramatically improved the efficiency of the check collection system, firms continue to use these disbursing techniques where they have established business relationships in each of these geographic disbursing points.

**Payable through Drafts.**    A draft is another instrument that is useful to the cash manager in eliminating idle and unproductive balances in disbursing accounts. A draft is an instrument drawn on the issuer and paid by the issuer. It is only an obligation against the corporate issuer when presented to the bank, which acts as an agent in the clearing process (presents the draft to the issuer for final payment). Several advantages accrue to the cash manager upon use of the draft. They are:

1.  The draft does not have to be funded by the company until presented; thus funds can be invested for longer periods of time.

2.  There is no risk of overdraft on using uncollected funds.

3.  Companies with regional offices can review local disbursements prior to making payments as well as reduce the number of local accounts needed.

Although banks dislike drafts because of operating problems associated with the handling and need to transfer funds, they continue to be used, especially by insurance companies, in payment of claims. They are also given to sales personnel in lieu of cash or check advances to extend disbursement float.

## INVESTING: INCREASING PROFITS BY INVESTING EXCESS CASH IN SHORT-TERM MONEY MARKET INSTRUMENTS

**CASH AVAILABLE FOR INVESTMENT.**   As previously discussed, the financial manager, through the use of collection systems, speeds up the flow of funds into the firm, and thereby creates incremental cash balances. Similarly, the employment of disbursement systems contributes to the elimination of unproductive idle balances, the extension of disbursement float, and creation of additional incremental cash balances. These "created" cash balances—formerly not available to the firm—are then invested or applied to the reduction of borrowings. This section will briefly discuss those instruments and vehicles that are used for the temporary investment of cash in excess of operating requirements. Additionally, the discussion that follows will also briefly cover short-range cash forecasting, corporate investment policy, and the criteria for selecting investments.

**The Short-Range Cash Budget or Forecast.**   The short-range cash budget, an integral component of the firm's profit planning and budgeting system, follows the complex assumptions incorporated in the budgets for the operating statement, the balance sheet, and capital expenditures. The inputs from these statements are utilized in the preparation of the cash budget. This forecast, covering a year, is further broken down into quarters and months. As each new month approaches, the forecast is further refined into weeks and days. This schedule is then used by the cash manager for:

1. Determining short-range operating cash requirements
2. Planning short-term borrowing
3. Planning short-term investments
4. Determining compensating balances

An example of a highly summarized cash forecast utilizing the cash receipts— cash disbursements method, is shown in Exhibit 5.9. This summary schedule is supported by schedules detailing receipts by type of revenue and operating

**EXHIBIT 5.9. Cash Forecast Using Cash Receipts-Cash Disbursements Method**

| | January | February | March | April | May | June | July |
|---|---|---|---|---|---|---|---|
| Receipts | $542 | $551 | $543 | $521 | $518 | $549 | $562 |
| Operating disbursements | 325 | 346 | 305 | 325 | 324 | 305 | 340 |
| Other disbursements | | | | | | | |
| Insurance | | 45 | | | 20 | | 15 |
| Interest | | | 180 | | | 180 | |
| Machine replacements | | 140 | | 35 | | 11 | |
| Dividends | 194 | | | 174 | | | 165 |
| Taxes (federal & state) | | | | | | | 170 |
| Total disbursements | 519 | 531 | 485 | 534 | 344 | 496 | 690 |
| Net cash inflow (outflow) | 23 | 20 | 58 | (13) | 174 | 53 | (128) |
| Beginning bank balance | 15 | 23 | 23 | 26 | 23 | 27 | 25 |
| Total available | 38 | 43 | 81 | 13 | 197 | 80 | (103) |
| Desired balance | 20 | 20 | 20 | 20 | 20 | 20 | 20 |
| Buffer | 5 | 5 | 5 | 5 | 5 | 5 | 5 |
| Total | 25 | 25 | 25 | 25 | 25 | 25 | 25 |
| Excess cash | 13 | 18 | 56 | (12) | 172 | 55 | (128) |
| Investment[a] | 15 | 20 | 55 | (10) | 170 | 55 | (130) |
| Type investment | | | | | | | |
| 90-day Treasury bills | 15 | 5 | | (10) | 10 | 10 | (10) |
| 120-day Treasury bills | | 15 | | | 120 | 30 | (120) |
| Commercial paper | | | 55 | | | 5 | |
| 1-year Treasury notes | | | | | 40 | 10 | |

[a]Company policy to purchase and sell investments in multiples of 5.

141

disbursements by type of expense. Starting with the beginning cash balance, and adding the change due to the net inflow or net outflow of forecasted cash for each period, a new cash balance is determined. Investment or borrowing decisions are then made, after incorporating compensating balances for bank services.

**CRITERIA FOR SELECTING INVESTMENTS.**   Safety and protection of principal and liquidity, and marketability of the money market instrument, are the principal criteria employed.

**Safety and Protection.**   The concern here is credit risk—will the issuer fail to pay off the principal and interest on the borrowed funds? Obviously the answer rests with the financial strength of the issuer. The preselection of debt instruments, and then continuous monitoring after investment, is mandatory.

Another aspect is market risk, which deals with the recovery of principal when the instrument is sold prior to maturity. The risk of loss of principal is a function of interest rate changes and the maturity of the instrument. When interest rates rise, the negative impact on principal is the greatest for those fixed rate instruments with longest maturities. The key here is the selection of money market securities with limited lives—a year and under is preferred.

**Liquidity and Instrument Marketability.**   How easily can the instrument be converted into cash when the company requires funds earlier than expected? A readily accessible secondary market for exchanges is necessary. The important point, of course, is not to invest in small debt issues (limited dollar volumes outstanding) in which few dealers make and maintain markets for these securities. The financial manager desires quotes that contain limited spreads between bid and ask prices when confronted with the need to raise cash immediately.

**Yield.**   In spite of the fact that the stress is on the return gained when investing funds, yield is only secondary to safety and liquidity of principal. The objective is to preserve principal, yet earn a market rate of return on the investment. Paramount is the consideration given to the trade-off of yield for safety and liquidity. The financial manager will be in a very unfortunate position when he or she has contributed to the loss of principal on investing the surplus funds of the firm.

**CORPORATE INVESTMENT GUIDELINES.**   As part of the firm's internal financial control system, corporate cash investment policy is frequently established by the board of directors or a finance committee. The purpose is to guide the daily investment decision process. This policy should contain, at a minimum, the following guidelines:

1. Investment criteria:—the preservation of principal, liquidity, only short-term marketable securities, and so on.

2. The person or persons designated to carry out this policy:—the specific responsibilities of the treasurer in connection with the management of cash.

3. Eligible investments:—domestic or foreign markets or both, eligible issuers or institutions, and so on.

4. Aggregate dollar amount limits for any one type of investment or institution

5. Whether investments can be denominated in other than U.S. dollars, and if so, under what conditions.

In some cases guidelines may not be available in smaller firms. In those instances it behooves the financial manager to suggest the drafting of such a policy by top management for the protection of all personnel associated with the investing process. As an example of the types of items to include, in addition to those discussed, see Exhibit 5.10.

Provision should also be made for an annual review of this policy. Investments that turn sour and generate losses can contribute to the hasty exit of the financial manager not operating within the firm's guidelines.

**Money Market Investments and Other Interest-earning Instruments.**
Short-term investing involves purchasing money market instruments whose lives extend one year or less. Much investing activity, however, centers on placing funds in interest-earning accounts for only a few days, or just overnight. To satisfy this time range of investing activity, an array of investment products are available. A number of the more popular interest-earning instruments are listed in the following section.

**Available Short-Term Investments.**    That which follows is a brief description of the outstanding features of popular investment vehicles selected by money managers. Covered are:

1. Bank money market accounts
2. Money market funds
3. Repurchase agreements
4. Negotiable certificates of deposit
5. Bankers' acceptances
6. Treasury bills

## EXHIBIT 5.10. A Typical Corporate Cash Investment Policy

**Purpose**

It is the objective of this company to invest excess cash within the following guidelines:

Investments shall be short-term

Investments shall be selected so as to preserve capital while maintaining liquidity

Investments shall earn market rate without undue risk to capital

**Responsibility**

The treasurer shall have the following responsibilities:

Selection of investments

Opening of accounts with brokers and/or dealers

Establishing safekeeping accounts

Custody of securities

Execution of any necessary documents

Review and modifications of investment guidelines as conditions warrant, subject to approval of the vice president for finance

**Types of Investments**

Domestic Banks. Banks with which the company has established a business relationship and/or the 25 largest U.S. banks—certificates of deposit or bankers acceptances. Aggregate investments with any one bank shall not exceed $ _____

Foreign Banks. A principal bank with which a division of the company has established a business relationship and/or a bank among the largest 100 foreign banks—time deposits, certificates of deposit, and bankers' acceptances. Aggregate investments with any one bank shall not exceed $ _____ .

Other investment areas include the following:

Repurchase agreements with the U.S. government or any of its agencies

Direct obligations of the U.S. government or its agencies, with maturities not in excess of two years

Commercial paper, not rated lower than A-1 by Standard & Poor, or P-1 by Moody Investor's Service. Investments with any one issuer shall not exceed $ _____

Eurodollar deposits placed with approved domestic or foreign banks. Aggregate deposits with any one bank shall not exceed $

**Curencies**

All investments shall be denominated in U.S. dollars or, if in foreign currencies, shall be covered by a hedge contract

7. Treasury notes and bonds

8. Commercial paper

9. U.S. government agency obligations

Refer to Exhibit 5.11, for additional information on short-term investment vehicles.

**Bank Money Market Accounts.**   Financial institutions are allowed to pay an unregulated rate of interest on balances of $1000 or more. Insured by the Federal Deposit Insurance Corporation (FDIC) for up to $100,000, many smaller companies use these accounts to invest funds in excess of those required for compensating balances. Simple, yet providing a relatively high yield, they are beneficial to the smaller company that wants to take advantage of the benefits of daily investing of excess funds.

**Money Market Funds.**   These funds invest in diversified portfolios of money market instruments. Securities approved for inclusion in a Money Market Fund (MMF) portfolio will give investors indications concerning a fund's investment objectives. The actual investment risk, however, is determined by a fund's current security holdings because money management fund shares are not insured.

Many funds allow businesses to transfer funds between the money market fund and the bank checking account at a minimum charge. This enables businesses to earn high money market rates on business checking accounts. In addition, the funds provide check-writing privileges, usually with a $500 minimum. Larger domestic companies utilize money funds for a number of reasons. Some are:

1. For "parking" excess cash until suitable investment opportunities are available

2. As portfolio managers, especially because fund portfolio managers are highly skilled

3. To eliminate many short-term portfolio management tasks, such as credit evaluation, interest rate forecasting, securities safekeeping, transaction processing, and maturity laddering.

**Repurchase Agreements.**   A repurchase agreement (repo) is an arrangement for securities to be sold to a customer under an agreement that obligates the seller to repurchase the same securities, at a specified date, a specified price, and with a specified rate of interest for the period held. Usually transacted for short periods of time (days), the agreements were created to provide an investment vehicle for the purchaser with the security of a U.S. government obligation or

**EXHIBIT 5.11. Partial Listing of Investment Vehicles Available to Corporate Cash Manager**

| Security | Minimum Denomination | Guarantee | Life | Interest Payments |
|---|---|---|---|---|
| Bank Money Market Accounts | $1,000 | Bank, FDIC up to $100,000 | Daily | Usually monthly |
| Money Market Funds | Varies—often $2,500–$50,00 | Underlying Investments of fund | Daily | Daily |
| Repurchase Agreements | varies—as low as $50,000 | Bank, underlying security | 1 day to over 30 days | Maturity |
| Negotiable Certificates of Deposit | $100,000 | Bank, FDIC up to $100,000 | 7 days to several years | Maturity |
| Bankers' Acceptance | $100,000 | Bank | 1 day to 1 year | Discount basis |
| Treasury Bills | $10,000 | U.S. government | 3 months to 1 year | Discount basis |
| Treasury Notes and Bonds | $1,000 to $10,000 | U.S. government | 1 year to 30 years | Semiannual |
| Commercial Paper | $25,000 to $100,000 | Issuing corporation | To 270 days | Discount basis |
| U.S. Government Agencies | $10,000 | Issuing agency of U.S. government | 30 days to 30 years | Maturity |

other appropriate security. Depending on the amounts involved in a repo, the rates approach the federal funds rate.

Popular until 1982, their use has diminished due to a New York bankruptcy court ruling (Lombard-Wall) that such an arrangement represents collateralized loans and not securities purchases. This meant that repo funds could be tied up indefinitely in cases of repo dealer bankruptcies. The Bankruptcy Act of 1984, however, has changed this, because the law states that repos are no longer subject to the automatic stay provisions of the bankruptcy code.

This still doesn't solve all the risks associated with a repo investment. A prudent financial manager will insist on physical delivery of the underlying securities, market-value-plus collateralization, and a written master purchase agreement. Barring these steps, the investor is subject to:

1. The pitfalls of additional government securities dealers failures
2. Institutions not governed by the bankruptcy code
3. Other undetermined risks not yet encountered.

**Certificates of Deposit.**   Domestic certificates of deposit are time-deposit obligations of banks that represent an investment in a financial institution in a minimum amount of $100,000. Not recommended for purchase with the intention of early sale, negotiable CDs (issued in bearer form) can be sold in actual secondary markets, with risk, because their marketability is limited compared with other money market instruments. Because the credit worthiness of the issuer stands behind this financial institution investment, the rates available on CDs issued by large, well-known money center banks are generally slightly lower than those offered by regional banks. Generally, the rates for CDs are 50 to 75 percent higher than comparably maturing U.S. government securities.

Dollar denominated deposit obligations issued by U.S. and foreign banks located overseas are known as Eurodollar certificates of deposit. The rates, usually higher than CDs, reflect the greater risk and the lessened security associated with this type of investment.

**Bankers' Acceptances.**   Used to facilitate international trade, the Bankers' Acceptance (BA), a negotiable time draft, represents a bank borrower's obligation to pay that obligation at a given date, with the payment guaranteed by the bank. By "accepting," the bank replaces the buyer's credit with the bank's credit. Returns are similar to that for CDs, because the risk of a BA is measured according to the perceived quality of the accepting bank.

**Treasury Bills.**   Considered the safest investment available, these are direct obligations of the United States backed by the full faith and credit of the U.S.

government. They are sold on a discount basis in minimum amounts of $10,000 with $5000 increments. Issued in maturities from 91 days to one year, the yields on treasury bills (T-bills) are generally the lowest of investment alternatives with similar maturities, because of safety and liquidity. The active secondary market for T-bills gives corporate investors the confidence that invested funds can be accessed quickly and easily.

**Treasury Notes and Bonds.**   Similar to T-bills, U.S. treasury notes and bonds are direct obligations of the United States backed by the full faith and credit of the U.S. government. These investments are issued at face amount and bear interest at the rate stated on the note or bond. Maturities range from one to 30 years, with the yields relatively low compared with other investments of comparable maturity.

**Commercial Paper.**   An unsecured promissory note of a corporation, issued on a discount basis, with a limited maturity (270 days). Issued either directly by the issuer or indirectly through dealers, many issuers obtain backup lines of credit from commercial banks to boost the purchaser's confidence in the issuer's ability to repay the borrowings. Some commercial paper issuers have no secondary market.

**United States Government Agency Obligations.**   These instruments represent indirect obligations of the U.S. government through certain government agencies. Agency obligations yield a relatively higher return than that of T-bills and treasury notes with comparable maturities.

## CASH POSITION INFORMATION

**THE DAILY CASH MANAGEMENT REPORTING AND CONTROL PROCESS.**   *Cash Position Control Systems* refers to techniques developed since the early 1970s for tracking (on a daily basis) information on corporate fund flows. Driven by the increasing cost of money, these manual and/or computerized systems provide information on fund amounts and locations to the cash manager. Thus on a daily basis, borrowing is required where shortfalls develop, whereas investing is the mode for cash surpluses.

**Daily Cash Management Reporting Flow.**   In order to take action to affect the end of day position of the corporate bank accounts controlled in the system, the cash manager needs to know the firm's cash position early in the morning each day. The process is initiated by the bank's demand deposit accounting system which processes, overnight, the corporate account debit and credit activity for the previous day's business. This reporting cycle is not completed until approximately 6 A.M., at which time the corporate account balances are sent to the branch and reporting service officers where reports can be made to the corporations. Major banks offering treasury management services gather account balance and transaction detail information on their accounts as well as other reporting U.S. banks, and offer this information to corporate clients through their proprietary treasury systems. The information can be obtained from these systems through a time-sharing terminal, CRT, or telex machine. Today, cash managers are also using microcomputers to retrieve daily balance reports from a network of bank accounts. With information on account balances (ledger and/ or collected) the cash manager forecasts individual account activity through the end of the day by estimating: (1) the deposits that will be "collected" today, and (2) the disbursements that will be "payable" today.

With this overall picture on a national basis, the cash manager will locate cash surpluses or shortages, determine whether compensating balances are being met, and define cash available for investments, pay downs, or other needs. Fund movements can then be initiated by wire transfers, advising banks of pay downs, or placing investment orders. These decisions are usually made prior to noon Eastern time—prior to the time that the New York money market begins to peak. Because there is a limited supply of investment instruments at any one time, the cash manager has to take early action before investment opportunities become lost (see Exhibit 5.12 for a summary of the daily cash management reporting process).

**The Elements of Daily Cash Forecasting.**    After the bank balances are received, the cash manager proceeds to forecast both the deposits and disbursements in individual accounts through the end of the day. The collection and disbursement systems already in place will provide most of the inputs for both of those important elements. In a previous section of this chapter (under "Cash concentration Methods") it was noted that funds are moved from local banks to the concentration bank through use of: (1) DTCs, and/or (2) ACH initiated transactions.

Additionally, the firm may use preauthorized payment systems, moving funds in either a paper-based mode through preauthorized checks, or an electronic mode using ACH initiated transactions. With the preceding means for the transfer of cash, it is known, with predictability, when these deposits will become "good" or "available" funds. Schedules are maintained, "tracking" time and amounts of both the DTCs and ACH transactions. Adding to these amounts the remittances received that day, which will become "good" funds that day, the total receipts can be forecast. Usually the deposit amounts received on the forecast day are translated into "good" funds that day by applying empirical experience. Funds wired would also be added to this total.

**EXHIBIT 5.12.    Daily Cash Management Reporting Process as of 9/26/8X**

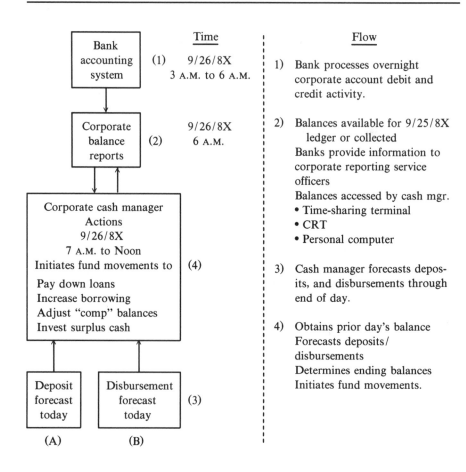

(A)  By schedule, track time and amounts of both DTCs and ACH transactions to determine collected funds today. Empirical experience applied to receipts received today, translating receipts into "good" funds today.

(B)  Disbursements clearing today through use of "days' outstanding factors," disbursement float summary schedules or controlled disbursements account information.

Several methods can be used for forecasting the disbursements that will clear the account at the end of the day. They are:

1.  Through judicial use of various disbursement points, the company can develop a highly reliable "days' outstanding" factor for its issuing locations.

2. Using disbursement services offered by banks (working in conjunction with account reconcilement services), the disbursement float summary schedule will report on the total number of days from issuance to clearance, for each check.

3. Through the use of a controlled disbursement account (see discussion under disbursing) information is provided early in the morning on the dollar amount of checks that will be paid later that same day.

The controlled disbursement account is the most effective technique because it reports debit information on the same day checks are paid. As previously mentioned, however, there may be obstacles in maintaining precise disbursement control through use of this method. By using the preceding techniques, information is developed to forecast the total clearings through the end of day. Wires are easily added to this amount, because they are controlled internally.

Exhibit 5.13 reflects the forecasts made for deposits and disbursements for Ultra Energy Corporation. The cash manager, after forecasting individual accounts through the end of the day, can now:

1. Initiate fund movements by wire
2. Advise banks of pay down or increased borrowing
3. Determine compensating balances required
4. Define cash available for investments

**Computerized Cash Management Reporting Systems.** Large money center banks have developed proprietary treasury management services for their clients. These systems provide a variety of services that enable the cash manager to perform cash management tasks effectively and productively. Security and confidentiality are built into these systems. Further, the information can be accessed through a time-sharing terminal, telex machine, or personal computer.

Some of the services offered are:

1. Bank account ledger balance and float amounts
2. Debit and credit detailed information
3. Lockbox reporting
4. Money market quotations for investment decisions
5. Money transfer reporter—provides a same day consolidated report of all incoming and outgoing wire transfers
6. Target balance information (compensating balances)
7. Account balance history

**EXHIBIT 5.13.   Ultra Energy Corporation Disbursement Float Position and Computation of Fund Transfer as of 9/26/8X**

Float Position

| | | |
|---|---|---|
| Opening bank balance 9/25/8X, reported by bank 9/26/8X AM | $ 449,000 | |
| (1) | | |
| Opening position books 9/26/8X, as of 9/25/8X | $(4,828,349) | |
| Total float (disbursement) | $(5,277,349 | |

Computation of Funds Transfer

| | | | |
|---|---|---|---|
| Opening bank balance, per above (9/25/8X) | | $ 449,000 | (1) |
| Deposited forecast - "collected" today | | 700,000 | (2) |
| | | $1,149,000 | |
| Disbursement forecast-"cleared" today | $2,288,000 (3) | | |
| Wires sent today (Fed Funds) | 61,000 | $2,349,000 | |
| Closing bank balance, forecast, 9/26/8X (overdraft) | | ($1,200,000) | |
| Compensating balance required | | (200,000) | (4) |
| Funds transfer amount, 9/26/8X | | $1,400,000 | |
| | | -0- | |

(1) Prior days' cash balances reported early morning today.

(2) Forecast of DTC's and ACH initiated transactions "collected" today, plus forecast for "immediately" available funds today.

(3) Through use of "days' outstanding" factors for disbursing locations, disbursements float summary schedules or controlled disbursement account information on clearings today.

(4) Forecast or through use of target balance information provided by proprietary bank treasury management services.

---

**8.**   International multibank reports—provides a consolidated picture of bank balances worldwide.

Additionally, treasury management consulting services are also offered to appraise and recommend solutions to optimize the firm's cash flows.

## SUMMARY

Many systems are available to the cash manager that help speed up the inflow of funds into the firm or conversely slow down the outflow. These are known as collection and disbursement systems. Newer collection products are highly automated and operate in an electronic mode. Zero balance and controlled disbursement accounts achieve the elimination of unproductive idle cash balances and extend disbursement float. These methods, when combined with proprietary bank reporting systems, provide up-to-the-minute information on corporate account balances. This information is necessary for the cash manager to take action on a daily basis, initiate fund movements, provide for pay downs, increase borrowings, adjust "comp" balances, and invest cash. Critical to cash investment, however, is the knowledge of cash forecasting, corporate investment policy, the criteria employed for investment selection and familiarity with interest-earning mediums and/or money market instruments.

The effective financial manager can integrate all these factors and in the short run contribute to the productivity of cash, increase profits, and greatly improve the company's bottom line.

## SUGGESTED READINGS

Akerley, Barbara H. "Money Management Plans Now Designed for Businesses," *The Cash Manager*, July 1983.

Beehler, Paul J. "Contemporary Cash Management: Principles, Practices, Perspectives," (2nd ed.), New York: Wiley, 1983.

Caruso, Robert L. "Paying Bills the Electronic Way," *Management Accounting*, April 1984.

Clements, Joel, and Woodall, Robert L. "Controlled Disbursements: A Cash Management Tool for Growing Concerns," *Management Accounting*, May 1983.

"Companies Learn to Live Without the Float," *Business Week*, September 26, 1983, p. 134.

Driscoll, Mary C. "Cash Management: Corporate Strategies for Profit," New York: Wiley, 1983.

Freimuth, Richard C. "Cash Management for Smaller Business: A New Technique," *Management Accounting*, June 1982.

Howe, Jerry T. "Managing Accounts Receivable Effectively," Management Accounting, August, 1983.

Lacey, Nelson J., and Chambers, Donald R. "Cash Manager's Guide to Money Market Mutual Fund Selection," *Journal of Cash Management*, March/April 1984.

McClintock, Ray M. "Impact of the Monetary Control Act," *Journal of Cash Management*, March/April 1984.

Meyerowitz, Steven A. "Repurchase Agreement Risks Reduced by New Bankruptcy Laws," *Cash Flow*, December 1984.

Peterson, Edward D. "Cash Management: A Guide to Increasing Profits," Belmont, CA: Lifetime Learning Publications, 1984.

# CHAPTER 6

# COST REDUCTION TECHNIQUES AND PROGRAMS

## Donald E. Keller

## INTRODUCTION

Cost reduction, like income taxes, suffers from a poor image. To many people, cost reduction means across-the-board cuts in the budget, with all the implications of reduced personnel and operations. There is no glamour in running a cost reduction program as compared with being in charge of implementing a new management information system or in launching a new product. The poor image of cost reduction is misdirected. Control of costs is necessary in all forms and sizes of organizations.

This chapter will cover many aspects of cost reduction, cost control, cost avoidance, and profit improvement. Each of these items will have a positive effect on the bottom line of an organization. Which one to apply, and in what circumstances, is a key component of effective management.

**Cost Reduction.** A cost reduction takes place when a cost that has been previously incurred is to be reduced at the time of next incurrence. In this context, the reduction is planned, deliberate, and relates to a past level of expenditure. Thus if a cost has *not* been previously incurred, we cannot have a cost reduction situation. For example, if a new product is to be manufactured and the cost of a raw material component drops from $40 to $38 before the material is purchased, there is no "cost reduction" but a windfall gain. The windfall resulted from outside factors unrelated to the activities of the business. The lower cost resulted in reduced cost to produce the new product, but it did not result from any deliberate action of the company and was not the result of a cost reduction technique or program.

**COST AVOIDANCE.**   A cost avoidance results from not incurring a cost, or from incurring a cost at a lesser amount than budgeted if this is the first time the cost will be incurred. Using the previous example, assume that a new product is to be manufactured and that the $40 raw material component is located at another supplier for $36. The $4 reduction in cost is a cost avoidance, not a cost reduction. In this case the planned and deliberate criteria are met, but there was no level of past expenditure. Accordingly, we have a cost avoidance, not a cost reduction.

**COST CONTROL.**   The techniques, procedures, and systems used to monitor and ensure that actual costs conform to predetermined allowed levels represent cost control. Management is concerned with control of costs effected primarily through the use of budgets and performance reports. Both the planning and control functions of management are tied closely to cost control.

**PROFIT IMPROVEMENT.**   Cost reduction, cost avoidance, and cost control all have a direct and positive effect on the bottom line for any organization. In addition to the techniques focused on costs, many situations contain both revenues and costs that can be managed to improve profits. For example, if a company is operating at full capacity and producing a variety of products, the question may arise as to which products should be produced and which should be cut back or eliminated. This is not a question of cost reduction, but is instead one of profit maximization. The focus should be on the mixture of products that will maximize profits, given the operating capacity of the company.

**UNIVERSAL NEED.**   Cost reduction techniques and programs are appropriate for all types of organizations: large and small; service, retail and manufacturing; profit, nonprofit, and governmental. The need is pervasive, because the effect on the bottom line —whether net income, loss or excess of tax revenues over expenditures (or the reverse, a deficit)—is of primary concern. It is not important *what* the bottom line is called, it is the effect on that bottom line which is important.

Most of the discussion and illustrations in this chapter will be for manufacturing organizations, with limited examples for service and nonprofit organizations. Many of the concepts for manufacturing organizations will be directly applicable to service and nonprofit organizations, however, with little or no modification. For example, cost reduction in clerical support used to record transactions would be equally beneficial to a manufacturer or a governmental unit.

# COST REDUCTION TECHNIQUES

Cost reduction techniques are many and varied. Techniques are a specific step or a single application of cost reduction. Cost reduction programs contain multiple steps in their implementation and completion. Cost reduction and cost control programs will be discussed later in this chapter.

**ACROSS-THE-BOARD COST REDUCTION.** Across-the-board cost reduction, expressed in terms of a percentage reduction in costs or in absolute dollar amounts, is probably the most misused cost reduction technique. The reason for its popularity is due to its simplicity. Almost everyone can understand a 10 percent reduction in a budget or a $100,000 reduction in a budget.

Despite the simplicity of the across-the-board cost reduction technique, it often is applied incorrectly. By reducing costs in all departments and activities by the same percent, it is assumed that all costs in departments and activities can be reduced by the percentage identified. This would be very difficult to implement in a manufacturing facility where 85 percent of the cost of a final product is raw material cost. An across-the-board 10 percent in cost may eliminate all factory overhead and one-half of the direct labor. It would be impossible to produce any product in this situation. Thus the percentage reduction mandated by management would be impossible to achieve without reducing production. Reducing production may have an adverse effect on net income because more revenue may be eliminated than the savings in cost.

One situation in which the across-the-board cost reduction would be appropriate and effective would be to reduce discretionary fixed costs by a set percentage, say 20 percent. Discretionary fixed costs are costs budgeted as a fixed amount for the period, but at a level based on management judgment. Costs in this category include employee travel for educational seminars and conventions, promotion samples, certain customer services, a company golf outing, and similar costs. An across-the-board cost reduction would probably hurt each of the different types of activities about equally and not eliminate any of them. Most managers could adjust activities to conform to a budget level of 80 percent of the original budget, if appropriate lead time is given.

If the across-the-board cost reduction is a certain amount of dollars, such as $100,000 per operating department, different inequities may be present. As in a percentage reduction, not all operating units can find or will be equally affected by the $100,000 cost reduction. One department may find the amount to be 10 percent of its budget, whereas another may find the amount to be only 1 percent of its budget. Presumably, it is easier to find 1 percent than 10 percent of a budget to eliminate, if everything else is equal.

Another inequitable aspect of the fixed amount of cost reduction relates to whether a department has discretionary costs that can be reduced without serious harm to the departmental activities. If one department has $800,000 of discretionary fixed costs and another has only $200,000, a $100,000 reduction per department would seem inequitable.

In summary, any across-the-board cost reduction, percentage or fixed dollar amount, should be made with caution and in light of all the facts. Often across-the-board cost reductions are made in the name of ease and equity, but in reality are very inequitable.

**PROGRAM ELIMINATION.**   Eliminating a program or activity is one way for management to identify priorities of different operating activities. Because of planned operations, budget constraints, or profit impact, a program or activity may be eliminated. For example, it may be decided that an in-house counsel is too expensive for the size of the organization. The decision may be to eliminate in-house counsel and to retain outside legal counsel on a retainer fee basis. Or, because of poor economic conditions, salespersons will be required to return company-leased automobiles and instead will receive $200 per month toward auto travel costs.

Program or activity elimination can be especially effective for colleges, transit systems, hospitals, and similar nonprofit organizations. Based on analysis of revenues and costs, often cost-ineffective programs can be identified, then combined with other programs or eliminated. Many colleges have reduced or eliminated their education schools because of low enrollments. Difficulty is encountered in eliminating programs because of redeploying tenured education professors or in terminating them. Similarly, hospitals can eliminate maternity, pediatric, or other cost-ineffective programs if other hospitals in the area are also underutilized in these program areas.

**ZERO-BASE BUDGETING.**   Zero-base budgeting (ZBB) is a management tool that received considerable attention during the 1970s. The ZBB technique first received notice in 1964 when the U. S. Department of Agriculture used it in the preparation of its budget. In the early 1970s, Texas Instruments was a prime developer of the technique in the private sector.

Zero-base budgeting has little applicability in manufacturing activities, but is applicable to support activities in manufacturing firms as well as to firms that are service oriented. Thus the benefits of a ZBB system are best realized in service firms, governmental organizations, and in service functions of manufacturing firms.

The major advantage of the ZBB technique is that management at different levels is involved in directing resources into the highest priority programs, whether the programs are long established or new ones. A key aspect of ZBB is that operating management is involved in the budgeting process in detail. Each manager must evaluate various options: (1) what alternatives are available to perform the functions within the manager's control; and (2) what costs are associated with each of the functions. Then, the manager must rank the various activities and associated costs in priority order. As these ranked activities and costs are integrated at the top organizational level, upper management can decide how many activities can be funded and the level of service that will be planned.

A key aspect of ZBB is that all activities and associated costs must be justified from base zero. Zero-base budgeting is a budgeting system more than it is a cost reduction technique. Thus further discussion of ZBB as a budgeting process is included later in this chapter under "Cost Control Programs."

**VALUE ENGINEERING.** As with ZBB, value engineering can be thought of as a cost reduction technique or as a cost reduction program. Discussion of value engineering as a cost reduction program is contained in the section entitled "Cost Reduction Programs."

The primary purpose of value engineering is to reduce costs. The concept was first used by the General Electric Company in 1949. Value engineering is a team activity, focused primarily on the relative worth of a product or service and its cost. The results of the team review should be a list of potential cost savings, ranked in order of desirability. The ranking, implications for top management review and associated cost savings will be forwarded to top management for action. In this sense, value engineering is parallel to ZBB in that activities are ranked in priority order and acted upon by a committee of top-level managers for implementation.

Proponents of value engineering indicate that it is most useful in two situations: (1) when there is a need for short-term cost reduction and other methods have been exhausted, and (2) when a competitive edge is needed in the marketplace where competition is acute. The implementation of value engineering requires the full support and commitment of top management, usually all the way to the chief executive officer.

# CONTROLLING MATERIAL COSTS

For manufacturing firms, the cost of raw materials and manufacturing supplies is often the largest component of product costs. Therefore control over the purchase, receiving, storage, use, and cost of materials is vital to the profitable operations of manufacturing concerns. Many techniques have been developed that aid in the control of materials and their cost.

**ABC INVENTORY CONTROL.**    ABC inventory analysis and control is a technique designed to reduce the cost of raw materials and supplies used in production. For most manufacturing firms a small percentage of materials or parts comprises a majority of the cost of all materials and parts used in the production process. Using this as a base, the ABC inventory technique was developed.

The ABC technique requires the inventory to be divided into three categories—"A" for the material representing a large percent of all annual material costs, "B" for the material with moderate cost, and "C" for material that has a relatively low total cost. In many organizations, the A category represents 5 to 10 percent of the items in inventory, but 60 to 80 percent of total material costs for the year, whereas the C category will often represent 50 to 80 percent of inventory items but less than 15 percent of total material cost.

For example, a manufacturer may carry 20,000 different parts and materials in inventory costing $500,000. Assume the following breakdown of inventory items and costs on an A, B, and C basis:

| Inventory Category | Items | | Cost | |
|---|---|---|---|---|
| | Number | Percent | Total | Percent |
| A | 1,000 | 5 | $300,000 | 60 |
| B | 5,000 | 25 | 140,000 | 28 |
| C | 14,000 | 70 | 60,000 | 12 |
| TOTAL | 20,000 | 100 | $500,000 | 100 |

Concentrating efforts on the 1000 items in the A inventory category would likely result in the greatest benefit. Saving 10 percent in cost for these inventory items would be $30,000, whereas only $6000 in savings would result if the same 10 percent could be saved on C inventory items. And, it would probably take considerably longer to find the $6000 savings among the 14,000 items in the C inventory category than to locate $30,000 savings in the 1000 A items. Thus concentrating on the inventory items where the potential for cost savings is greatest—the large-dollar items—will likely result in the greatest benefit to the organization.

The ABC inventory control technique is used by many manufacturing firms and by equipment and vehicle parts supply houses. Generally, the old 80 to 20 percent rule of thumb applies here—80 percent of the cost of inventory is often made up of 20 percent of the items, whereas the other 20 percent of the cost of the inventory is made up of 80 percent of the inventory items. Therefore concentrating on 20 percent of the items will generate savings on 80 percent of the cost of inventory.

**MATERIAL SUBSTITUTION.** Substituting a lower cost material or component for a more costly one is an established business practice in many firms. The essence of this cost reduction technique is to determine where a less costly material or product component can be substituted for a more costly material or component. Ideally, the new material or component will perform as well as the prior item, but with a lower cost, or the performance will be reasonably close to the prior material or component.

This substitution technique has been used extensively in the automobile, appliance, and furniture industries. For example, many interior parts and some peripheral engine components on automobiles are now made of plastic instead of more costly steel or aluminum. Most of these changes have resulted in lower manufacturing cost of the components and also ease in handling and installing the lighter components.

Another example of material substitution is where a large appliance manufacturer replaced a brass mixing valve component with one that was primarily plastic. The change resulted in two benefits to the manufacturer: the cost of the mixing valve assembly was reduced to less than one-half its prior cost and the weight was also reduced to less than one-third of the brass component. Three cost savings resulted from this change: lower cost of the component part, lower shipping and handling cost of purchasing the part, and the lower cost of shipping the completed appliance to retailers. The cost per unit savings for this appliance was just over $2, but with over 200,000 units produced per year the total estimated savings was close to $500,000 a year.

**MATERIAL STANDARDS.** Standard costs are used by many manufacturing firms for both the planning and control of costs. The benefits of using a standard cost system include the control of material costs, the control of material quantity usage, and reduction of clerical costs. Standard costs are used primarily as part of the management planning and control system, not as a cost reduction technique.

Cost reductions can result from the use of a standard cost system. Standard costs are carefully predetermined physical and cost estimates that should be attained in normal efficient operations. Using this definition, the standard cost to produce a given product is the quantity of the various material components that is included in the bill of materials and the cost that should be incurred to purchase and make ready the raw material for production. Effective management control and reduced cost should result from the use of performance reports indicating material usage variances and material price variances. Price variances normally are the responsibility of the purchasing department, whereas usage variances are usually the responsibility of production departments. Effective cost control of material should be accomplished by using standard costs, performance reports containing variances from standard, and a reporting system for all levels of management.

**MATERIAL REQUIREMENTS PLANNING.** The relative availability of data processing capabilities has brought to the business community the concept of material requirements planning (MRP). The essence of this concept is an inventory planning and control system integrated with the manufacturing process for the planning and control of production and material flows. This highly integrated computerized system is based on the premise that the demand for material, parts, components, and manufacturing supplies depends on the demand for product output.

An MRP system is comprised of four critical elements. These elements include the master production schedule that is the heart of the system, the bill of materials file, the inventory data file containing the status of inventory items, and the logic that makes up the materials requirements planning package. The elements of the MRP concept result in a manufacturing planning and control system that should minimize inventory stock while maintaining delivery schedules.

Because of the extreme detailed nature and technical aspects of MRP, the concept will not be fully discussed here. Other sources explaining how MRP operates should be studied to determine whether the technique is appropriate for the operations being evaluated.

**LINEAR PROGRAMMING.** Accountants increasingly utilize mathematical and computer models to help solve business problems. Linear programming (LP) is a mathematical technique and a tool used by the accountant to help solve certain profit maximization or cost minimization situations. The basic premise in LP is that all aspects of the problem can be stated in linear functions (fixed or variable costs and sales revenues) and that the costs or revenues are known with certainty. Although these constraints are never completely true, the mathematical solution will be reasonably close to a more accurate but much more complicated computation if the constraints are not accepted.

To minimize costs, the application of LP would be appropriate for formulating shipping schedules, production schedules, or for varying ingredients in a product. When determining shipping schedules and selecting carriers, such factors as weight, distance, time of arrival, time of pick-up, and cost would all be used to determine the optimum shipping arrangement for the lowest cost.

Meat processors often have a variable (within certain limits) range of ingredients that go into bologna, salami, or sausages. With the aid of LP, the ingredients selected can have the lowest cost per pound of output given the relative prices of the various meats and fillers that can comprise the finished product. For example, assume the price of beef increases and the price of soybean meal decreases for the processing of bologna; then, the relative proportions of the beef can be reduced and the relative proportion of soybean meal can be increased, within certain limits of taste and texture of the final product. If there were seven different ingredients going into the production of the bologna, the relative proportion of more than the two ingredients may change.

Often LP is used to maximize profit (gross or contribution margin), not to minimize cost. The combination of products to produce, given the constraints on machine time, materials, or skilled labor, will determine which combination of products will maximize profits in the short term. With the aid of a microcomputer, almost any LP problem can be quickly and easily solved. In complex situations, deriving a hand-calculated solution would be very time-consuming; using a computer makes the calculation relatively quick and simple.

## CONTROLLING LABOR COSTS

Salaries, wages, and fringe benefits comprise a significant portion of almost every organization's total cost. In many service, governmental, and not-for-profit organizations, these costs often represent 80 percent or more of the total budget. Therefore controlling labor costs is critically important to the success of the organization.

**LABOR (PROCESS) SUBSTITUTION.**    A technique for reducing labor costs is to substitute lower cost labor for more expensive labor. If a function such as customer product complaints typically has been performed by a customer relations manager, but could have been performed by a clerk with minimum training, the potential for cost reduction is good. Perhaps 90 percent of the customer complaints are relatively routine and could be handled by a clerk — a lower-cost person. And, this will free the customer relations manager to give full attention to complaints, and may provide more time to perform his or her function more effectively or to do other tasks now performed outside the organization or by other high-cost personnel.

Another opportunity exists for labor process substitution where two or more prior steps in a manufacturing process can be combined into a single step or with a single set-up of the machine or equipment. The reduction in cost will result from the combining of prior steps into a single step, thus eliminating starting and stopping time and the need for handling the component two or more times. A cost savings also results from the reduction in set-up time—now only one set-up is needed where two or more set-ups were needed in prior production schedules.

**INCENTIVE PAYMENT SYSTEMS.**   Techniques used to encourage employees to be more productive include various incentive payment systems. The basic premise is that the incentive payment will be less than the increase in earnings from the production of additional units. There are many incentive systems in use, both for industrial and clerical-type activities.

The incentive systems can be categorized into individual incentive systems and group incentive systems. The individual incentive systems include piece-rate systems and bonus premiums. Similarly, group incentive systems are comprised of group piecework systems and group bonus plans.

An individual piecework system is designed so that the worker's wage is calculated only on the number of pieces of product produced. The rate of pay is per piece produced, based on agreement or set by management. Total pay is then computed by multiplying the rate per piece times the number of units produced. This is the simplest pay rate per piece system that can be used.

However, different rates may be paid for the units produced. One such system is where the rate per piece is higher for *all* units produced if production exceeds a given level, often called the standard level. Another piece-rate system will pay different rates per piece, depending on how many pieces are produced. For example, one rate may be paid for the first 100 units produced in a day, another higher rate per piece for the next 25 units produced that day, and a still higher rate for units produced in excess of 125 per day. The choice of the piece rate of pay system depends on management and employees and their relative bargaining positions.

An employee bonus system results when a bonus is paid for producing at a rate above some level, often called the standard level. In the bonus system, the payment will be for production in excess of the standard for a week (or day) and usually is based on the time saved because production exceeded standard. Often the time saved multiplied by the employee hourly rate of pay will be split between the employee and the employer.

Group incentive piecework and bonus systems are similar to the individual systems discussed earlier. The major problem in group systems which is not present in individual systems is how to divide the rate or bonus; usually the division is made in a way that gives skilled-labor employees a larger share of the total payment than the amount given to nonskilled labor employees.

**AUTOMATION.**   Replacement of human labor with machine power is occurring in both factory and office. The largest gains so far have been made in the factory where some robots have been successfully introduced and are being utilized to perform many routine repetitive functions. The advantages of the change to automation are many, the primary being lower cost per unit of good product output. With fewer repetitive functions for employees to peform, monotony and disenchantment with the job are less likely. Also, machines do not become tired, require lunch breaks, or daydream.

The economics of automation are rather simple. If the total operating cost of the new equipment, including depreciation and labor to operate it, is less than the total labor and other costs of performing the same function, then in that situation the change to automated equipment is desirable. All factors should be considered when comparing the costs of the two approaches with performing a task. If the change to automated equipment will reduce the number of supervisors or forepeople needed in the production facility, the cost of reduced supervision should be considered.

In recent years there has been considerable discussion about office automation. Significant potential exists for reduced cost and better performance in the office. The gains in office automation have been small and slow, however. The most significant gains have been in the utilization of word processing equipment and microcomputers in the office environment. Because of the similarities among some word processing equipment and microcomputers, it is difficult to distinguish between them in some situations. Gains in both quality and quantity of letters and reports from organizations utilizing word processing units have been gratifying. This trend should continue.

The utilization of microcomputers in the office, primarily for accounting and certain purchasing, personnel, and marketing functions, is encouraging. In many cases, the cost of these functions has not been reduced, but the amount of timely data available to make management decisions has increased significantly. With the availability of low-cost equipment, and as software becomes increasingly available, the increased use of microcomputers in business will continue. The primary obstacle to better and faster office automation now resides in the development of available low-cost software.

**STAFFING PHILOSOPHY.**  Staffing a function so that it can meet the peak demands of that function within its normal operating day may not be very efficient. The problem of maximum staffing is that frequently there are one or more persons who have nothing to do or are underemployed. This may lead individuals in that function to believe that this average level of activity is "normal" and that management expects them to work less than a full day.

For example, assume the factory maintenance department has functions that would require five and one-half people to perform each day. Should the department hire five or six employees? Assume that a one-half person cannot be hired. If five persons are hired, overtime will be required for each. And if six employees are hired, there will be excess time (idle time) to the extent of one-half employee each day.

The economics of this staffing problem are as follows. Assume that all maintenance employees are paid $10 per hour worked and time and a half for overtime. If the sixth employee is hired, the cost per week is $400 (40 hours × $10). If the five employees each work 4 hours per week overtime—20 hours total—the cost per week is $300 (20 hours × $15). Thus the direct savings is $100 per week, which may seem immaterial. If fringe benefits average 40 percent of pay, however, the savings become much larger. The fringe benefits for the new employee would be $160 per week ($400 × 40 percent), whereas the fringe benefits for the overtime worked would be very low, probably not more than $20 or $30 per week. Thus the total savings of not hiring the sixth person would be $230 to $240 per week.

Savings in fringe benefit costs would result from the current five employees' costs that would not change—for such items as federal unemployment tax, state unemployment tax, medical insurance cost, life insurance cost, and vacation pay. Fringe benefits that may continue with the overtime pay would be social security taxes and pension contributions by the employer. Because of the total cost of fringe benefits, many employers are looking carefully at how and when to add an additional employee to the staff and when current employee overtime is a less costly solution. It is estimated that fringe benefits cost the average company approximately 37 percent of the base salary for each employee.

**LABOR STANDARDS.** Standards developed and used for labor are part of a standard cost system in many manufacturing firms. Labor standards are used by manufacturing firms for both the planning and control of labor costs. The benefits of using a standard cost system include the control of labor rates, labor time usage, and reduced clerical costs. Standard costs are used primarily as part of the management planning and control system, not as a cost reduction technique.

**LEARNING CURVES.** The learning curve is a mathematical expression of what happens to labor productivity in the production process when a new product is introduced or a change takes place in the manufacturing process. As employees become more familiar with the steps involved in producing the product, the labor time involved to complete a unit of product will decrease by a set rate. The rate of learning is referred to as the learning curve.

Learning curve theory states that, as cumulative quantities double, the average cumulative time decreases by a certain percent. The rate of learning is usually stated as a percent—75, 80, 90, or a similar amount. Assuming a 75 percent learning curve, each time the cumulative number of units produced doubles, the average time for all the units produced will be 75 percent of the previous average.

An example will be used to explain the application of the learning curve theory. Assume that 10 units are produced in the first batch and that the time to produce these 10 units was 50 hours. With cumulative production of 10, 20, 40, and 80 units, and a 75 percent learning curve, the following would result:

| Cumulative Quantity | Cumulative Average Time Per Unit (Hours) | Cumulative Total Time Needed(Hours) |
|---|---|---|
| 10 | 5 | 50 |
| 20 | 3.75 (5 × .75) | 75 |
| 40 | 2.81 (3.75 × .75) | 112.4 |
| 80 | 2.11 (2.81 × .75) | 168.8 |

The primary benefit of learning curve theory is that when a new product is being produced or the manufacturing process is changed, the labor time that should be incurred can be estimated. This technique allows projections of the cumulative average unit cost at any stage of production. Also, after producing many units, the gains in reduced labor time per unit are extremely small—this is when the standard time may be set at a constant amount. The basis for standard cost variance analysis is also established as is the basis for production control, by increasing lot size so that a level work force can be maintained.

## CONTROLLING OVERHEAD COSTS

Overhead costs are comprised of a wide variety of costs for a relatively large array of services in almost all organizations. Cost reduction techniques (discussed near the beginning of this section) apply to overhead costs—including all the advantages and disadvantages of those techniques. Across-the-board cuts, program eliminations, ZBB, value engineering, and other reduction techniques may be applied to overhead costs to reduce them.

**SERVICE SUBSTITUTION OR REDUCTION.**   Potential for the reduction in cost is present in many of the varied functions covered by overhead services. In some functions the opportunity is available to fund internal services versus purchasing outside services. This opportunity is available for motor vehicle maintenance, computer services, medical insurance, and other functions. Should the company maintain and staff a motor vehicle pool for 10 small delivery trucks? Or would it be less expensive to contract with a local service station to park, service, and fuel the vehicles? When comparing total cost of the motor vehicle pool with the cost of contracting for outside vehicle maintenance, the cost of maintaining a motor pool may represent an expensive luxury.

Similarly, many companies purchased computers when the purchase of outside batch or time-sharing computer services would have been cost-effective. The "status" of owning a computer sometimes overshadowed the cost/benefit analysis. With the relatively inexpensive microcomputers now available, the key question seems to be: what the needed software will cost to make the system work for your organization. The total cost of the in-house computer versus the total cost of using an outside facility should be the key question answered before an investment decision is made.

Savings in the cost of insurance can often be achieved with little or no effect on the desired coverage. One simple change in casualty insurance coverage that would increase the deductible per accident from, for example, $100 to $1000 or from $500 to $10,000 may cause a significant reduction in premiums. Insurance companies do not want to process small claims, because the cost is almost as great as processing a claim five to 10 times as large.

Also, during recent years some companies have been self-insuring for medical insurance while maintaining outside major medical insurance coverage. The cost, speed, and simplicity of self-insurance is more advantageous than dealing with what often seems to be a very slow-paying insurance company. Usually, coverage can be maintained or increased when the self-insured medical plan is adopted — plus insurance coverage and protection from very large medical bills is covered by the use of a major medical plan.

**OTHER TECHNIQUES OF COST CONTROL.** Other techniques sometimes applicable to help control overhead costs include the ratio of direct laborers to indirect and supervisory labor, the ratio of prime costs (material and direct labor) to total overhead, comparing your company averages with industry averages, and probably most important, the philosophy of management regarding cost control. When using ratios to track costs, both the trend of the ratio and the recent change are important. What is the reason for the change (trend) and is the change (trend) justified? As in so many other situations, management judgment and philosophy are often the critical ingredients to effective cost control.

# COST REDUCTION PROGRAMS

In large businesses and in smaller, growing ones, management often becomes removed from the day-to-day operating activities of the organization. Therefore the business systems operations and practices become obsolete, reports are inadequate for current internal and external needs, and necessary information is not included in the current system. Although some of these problems arise from external pressures over which the company has little or no control, others arise from internal factors that can be altered.

Often a company will try one of the cost reduction techniques discussed earlier in this section to improve profits. They may institute across-the-board cuts, incentive programs, hiring freezes, or program elimination. These techniques are often only a quick fix that renders some short-term benefits, but usually has no lasting effect. Only a structured cost reduction (profit improvement) program will have the lasting effect desired by management.

**ORGANIZING A COST REDUCTION PROGRAM.**  All long-term effective cost reduction programs are well-planned, structured, time-consuming efforts. The structure and design of the program will differ from company to company, but the process has many similarities. The necessary steps in a cost reduction program include:

1.  Top management supports and should take the initiative in establishing a cost reduction program.

2.  A committee is established comprised of senior-level managers and other key employees to oversee the cost reduction program.

3.  A general review is performed, including industry data analysis and marketing position. This review will take from 2 days to 2 weeks, depending on the size of the organization, the amount of detail considered, and the charge of management.

4.  After an analysis of the general review data, a preliminary review is performed. This step will take from 2 to 5 weeks. In this phase specific areas of potential profit improvement will be identified and the potential for success estimated. This step is done so that action can be taken in those areas where profits can be improved most quickly.

5.  The company conducts detail analysis of the areas showing the greatest potential for success as identified in step 4. This step may take from 4 to 12 weeks. This is where the identified opportunities for improvement are converted into specific recommendations and a management plan for action is created. This is the most detailed of the cost reduction steps, and should result in specific step-by-step recommendations for cost reductions.

6.  The committee reviews and identifies opportunities for implementation of cost reduction. The specific areas for cost reduction, the priorities of each area, and the steps to be followed in their implementation will be decided by the committee. Implementation of the recommendations will be left to the operating managers or subcommittees.

7.  Implementation of the plan. In some cases testing on a small scale will be desirable. If successful, then the complete change will be made. Testing

of the possible cost improvements is a good method to identify and solve the problems that may result from change and also is a way of gaining acceptance for making major changes in procedures.

8. The final but extremely important step is follow-up control. Follow-up is needed by top management to ensure that the plan is properly implemented, to review periodic reports on the progress of the plan, and to ensure that the cost reductions remain and that the old cost inefficiencies do not creep back into the system.

This eight-step cost reduction program may be thought of as a generic program. The number of steps in the program will depend on the formulation of the plan of action. For example, steps 1 and 2 and steps 3 and 4 could be combined into two steps instead of the listed four. If time is of the essence, this combination may be necessary—or it may be desirable because the organization is relatively small. Accordingly, think of the steps above as necessary processes to be performed, regardless of how they may finally be packaged.

**COMMITTEE AND TASK FORCE SELECTION.**   The key ingredient of a cost reduction program is the complete commitment of senior management in setting the climate, setting priorities, and in making decisions. Top management's primary task is to instill a concern for profit improvement throughout the organization.

In most companies it will be necessary to establish a committee to oversee the cost reduction program. The committee will be responsible for determining the parameters of the review, determining which organizational units are to be included in the study, setting review policies, making recommendations, and resolving any conflicts that may arise. This committee will guide the process from steps 1 through 8. Often the chief executive or chief operating officer will serve as committee chairperson.

The composition of the committee may include the president (chief executive officer), the controller, one or two key vice-presidents, and a few other key management employees. The committee should contain between seven and 12 persons so that sufficiently different ideas are represented and so the committee does not become too large and cumbersome. The purposes of the committee are to be authoritative, action-oriented, and responsive to subcommittee or task force needs. By careful planning, the composition and size of the committee will be effective and efficient.

After the cost reduction committee has ben formed and met, subcommittees or task forces should be established. These task forces will contain membership from all departments within the task force scope. Selecting persons for the task forces requires tact, because persons serving on the committees should be of about the same managerial level. The task forces will have a charge to look at product design, salaries and fringe benefits, materials, support activities, sales and administrative costs, and other areas.

These subcommittees or task forces are vital to the success of the cost reduction program. Each task force member provides motivation and can exert pressure to give up or modify nonessential resources. The identification of possible cuts, commitment to the top-management committee, and open discussion with peers should help achieve the cost-cutting goals.

Chrysler Corporation, in their financial turnaround, reported the following information regarding their cost reduction program committee structure:

> We found that the formation of a standing committee at the corporate level was useful, consisting of representatives from each operating group and chaired by a representative from the controller's office. This committee has the mandate to establish guidelines and act as final approval authority for all nonproductive expenditures not immediately required to support production activities. Such a committee can also serve in an advisory capacity to aid locations in developing cost reduction programs that fit their specific needs. Plant-level cost control activities should be an extension of the corporate-level cost control committee. A plant-level committee can also establish a program in which cost reduction proposals are solicited from plant employees[1]

**GOALS AND GOAL CONGRUENCE.**   Setting cost reduction goals is an important part of an effective program. The goals should be set by top management and communicated throughout the organization. The company target cost reduction will have to be divided into individual department, cost center, or other segment goals. Identifying the cost reduction goals for subunits in the organization should be performed by the cost reduction committee and the task forces.

The goals selected by top management may be a certain return on assets, a return on sales, or simply a percentage or dollar amount of reduction in costs. If a percentage return on assets or sales is selected, it will usually be converted into an absolute dollar amount. For example, a 10 percent return on assets may be determined as $70,000 (10 percent × $700,000 assets employed). Thus if the company is currently earning only $25,000 per year on the assets employed, there is a shortfall of $45,000. The $45,000 then becomes the targeted cost reduction goal.

The organization goal of $45,000 cost reduction must then be converted into goals for individual operating units. Each operating unit must contribute to the cost reduction effort, but not necessarily by equal amounts. In some operating units, a high goal may be exceeded. In others, a smaller reduction may be difficult to achieve. In each case, the question should be: If the cost of this

[1]Steffen, Christopher J., "Tightening Industry's Belt," *Financial Executive,* May 1982, pp. 17–18.

operating unit is to be reduced by $XX, what is the least harmful way of accomplishing this objective? Determining the cost reduction target of each operating unit is one of the major tasks of the cost reduction committee and the task forces.

Establishing a goal to improve an organization's operating performance and selling the goal to operating units is the essence of management effectiveness and goal congruence. Both the setting of the goal and the acceptance of the goal are key elements to achieving long-term cost reductions.

**IMPROVEMENT OPPORTUNITIES AND RECOMMENDATIONS.**   The process of identifying cost improvement opportunities and making recommendations for change represent the implementation of steps 3 through 5 in the preceding list. This process begins with gathering data for the organization and concludes with analysis of detail from various operating units.

The initial step is to document that there is a need for a cost reduction program. This is difficult to do if your organization is profitable, has a return on investment greater than the industry average, and the general economy is healthy. Often, the reverse is true. The company is losing money, has a negative return on investment, and the economy is in a downturn. Determining the magnitude of the problem is the first step in cost reduction and profit improvement.

To peform the general review, a number of information items will be needed. First, financial statements for the company for at least the last two years will be needed. Also, outside sources of information will be needed for comparison purposes. These items would include financial statements of competitors in the same industry, industry statistics from Dun & Bradstreet, Robert Morris Associates, the Labor Department or Department of Commerce, and other sources. One place to check for good recent sources of industry information is the industry associations or accounting associations in which the company is a member, or in which employees are members. The sources of information are many and varied.

Once the various sources of information have been identified and received, the data must be summarized and analyzed. From this analysis we may find that both the cost of goods sold and marketing expenses are significantly higher than the main competitor companies. This may indicate a prime source for cost improvement. Or, the preliminary analysis may indicate that all expenses, cost of goods sold, marketing, and general and administrative, are slightly higher than the industry average and that the ratio of sales to total assets is lower than the industry average. This may indicate different problems and possibly an approach to cost reduction and profit improvement.

After the general review and analysis are performed, areas are selected for preliminary review where specific areas of potential profit improvement will be identified. The primary purpose of this step is to determine where action can be taken and profits improved most quickly.

The preliminary review will be performed by task forces. Much of the information used by the committee in the general review will be passed along to task forces to help them in the preliminary review. If outside sources of data are available, the task force will use them in this preliminary detail analysis. Areas that may be studied by the task force include direct material cost and usage, direct labor usage, indirect labor utilization, clerical costs, sales force assignments and performance measurement, transportation/distribution costs, systems and data processing costs, and others.

The data needed by the task forces would include at least two years of operating results. Utilizing this historical information and analyzing the data for trends, cost per unit of output (units produced, invoices processed, customers serviced, or other measures of activity), and changes in the cost per unit or total cost, would indicate where potential cost reductions may be possible. Then, comparing these internal data with outside sources from Dun & Bradstreet, U.S. Department of Commerce or Department of Labor, other industry sources, or other operating units in the same company is desirable. Measuring, or attempting to do so, the performance of an operating unit with internal and external operating units is one indication of the relative efficiency of operating units. For example, if the warehousing and distribution costs represent 12 percent of sales revenues for Division B, whereas the industry average is 9 percent, we have identified a potential cost reduction area. Or, if raw material costs are 33 percent of final product cost, whereas the industry average is 31 percent, we have identified another potential cost reduction area.

When the preliminary review and analysis has been completed by the task forces, the information will be taken to the committee for further discussion and analysis. Based on this committee activity, the areas for detail analysis will be identified and prioritized. This process will give the task forces guidance in the next step, the detail analysis of areas in which the potential for cost reduction is greatest.

An area identified in the preliminary review process for potential improvement may be the order entry/billing department. Information from the preliminary review plus additional data and analysis may reveal the following statistics:

|  | Increase in Cost of Function | Increase in Sales Revenues | Increase in Sales Orders |
| --- | --- | --- | --- |
| Year 1 | 12% | 2% | 3% |
| Year 2 | 15% | 4% | 5% |
| Year 3 | 14% | 2% | 5% |

The costs of this department are from processing orders received from field salespersons, customer credit checks, invoice preparation, and shipping release for the order. Based on this data, questions that should be asked include: Why is the cost of the function increasing much faster than both sales revenues and the number of sales orders? Why have the number of sales orders increased faster than sales revenues? Are functions other than processing of sales orders being performed by this department?

Further analysis by the task force revealed these three contributing factors to the increased cost of the department:

1. Fewer items than in prior years were being ordered per each order received from salespersons.

2. Many customers were near or at their credit limits.

3. The average days that accounts receivable were outstanding had increased from 40 to 44 to 49 days during the last three years.

Discussions with the order entry/billing personnel and sales manager revealed that the three factors were related. Many customers were near their credit limit because of the high cost of borrowing money; thus they slowed down the payment of liabilities and placed smaller orders. The latter item was an attempt to keep operating inventories low, thus reducing their investment in working capital and reducing their need to borrow at very high interest rates.

Another critical factor was the relative inattention of the credit manager to follow up on delinquent accounts. The company policy was credit terms of net 30 days. The most recent year indicates that the average payment was being received 60 percent later than the credit terms allowed. One of the factors contributing to this lack of timely follow-up in collections was that the accounts receivable aging schedule was often received late from accounting.

The solution to this problem is now evident. First, the follow-up on delinquent accounts must be timely and consistent. This means that the aging of accounts receivable schedule from accounting will be given priority; it is to be given to the manager by the fifth working day after the end of the month. Second, salespersons will be given daily a list of customers who are at or very near the credit limit so they can discuss this with the customer, and also so they will not accept a large order from a customer when only a small one can be shipped.

An unexpected benefit resulted from this analysis. The company was able to reduce its salespersons in the field from nine to eight because it felt it was not necessary to call on certain of its customers twice weekly—that once each week would be sufficient. If these smaller customers needed items, they were to call a toll-free number, direct to a senior order entry person, and place the order, which would be shipped the next morning on one of the delivery trucks.

The result of this cost reduction analysis was that, one year after the recommendations were made, the cost of the order entry/billing process rose less
than the increase in sales revenues, the estimated net savings of the eliminated
salesperson, and the added cost of the toll-free telephone number was $22,000
net savings, the accounts receivable days' outstanding was reduced to 42 days,
but the average number of items per sales order remained unchanged. The
primary reason for the low number of items per sales order was because of high
interest rates—customers were still trying to keep inventories low, thus placing
more but smaller orders.

Cost reduction can be found in manufacturing functions as well as in other
areas. Reductions can be achieved in material costs, perhaps by material substitution, in direct labor costs, perhaps by automation, and in the area of factory
overhead. In the following discussion is an analysis by a task force or value
engineering analysis in a manufacturing firm that will result in cost savings on
one of its machine items.

Assume a machine shop performs many steps on many different kinds of
equipment, including farm implements, and auto parts. One part is a large pulley
that is used on farm tractors. Annual production of this part is planned at 3200
pulleys. Two processes, steps 8 and 11, relate to machining the hub of the pulley
and deburring. These two steps are done with different machines, with setup
needed for each. After discussion and analysis, it is determined that the two
steps can be peformed with the same machine, eliminating one setup. The added
cost of the necessary machine attachment to perform the two steps in one
operation is $4000. Comparison of the two methods to machining and deburring
the pulley follows:

| | Two Separate Steps | Combined as One Step |
|---|---|---|
| Annual production | 3,200 units | 3,200 units |
| Cost of step 8 | $3.00/unit* | — |
| Cost of step 11 | $1.00/unit* | — |
| Combined step 8 & 11 cost | $4.00/unit* | $3.20/unit* |
| Cost of machine attachment | — | $4,000 |
| Estimated life of machine attachment | | 5 years |

*Includes direct labor costs and manufacturing overhead costs.

| Cost to produce 3,200 units (steps 8 & 11) | $12,800 (3,200 × $4.00) | $10,240 (3,200 × $3.20) |
|---|---|---|
| Depreciation on attachment | -0- | 800 |
| Estimated annual cost | $12,800 | |
| Less cost if steps combined | 11,040 | $11,040 |
| Estimated annual savings | $1,760 | |

Cost reduction opportunities such as the ones outlined in the preceding examples result from value engineering analysis or task force cost reduction recommendations. These recommendations are then evaluated by the committee to determine which opportunities should be tested, implemented, or revised. Some changes are relatively simple and will be made by management directive, whereas others will be more complex and will require more time and involvement. Often task forces will be assigned the responsibilities of seeing that cost reduction steps are carried out and monitoring their progress.

**IMPLEMENTING COST REDUCTION CHANGES.** This phase of the cost reduction program can be efficiently achieved if the prior steps were carefully performed. If the reduction is a single-step change, all affected employees can be quickly informed of the change in material, method, or routing in manufacturing the product, in processing a document in the sales office, or similar activity. Because of the single-step nature of these changes, they can be made quickly and with little confusion.

Other cost reduction opportunities will be more complex. In these cases, testing the new technique may be desirable. Or, the change may be broken down into smaller steps that can be easily understood and implemented. In a manufacturing firm it is usually desirable to document the change, such as on Exhibit 6.1. A slightly modified version of this form can be used in nonmanufacturing firms or activities. The purpose of the form is to have consistency in reporting from one organizational unit to another.

Exhibit 6.2 is a filled-in version of Exhibit 6.1 for the cost reduction expected for combining the machining and deburring steps in manufacturing the pulley discussed earlier. Detail on this form indicates the department making the change, the budget year and quantity, a description of the change, and the cost reduction expected. This is primarily a planning document, but it will also be used as a control document when follow-up analysis is performed to see if the cost reduction was in fact realized and continues.

Another type of document is often used in implementing cost reductions. Exhibit 6.3 is a cost reduction project schedule for the credit/order entry/billing

**EXHIBIT 6.1.    Cost Reduction Report Form: Manufacturing Activity**

Description:

Department:_____          Budget Year:_____

Department Manager:_____          Budget Quantity:_____

|  Old Process  |  New Process  |
|  ---  |  ---  |

|  |  | Unit Costs | | |
|  ---  | ---  | --- | --- | --- |
|  |  | Old | New | Change |
| Raw Material |  |  |  |  |
| Direct Labor |  |  |  |  |
| Manufacturing Overhead |  |  |  |  |
|  | Depreciation: |  |  |  |
|  | Other Costs: |  |  |  |

Effective Date:

|  |  | Cost Reduction Summary | |
|  ---  | ---  | --- | --- |
|  |  | Unit Cost | Total Cost |

Approvals

|  |  | | |
|  ---  | ---  | --- | --- |
| Finance_____ | Raw material |  |  |
| Manufacturing_____ | Direct labor |  |  |
| Engineering_____ | Manufacturing Overhead | _____ | _____ |
|  | Total |  |  |
|  | Depreciation |  |  |
|  | Other costs | _____ | _____ |
|  | Net reduction |  |  |

area. Using the information presented earlier, five major steps have been identified and listed for reducing costs and increasing the effectiveness of the activity. This form contains the major steps to be performed, the initiating date of each step, the frequency of the step identified, the person responsible for performing the step, and additional comments. Estimated cost savings are not part of this report, because they would be reported on a Cost Reduction Report Form (Exhibit 6.2).

**EXHIBIT 6.2.   Cost Reduction Report Form: Manufacturing Activity**

Description:

Department:_____          Budget Year:_____

Department Manager:_____          Budget Quantity:_____

|                Old Process                |                New Process                |
|-------------------------------------------|-------------------------------------------|

| | Unit Costs | | |
|---|---|---|---|
| | Old | New | Change |
| Raw Material | | | |
| Direct Labor | | | |
| Manufacturing Overhead | | | |
| Depreciation: | | | |
| Other Costs: | | | |

Effective Date:

|  | Cost Reduction Summary | |
|---|---|---|
|  | Unit Cost | Total Cost |

Approvals

|  |  |  |  |
|---|---|---|---|
| Finance_____ | Raw material | | |
| Manufacturing_____ | Direct labor | | |
| Engineering_____ | Manufacturing Overhead | _____ | _____ |
| | Total | | |
| | Depreciation | | |
| | Other costs | _____ | _____ |
| | Net reduction | | |

Achieving cost reductions is often as much a good selling effort by management as it is the need to improve operating performance. If management can convince employees of the necessity for change and the long-term benefits of change, the cost reduction (profit improvement) program should be a success. Often the human behavior factors are as important as the quantitative factors in managing a successful cost reduction program.

**EXHIBIT 6.3.  Cost Reduction Project Schedule: Increase Control Over Order Entry/Billing/Collection Process, Fiscal Year Ended August 31, 19X5**

| Steps to Be Performed | Beginning Date | Frequency | Person Responsible | Comments |
|---|---|---|---|---|
| 1. Inform salesperson daily about accounts receivable balances of customers | | | | |
| 2. Aging of accounts receivable schedule to be given to credit manager on fifth woking day of each month | | | | |
| 3. Establish collection procedures for delinquent accounts | | | | |
| —Contact delinquent customers by telephone | | | | |
| —Send letter to delinquent customer not responding to telephone call | | | | |
| —Telephone and follow-up letter to delinquent customers not responding to previous letter | | | | |
| 4. Monitor progress of cost reduction program | | | | |
| 5. Perform post-cost reduction evaluation | | | | |

**PROGRESS REPORTS AND FOLLOW-UP EVALUATION.**   This final but very important step in the program must have the sustaining commitment of top management. To fully realize the benefits of a cost reduction program, progress reports and follow-up evaluation must be performed.

Progress reports prepared monthly will keep top management informed of progress and enable them to take corrective action if it appears that the program is not attaining its objectives. A committee meeting, with chairpersons of all task forces attending, should be scheduled soon after the monthly progress report is completed. Each task force chairperson can report on changes implemented in his or her area, changes in progress, and the difficulties encountered. This is the time that requests should be made for needed assistance and to identify unexpected benefits and costs that were not identified in the study phase.

Separate monthly progress reports prepared by task force chairmen will be used by accounting personnel to summarize progress of the profit improvement program as a whole. The summary report may show the target savings for each time period and the achieved savings for each period completed. Gaps in the achievement amount or percentage will be one of the agenda items at the meeting of the committee and task force chairpersons. The meeting will be used to identify new action steps to be taken in the implementation of any changes in the cost reduction steps or targets. These changes are necessary because the items causing the change were not identified or not in existence at the time of the study phase.

Cost reduction programs have limited lives. When a program is undertaken it should be remembered that the program will be completed and replaced with a cost control program integrated with the budgeting process. Phasing out of the cost reduction mode and into the cost control mode should be accomplished as soon as costs have attained levels compatible with organization goals. Benefits of the program should not be limited to achieved and continuing cost reductions. An increased awareness of how costs can be reduced may be carried into the budgeting process where, in essence, the cost reduction program becomes part of the annual budgeting process. Once this level of cost consciousness is achieved, maximum benefits from the cost reduction program have been transferred to the cost control program.

## COST CONTROL PROGRAMS

Cost control programs refer to all the policies, practices, and procedures used in an organization to control costs. They do not include the formal *cost reduction techniques* or *cost reduction programs* discussed earlier. Thus cost control programs are the ongoing practices and systems used in an organization for cost control.

**BUDGETING FOR CONTROL.**    Budgeting is planning for the future. The budget is a quantitative expression, usually in monetary terms, of the organization's plan of action for a period of time. The master budget summarizes the plans of the organization, or of a subunit, regarding its objectives, the input needed to achieve those objectives, and the expected output. The master budget is usually supported by other special budgets that contain more detail. There are many types of budgets and many uses of budgets.

Without planning there can be little control. It is difficult to know if you are near an objective if you have no plan of action and don't know in which direction you are headed. If a person starts driving an automobile without knowing where he or she wants to go or the purpose of the trip, how will the person know where to go? Wherever the trip ends is the goal! Businesses cannot operate with this type of uncertainty without serious consequences.

Utilizing budgets as the plan for action and as the basis for control is good management. When used effectively, budgets can help in managerial planning, provide information for performance evaluation, and promote communication and coordination. Without planning, effective control is not possible. The exact execution of a defective plan will result in undesirable results.

**GOAL CONGRUENCE.**    The accounting system should be designed to encourage managers to achieve overall company objectives. This means that the budgeting system, cost accounting system, and reporting system all are coordinated so that managers are encouraged to peform in accordance with broad company goals.

To achieve company objectives, the objectives must be reduced to individual goals for individual managers. Goal congruence is an ideal that is difficult to achieve because each manager has personal goals that may not be identical or parallel to those of the organization. For example, an individual manager may prefer to operate a department with long production runs, with changes coming on Mondays only. Because of product demand, this may not be possible. Shorter production runs may be necessary, with changes occurring on almost any day of the week. Shorter production runs and more set-up time is not the most efficient method of operating a department, but may be necessary for the company to meet product shipping schedules. Thus the needs of the total organization may supersede the desires of the individual manager.

Although goal congruence is difficult to achieve, managers should communicate the company goals so that employees can understand their responsibility in achieving these goals. Good managers will set company goals so that employee goals and company goals will be achieved simultaneously. The company's goals should be stated in such a way that employee performance does not conflict with, but in fact supports, organizational goals.

Top management should see that the management performance measurement system is designed so that each manager seeking to achieve personal goals will also be working toward the overall company goals. Although this goal congruence is difficult to achieve, top management must guard against suboptimization where each manager may benefit but at the expense of the total organization. Keeping everyone working toward the same organizational objectives is one of the major challenges to management.

**RESPONSIBILITY ACCOUNTING.** Responsibility accounting has been referred to as personalizing the accounting system. The essence of responsibility accounting is in designing an accounting system that recognizes various responsibility centers throughout the organization; and that the plans and actions of each center will be assigned responsibility for its performance. The responsibility centers should be the same as the managerial levels shown in the company's organization chart.

From an accounting perspective, responsibility accounting begins at the lowest level of the organization for which costs are accumulated and flows upward in the organization. This system of accounting is tailored to the organization in a way that costs are accumulated by levels of responsibility within the organization. Each responsibility center manager is charged only with the cost for which he or she has responsibility and control.

The lines of authority and levels of reporting in a responsibility accounting system for a manufacturing firm may include the line supervisor, department manager, factory general manager, vice-president of manufacturing, and the president of the company. These five levels of responsibility would receive accounting reports with successively more summarized data as we move up the hierarchical levels of the organization. For example, the line supervisor may receive detail information on raw material usage and direct labor usage for the latest period (week or month) and for year-to-date. In contrast, the vice-president of manufacturing would receive reports for the factory level of total performance for labor, material and overhead, research and development, engineering, and purchasing and inventory control. The amount of detail in the reports is greatest at the lowest reporting level and summarized at the upper levels. Of course the detail information is available if needed and can be secured by managers higher in the hierarchy line of authority.

Often a distinction is made among responsibility centers, identifying them as cost centers, profit centers, and investment centers. A cost center is one in which the manager has control over costs only and has no sales- or revenue-generating responsibility. The next higher level of responsibility center is the profit center, where the manager does have control over both costs and revenues. In this type of center, the planning and reporting would be for both costs and revenues. The highest level of responsibility center is the investment center where the manager has control over the incurrence of costs, revenues, and over the investment funds. The line supervisor in a manufacturing plant would be a cost center manager, whereas the president of the company would be an investment center manager.

Budgets and performance reports should contain all the costs (and revenues) controllable by the person responsible for that activity or center. As mentioned earlier, the line manager in a manufacturing plant may be responsible for a cost center, but a salesperson may be responsible for a profit center if he or she has some control over the sales price of the products being sold. Thus a performance report for the salesperson would include the revenues, costs, and expenses under direct control.

Controllable costs refer to any cost that is subject to the influence of a given manager of a responsibility center for a specific period of time. The key words in this definition are influence, manager, responsibility center, and period of time. All costs are controllable at some level of management and if the time period is long enough. At the production department manager level, costs such as building rent, machine depreciation, insurance, and employee fringe benefits would not be considered controllable. These costs, however, would be controllable at the factory general manager level, vice-president, or the president level. All costs are controllable by the president in the long term.

Who has significant influence on costs and revenues is of critical concern in budgeting and controlling costs and revenues in a responsibility accounting system. Both top management and individual managers will be informed about their performance with the proper use of a responsibility accounting system.

**COST BEHAVIOR ANALYSIS.**    Management needs to know how costs function for planning and control purposes. Effective planning is based on information on how volume and time affect each item of cost and revenue. Effective control is best achieved if each cost item and revenue can be estimated in advance for different volumes. Responsibility accounting would indicate that each cost and revenue item be assigned to time periods and to company segments.

Costs can be classified by determining whether they vary with time, volume, or rate of activity. The major classifications of costs include variable, fixed, semivariable, and semifixed. These costs are illustrated in Exhibit 6.4. Determining cost behavior is both a science and an art. Cost behavior can be determined by engineering analysis, statistical analysis, or management judgment. Methods of determining cost behavior are beyond the scope of this book.

Variable costs are illustrated by the graph in Exhibit 6.4a. Variable costs increase proportionally with some activity, such as sales, production, labor hours, or some other activity. Examples of variable costs include raw material usage, direct labor costs, operating supplies, and freight-out on units sold.

Costs that will not change during the budget period, usually a year, are classified as fixed costs and are illustrated in Exhibit 6.4b. Often, fixed costs are further subdivided into committed fixed costs and planned fixed costs. Examples of committed fixed costs would be depreciation on buildings, property

**EXHIBIT 6.4**

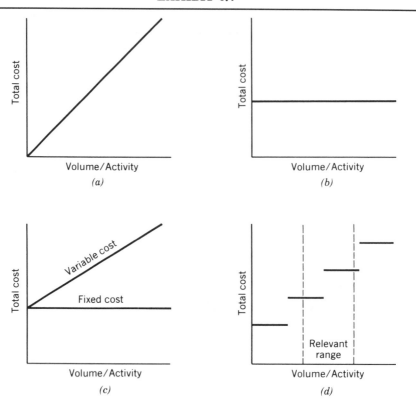

taxes, casualty insurance, and the president's salary. These costs will need to be incurred, or committed, in order to operate and should not change as long as operations are confined to some normal range of activity.

Planned fixed costs are costs that are planned by management judgment, but are useful in the operation of the firm. Examples of this type of fixed cost include research and development, advertising, education and training, and travel costs. These fixed costs can usually be significantly reduced by management decision, although to do so may have a major negative effect on employee morale.

Semivariable costs are those that are influenced both by the volume of activity *and* time. Usually these costs will be separated into their fixed and variable components as indicated in Exhibit 6.4c. When this is done, the fixed and variable components are treated as separate fixed and variable expenses.

Semifixed costs are layers of fixed costs added for each significant increase in activity as shown in Exhibit 6.4d. These fixed costs, also called step-fixed costs, are often treated as fixed costs for planning purposes. For control purposes, semifixed costs are based on the level of activity actually attained.

Identifying the factor that causes total cost to vary will determine whether a cost is fixed, variable, semivariable, or semifixed. Costs are influenced by many factors, but if part of the variation in total is caused by volume of activity, that cost item will be considered a variable cost. With this understanding of cost behavior we will now look at the budgeting process.

**FLEXIBLE BUDGETING.**    Only in a few situations will a fixed or static budget be a satisfactory method of budgeting. In these rare situations, comparing actual results with budget will yield reliable data. If actual volume differs from planned volume, a comparison will be misleading.

The basic premise of flexible budgeting is that after determining cost behavior patterns, and determining cost equations for each cost item, a budget can be prepared for any level of activity. A simplified budget is given in Exhibit 6.5.

### EXHIBIT 6.5    Flexible Overhead Budget

| | Cost Formula | Range of Production in D.L.H. | | | |
|---|---|---|---|---|---|
| | | 15,000 | 16,000 | 17,000 | 18,000 |
| Variable Overhead: | | | | | |
| Indirect Material | $   .20 DLH | 3,000 | 3,200 | 3,400 | 3,600 |
| Indirect Labor | 1.00 DLH | 15,000 | 16,000 | 17,000 | 18,000 |
| Power | .30 DLH | 4,500 | 4,800 | 5,100 | 5,400 |
| Total Variable Overhead | 1.50 DLH | 22,500 | 24,000 | 25,500 | 27,000 |
| Mixed Overhead: | | | | | |
| Utilities | 1,000+ <br> $   .20 DLH | 4,000 | 4,200 | 4,400 | 4,600 |
| Maintainance | 2,500+ <br> $   .50 DLH | 10,000 | 10,500 | 11,000 | 11,500 |
| Other | 1,500+ <br> $   .30 DLH | 6,000 | 6,300 | 6,600 | 6,900 |
| Total Mixed Overhead | $ 5,000+ <br> $ 1.00 DLH | 20,000 | 21,000 | 22,000 | 23,000 |
| Fixed Overhead: | | | | | |
| Rent | 3,000 | 3,000 | 3,000 | 3,000 | 3,000 |
| Salaries | 15,000 | 15,000 | 15,000 | 15,000 | 15,000 |
| Depreciation | 7,000 | 7,000 | 7,000 | 7,000 | 7,000 |
| Other | 5,000 | 5,000 | 5,000 | 5,000 | 5,000 |
| Total Fixed Overhead | $   30,000 | 30,000 | 30,000 | 30,000 | 30,000 |
| Total Overhead | $   35,000+ <br> $ 2.50 DLH | $72,500 | $75,000 | $77,500 | $80,000 |

The major use of the flexible budget is as a control technique and in planning and coordinating company activities. On a monthly, quarterly, and yearly basis, comparisons can be made of the actual results with the flexible budget amounts. With the use of the flexible budget, actual results will be compared with costs that should have been incurred, given the level of activity attained. Thus the comparison of budget and actual costs will be for the same level of activity.

Exhibit 6.6 contains actual results for the level of performance for the month. Actual costs and the budget for the same level of sales activity are compared. The difference is a budget variance, identified as either favorable or unfavorable. Although this budget is simple and has few expense items, the major point is that the flexible budget can be used for control purposes. The variances direct management's attention to items that are not in line with expectations. Managers would be most interested in why the large variances, both favorable and unfavorable, have occurred.

The flexible budget and report was company-wide. The budget and report could have been prepared for a department or cost center with the variances for that segment of the organization. Segment reports let segment managers evaluate

**EXHIBIT 6.6.   Overhead Cost Report**

| Actual Direct Labor Hours: | 17,400 Budget Based On 17,400 DLH | Actual Cost for Month | Variance Favorable (F) Unfavorable (U) |
|---|---|---|---|
| Variable Overhead: | | | |
| Indirect Material | 3,480 | $  3,550 | 70 U |
| Indirect Labor | 17,400 | 17,200 | 200 F |
| Power | 5,220 | 5,500 | 280 U |
| Total Variable Overhead | 26,100 | 26,250 | 150 U |
| Mixed Overhead: | | | |
| Utilities | 4,480 | 4,650 | 170 U |
| Maintenance | 11,200 | 11,550 | 350 U |
| Other | 6,720 | 6,600 | 120 F |
| Total Mixed Overhead | 22,400 | 22,800 | 400 U |
| Fixed Overhead: | | | |
| Rent | 3,000 | 3,000 | -0- |
| Salaries | 15,000 | 15,600 | 600 U |
| Depreciation | 7,000 | 6,900 | 100 F |
| Other | 5,000 | 5,400 | 400 U |
| Total Fixed Overhead | 30,000 | 30,900 | 900 U |
| Total Overhead | 78,500 | 79,950 | 1450 U |

their performance and correct inefficiencies. Flexible budgeting and performance reporting is a means of cost control for many organizations.

**ZERO-BASE BUDGETING.** The ZBB is different than traditional budgeting in which budgets are prepared on an incremental basis, adding to or deducting from last year's budgeted amounts. In traditional budgeting, managers don't have to start from zero base each year to justify costs for existing programs.

Because of its nature, ZBB is cost control in action. Each manager evaluates operations to establish "decision packages" in a priority order. Review and analysis by managers higher in the organization should help in identifying which packages are cost-effective and should be funded. Performed annually or less often, ZBB reviews can be helpful in both the budgeting and cost control processes.

Integrating the budgeting process in a responsibility accounting system with performance reporting provides management with the tools needed for continued cost control. Without well-defined plans, it is difficult to control operations to meet management objectives.

# REFERENCES

Bulloch, James, Donald E. Keller, and Louis Vlasko (eds.), *Accountants' Cost Handbook,* New York, Wiley, 1983.

Bumbarger, W. B., "Key to Lasting Overhead Productivity Improvement," *Financial Executive,* September 1977, pp. 40–48.

Chastain, Clark E., "Managing Your Way Through the Recession," *Cost and Management,* January–February 1983, pp. 5–9.

Edwards, James B., and Julie A. Heard, "Is Cost Accounting the No. 1 Enemy of Productivity?," *Management Accounting,* June 1984, pp. 44–49.

Higgins, Lindley R., and Ruth W. Stidger (eds.), *Cost Reduction from A to Z,* New York, McGraw-Hill, 1976.

Jordan, Raymond B., *Cost Accounting: A Practical Approach,* New York, National Association of Accountants (Self-Study Course), 1984.

Jordan, Raymond B., "Cost Reduction: A 'Get Tough' Action Plan," *Management Accounting,* May 1984, pp. 37–46.

King, William D., "The Six Phases of Cost Reduction," *Business Horizons,* August 1973, pp. 37–46.

O'Halloran, James P., and Joseph F. Berardino, "The Profit Improvement Review: Cutting Out Costs and Increasing Revenues," *Corporate Accounting,* Winter 1983, pp. 54–59.

Scott, Robert C., "Protecting Jobs and Profits with Automatic Cost Reduction System," *Journal of Systems Management,* March 1979, pp. 24–26.

Steffen, Christopher J., "Tightening Industry's Belt," *Financial Executive,* May 1982, pp. 14–18.

Warren, Gorham & Lamont, "Value Engineering: Cutting Costs Not Services," *Corporate Controller's and Treasurer's Report,* May 1981.

Steffen, Christopher J., "Tightening Industry's Belt," *Financial Executive,* May 1982, pp. 17–18.

CHAPTER **7**

# FIXED ASSET MANAGEMENT

## Felix Pomeranz

## INTRODUCTION

Management of property, plant, and equipment (the chapter author prefers the older term *fixed assets*) may not have received the attention that it deserves. Yet, replacement of fixed assets, given today's inflated prices, poses a serious problem for the "private sector," as well as for not-for-profit and public agencies; the need to repair or replace the nation's "infrastructure" has become an important public issue. Often, entities of all types must extract longer service from their existing fixed assets. And, assets must be made to do double duty wherever possible; assets may need to be "liquefied" (i.e., turned to cash), and assets may have to be made to "turn" more rapidly in terms of utilization. The ability to employ fixed assets to greater advantage is a hallmark of business excellence in a mature economy; in other words, the balance sheet, and the deployment of the assets appearing thereon, are likely to be of overweening importance.

An accountant, trained in the optimum utilization of financial resources, plays a critical role in aiding a business to use assets profitably; virtually all of the techniques discussed in this chapter relate to record keeping, to internal accounting and operational controls, and to well-known analytical techniques. Moreover, improved fixed asset management offers substantial opportunities. In this connection, a 1983 survey indicated that the sophisticated techniques and practices advocated in the capital budgeting literature typically are found only in the very largest of firms. Considerable territory remains unexplored in the search for ideas, better classification methods, reliable preliminary screening methods, appropriate estimating techniques, and *ex post facto* control information.[1]

---

[1] Pike, R.H. "A Review of Recent Trends in Formal Capital Budgeting Processes," *Accounting and Business Research,* Summer 1983, pp. 201–208.

The need for focusing additional attention on property management was highlighted in a study sponsored by the National Association of Corporate Real Estate Executives which, relative to the real estate held by American corporations, found that basic elements of an asset management system were generally lacking, to wit:[2]

> An up-to-date, easy to use, consolidated inventory of all properties owned and leased, including, at a minimum, address, use, general description, size age, zoning, acquisition costs, capital improvements, and capital needs.

> A real property management information system, which tracks, on an individual property basis, income and expense.

> A schedule of rents, including internal rents, based on fair market value.

This chapter discusses when and what to purchase, how to select an optimum financing method, how to manage the asset, and how to plan and control the property investment. Attention is given to record-keeping aspects, and to the need for meeting the information requirements of various constituencies through one data base.

In general, all companies should lay down guidelines for determining when a new property investment should be made, how the investment should be financed, how the investment should be controlled, and how the actual performance of the investment should be compared with expectations existing at the time the investment was authorized. In managing property, as well as in other corporate endeavors, emphasis ought to be placed upon management processes, on the qualifications of the people who execute those processes, and on the system that links processes, and people.

## THE UNINTENDED EFFECT OF THE FOREIGN CORRUPT PRACTICES ACT

The Foreign Corrupt Practices Act was designed by its author to enjoin bribery of officials of foreign governments. The Act dealt with three main subjects: foreign corrupt payments; "accounting standards" relating to registrants' books, records, and internal accounting controls; and disclosure of information when a significant beneficial ownership is acquired.

---

[2] Harvard Real Estate, Inc. in cooperation with the National Association of Corporate Real Estate Executives, "Corporate Real Estate Asset Management in the United States," 1981.

Although, as has been noted, the Act was intended to redress a specific problem, the response of the American accounting profession represented over-kill, in terms of the profession's input to the Act's sponsor. As a direct result, the Act's accounting standards section requires companies subject to the registration and reporting mandates of the Securities Exchange Act of 1934 to

> Make and keep books, records and accounts which, in reasonable detail, accurately and fairly reflect the transactions and dispositions of the assets of the issuer, and to devise and maintain a system of internal accounting controls sufficient to provide reasonable assurances that:
>
> Transactions are executed in accordance with management's general or specific authorization
>
> Transactions are recorded as necessary to permit preparation of financial statements in conformity with generally accepted accounting principles or any other criteria applicable to such statements, and to maintain accountability for assets
>
> Access to assets is permitted only in accordance with management's general or specific authorization
>
> The recorded accountability for assets is compared with the existing assets at reasonable intervals and appropriate action is taken with respect to any differences

Despite the similarity of the foregoing abstract to the professional liturgy, the Act's impact on property appears to have been little noticed by public accountants, management accountants, and internal auditors. Nonetheless, the fact that this Act is still on the books poses a risk of legal noncompliance for those who do not maintain appropriate records and controls pertaining to property.

# PROPERTY ACCOUNTS AND REPLACEMENT COSTS

The Financial Accounting Standards Board, the accounting profession's rule-making body, as well as the Securities and Exchange Commission, have for almost 10 years aimed at the disclosure of replacement cost information in the financial statements of public corporations. This thrust occurred despite indications that analysts and other financial statement users to not entirely support the disclosure of the information, or else do not know how to use the information properly. Compliance with the related rules has probably added to the cost of record keeping. On the plus side, such replacement cost information, if properly understood and adjusted as necessary, could be of value to management, especially with respect to valuation for insurance purposes, and capital budgeting.

## THE INCREASINGLY SOPHISTICATED ACQUISITION DECISION

Moustafa H. Abdelsamad[3] noted that in finance theory, the financing decision is separated from the investment decision, although, practically speaking, the two decisions are often considered simultaneously. He felt that the acquisition decision increasingly involves use of discounted cash flow methods. On the other hand, he pointed out that the older internal rate of return method still predominates. (Brief definitions appear in succeeding paragraphs.) And, payback to be received from an investment in fixed assets continues to be a popular method of evaluation.

Abdelsamad emphasized that the forecasting of future cash flows remains difficult; considerable progress remains to be made with respect to the adoption by industry of more sophisticated capital budgeting techniques. At the same time Abdelsamad suggested the following:

Make sure that those involved in capital budgeting decisions are familiar with the uses and limitations of capital budgeting methods and techniques, and with the underlying assumptions.

Ensure that the decision makers realize the value of capital budgeting methods, but are not viewing such measures as unduly precise.

Decision makers should consider and deal with the risk an investment is subject to, and use past experience to monitor performance.

Finally, the system should be checked annually to see that it is working as planned.

The state of the art was succinctly summarized in an article by John W. Hardy.[4] This author indicated that four common capital budgeting tools are used to evaluate capital budgeting decisions: (1) the net present value method, (2) the internal rate of return method, (3) the average rate of return method, and (4) the payback method. Only the first two methods recognize the time value of money. The author described the methods briefly:

Net present value compares the present value of the future cash flows of a project with the initial investment. Internal rate of return identifies the yield that an investment is earning over its useful life.

Contrariwise, average rate of return treats cash flows received in year one, as equal

---

[3] Abdelsamad, Moustafa H., "Spending Smart," *Management World,* June 1983, pp. 38–39.
[4] Hardy, John W., "How ERTA and TEFRA Affect Capital Budgeting Decisions," *Management Accounting,* May 1983, pp. 20.

in worth to cash flows received in other years. And the payback method measures the time that it will take for an investment to generate cash flows sufficient to pay back the initial investment; it seeks to identify how long a company may be at risk in terms of its investment.

Hardy also mentioned the impact of tax legislation on property transactions; he noted that the additional cash flows provided by depreciation writeoffs under the Economic Recovery Tax Act of 1981 (ERTA) and Tax Equity Fiscal Responsibility Act (TEFRA) laws would improve the results of analysis generated by capital budgeting techniques.

To plan a capital investment, and bring it to successful completion, requires recognition of risk, both short-term and long-term. The principal risks confronted by a fixed asset manager are external; examples are energy shortages, inflation, and competition. But internal risks, such as those involving inability to distribute materials on a site, coping with technological change, or meeting quality standards, must also be taken into account.

Some exposures can be avoided entirely by careful planning. Those that cannot be avoided must be assumed (which is normally done unwillingly except where the potential loss is insignificant) or shifted, either to other entities connected with the project or to an insurer. What has come to be known as risk management is predicated on the theory that, to some extent at least, unfavorable possibilities can be anticipated and their risks mitigated. As a project is implemented, it is necessary to perform a variety of tests to determine whether the preventative controls are functioning as planned, and whether the unfavorable conditions guarded against are not indeed occurring. Some risks of particular interest to asset managers are:

**Material Shortages.**    The usual approach is to shift the risk to vendors via long-term contracts. Simply having more than one vendor to choose from may afford a certain degree of protection.

**Inflation.**    It is often possible to shift the risk of inflation to vendors. One way to do this is to negotiate hard money or fixed price contracts; another is to cap escalation in contracts.

**Capital Shortages.**    It is necessary to synchronize cash inflow and cash outflow.

**Noncompliance with Laws.**    It is usually advisable to comply with a law rather than ignore it and run the risk of being brought into compliance at additional cost.

**New Technology.**    Major projects are usually "state of the art," that is, planned on the premise that the latest technology will be reflected in the design of the finished facility and in the techniques for construction. Anticipation of technology "in the pipeline" can avert costs of redesign.

# THE IMPORTANCE OF THE FINANCING DECISION

The capital investment decision is theoretically separate from the financing decision. After a decision has been made to undertake the project, the evaluation procedure moves to the financing decision. It is recognized that interest rates, especially for long-term debt, are historically high; short-term rates are considerably lower. Consequently, it may be possible—especially for a governmental or not-for-profit entity—to secure a short-term "bridge" loan to be replaced eventually by long-term financing; the expectation in such an arrangement is to realize the benefits inherent in the rate differential, to say nothing of the possibility that long-term rates may decline.

The usual choice is whether to borrow money and buy the asset, or whether to lease.[5] Some definitions may be appropriate:

A finance lease transfers the risks and rewards of ownership to the lessee. Normally, the lessee is required to provide insurance and maintenance. The lessor retains legal ownership to be able to qualify for capital allowances and grants which may be claimed by the purchaser alone.

All other leases are classified as operating leases. The assets are hired for some part of their useful lives; the rental paid is written off to the profit and loss account.

Companies are beginning to realize that the wrong choice can cost thousands of dollars.[6] The computation must take into account complex tax options that seem to change every year: tax credit eligibility; the depreciation schedule; first-year expensing; corporate marginal tax rate, including federal, state, and local taxes. The tax aspects together with time value of money must be evaluated individually, and weighed collectively.

It is often in the interest of an organization to maximize investment tax credit benefits. Close attention should be given to the *latest* rules of the Internal Revenue Service to minimize tax credit disallowances. Accounting and valuation engineering inputs will be desirable.

Careful planning may reduce exposure to sales and compensating use taxes.

---

[5.] Cooke, Terry, "To Lease or Not to Lease," *Accountancy,* May 1983, pp. 102–108.
[6.] Held, Gilbert, "Tax Options and New Equipment: Buy versus Lease," *Data Communications,* Mid-September 1983, pp. 39–48.

The general rule is that where an entity becomes the final user of a particular product, it is subject to sales and compensating use taxes; on the other hand, if the entity makes further use of the product in its own manufacturing operations, it may be possible to exempt the product. The taxability of particular fixed assets may be in doubt in some jurisdictions; accounting inputs can be beneficial. It is fair to say that the importance of tax legislation—federal, state, and local— on capital budgeting decisions cannot be overestimated.

Buy/lease decision criteria can be conveniently recapped as shown in the following table:[7]

| Decision Criteria | Lease | Purchaser |
| --- | --- | --- |
| Title | With lessor | Purchaser |
| Payments | Lower but repetitive | Large, one-time |
| Maintenance | Usually included | Usually separate agreement |
| Tax credit | May be available if passed to lessee | Normally available |
| Depreciation | Not available | Available |
| Discount potential | None to minimal | Higher |
| Replacement | End of lease or anytime with penalty | More difficult because of investment |
| Price rise | Can occur at equipment renewal time | Purchase results in fixed cost |

Perusal of the table will show that accurate records make it easier to assess the effects of various techniques so that an optimum approach may be selected.

# THE ACCOUNTING PROFESSION AND LEASING

The regulatory bodies of the profession have issued dicta[8] concerning the proper accounting for leases when such leasing transactions have characteristics similar to purchase transactions. For a lessee to be able to acquire the use of assets

---

[7] Stephens, William L., "The Lease or Buy Decision: Make the Right Choice," *Financial Executive,* May 1983, pp. 41–49.

[8] Ibid.

with "off balance sheet financing" can mean that the financial statements will reflect improved measures of profitability, liquidity, and solvency. Although the effect on key financial ratios may be an important consideration for a firm deciding whether to lease or buy, other considerations are at least equally important:[9]

Is the available credit different under the alternatives of lease or buy?

Can the risks and costs of obsolescence be reduced by leasing?

Do the fully deductible lease payments relate to any nondepreciable assets that would not be tax deductible if bought?

Is there a residual value for the asset at the end of the lease terms which would be lost through leasing?

Are the benefits of the investment tax credit which can be passed from lessor to lessee more valuable to a buyer or a lessee?

How does the implicit rate of interest in the lease compare with the cost of financing the purchase?

Consideration must be given to the following variables:[10]

"Discount rate. Is the rate the cost of borrowing, or the weighted average cost of capital?

Implicit interest rate in the lease. Is the implicit rate of interest in the lease the same as or different from the cost of borrowing? Is it appropriate to assume that a purchase would be financed through borrowing? (Because leasing is a form of financing and is quite similar to a debt arrangement, the usual approach is to compare leasing to borrowing. But, funds can be generated from other sources and it might be necessary to consider financing costs other than those for debt.)

Methods of analysis employed. Is it possible to compare lease and buy outlays? (This might be accomplished by either showing the debt repayments related to the required asset substituting for the initial outlay, or by determining the prepayment that would be necessary at the inception of the lease that would be comparable to yearly lease payments.)

Tax savings from interest on borrowed funds. How should the tax savings from the deductibility of interest be included in the analysis of the buy decision?

---

9. Ibid.
10. Galper, Harvey, and Eric Toder, "Owning or Leasing: Bennington College, and the United States Tax System," *National Tax Journal,* June 1983, pp. 257–261.

The author concludes: "The decision to lease or buy can be quite difficult because of these interacting variables. A firm trying to decide whether to lease or buy should be aware of the effect of those variables when using the typical decision model."

# GOVERNMENTAL AGENCIES, OR NOT-FOR-PROFIT ENTITIES MUST MAKE INFORMED LEASE OR BUY DECISIONS

Municipal buildings, university dormitories, and the like are being sold to private investors who then rent these facilities back to the sellers so that service can continue.

The scope for tax-motivated leasing was significantly broadened by the safe harbor leasing rules enacted as part of ERTA. Safe harbor leasing provided a convenient means by which entities with limited tax obligations could take advantage of investment incentives by leasing equipment from companies able to use the tax deductions and credits.

Because tax exempt institutions already acquire the services of capital tax free, it might appear that leasing would provide no benefits. But, such an analytical focus is too narrow. To determine whether leasing or owning assets is appropriate from the exempt institution's point of view, it is necessary to consider net return on the entire asset portfolio. Taxpayers generally sort out their portfolios according to their tax brackets in order to maximize their after-tax income flow. Consequently, tax exempt investors would generally want to hold the most heavily taxed assets; after allowing for risk, such assets would tend to carry the highest before-tax returns.

Government agencies have the further advantage of being able to issue tax exempt bonds to finance capital acquisitions. Traditionally, they have acquired new capital by owning rather than leasing, because the tax exempt interest rate is lower than the pretax cost of funds implicit in leasing. However, because sale and leasebacks of municipal facilities in many circumstances can also be financed by tax exempt bonds, state and local governments can simultaneously avail themselves of the twin advantages of tax exempt financing and accelerated depreciation, increasing the attractiveness of leasing.

The sale and leaseback of existing state and municipal facilities allows state and local governments to realize benefits of tax arbitrage because the proceeds from selling the facilities, unlike the proceeds from issuing tax exempt bonds, can be invested in taxable securities.

## CONSTRUCTION CAN POSE SPECIAL PROBLEMS

When an owner decides to perform major construction either by using its own forces, or by contracting to have such work performed by a general contractor, or by contractors directed by a construction manager, the owner incurs control problems, together with the related opportunities. If the dollars involved in such construction are very large—more than $50 million—a comprehensive approach to control should probably be taken. This is particularly true where an owner engages in construction on a sporadic or discontinuous basis. The various elements of risk, together with the owner oversight issues, have been discussed by the chapter author in another work.[11] Where the project tends to be below $50 million, however, the owner may improve its oversight capabilities by following the recommendations appearing in the Appendix to this chapter, entitled "Owner Checklist."

## VARIOUS CORPORATE OBJECTIVES DEPEND ON ACCOUNTING INFORMATION

There are sound operating reasons for achieving control over fixed assets within an industrial company, a nonprofit organization, or a government entity. Objectives of fixed asset accounting include:

Protection of assets from waste, diffusion, or loss

Information necessary for the development of depreciation policies which would enhance cash flow and complement replacement actions

Assistance in repair/replace decisions

Data required for capital budgeting and financing determinations

Management of risk, including development of information for insurance purposes

Purchasing/warehousing of spare parts and other materials so as to provide timely and cost-effective support to operations

Promoting greater use of fixed assets. (For example, a company might farm its timberlands; a church might rent its premises to a company, accepting a donation in return; a concern might rent nonprime shift computer time to outsiders—assuming that appropriate security and controls over usage have been established; idle plant or warehouse space could be leased either to company units or outsiders.)

---

[11.] Pomeranz, Felix, *Managing Capital Budget Projects,* New York, Wiley, 1984, pp. 27–36.

# THE COMPUTER OPENS NEW RECORD-KEEPING OPPORTUNITIES

The emergence of minicomputers and microcomputers offers improved tools to the fixed asset manager, in terms of both hardware and software. For instance, new control possibilities could stem from "relational data bases," such as PERSONAL PEARL, LOTUS 1, 2, 3, and dBII; a fixed asset manager using one of these programs, creates a record; he or she specifies the nature of the desired report—the software performs the intermediate programming. The record can accommodate the needs of different users of fixed asset accounting information and can be customized to meet overseer as well as doer requirements.

Given the present state of the art in personal computers, it is possible to "down load" microcomputer files to a main frame—and vice versa—and to perform analytical operations on the down loaded data, to identify variances from desired cost, schedule, and quality. The relational data bases mentioned (no doubt others will be created in the future) permit linkage to other programs, including the well-publicized "spread sheets," as well as to report and letter-writing programs. Output can be used in the preparation of reports, and even in their typesetting.

The fixed asset manager must be judicious in the choice of a data base. If the project is elaborate, the data base should incorporate cost control, accounting, resource allocation, and scheduling aspects. At the latest count, well over 100 construction management packages alone were on the market, and many are being promoted based on extravagant claims. In the experience of the chapter author fewer than 10 packages are likely to meet the needs of an activist owner. How does a property manager protect against purchasing an unsuitable package? Essentially, by specifying his or her own needs in the form of the criteria the package is to meet; the property owner's accountant can play a significant role in criteria definition, as well as in package evaluation and testing.

# PURCHASE OF ARTICLES INVOLVES "SHOPPING" DECISIONS

After a need to purchase has been recognized, it becomes necessary to "shop" the market. The buyer must know what the item is expected to accomplish. And, he or she must have adequate time to shop. Stated differently, "performance specifications" should permit alternative products to be considered. (The time to shop cannot exceed the vendor's lead time, plus the necessary clerical processing.)

A purchase requisition is prepared by the "user" and forwarded to the buyer, to initiate the shopping process. The buyer selects potential vendors, hopefully on the basis of their previous cost, quality, and delivery performances. Several vendors—usually three or more—may be asked to quote, by reference to the performance (and physical) specifications provided. In evaluating competitive bids, it is necessary to temper awards based on price, with an evaluation of other factors, such as the vendor's reputation for quality and service, and life-cycle costs.

The merits of competitive bidding are subject to controversy. In some cases, astute bargaining with one vendor could be more effective. In other cases, potential shortages have caused allocations of purchases among several vendors. But, where competitive bidding is utilized, awards to other than the lowest bidder should be subject to special review and clearance by management.

## PURCHASE ORDER

The buyer records his or her understanding of the terms of a transaction on a formal purchase order. Almost every line on the order carries business implications:

**Date.**    The time from the order's date to the required delivery date should be well within the vendor's lead time requirements.

**Purchase Order Number.**    Generally, prenumbered purchase orders will facilitate control (i.e. the tracking of "open" transactions).

**Product Description.**    The product should be identified with care. Performance as well as "physical" (i.e., indications of product composition) specifications are superior to brand names.

**Quality.**    Test requirements must be carefully spelled out; requirements may include certifications of tests to accompany delivery, where articles are subject to tests on a lot basis.

**Price.**    In general, prices should be stated together with trade or cash discounts. (Where cash discounts are received on fixed asset purchases, it may be advantageous to reduce the fixed asset cost by the amount of the discounts. This handling, although lowering overall depreciation expense, will minimize income taxes over the near term, because it removes cash discounts from revenues.)

**Legal Convenants.**    As required.

**Freight on Board Points.**    These terms govern when title passes, who assumes risk and, usually, who files claims.

**Shipping Methods.**    They should be specified to enhance the buyer's profit picture and may be based on comparative analysis of shipping costs from particular areas. (The usual determination involves unit costs based on volume.)

**Receiving Directions.**    These may be governed by the buyer's unloading and/or materials handling facilities. The avoidance of demurrage is an important consideration.

**Signatures.**    Should conform to corporate authorization policies.

# RECORD KEEPING SHOULD COVER ARTICLES ON A CRADLE-TO-THE-GRAVE BASIS

Complete, accurate, and up-to-date records must be kept. Accounting control should be established over purchase orders, receiving reports, inspection reports (where appropriate), accounts payable, retirements and disposals, and adjustments resulting from physical inventories. And, locator files should be kept up to date.

Duplication in record keeping should be minimized; electronic data processing (EDP) data bases permit a variety of data to be associated. The information needs of the following functions should be considered in the design of the record: accounting, maintenance, insurance, tax, and engineering.

From a data processing point of view, the purchase order should permit subsequent massaging of information without repetitive data reentry: expediting, receiving, inspection, and intraplant movements are facilitated by information that drives off the purchase order, as discussed in subsequent paragraphs.

After a purchase order has been issued, it becomes necessary to track the open transaction, and to expedite, to ensure the vendor's conformance to terms, especially to delivery dates.

The methods for receiving incoming fixed assets parallel those for materials generally:

Weights, measures and counts, at least on a sample basis

Inspection of the condition of packages and initiation of short, over, freight, and damage claims, if necessary

Establishment of accounting control over receipts and claims

Relative to claims, the advantage rests with those who discover, record, press, and settle quickly. For example, if short shipment is experienced, steps must be taken immediately (1) to avoid overpayment and (2) to make sure that the missing articles are shipped with premium freight charged to the vendor. On the other hand, if overshipment has occurred, then it could well be advantageous to negotiate a special price with the vendor so that he or she may be spared the return freight, and attendant handling. If the delay involves a carrier, it is not only important that the claim be registered, but that it be settled expeditiously — there is a two-year statute of limitations.

Significant items should be shown on locator files. After such files have been established, it becomes necessary to control posting at the time of receipt, at the time of change of a location or installation, and at property retirement.

With respect to certain types of property, it is desirable that permanent, or, at least, semipermanent tags be affixed to the property. Imaginative vendors have faciliatated the creation of tag information via EDP processing. Also, the tag, appropriately annotated for surplus disposal or condemnation, can serve as an exit pass out of the premises, on the way to a disposal site. In this way, the exposure of selling "good" property at a surplus sale tends to be minimized.

Reorder points and quantities conceivably should be shown on records. One of two techniques may be suitable: (1) For machine spares, reordering when an existing spare is used. (*Caution*: Borrowing arrangements may be necessary to protect the continuity of operations if an additional spare is required during the replenishment period.) (2) Repetitively used articles can be stratified, based on usage values, and reorder routines determined for a homogeneous stratum.

## MAINTENANCE MANAGEMENT

Records also facilitate maintenance. Maintenance includes daily maintenance/housekeeping pertaining to individual machines as well as to an entire system, such as heating and air conditioning. Because breakdowns can disrupt operations or impair effectiveness, the records should facilitate the planning of major maintenance and of the related downtime, and help to control costs.

The importance of the information needs of maintenance management has been discussed by the chapter author in another book.[12] Some factors are listed:

Do equipment and machinery records show

　Age and location of item?

　Servicing dates?

---

[12] Pomeranz, et al, Felix, *Auditing in the Public Sector,* Boston, Warren, Gorham & Lamont, 1976, pp. 237–260.

Warranty details?

Manufacturer servicing record?

Costs and number of hours required for each servicing?

Major parts replaced?

Are planned major repairs staggered to facilitate both scheduling and funding? Does the system provide for the accumulation of financial and operational data?

If so, does the data show

Comparison of actual costs and hours to budgeted and/or standard amounts?

Maintenance costs per major item or group?

Frequency of repairs for major items of equipment?

Analysis of unscheduled maintenance and repair?

Analysis of machinery and equipment downtime and facility shutdowns due to repair and maintenance?

Are standard reporting formats and cost codes used?

Are maintenance project reports

Complete and up to date?

Submitted on a timely basis?

Accurate?

Prepared in the standard or required format?

Are the data collected used to evaluate the maintenance function?

Are analyses made of the effectiveness of the preventive maintenance program? (For example, a decrease in emergency work orders may be an indication of the success of preventive maintenance.)

Are breakdown reports analyzed for the detection of failure patterns that might be corrected through preventive maintenance?

Are actual work order results compared with established standards, with explanations sought for variances?

Are the performance reports analyzed with regard to recurring maintenance problems? (Recurring maintenance problems can signify a need for more frequent preventive maintenance, a deficiency in particular pieces of equipment, or a need for replacement.)

Is the cost performance data used in planning and scheduling future maintenance?

Is the data used to evaluate the results of improvement programs?

Is the data used to perform cost/benefit analyses of work methods and maintenance technology?

## INSURANCE CONSIDERATIONS

Complete and accurate fixed asset records also aid decisions concerning insurance. Carriers pool the risks of customers; they add a loading factor beyond the cost of perceived losses to allow for reserves, profits, and administrative expenses. This makes it desirable for an owner of property to examine its own risk situation. For a company with dispersed risks, total self-insurance, or a degree of self-insurance, may be appropriate; the willingness of an owner to assume risk may be influenced by risk averseness. (The point is that an accountant/financial advisor may help the owner to gain a better appreciation of his or her philosophy toward risk.) Insurance costs may be diminished by (1) introduction of deductibles, and (2) programs to control or minimize risks or losses. All costs and benefits—including deductibles and the attendant risk, and the expense of a loss control program—must be weighed to determine the best approach.

Some insurance policies require reporting current replacement costs. (We have previously mentioned the somewhat related rules of the Financial Accounting Standards Board.) The manner in which such costs are determined should leave a clear "audit trail." [Essentially, three techniques may be used to determine replacement costs: (1) referring to invoices or vendor catalogs, (2) appraising, or (3) indexing—that is adjusting historical cost information based on changes in the prices of the asset categories bought.]

Detailed records are helpful in calculating depreciation, particularly when alternative methods, such as straight line, sum-of-the years' digits, and such are compared. Automated computations and simulations using different depreciation methods may be utilized for a variety of purposes, such as product pricing, capital budgeting, and replacement value computations.

Within the restrictions of the Internal Revenue Code, certain changes in depreciation policy are permissible; once changes have been made, they may not be reversible. From the point of view of cash flow, speedier depreciation may well be in order; one might think that the recognition of tax advantages would have a beneficial effect on the valuation of a company's securities in the marketplace. However, research indicates that where similar changes were reflected in earnings because of tax laws, and a decrease in earnings resulted, market values tended to be depressed. Thus, accounting changes should be undertaken only as a result of a complete study of all factors.

# PHYSICAL INVENTORIES MAY BE NECESSARY TO CREATE RECORDS INITIALLY

The following actions relate to the *initial* establishment of fixed asset records, the first inventory:

**Arrange for Preinventory Preparations.**    This includes allocation of storage space when necessary.

**Design Count Tags.**    Consider prenumbered tags to safeguard completeness of the count. Multipart tag forms permit one part of the tag to remain attached to the asset; other portions of the tag can then be used to prepare permanent tags. (Supervisors can gain assurance that all items have been counted by touring the premises.)

**Consider the EDP aspects.**    When designing the tag, keep in mind how the information is to be processed. This consideration affects the layout of the tag and bears on the sequence in which items are input.

**Develop Count Instructions; Take the Inventory.**    In some cases, skilled craftspersons may be the only individuals with the technical skills to identify articles or describe them accurately. Use the appropriate unit of measure — for example, units, tons, hundred-weight — on the inventory forms. Where weights are necessary, logarithmic scales—duly calibrated— may be useful; whenever required, packages should be opened to permit counting. Counters should initial inventory tags. Checkers should also initial inventory tags, at least on a sample basis.

**Assign Values.**    Two approaches may be followed: (1) Values may be assigned, based on invoices and/or vendor catalogs. (2) Appraisal techniques may be used. It may be advisable to engage qualified appraisers who follow written guidelines. Write-ups could invite taxable income; similarly, higher book value may result in higher personal property taxes. (The important element in control is to see that the item is recorded on the books, not necessarily that a value is shown.)

**Design a Reasonable Coding System.**    Two approaches might be suitable: (1) Items used repetitively may be coded, by commodity, to facilitate negotiations with vendors; commodity coding can incorporate the nature of the commodity, size, and material. (2) Spare parts may be correlated with the machines on which they are used to speed identification when breakdowns occur. If the design of the code is sound, it should be easier to:

Develop commodity volume statistics to permit the company's purchasing power to be leveraged.

Eliminate overlapping and duplication of acquisitions and inventories, and standardize on usage of preferred items.

Ensure availability of parts for maintenance and operating purposes.

Analyze depreciation practices and their effect on cash flow.

**Enter Codes on the Inventory Sheet.**   (The degree of elaboration in a code depends on the nature of the property, on the production process, and on the EDP system.) If the code is lengthy, it may be desirable to set up teams to assign code numbers based on a preestablished coding framework. (The nature of selfchecking devices—repeat keying, check digits, programmed checks, etc.—in code assignments/machine language conversion, represents an accuracy/cost tradeoff.)

**Process Information.**   Keypunching might be minimized by creating the machine-readable media as by-products of typing. Indeed, the *typed* information could be converted to *typeset* information, using a program such as WORDSTAR, thereby furthering catalog creation.

Subsequent to the physical inventory, periodic "cycle counts" may be appropriate. Again, reasonable control procedures are needed:

Assign responsibility for inventory taking.

Develop methods to ensure that, where necessary, each significant item will be counted within an appropriate time cycle. (Where construction is involved, special precautions should be taken to be certain that the item will be there when needed by the constructors.)

Assign personnel, other than the custodians, to participate in the counts. Consider allocating some inventory-checking responsibilities to internal auditors.

Develop techniques to safeguard the accuracy and completeness of counts.

Evaluate adjustments to the records, and make adjustments only upon careful consideration of the related reasons.

# OTHER ASPECTS—CATALOGS, SECURITY, AND SURPLUS DISPOSAL

Consider creating a catalog of spare parts. Such a catalog should establish a common language for storekeepers, purchasing agents, and operating personnel; pictures may enhance the catalog's effectiveness. Both design and format should be adaptable to updating and reproduction at minimum expense.

Security over fixed assets may need strengthening. Where fixed assets are subject to pilferage, it may be desirable to police parking areas, inspect outgoing commercial and passenger vehicles, install surveillance techniques, and consider other security measures. In essence, the more "marketable" the article, the greater the degree of security to be applied.

Procedures must be created to identify, evaluate, and dispose of surplus, obsolete, or retired articles. The following steps are suggested:

Establish procedures to identify surplus items with a view toward minimizing losses from their disposal.

Inform other company entities of the existence of these items so that needs within the organization may be met before disposal to outsiders.

Consider establishing a fixed asset review committee, representing the different constituencies—procurement, maintenance, finance, and so forth.

Segregate surplus into components based on market ability. Develop rules relating to the evaluation of the components.

Formulate disposal rules based on recovery priorities; for example, return to vendors, transfer to other company units, sale to employees (if practicable), donation to a charity or university, sale as used equipment, scrapping based on sorting and, finally, bulk scrap.

## CONCLUSION

The accountant/business advisor can play a seminal role in all decisions involving fixed assets, starting with recognition of a need to obtain a fixed asset and ending with scrapping of the obsolete article. His or her primary role will be to assist in the design of forms, procedures, records, and reports which provide corporate decision makers with accurate, timely, and complete information. And, the needs of a variety of functional users will have to be met in a cost-effective manner, drawing upon all of the skills in the accountant's repertoire.

# Appendix to Chapter 7

## Owner's Checklist for Construction Projects

|  | Yes | No |
|---|---|---|
| **1.** Have you conducted a feasibility study? | ☐ | ☐ |

Does it include the estimated costs and an assessment of the project's benefits?

*In general, a feasibility study should show the ongoing projected revenues and operating and maintenance costs of a proposed project, as well as its estimated acquisition and construction costs. The study should also present the underlying assumptions related to the project's size, its timing and scheduling, its quality and design and the risks involved.*

**2.** In selecting the site for your project, did you consider all available alternatives?  ☐  ☐

*Site selection will be influenced by these factors, which should be considered before construction begins:*

*Proximity to markets*

*The availability of raw materials*

*Transportation facilities*

*Proximity to energy sources*

*Real and personal property taxes*

*The quality of life in the area*

*The availability of labor and the nature of the labor relations prevailing in the community*

*Environmental and licensing regulations and their impact.*

**3.** Have you developed a project plan that sets out the    ☐          ☐
fundamental objectives that must be achieved?

*Your project plan should include these items:*

*A description of the project.*

*An estimate of the project's cost.*

*A timetable for its completion.*

*An organizational plan.*

*Designation of responsibilities for management of all project functions.*

*Significant project risks.*

*The approach toward identifying and complying with all licensing and regulatory requirements and the level of expenditures that can be reached before all licenses and permits must be acquired.*

*The approach toward construction (e.g., general contractor vs. construction manager).*

*The construction techniques to be used. You can either wait until all design work has been completed before starting construction or "fast track" your project. Under the fast track approach, construction starts as soon as the drawings for a particular section are completed, even though drawings for other sections may still be in the preparation stage. The advantage of the fast track approach is that it may result in earlier completion of a project, but it may also increase construction costs and coordination problems. Before deciding whether or not to use the fast track approach, make sure you analyze its pros and cons as they relate to your particular project.*

**4.** Have you thoroughly considered and defined your ap-    ☐          ☐
proach to risk management?

*Early in the planning stage, you should identify the risks your project may face and determine the approach you'll take toward managing them. For example, your project may be affected by labor stoppages, energy shortages or inflation. These risks-or any others-may be disregarded, shifted to others or managed by strong control procedures; or you may use a combination of these approaches.*

**5.** Have you selected an architect/engineer? ☐ ☐

*Have you decided whether his fees measure up to his professional skills and reputation?*

*When you're selecting an architect/engineer, you must weigh his fees against his professional skills. Take a look at the reputation of the individuals assigned to your engagement and determine beforehand how much of their time will actually be spent on your project. You may also want to verify the firm's asserted achievements by talking to some of its other clients.*

**6.** Have you determined what the full extent of the architect/engineer's role will be? ☐ ☐

*Initially, the architect/engineer's work will involve preparing preliminary designs, drawings and specifications and putting together a cost estimate. Any major changes to the initial design should be evaluated for their cost/benefit, since the design of any project is an important device for controlling costs.*

*In addition, you should decide as early in the project as possible whether you also want the architect/engineer involved in quality control activities during the construction phase. You may decide that a third party should be involved in that process. Whatever your decision, however, be sure you set up procedures for overseeing the quality of the construction work.*

**7.** Have you established a realistic budget? ☐ ☐

*A sensible, realistic budget will include:*

> *Prices for materials that are based on recent costs and on current and foreseeable escalation rates*
>
> *Labor costs that are based on drawing quantities,*

*realistic productivity, current wage rates and current and foreseeable escalation rates*

*Overhead cost allocations*

*Contingencies for both design and construction, as well as a general contingency plan.*

8. Have you arranged for financing? Have you fully explored all possible arrangements?    □        □

*Depending on the nature of a project and on your borrowing power, you may either fully own a project, pursue a sale/leaseback arrangement, mortgage the property or use a combination financing arrangement. Since each approach has its advantages and disadvantages, the one that's best for your project should be determined with the help of your financial and tax advisers.*

9. Have you decided whether you, your construction manager or a general contractor will manage the actual construction process?    □        □

*Have you evaluated the pros and cons of each approach?*

*Each approach has its advantages and its disadvantages.*

*If you decide to manage construction, you'll need to have individuals on board who have the requisite skills. For owners with infrequent construction projects, this approach can be very costly.*

*For standard, "cut-and-dry" construction projects, it may be best to have a general contractor manage your project. However, you should be aware that some general contractors will base their decisions on their own interests—not necessarily on yours.*

*Having a construction manager in control means that you can rely on the judgment of an independent professional. But make sure that whatever compensation he receives is based on the value of the services he performs—with appropriate incentives—and not solely on the achievement of targets he has set.*

**10.** Have you set up a realistic project schedule?    ☐    ☐

*The two most common methods of project scheduling are:*

*Bar charts, which are fairly easy to produce and understand. However, bar charts don't always show task relationships and their priorities.*

*Networks—or the critical path method—which identify the most important tasks relative to all other construction tasks and which can be more comprehensive. Since most network schedules are computerized, however, using this method often requires greater technical know-how.*

*The scheduling method you choose will depend on the complexity of the project, the construction approaches and techniques selected and how much control is needed over the project. Your overall schedule should also include several specific sub-schedules for design, procurement, construction, testing and start up.*

**11.** Is your schedule linked to your financing plan?    ☐    ☐

*It's vitally important that your project schedule be integrated with your financing plan. As the owner, you may choose between drawing immediately on monies set aside for the entire project or using these funds as contractor billings come through. If you use the entire proceeds immediately, you should make some provision for temporarily investing unneeded funds. If your take-down is based on construction progress, banks generally will charge a relatively nominal standby fee.*

**12.** Have you determined which type of contract is best    ☐    ☐
for your project?

*Contract policies are subject to local requirements and are affected by the nature of a project, by the supply and demand of local labor forces and by the extent of design completion. Whatever policies you choose, make sure you've investigated all possible choices.*

*Essentially, there are three major types of contracts, which may be used individually or may be combined, depending on the requirements of your project:*

*The lump-sum contract, which is for a fixed amount, including overhead and profit. This type of contract passes the risk of overruns on to the contractor, but it also tends to increase the amount of claims and change orders for various reasons, including unanticipated conditions, additional work referred or alleged owner-caused problems.*

*The unit-price contract, which sets a price—either fixed or sliding—for an established number of units. Overrun or underrun provisions may or may not exist, and there may or may not be an overall quantity or dollar cap provision in this type of contract.*

*Cost-plus-fee contract. Here, the contractor charges actual cost, plus a fee for his services; the fee may or may not depend upon the value of costs, and it may or may not include provisions for savings incentives. In addition, the fee may or may not be subject to an overall cap.*

**13.** Have your contracts been reviewed to ensure that they're clearly written and protect your interests?     ☐     ☐

*Vague contract provisions are almost always a source of additional costs. And since many construction contracts are originally drafted by contractors, your interests won't necessarily be protected. To make sure your rights are protected, review your contracts with the appropriate experts before you sign them.*

**14.** Have you set up contract administration procedures to make sure the terms of contracts are being met?     ☐     ☐

*Effective, ongoing contract administration proce-
dures should be established so that you can be sure
the terms of any contracts you have are being met
on a daily basis. You should set up procedures to
oversee the contractors' activities, especially in such
areas as cost accumulation, invoicing, retention, materials management, safety, site security, productivity
and labor relations. By effectively monitoring these
activities, you'll help control time, cost and quality
of performance—the essential elements of any contract.*

15. Have you set up a system to make sure that minority    ☐         ☐
    business enterprise goals and Affirmative Action/Equal
    Employment Opportunity (AA/EEO) requirements are
    being met?

    *Complying with MBE rules may involve goals that are
    set for contract value, for the number of contracts
    and for the number of minority workers. To help
    meet MBE and AA/EEO requirements, you should
    consider:*

    *Setting goals that have reasonable parameters.*
    *Identifying minority groups within the community
    who can refer minority workers to you.*
    *Training minority employees.*
    *Monitoring MBE performance to detect shortfalls.*
    *Creating objective fact-gathering mechanisms.*
    *Reporting against goals.*

16. Have you set up a system that will allow you to select    ☐         ☐
    vendors on a truly competitive basis?

    *To objectively evaluate vendors, you should:*

    *Select those vendors eligible to receive bidding
    invitations.*

    *Mail comprehensive bid packages, including pro
    forma terms and technical and general specifications
    to the vendors chosen.*

*Arrange for prebid conferences.*

*Make the award to the lowest responsible bidder —subject to exception routines and controls.*

*Monitor pre-award negotiations to make sure the objectives of the competitive bidding are not invalidated.*

**17.** Have you set up a system to identify any deviations    ☐    ☐
from targets and schedules in time to correct them?

*Although you may choose to delegate information systems details to your construction manager and rely on his reports, be aware that this can be dangerous unless it's reinforced by some sort of owner monitoring.*

*To monitor construction progress, you can evaluate these key systems:*

*Planning and scheduling, which allow for controlling time and productivity*

*Procurement, which includes handling vendors and contracts*

*Control over materials*

*Production control, which can track physical progress*

*Quality control, which will help you maintain the appropriate quality*

*Cost engineering/forecasting, which generates prospective information on estimates to complete the project*

*Cost reporting/accounting, which accumulates financial results.*

**18.** Have you set up a system to measure a project's phys-    ☐    ☐
ical progress against its financial progress?

*These simple formulas can be used to evaluate and compare a project's physical and financial progress:*

*Cost to date + estimated cost to complete = total project cost*

*Total projected cost – budget = budget underrun (or overrun).*

**19.** Have you set up a contractor claims coordination system? ☐ ☐

*A contractor claims coordination system helps ensure that, through scheduled meetings and exchanges of written information, any problems with contractor claims are identified. Usually, contractor claims are based on assertions that delays were created by activities outside the claimant's control or were the result of faulty work allegedly caused by the owner, by other contractors or by inadequate design. In addition, claims may also be made for unforeseen reasons. You or your representative should monitor claims assertions to make sure that steps are taken to minimize their damage and that all parties are treated equitably.*

*If you decide to disregard contractor complaints and/ or claims, you do so at your own risk. Remember, unchallenged claims acquire an aura of authenticity simply by not being challenged.*

**20.** Do you have plans to visit the site and monitor the actual construction in progress? ☐ ☐

*Periodically, visit the construction site to make sure that activities being reported are actually taking place. Observe the workers, and try to assess their productivity—even if you have a fixed price contract. If workers appear to be extensively idle, this could indicate that your contracts are not cost-effective.*

*Also pay attention to engineering changes, which are usually triggered by design changes, regulatory considerations, unforeseen events or claims.*

*Examine these changes to determine whether they are in scope (in which case, the contractor is responsible for them) or out of scope (in which case, you're responsible for them). If the changes involve significant amounts of money, consider competitive bidding—if practical.*

**21.** Have you established a way to periodically monitor costs and schedules? ☐ ☐

*You should require that some means be set up to compare performance during construction to defined cost, schedule and quality milestones. And you should make sure that all on-site contractors receive any proper technical documentation they need to keep the project on time and within budget.*

**22.** If you're moving to a new site (e.g., new company headquarters), have you considered appointing a "move coordinator"? ☐ ☐

*A "move coordinator" can help make sure that the actual physical move from one site to another goes more smoothly by:*

*Integrating any move-related activities of the architect/engineer, construction manager or general contractor with the mover's*

*Determining which assets should be left at the old facilities and which should be moved*

*Procuring new equipment on a timely basis so that it's available when needed to start operations at the new facility*

*Finding a cost-effective way to dispose of surplus equipment*

*Making sure the move proceeds as cost-effectively as possible and with minimum disruption to operations by identifying, routing and dispatching all necessary equipment.*

*Source:* Reprinted with the permission of Coopers & Lybrand.

# CHAPTER 8

# SYSTEMS AUTOMATION

## Kenneth O. Cole

## INTRODUCTION

The accountant, in the position of external auditor, internal auditor or management accountant, has a unique perspective in dealing with his or her client/employer. In this perspective the accountant must be able to:

Identify problems

Communicate these to the client/employer

Know where to go to seek help from experts

The information presented in this chapter will arm the accountant with information to help identify the problems.

The job of the accountant as a business advisor is getting more complex each day, especially in the area of systems automation. He or she needs to have a broad knowledge of computer software (both operating and applications); hardware (micros to super mainframes); communications (local area networks and digital private branch exchanges); office automation (word processing, micrographics, reprographics), and so on. The accountant/business advisor has an obligation to keep up with the changing technology—first understanding it, then imparting that knowledge to the organization for its benefit.

Obviously, the accountant is not expected, in this business advisor role, to be an expert in each of these areas. In most cases, after identifying a problem, the accountant will need to seek additional help from experts. An accountant who is a member of a public accounting firm will seek help from the Management Advisory Services (MAS) Department. Similarly, an internal auditor or a management accountant will seek help from the Internal Consulting Department or from outside consultants.

# SOFTWARE

A new technology in software development is taking shape, that is, the ability to automate fully the development process—from design through installation.

**FOURTH-GENERATION SOFTWARE LANGUAGES.**   These languages have been in existence for at least 10 years. They represented a step in the direction of reduced complexity and greater economy of expression when programming application software. Despite vendor claims, however, no fourth-generation software language is "nonprocedural." They still require specification of the sequence of steps necessary to achieve the desired result. The "how" must be given in order to achieve the desired "what."

This requirement entraps the fallible human programmer into the same morass as first through third-generation languages; that is, out-of-place statements, erroneous logic, multiple logic paths, and if-then-else constructs inevitably leading to bugs and the requirements for testing, recode, retest, and so on.

**FIFTH-GENERATION SOFTWARE.**   The use of the term *fifth-generation software* is now used to label accurately the new technology. This is software with which the man/machine interface is only at the specification level, whereas the organization of specifications into the facts needed to create an information processing system is carried out by the software development system. Fifth-generation software always produces programs that work. They may not function as the specifier intended, but they always perform the functions specified.

Because post-initial development activity (maintenance enhancement) typically consumes more than two-thirds of the programming effort required during the lifetime of an effective system, saving in these areas is even more rewarding than saving in initial development. By getting fallible humans out of the rework/refit process, the fifth-generation tool can impressively affect life-cycle costs of application production. Fifth-generation technology is changing organizations and functions. Management must be prepared to reassign talents now that many repetitive tasks need no longer be performed by people.

The program development manager must recognize the tremendous desire on the part of the expanding personal computer population within the company for software and data, specifically data from the corporate data base. A fifth-generation product should provide the ability to specify applications on either the maintenance or the micro, and upload or download the specification for target application creation as needed. With the power of this approach realized, a conceptual merging of the development center and the information center is possible. No data processing manager can afford to ignore this emerging technology.

**APPLICATION GENERATOR.**   Another software development that can be helpful to the programmer is the application generator. This is a tool kit that assists in automating selected tasks in the programming process.

Application generators develop the data structures and the data base management system calls, or all but the program logic. They invariably require the skills of a programmer to complete the missing pieces. They improve programmer productivity manyfold. Today there are commercially available systems that allow an individual to generate programs via either a question-and-answer or fill-in-the blank interaction with computers. The application generator (written by programmers) then automatically develops software to perform some function based on user answers.

Application generators are inherently data base oriented, not process oriented, and are built to interface with a data base management system. This means that the new system will be built around the data base and not vice versa. This requires that the data base design issue be addressed sooner in the development life cycle.

Approaching the design of a system with the application generator and its data base orientation involves a recommended sequence of events:

Define the functional requirements

Build a data model

Understand the application generator

Create the specifications

Conduct design walkthroughs

Consider phototyping

Design the physical data base

This is the traditional functional decomposition of the user's requirements, one where the system is broken down in a top-down fashion until the lowest subfunctions can be identified with some transaction (unit-of-work) process that can then be related to some number of programs and screens.

**Building a Data Model.**   Numerous books and vendor products address this effort. Very simply stated, this is the grouping of related fields into segments and the segments into logical views that depict the segment relationships within subject data bases.

**Understanding the Application Generator.**   Every application generator has a number of options, considerations, and restrictions that must be understood if it is to yield the productivity gains stated by the vendor.

**The Specifications.**   If the application generator is data base oriented, it seems natural that the programming specifications should use a data base oriented technique, one that insists that the preparer identify all the required segments and keys in the data model required for a particular transaction process.

This access map shows the interaction with the data model and will be the basis for the specification. The specification is the access map expanded to include the transaction logic (field editing, processing, document generation, and so on.) Accompanied by appropriate attachments (screen layouts), the next step is a walkthrough.

**Design Walkthrough.**   The design walkthrough usually involves the preparer, a knowledgeable user, and an experienced application generator developer. Together they will determine, through an iterative process, whether the transaction will meet the user's needs and whether it can be programmed with the application generator. Some developers make the *fatal* mistake of thinking that walkthroughs are unnecessary.

**Prototyping.**   Because application generators are excellent for creating skeletal versions of the transaction process, a prototyping step may be useful or required to confirm user satisfaction.

**The Physical Data Base.**   Define the physical characteristics of the data base, load it with some test data, and start. Follow these steps when appropriate, and you can usually guarantee success; not following these steps can almost always guarantee dissatisfied users, unnecessary delays, substantial technical problems, and a group of developers and designers ready to blame the application generator for their failures.

**SOFTWARE TECHNOLOGY LAGS BEHIND HARDWARE.**   Even with the new technology in software development, software has not kept pace with hardware technology. The Western world has chosen to rely increasingly on computers. The computer industry has responded by developing a virtual continuum of more powerful machines. It has been a remarkable progression matched only by an accompanying steep decline of costs.

At the same time, we are implementing increasingly complex functions in software to execute on these computers, but the technology of software has not advanced nearly as far as that of hardware. And because software is still an emerging technology, the cost, the performance levels, and the management problems involved in implementing a function in software continue to be high.

The three strategies for improving both software productivity and quality are: consolidation, evolution, and revolution. Each strategy will have an effect in a different time period.

**CONSOLIDATION.** This means applying existing tools to software development projects. Many tools have been developed which, although not integrated, can provide immediate improvement. Consolidation will have an effect today, and it should readily and immediately yield improvements of 25 percent in productivity and up to 50 percent in quality.

**Evolution.** Evolution is providing integrated tool sets to aid and support the software engineer so that he or she will be able to produce an improved product more efficiently than is possible today. The evolutionary strategy will affect system development and support several years from now, and should yield improvements of 50 to 300 percent in productivity and up to 100 percent in quality over that typically found today.

**Revolution.** Revolution means changing the software development track, developing methods and tools so that the software developer does not have to write each line of code anew for each application. Software itself must be used to write the bulk of the applications, and the users, rather than the programmers, must determine the design of software. The revolutionary strategy requires more elapsed time to take effect, but it could yield improvements of up to 1000 percent (10 times) in productivity and two to four times in quality.

The objective of consolidation is to apply a wide application of the software support facilities that already exist.

Improved software tools that are needed now include:

High-level language compliers

Microcode compliers

Screen editors

On-line, source-level language debuggers

Configuration management documentation systems

Upgrade work processing

**INTEGRATED SOFTWARE PACKAGES.** With the introduction of new, integrated software packages, the door is now open to customize software with a minimum of effort. Most business computer purchasers aren't very interested in buying computers hardware or software—instead, they are willing to purchase a solution to a particular business problem. That solution could take the form of another bookkeeper, a computer system, or whatever. But it must solve the business problem being faced.

Computers, when programmed with the proper applications software, can be great problem-solvers. They can solve accounting problems, bookkeeping difficulties, inventory tangles, sales lead difficulties, and a myriad of other problems that businesspeople face daily. But, computers and their software can also, in and of themselves, confront the businessperson with a whole new problem— how to make it work.

Making computers work is the job of software, and making software work has traditionally been the job of programmers and systems houses. With the advent of "user friendly" software, more and more businesspeople learned their way around programs such as Lotus 1-2-3 and the Visi or Perfect series of software, but a great many more potential business customers have neither the time, inclination, nor courage to even give it a try. Consequently, they have to contract with high-priced programmers, Independent Sales Organizations (ISOs), or system houses to get their job done. Businesspeople's time is valuable too, and most subscribe to the age-old notion of doing what you do best and hiring out what you do poorly.

The user-friendly, powerful, new integrated software packages allow the users easily and inexpensively to customize applications for their businesses.

**Quick and Easy.**  This new generation of programs offers the capability of quickly and easily generating data entry screens, printout formats, sort routines, and interactive mathematical modeling. All within a menu-driven, user-friendly environment.

After just an hour or two of configuration, the business purchaser can be presented with a default screen on boot-up, which says the company name, asks if he or she wants to take orders, print invoices, do last month's bookkeeping, or whatever, and checks to make sure that only the appropriate people can use various modules of the program. Because most of this type of software can be arranged to be completely and only menu-driven, it's impossible for the program to crash around the poor user's ears because he or she forgot to precede a command with an exclamation mark, or misplaced a comma.

These newest of the integrated software programs have virtually rendered obsolete the notion of programming. Imagine being able to offer any business user any application; and offer business solutions, completely customized and virtually off-the-shelf, to just about any imaginable type of business problem.

**Know the Package.**  The first step, of course, is to get to know a new package, such as Aura; Symphony; Ovation; MBA; Framework and Lotus. The second step will be to become proficient with one particular system, the one that seems the most powerful and versatile, and the easiest for you to use once it's configured.

**DATA BASE MANAGEMENT SYSTEMS,**  A data base management system (DBMS), in terms of its use for a business, is to provide all Management Information Systems (MIS) users with the ability to access the organization's data quickly and easily, and through the use of that data, enable users to develop programs and produce their own information outside the constraints of the MIS Department. The goal of the DBMS process will be, insofar as is practical, to capture all the organization's data, one time at the source, and then make that data available throughout the organization. The purpose of the development of the DBMS environment is to provide a vehicle to manage the organization better.

It follows that once a concept of the DBMS' role has been identifed, the next step is to consider the individual criteria that affect the success of that concept. Building an effective DBMS environment is a massive task. The value of defining DBMS goals and criteria is that it forces people to raise and consider the real DBMS issues before the DBMS environment has become entrenched.

Building the DBMS environment is indifferent, in terms of planning, from any other MIS project. The basis of project management applies here as surely as anywhere else. The key to success, just as with any MIS application project, is to have the clearest possible vision of the ultimate goals of the project prior to commencing.

**OPERATING SYSTEMS SOFTWARE,**   End users should never see the operating system. It's up to applications developers to provide the front ends. Today, when we discuss front ends, we think of terminals, but it could be voice or other types of input. The interest of an end user in an operating system should be no more than intellectual curiosity.

Users are banding together into user groups to help each other. Many professional organizations research the best operating software and recommend it to their members.

Standard operating systems cost just a fraction of what they would cost to provide the same capabilities in a proprietary operating system. The operating system is the master control program that runs the computer, acting as an intermediary, a traffic cop and a master scheduler. Among the many tasks the operating system performs are executing application programs, handling I/O (input/output), and understanding different media configurations.

Put simply, and ignoring such important activities as high-level language interpretation and compilation, the operating system links a user's program or package to the hardware by converting a logical request into a physical set of commands.

**Features.**   Among the features that make one operating system better than or different than another are whether it is: (1) a single-user or a multiuser operating system, (2) single or multitasking, (3) floppy or hard disk oriented. Each operating system has different capabilities for handling the screen (particularly graphics and windows), communications, and storage devices.

**SPREADSHEETS AND FINANCIAL PLANNING SOFTWARE.**    The electronic spreadsheet is the software that moved computers from hobbyists' garages to executives' desks. Spreadsheets are the number one best-selling category of business software. They are easy-to-learn management tools that are excellent for a wide variety of number-crunching tasks. But that doesn't mean spreadsheets are best for all financial applications. There is a whole other class of financial planning software that is far more powerful than the spreadsheet.

Many of the programs in this class evolved from mini and mainframe-based decision support packages. They are more difficult to use than spreadsheets, but they can do quite a bit more.

**Financial Planning,**    This software can handle larger amounts of data than spreadsheets, and it includes a large number of statistical and financial functions unknown to the spreadsheet software. It has regression analysis and depreciation calculations, together with goal-seeking capabilities. The price the user pays for this added power is the extra effort it takes to learn and use these programs.

Rather than enter data and formulas into cells, the user creates a model by writing a series of programming-like commands. Results are not displayed until the model is run. Although the process is straightforward, it requires experience and careful thought up front. Financial planning software is ideal for the professional whose everyday job is to prepare financial plans. The time saved over the long run will more than offset the initial effort in learning how to use these powerful planning tools.

**Spreadsheets.**    If financial planning is only one of the user's many duties, then the easier-to-use spreadsheet may be better. The user needn't limit the use of the spreadsheet to financial applications. It can be used to maintain mailing lists, write reports, or create graphs for presentations.

Spreadsheet users routinely make three common mistakes: relying on spreadsheets that contain errors; not documenting their spreadsheets; and overusing their spreadsheets.

A spreadsheet can easily contain a minor error that can cascade into a major catastrophe. As the user develops a spreadsheet he or she tends to insert, delete, and change constants, formulas, and locations of data. In the process it is easy to introduce an error, and the error can be multiplied many times over by successive formulas that depend on the erroneous cell.

Here are four typical spreadsheet errors: specifying the wrong ranges in a formula; entering data on top of a formula; copying a formula incorrectly; and entering an otherwise correct formula with an incorrect reference. One way to prevent these errors is to check manually any figure that seems wrong. If it looks out of line, it probably is.

Another technique is to scan the entire spreadsheet, keeping track of the formulas as you look at the individual cells. This approach is time-comsuming, and following the interdependencies of formulas is difficult, especially when the spreadsheet is larger than the display. Despite the drawbacks, the electronic spreadsheets remain one of the most versatile financial tools in use today.

**GRAPHICS.** Graphics software presents a significant area of opportunity. The business-type graphics software—bar, line, pie, scatter charts, and such—offered by these packages to busy professionals, will experience a significant growth curve in the future. The visual excellence provided by contemporary end-user packages will be enhanced even further with the increased resources presented by new computer-based architectures.

**WORD PROCESSING.** All word processing software can store and retrieve text and add or delete information. All modern products also have the ability to automatically "wrap" a word to the next line if it intrudes into the right margin. Support for special print attributes such as underscore and bold text is similarly universal. What makes a given word processor desirable is not the support of basic word processing, but the way in which basic features are provided and the number of advanced features that accompany them.

In corporations, the average word processor user tends to be a frequent user, so products that provide ease of learning at the expense of functionality should be avoided; concentrate on the formula of features, functions, and benefits. In addition to the traditional ability to manipulate text and to read and store documents, look for mail/merge facilities; spelling; multiple text windows that permit several views of one or more documents; multiple document editing, either through the use of windows or through document selection features; and background printing that permits the central processing unit (CPU) to remain available for another simultaneous task.

Other features consist of: cursor control and function keys for easy and consistent operation; ability to undo the most recent operation; backup and recovery facilities; system command entry, either via menu or through special key sequences; edit command techniques that include the use of function key and control key sequences; and the ability to format and reformat data that is keyed or changed. It may also be desirable to support special documents such as indexes, tables of contents, and footnotes. An added feature is the ability to use foreign languages.

Because written communications is both a very important part of business, as well as a very personal and subjective matter, it is not suprising that word processors are among the most hotly debated of software products.

**EVALUATING SOFTWARE VENDORS.**    Vendor responsiveness is included in most checklists for evaluating end-user software. Usually this criterion is low on the list. All too frequently, software selection teams give this qualification only cursory attention. And rarely is the vendor's ability to meet the inevitable demands for technical support put to the test before the software is acquired. Fortunately, it is not difficult to access a vendor before you sign away a major chunk of your software budget. Expect the vendor's marketing presentation and product brochures to be slick. A sloppy marketing pitch could be the first clue to stay away from the product.

**Question the Vendor.**    When you've evaluated enough products to narrow the list to three or four candidates, ask the vendor some questions.

How long will installation take?

Will the vendor be available during the installation?

Find out if the vendor has a hot line for technical support. Does it have an 800 number? A hot line without a foll-free number could be indicative of a vendor that is not interested in hearing your problems. The expense of repeated long-distance calls may be a deterrent for your company to seek adequate support.

What kind of telephone support can you expect? Every question answered in thirty minutes? Sixty minutes? Twenty-four hours? Is technical support available during evening hours? During the weekend? If the vendor is on the West Coast, and you are on the East Coast with a problem at 8:00 A.M., will you be able to get help?

How quickly can the vendor get to your site? Is the vendor willing to send a technical heavy hitter to you on short notice in an emergency? A vendor one hour away by shuttle might as well be on the other side of the world when traffic and weather conditions don't cooperate.

Do some checking on your own. Choose several questions with obvious answers; for example, does the product offer graphics? Ask a few questions with answers requiring technical knowledge of the product and some data base aware-ness. Call the technical support department at various times and ask these questions.

Call the marketing representative servicing your region. Chances are he or she will be out seeing customers. Leave a message, and note how long it takes for the call to be returned. When you make contact with the representative ask that some product literature be sent to you. See how long it takes to arrive.

Get the names of companies where the products are in use. You can start with a list of references from the vendor. Assume, however, that these will be companies the vendor wants you to know about.

Ask each reference for the names of other companies using the product. Contact the local or national users' group, if there is one. Even better, try to attend a users' group meeting.

You may also want to ask about training. Many vendors stress the importance of training for efficient and effective use of the product. Ask the vendor how far in advance you must schedule on-site training; does this fit your training plans? Ask references about the quality of this training. Find out if the vendor is willing to customize training to your organization's unique needs. Again, the vendor's response may be useful to you in gauging its interest in serving you.

Vendors, of course, have problems just like everyone else. For many, the success of their products has exceeded even their most optimistic expectations, and they are experiencing growing pains. Some vendor support managers comment freely about their concerns in keeping up with customer demands for support. Other vendors are happy to collect monthly license fees and consider training, consulting, and technical support a tedious, but necessary, cost of doing business.

Information center and data processing staff need to determine the importance of vendor qualifications in an overall evaluation. Regardless of the relative importance of these criteria, knowing what you can expect from a vendor will contribute to effective planning of the best possible level of support for your users.

# HARDWARE

The classification of hardware is diverse, starting at the top end with super-mainframes; mainframes; superminis; minis; supermicros; and micros. Data processing executives look for raw computing power capable of supporting the needs of multiple users. Users of minicomputers and microcomputers, on the other hand, tend to seek a solution to a specific set of business problems. For them, computing power becomes less of a consideration. Computing power for mainframes and superminicomputers is measured in millions of instructions per second. Because many microcomputers have been designed around a handful of industry-standard microprocessors, providing performance figures is less meaningful than with more unique mainframe and superminicomputers. Actual performance of any computer can vary greatly depending on the system work load, configuration, number of concurrent users, and the quality of the software, application, and operating.

What is needed now is better quality hardware; increased videoscreen size; resolution and display/redisplay speed and more computing cycles allotted to programmers to speed up the way in which they can peruse and interact with existing code, prose, and data.

**MAINFRAMES.**   The mainframe vendors will have to depart from their aging systems architectures in order to meet users' demands for increased performance.

**MINIS.**   The minicomputer has grown from a one-time novelty to a mature industry. Some of the original minis have become so well-known that their performance has become an industry standard. There have been rumors that minis were dying out; however, three trends have developed to extend the life span of minis. The first trend is the reluctance of the huge installed base of traditional mini users to switch over to the larger mainframes. Existing mini users often find it more economical to install more minis than to absorb the high conversion costs associated with migration to another computer system architecture.

Second, some dissatisfied micro users have decided they need systems capable of providing more power, a common data storage facility, and the ability to support multiple users. Although minis seem to be the ideal solution for these needs, the trend has sparked a new type of system—the supermicrocomputer—to provide more competition for the already embattled mini. Micro users who have determined that they need more power or additional capabilities seem to slip away from minis because they think the systems are too complex.

The third trend is that the quest for micro-to-mainframe link has opened up another market for minis as file servers in large computer networks.

There is little doubt that the mini marketplace has undergone dramatic change. The mini has been assailed at both the high and low ends by newer technology products, the traditional definition of a mini—a 16-bit general purpose computer system—has become a blur.

Powerful 32-bit superminicomputers have taken over the scientific and engineering markets and are now being repackaged in small configurations for office or stand-alone use.

Based on the encroachment of the 32-bit superminis at the high end and of micros at the low end, many industry watchers predict the eventual demise of the mini in spite of the three trends previously mentioned.

**MICROS.**   Most microcomputers are either 8-bit or 16-bit machines; however, there are some 32-bit micros coming on the market. The "bit" designation refers to the internal word length (e.g., eight bits) of the microcomputer.

**Differences.**   There are several major functional differences between 8-bit and 16-bit microcomputers. First, because 16-bit machines have a larger word length, they can process data faster than their 8-bit counterparts. Second, 16-bit microcomputers can address more memory than 8-bit microcomputers. Another difference is that 16-bit microcomputers have different operating systems than 8-bit machines.

**Microcomputer Software.** There is an abundance of microcomputer software on the market. It is written for specific word-length machines and is also written for specific operating systems. Common 8-bit operating systems are CP/M, Apple DOS, and TRS-DOS. Common 16-bit operating systems are PC-DOS and TRS-DOS. Common 16-bit operating systems are PC-DOS, MS-DOS, and UNIX.

General application software exists for most hardware/operating system combinations. General accounting, spreadsheet, and word processing packages exist for 8-bit and 16-bit machines for the most popular operating systems. The 16-bit micros are more expensive. Similarly, software for 16-bit systems will cost more than for the 8-bit systems.

**USER-FRIENDLY CAREER ADVANCEMENT.** After nearly three decades of frustration in dealing with centralized business systems and user-hostile terminals, users have become aware of the beginnings of a new form of data processing (DP) life. That life is organized around personal systems and user-friendly interfaces and, according to users' perceptions, offers to liberate them from the bondage of the vast bureaucracies of computer departments.

One reason for the current ground swell of personal computer excitement in user camps is because the users view the micros as devices that can help them personally, as distinguished from helping the business. Users see the potential for these machines to enable them to perform better on the job, certainly by increasing productivity, but much more important, by increasing the quality of their output.

The astute go-getters have found a red-hot link between their abilities to handle a personal computer at the office and the advancement of their careers. Those knowledgeable in a spreadsheet program are heading rapidly toward their personal goals, as opposed to colleagues without the capability who are trudging ahead on the treadmill, if not losing their competitive standing altogether.

Indeed, these days, if a DP center wants to heal the long-standing divisions that have separated it from the user population, it can establish in its user support group an individual to consult with the user departments on the acquisition, operation, and support of personal computers. This one person can be instrumental in building friendships anew and rekindling cooperative attitudes.

**Portables.** The portable personal computer is considered by many to be an excellent concept, even though the idea configuration is still to come. The notion of providing a company-paid personal computer for both den and office is indeed attractive, but dragging a 20- to 30-pound piece of hardware home every night lessens the appeal. It's far better to choose notebook-style lap systems for their high coefficient of carrying ease, with a tie-in to full function desktops, as long as there is sufficient compute ability to handle their specific jobs.

There is available to users a lap-style portable that plugs into an office station, together making up the desktop configuration. The station houses a video monitor controller and provides attachments to one or more diskette drives. This enables the users to download programs and data from the desktop to the portable. Then they can plug the portable and go work wherever they wish.

**Computer Literacy.**   This is still a matter of concern in some quarters, but is rapidly giving way to considerations of personal productivity with the undeniable success of personal systems such as workstation access to micros, minis, or mainframes.

This is the era when busy executives everywhere must be thinking about acquiring personal computers or terminals, particularly if the machines provide easy, low-cost methods for saving time and/or avoiding tedious tasks. For example, those on the run surely must be looking closely at simple notebook-style machines to allow them to type in short notes and reports for immediate transmission via phone lines to a host machine at the home office. And the notion of using an in-transit hookup from a train or plane is now practical.

As another illustration, spreadsheet facilities are a must in the hands of the executive. The insight gained by varying input parameters and watching projections—those fundamental to the business—change over a period of years should not be a delegated task. The availability of reliable spreadsheet software, plus its ease-of-use and low cost, make it a natural for top managers.

One consideration is the choice of the integrated package of applications (spreadsheet, word processing, data processing, and graphics). Such packages eliminate the need for learning individual sets of commands; however, there may be some sacrifice in performance. Each situation must be justified on the merits of particular programs and their ability for the user.

**STATE-OF-THE-ART.**   State-of-the-art implies use of the latest hardware and software advances, including DBMS, fourth-generation languages, and information centers. However, the true measure of success of an MIS organization lies in the degree of support provided to the attainment of corporate strategic and operational goals, not in attainment of some nebulous measure of state-of-the-art technical advances. To provide such support effectively, the MIS director must naturally become part of the corporate management team. For this to happen, however, MIS people must be capable of acting as business managers, not as data processing technicians.

Undue emphasis upon the tools of our trade, rather than on the effective application of these tools, can only result in a less effective and less useful MIS organization. These tools, as well as the more established ones, must be applied within a sound business plan after careful analysis of the organization's current and future information processing requirements.

**Fifth Generation Computing.**    Fifth generation computing will employ artificial intelligence techniques to make computers easier to use and able to mimic several characteristics of human intelligence. The plan is to make hardware that can speak, understand verbal communications, make inferences, and generally deal with "knowledge" instead of raw alphanumeric data.

# COMMUNICATIONS

Without communications, there is no information revolution—no office automation, no computer integrated manufacturing, no telecomputing, no 50-acre teleports packed with disk antennas. The telecommunications function is becoming more important and consequently more visible. Telecommunications decisions are much more frequently major ones, requiring involvement of senior corporate management. There is increasing talk about a chief information officer, but few enterprises have yet adopted this terminology.

The most common consolidation of telecommunications components is voice, data, and image transmission (i.e., facsimile). In addition to being responsible for an evolving telephone system, telecommunications people are generally leading the way in new initiatives, such as local area networks (LANs) and private branch exchanges (PBXs).

**LAN AND PBX.**    The local area network (LAN) and the digital private branch exchange (PBX) are the principal technologies competing to provide in-house data communications for systems automation. The two technologies are independent developments of two distinct industries; data processing vendors developed the LAN, and telecommunications processors developed the digital PBX.

Both LANs and PBXs offer the ability for any attached station (computer or workstation) to communicate with any other. Both offer communications independent of any host computer or applications processor. Both allow users to move hardware and software from one physical location to another without either rewiring the office or regenerating an operating system. From a strict data communications viewpoint, even the cost of connecting a station is roughly the same for both techniques.

Charges and countercharges between the LANs and PBXs continue. According to many vendors from the LAN side, the up-front cost of a PBX is enormously higher than for a LAN; the PBX constitutes a central point of failure without which the entire network is useless; and the PBX cannot possibly offer the high data rates and throughput available with a LAN. According to the PBX vendors, on the other hand, LANs require even more rewiring for growth; LANs offer no central facility for management and diagnostics; and LANs represent an infant technology that has yet to prove itself in the market.

To some extent, all the charges are true, and to some extent they are all exaggerations. The initial cost for PBX is very high, but most PBX vendors justify that initial cost only on the system's function as a telephone switch. Every office with more than about 50 telephones needs some sort of switch, either a PBX or Centrex service from the local telephone company. With the advent of a number of new telephone features, any PBX acquired before about 1980 is obsolete; thus most PBX users will probably have to install a new switch in the next five years whether or not they plan to use it for data. The addition of a data station to an installed digital PBX carries about the same cost as the addition of a data station to a local area network.

The PBX does offer a central point of failure; if the PBX crashes, so does the data network. However, all PBXs are specifically designed not to crash; for most businesses, the loss of the in-house data network is unfortunate, but the loss of the telephone network is catastrophic. Thus the PBX may be the most reliable complex appliance commonly installed in offices today. The probability of a total PBX crash is close to zero.

Data throughput over any medium depends on the specific application. Most data terminals transmit at rates between 2400 bps and 9600 bps; most PBXs can handle data transmission up to 19,200 bps while transmitting voice over the same circuits. Some can handle individual data circuits at 64K bps. Some applications, notably file tranfers between computers and detailed interactive graphics, require greater throughput. Users with large file transfers or CAD/CAM applications should favor a LAN over a PBX. Any others can use a PBX with ease.

From the other side, local area networks do require that new cable be installed in addition to the wire used for the telephone plant. However, such networks usually require only a single, very long cable run with short attachments for the stations. Users designing new offices or, especially, new buildings, should be able to design the LAN into the construction with ease. Users installing LANs in current facilities can run cable over drop ceilings with relative ease.

Growth can be a problem with LANs, both in the number of stations users can attach to the cable, and in the amount of traffic offered to the network. Cable networks often require expensive repeaters to extend their lengths; these repeaters require an additional cost over the possibly significant cost of installing extra cable. A LANs performance under heavy traffic depends on its access method; networks that use CSMA/CD perform poorly under constant, heavy traffic, whereas networks that use token passing degrade as users add more stations.

Local area networking is a young technology, but so is digital telephone switching. Neither has been developed to its full potential, and neither can solve all communications problems. Specifically, neither technology has adequately addressed the problem of end-to-end communications among dissimilar devices. The problem of installing a complete, local communications plant remains complex. Although it is not complex beyond solving, it demands more attention and study than simple charges and countercharges among vendors indicate.

**PROTOCOLS.** The standardized sets of procedures known as protocols govern the interaction of terminals, computers, and networks. With the increasing interdependence of data processing and data communications, and the increasing variety of products and services offered by telecommunications vendors, a basic knowledge of protocol is vital to every accountant/business advisor. But as the complexity of the communication task has increased, so has the number and complexity of the protocols. The accountant/business advisor attempting to understand a data communications system is often overwhelmed by the resulting jargon and confusion.

The physical interconnection protocols are those dealing with the physical interconnection between the communications system and the data terminal or computer. They specify the shape and size of the interconnecting plugs, the electrical characteristics of the signals appearing on the plugs' pins, and the meanings of those signals. Some pins carry data, some carry timing and synchronization signals, others carry control signals used to coordinate the actions of network and terminal (e.g., a signal indicating that the modem is ready for operation.

The next one is the data link control protocol. A simple physical connection is not sufficient to guarantee accurate transmission of data. Both sender and receiver must agree on a protocol to detect and recover from errors, to initialize operations, and to handle multiple terminals on computers on the same physical line. The data link control protocol handles these functions. Software or hardware programmed to handle the rules described in the protocol standard are installed in terminals and computers where they can process data just before the data is transmitted over the physical interface, or just after the data is received from the interface.

The start/stop protocol, which is virtually no protocol at all, is normally used for asynchronous (teletype-like) communications where characters are transmitted individually, without first being collected into groups of characters, or blocks. It specifies only a simple error-detecting parity check scheme and provides synchronization for individual characters.

Network connection management protocols define the formats to be used in transactions between user equipment and the network's switching systems. It is possible to interconnect different networks, allowing data traffic to flow from one network through others to reach a remote destination. Specialized gateway protocols are used to control the transfer of addressing, billing, and supervisory information among the participating networks.

End-to-end transport protocols can be used to carry data and ensure that it is delivered accurately, despite any failures on the part of the network.

Service protocols are usually run as applications programs and use formats that are standardized by the service protocols to transfer files, mail, and terminal traffic over the connections provided by the other protocols discussed.

A respectable number of stable, well-defined, vendor-independent protocols are available. Users must rely on vendor-specific protocols that are usually not constructed to handle traffic between different vendors' equipment.

**WALL-TO-WALL CARPETING, AIR CONDITIONING, AND COMMUNICATIONS.**   The landlord is called when the plumbing breaks down, or when the air conditioning suddenly dies—why not when communications and data processing equipment fails? You're more likely to do that now than ever, as real estate developers and owners identify shared tenant telecommunications services as part of the value-added sales pitches for their office space. These services— from the simple management of telephone installation to development of a national network offering shared data processing—will draw tenants who, perhaps, could not afford them individually. Some of the shared tenant services include voice terminals, intelligent workstations, personal computers, key systems, PBXs, local area networks, facsimile, electronic mail, and teleconferencing.

**MAIN ISSUES AHEAD.**   The major challenges for telecommunications as well as for data processing and office automation are compatibility and integration. For years, few words passed between the telecommunications manager and the data processing manager. In addition to the fact that neither had much interest in the other's operations, they also spoke different languages. The bands and bandwidth banter of the telecom group was unintelligible to the data processors who spoke in bits and bytes. The fields of voice and data were miles apart.

Now, these turfs are not only closer, but in many cases they overlap. A voice/ data PBX can serve as the cornerstone of a corporate communications system or as the backbone of an office automation system. Financial consolidation and reporting systems are as dependent on effective telecommunications as on efficient data processing. Technologies are becoming relatively easy to integrate; job functions are more difficult to integrate. It's time to bridge the divide between telecom managers and managers. And the gap is great.

Although telecom managers have been around twice as long as DP managers, their role through the years has remained more static. Trained largely by the Bell System, telecom managers functioned in a relatively controlled environment. They operated a budget based on current, and recurring, costs. Corporate communications was an expense item that was predictable at least five years out. "Ma Bell's" steady rate hikes had to be anticipated and taken into account, but there were few other variables. The work of telecommunications managers (often thankless) was seldom challenged—either technologically or by corporate management.

Situated in another corner of the corporate basement was the DP department. Masters of mystique, these DP types had quite a different budget to manage. Weighted down with multimillion dollar capital expenditures, the DP budget was not only mammoth, but also unpredictable. With so much money and human resources funneled into their departments, DP managers had frequent and often frustrating accountability sessions with corporate management. What's more, the expertise of the DP department was constantly being challenged by young whippersnappers, those fresh, feisty computer science graduates armed with the latest in this fast-changing technology.

What happened, of course, is history. The DP department moved up fast. Having tackled the challenges of constant change, ever-bulging budgets, and a growing dependence on them by corporate management, data processing managers had gained—whether by force or by fiat—valuable management expertise. Soon, DP managers were within earshot and arm's reach of top management. And where was the telecom manager all this time? Still plugging away at the formula for assessing next year's corporate telephone costs.

The tables have turned on telecommunications managers. Today they face the management challenges that were met head-on by DP managers 10 to 15 years ago. Job responsibility includes both voice and data, and often spreads into the realms of data processing and office automation. And just when the pace of technological change picked up, the long-incumbent telecom supplier packed it in. The dismantled AT&T can now be eyed as an option rather than an assumption. That means capital expenditures loom large; indeed, corporate management is banking on its ability to depreciate some telecom equipment over time to keep communications costs down. The telecom manager-turned-purchasing agent has a much bigger budget to manage—and it's an elastic one at that.

Telecom managers are now in the limelight. Their challenge is greater than the management of what's traditionally been considered the telecommunications turf. It stretches well into the field of DP. That same challenge, in reverse, holds for the DP manager.

The technologies now talk to each other. So should the managers.

# EDP AUDITING

The EDP auditor must have programming knowledge, an understanding of computer operations, the ability to report uncomfortable truths to upper management, and the ability to provide computerized support and advice to financial auditors. The EDP auditor has to keep abreast of federal regulations and be aware of innovations in hardware and software technology within the industry. Many of the functions the EDP auditor provides are as a business advisor with respect to the EDP function.

The two main functions of an EDP auditor are to verify controls and identify exposures.

The heart of the word *exposure* is a reasonable chance that something bad may occur. To a corporation, losses or bankruptcy are the possibilities. The EDP auditor looks for the possibility of loss and the degree of risk involved. If the risk is low and the chance of loss is low, odds are that management will elect to accept the risk. Most of the time, the EDP auditor will find low-loss and low-risk exposures, but will still report them to management. It is the EDP auditor's duty to report all significant findings to management, and this includes any and all exposures. It is up to management, not the EDP auditor, to decide what action will be taken. If the EDP auditor did not report his or her complete findings and a loss occurred from some nonreported exposure, legal action would be likely.

Reporting exposures and recommendations to management is relatively easy, but finding the exposures is another matter. About 70 percent of an EDP auditor's time is spent gathering information. In order to get this information, he or she uses a variety of tools. Some of the more common ways to gather data include the use of questionnaires, checking documentation, checking the source code, and testing the master files.

Interviewing personnel is the most basic tool an EDP auditor has because it permits greater insight into the area being examined. Although structured questionnaires can be used as guidelines, the EDP auditor also relies on experienced department personnel to find the necessary information. Although interviews are useful, they do have drawbacks. Most people are nervous when questioned by a member of the Auditing Department. They believe the EDP auditor is trying to find fault with them or their jobs, but EDP auditors are far more concerned with finding fact than fault.

Examining documentation is another way the EDP auditor learns about a particular operation. This is not as effective as many other tools, because documentation is usually out-of-date or nonexistent. Up-to-date system information is actually much more valuable to the programmers, operators, and users than the EDP auditor. That's why he or she informs management of the lack of documentation for the benefit of the operations as a whole.

Checking the source code is an excellent tool for EDP auditors who understand a particular language, and an aggravation to the programmers who wrote it. Many programmers believe that the auditor is criticizing their coding ability or attempting to find some code that has been defrauding the company for years.

In reality, the EDP auditor uses source code to try and follow the flow of data in the system to understand how the computer is used in a particular application. But also he or she will look at certain sections of code to see if interest is being skimmed or if accounts that should be charged are not. This should not automatically convey suspicion upon the programmer. Rather, it is a general scan that is used, "just in case." He or she needs the knowledge to write a program, but not the ability to compile or run that program in the system. The EDP auditor should have a programming tool available, but it must be more controllable than COBAL or BASIC.

EDP auditors should be able to verify information in the master files themselves to see if it is complete and accurate, that no invalid codes are present, and to verify balance information when necessary. File information is usually checked against the output from the system or from general ledger balances.

Audit software can be used by the EDP auditor to perform all of the functions mentioned, plus some specialized ones, without causing any damage, updates, or modifications to the master files. And, audit software has more controls built into it to help prevent errors. Even a generalized report writer can be used effectively by auditing without damage to the system.

The greatest concern of an EDP auditor is finding exposures. Fraud is one exposure; others include business interruptions, competitive disadvantage, erroneous management decisions, errorneous record keeping, excessive costs, loss or destruction of assets, and unacceptable accounting.

Potential problems include data entry errors, mounting the wrong input, eating or drinking near the computer, taking tapes or master file printouts home, and firing an employee but not restricting access to the computer.

Internal auditors keep a close watch on the EDP auditor to assure that he or she is doing the job properly and checking the areas that most concern management. External auditors (both financial and EDP) examine the reports and working papers filled out by the EDP auditor, and also check that the EDP auditor is following the guidelines set forth in the EDP auditor manual. Regulating agencies double-check the work done to see if their guidelines for auditing are being followed. Management makes sure that the EDP auditor is adequately addressing its concerns. Data processing programmers and operators check to ascertain that the EDP auditor is following their department guidelines.

In summary, typical EDP audit tasks include:

Normal financial audits (i.e., without significant EDP aspects)

Traditional post installation reviews (e.g., of controls in an installed application)

Computer installation review (simple review of security and operating procedures; nonpolicy, nonmanagement review)

Operational audit of EDP Department (review of efficiency, effectiveness, adherence to policy and so on, of EDP Departments; may include EDP management)

System feasibility studies (participation in or review of hardware - software purchase or make decisions)

System design control: reviews (review of controls in a proposed EDP system)

Project control review of timeliness, cost, and the like in an ongoing EDP project

User of an audit software package

Consultant to other auditors on use of audit software

Writing computer programs for audit or usage

EDP consultant or team member responsible to EDP for non-EDP audit staff

Designer of generalized audit software

Traditional test checking of installed system

Acceptance testing of new EDP systems (i.e., before installation of system)

Supervise or sign-off on EDP system, work of non-EDP auditors

Supervise other EDP auditors

Conduct training of auditors in EDP topics

Use of integrated test facility approach

Use of COBOL missed branch indicator or other analyzer of tests

Use of (DBMS) as an audit tool

Review of EDP adherence to recent legislation (e.g., privacy legislation)

# OFFICE AUTOMATION

In the world of office automation (OA), the past few years have been relatively serene. It has been a time of consolidating technological resources, starting to take advantage of OAs potential and assessing the importance of the personal computer. The next few years, on the other hand, look as if they will be years of explosive change.

The forces of change, frustrated by a lack of standards, unworkable systems, and business's sensible reluctance to commit capital to short-term solutions, seem about to break free. This means that some of the long-promised benefits of an integrated approach to office automation will become a reality.

Technology is not going to take a dramatic leap forward, but, rather, the last pieces of the OA puzzle are falling into place: the matrix of available tools, users' perception of the application of these tools, and users' understanding of their needs.

**INTEGRATION.**    Office automation is moving toward integration. Users have had enough of isolated OA tools. It's time to get these machines talking to each other. This push toward getting things to work together is the driving force behind the three primary product areas that users and vendors believe will be at the forefront of OA for the next few years: local area networks (LAN), integrated software, and laser printers.

Local nets offer the promise—and are finally starting to deliver on that promise—of tying dissimilar machines together so that users can easily share and exchange information. Integrated software has the potential to make what's done at each user's machine easier, more consistent, and better integrated. Compact, relatively inexpensive laser printers tie the package together by working possible widespread distribution of departmental print servers on a network.

The integration of information resources also manifests itself in the micro-mainframe connections; optical storage and ergonomically designed offices. Micro-mainframe links allow integration of departmental-level personal computer (PC) clusters with corporate mainframes. Optical disks give users the capability to pack the storage capacity of a tape drive or disk pack or two into a desktop cabinet the size of a typewriter. People are now focusing on how best to support their equipment and the people who use it.

One item to look at is the high-bandwidth cabling for networks, which allows the mixing of voice, data, and video information on the same wiring. The megabits-per-second are impressive. This all-purpose voice, data, video highway is of interest to companies, especially the Fortune 100. The combined voice-data workstation is beginning to appear. It is a logical blending of computer and telephone.

Other items to consider are voice, mail, and portable computers. The OA market has been disjointed, confused, and suspicious of the impact the personal computer might have. The chaos the PC proliferation engendered, together with the infusion of other technologies into the OA domain, did little to improve the OA situation. Things are beginning to clear up, and to calm down a little. Businesspeople are beginning to see how they can actually use the various technologies.

The learning curve has been steep. MIS managers, OA coordinators, telecommunications managers, microcomputer support people and planners have all had to learn a new language and have had to begin working closely with people whose jobs didn't exist before now. Office automation buyers can start hooking up the disparate bits and pieces of OA and watch that very real synergy of integrated office systems come to life on users' desktops.

**ELECTRONIC MAIL.**    Alternative delivery methods, new applications, integration of text with voice messages and images, and the use of personal computers to exchange messages are among the trends in electronic mail. Electronic mail will work for most businesses and should be used to process text, voice messages, and images. Electronic mail is a dynamic, changing industry and it is essential to OA.

Alternative methods of delivery allow electronic mail users to send electronic messages to recipients who have the proper equipment and written messages to others. There are new services that transmit, electronically, messages across the country to dispatch centers where the messages are printed and hand-delivered within two hours. Applications in electronic mail permit an organization to track transactions such as sales and orders and to relay the reports to remote offices.

Integration means giving the user the option of leaving a verbal message instead of typed message or the opportunity to attach documents such as contracts or graphs to messages.

The use of PCs as workstations for accessing electronic mail systems will increase as will the use of integrated message systems where voice and text complement each other. Voice messages are better suited for short, personal messages, whereas text is better for longer messages or communications that may require a paper record for legal reasons. Additionally, text allows easy scanning of messages for key points, data extraction, message reuse, and conversion of text into voice.

**VOICE STORE AND FORWARD.**    A voice store and forward messaging system is similar to electronic mail. At the heart of the system is the capability of digitizing analog speech and storing it on hard disk for late retrieval. Typically, users are assigned voice mailboxes and access codes. In order to use the voice mail system, the user dials the system's extension on his or her telephone and logs on as if logging onto a terminal. The user then listens to messages sent to him or her and disposes of them by saving them on disk for future reference, deleting them, forwarding them (with, if desired, a brief annotation) to another person, or answering them directly. Or, he or she can record a new message and send it to some subset of the total number of users. Once installed, these systems become addictive.

The key is to have a complete voice mail system, with overflow capabilities, message waiting signals, and ease of use along with return receipt and private designations for messages that users either want to know have been received or want to prevent from being forwarded on to other persons.

Voice mail will be offered as a standard service to most private automatic branch exchanges users by the end of the 1980s. Voice store and forward will become an added value to office systems, especially for managers and executives.

# CHAPTER 9

# THE ACCOUNTANT AS TAX ADVISOR

## Leon Lipner

## INTRODUCTION

The basic objective of any business is to give its investors a return that is greater than can be earned in an entity over which investors have no direct control (such as holding stocks or bonds in publicly held corporations, or investing in governmental securities). The return on investment in a business may take one or more forms.

The most common conception of return on a capital investment is a direct return, such as in the form of dividends from a corporation, or withdrawals of capital from an unicorporated entity. However, there are other concepts to be considered as a return on capital. In a closely held business, the return may also be in the form of salaries to employees-shareholders, and in receiving "fringe" benefits not subject to income taxation at the recipient level, but nevertheless deductible as "ordinary and necessary" business expenses by the paying entity. Or, it may well be potential appreciation in the value of the entity. Obviously, the maximum retention of after-tax dollars is the prime objective to be considered.

There are other nonfinancial rewards that may be obtained from the operation of a business, such as the feeling of well-being or additional freedom (frequently illusory). An analysis of these objectives, however, is best left to the owners themsleves rather than the accountant, and will not be considered herein. This chapter will devote itself to considering those tax factors that allow for the greatest retention of funds from operating a business.

The type of business on which we will primarily concentrate will be the closely held one (whether it be an individual proprietorship, partnership, or corporation) as distinguished from that of a publicly held entity. The accountant or auditor to such a business is in a unique position to be an advisor when considering tax issues. As with other technical areas in this book, however, the accountant should seek help from tax experts, where necessary.

Throughout the chapter, there are various tax citations in footnotes. These will provide valuable reference sources for those who have a basic familiarity with tax research.

# DETERMINING THE FORM OF OWNERSHIP OF A BUSINESS

**TAX AVOIDANCE.**   It is the inherent right of taxpayers to use all legal forms at their disposal to limit the amount of taxes that must be paid. Proper planning to minimize taxes is not an immoral activity. Whereas tax evasion is illegal, tax avoidance is perfectly proper. The words of the late Justice Learned Hand, formerly of the Circuit Court of Appeals, written in a decision in the case of *Commissioner* v. *Newman*, best reflect this. In that case, Justice Hand wrote:

> Over and over again courts have said that there is nothing sinister in so arranging one's affairs as to keep taxes as low as possible. Everybody does so, rich or poor; and all do right, for nobody owes any public duty to pay more than the law demands: taxes are enforced extractions, not voluntary contributions. To demand more in the name of morals is mere cant.[1]

**UNINCORPORATED ENTITIES.**   The first tax consideration in orgainizing of a business is choosing the form of business entity. All business entities can be classified as either unincorporated or incorporated. In the unincorporated sector, we may have either an individual proprietorship or a partnership. Obviously, in an individual proprietorship, there is only one owner. As soon as you have an unincorporated entity with more than one owner, you have a partnership of one form or another. The term *partnership* encompasses such things as *joint ventures*, *syndicates*, *pools*, and any other type of unincorporated entities not otherwise classified (such as trusts or estates).

In the case of both individual proprietorships and partnerships, the income (or loss) is not taxed individually to the entity but rather flows through to the owner (or owners) and is co-mingled with other elements of income, gains, or losses which go into the determination of taxable income. The nature of the

---

[1] *Commissioner* v. *Newman*, 159 Fd.2d 848(2nd Cir. 1947). Also cited in 47-1 USTC 9175, and 35 AFTR 857.

income or deduction generally retains its character in the flow-through and is unchanged. There is no provision in federal statutes for the taxation of income at the unincorporated entity level.[2] The entity is merely a conduit to the owners.

The federal partnership return (Form 1065) serves merely as an information return and lists each partner's distributive share of partnership income or loss. Where the items that comprise such income or loss are specifically treated on the owner's return, they are separately delineated on the partnership form. They then pass through to the owner with the character of the income, deduction, or credit remaining unchanged, and are shown separately from the distributive share. These include items such as charitable contributions and the investment tax credit which have limitations on the individual 1040 federal tax return.

Choosing the form of business entity is the first major decision in organizing a business. This is a decision which should be based on factors other than income taxation. That does not mean that income tax considerations should not enter into the picture, but instead means that there are other considerations as well. Probably the major single nontax factor to be taken into account is the fact that in the unincorporated entity, the owner (or partners) will have unlimited liability, whereas in an incorporated entity there is limited liability.[3]

Once the nature of the entity is determined, the business utilizes this form in its operations. However, the decision as to form is not irrevocable forever. A change from unincorporated to incorporated form may be made, frequently without triggering any tax consequences. A change from the incorporated form to the unincorporated form, however, will generally trigger some tax consequences. The severity of such tax consequences will depend on the method used to change the form of entity and will be discussed later on.

The major emphasis of this chapter will be on corporate taxation, on the assumption that the concept of limited liability is of such overriding importance

---

[2] This is not necessarily so at the state or city level. For example, New York City taxes the unincorporated entity by the imposition of an unincorporated business tax, as well as taxing the same income on the owners' tax returns. New Jersey and Connecticut have, at one time or another, also imposed taxes upon the unincorporated entity which were related to the income of the business (even though it may be gross income). There may be other state or city jurisdictions that also assert some form of tax on the unincorporated entity.

[3] This statement is narrowed when there is a limited partnership. In a limited partnership, the limited partners' liability is only to the extent of their investment. In such a situation, it is frequently feasible to have the best of two possible worlds—limited liability, and taxation as an unincorporated entity. Even in a limited partnership, however, there must be at least one general partner whose liability is unlimited. A corporation may be a general partner, but the Internal Revenue Code (IRC) imposes restrictions so that the general partner cannot be a "dummy" corporation with no (or insignificant) assets. However, any individual (no matter how limited his or her assets may be) can be a general partner.

as to make the corporation the entity of choice. However, some of the topics covered herein, such as methods of accounting, financial versus tax reporting, the use of the installment method and deferred compensation plans (covered elsewhere), apply both to the unincorporated entity as well as the corporation.

Every business, regardless of its nature, must file a federal income tax return, although the partnership return does not use the word *tax* in its title, because of its conduit nature. The period of time to be covered cannot be for more than one year. A new business will have to select a fiscal year. If the entity is a sole proprietorship, then the year must conform to that of the individual owner (usually a calendar year). If the entity is a partnership, the year is usually required to be a calendar year, although there are certain exceptions provided for in the law. If the entity is a "C" corporation (as distinguished from an "S" corporation), there is a wide latitude in the selection of the fiscal year. The last day of any month can be selected as the end of the fiscal year. The first year may therefore be a short year (one that is less than 12 months). Under no circumstances can it ever exceed one year.[4]

# SELECTION OF AN ACCOUNTING METHOD

Selecting a method of accounting is another major decision. No uniform method is mandated for all taxpayers, and taxpayers should select the method most suitable for their individual purposes. In some instances, however, a method of accounting may be mandatory. The IRC provides that "if no method of accounting has been regularly used by the taxpayer, or if the method of accounting does not clearly reflect income, the computation of taxable income shall be made under such method as in the opinion of the Secretary or his delegate, does clearly reflect income."[5] The phrase "clearly reflects income" gives the IRS the power to attempt to change a taxpayer's method of accounting when it is felt that there has been unreasonable application of a method. Fortunately, the IRS has generally not attempted to exercise such right except in cases where the facts would indicate a clear-cut distortion of income.

---

[4] The 52- or 53-week year is not an exception to this rule. This is a tax year that varies from 52 to 53 weeks and always ends on the same day of the week. The use of such an accounting period is merely one that allows certain businesses (such as retail department stores, food establishments, and theaters, among others), which normally end their accounting period on the same day of the week, to adopt the same method for federal income tax purposes. This eases the bookkeeping and accounting problems for such businesses.

[5] IRC Section 446(b). Reference to the "Secretary" is to the Secretary of the Treasury. "Delegate" means the Commissioner of Internal Revenue (or any duly authorized employee of the IRS).

**TYPES OF PERMISSIBLE METHODS.**    The permissible methods outlined in the IRC are:

1. Cash receipts and disbursements method
2. Accrual method
3. Any other permitted method (such as the installment sales or long-term contract methods)
4. Any combination permitted under the regulations prescribed (commonly called "the rags")

A cash basis taxpayer takes income into account only when received (actually or constructively), and deducts expenses only when paid. An accrual basis taxpayer takes income into account when earned (regardless of when it is received) and deducts expenses when incurred rather than when paid.

In the case of a business where inventories are involved, the accrual method is mandatory (at least in the area of sales and purchases or in the calculation of gross income). Furthermore, the valuation of the opening and closing inventories must also be taken into account. At a later point, there will be a discussion as to how an inventory may be priced, and of some of the alternate methods available.

**CASH METHOD.**    Generally speaking, in a business where inventories are not an income-determining factor (as in a service business, or a professional practice), the cash method will frequently be selected as the method of choice. In such a business, income tends to be realized at a later time than expenses. Accounts receivable, although they may exist, are not recognized as income. Rather, the income is reported only when the account receivable is paid. Expenses, on the other hand (especially salaries and wages), usually are paid out earlier than the income is received. Utilization of the cash receipts and disbursements method will generally result in a permanent deferment in the payment of taxes.

**ACCRUAL METHOD.**    Ideal as the cash method may appear to be from a tax savings point of view, it is not permitted (as has been mentioned) where inventories are involved. There the taxpayer *must* normally use the accrual method. If the taxpayer is engaged in two or more separate businesses, however, a different method of accounting may be used for each, so that one business can use the accrual method and another the cash method. Separate records must be kept for each business to reflect the income according to the method used.

If the taxpayer has unwittingly adopted a method that is not permissible under the IRC, but has consistently followed such method (although clearly erroneous), the IRS, on audit, may choose to allow such an erroneous method. The theory is that, once a method has been used consistently over the years, the distortions in the reporting of income have tended to be equalized. It should be noted that this discretion is left to the IRS and should not be relied on by the taxpayer. The IRS may also attempt to institute an accounting method change if it feels that it is advantageous to do so.

**INSTALLMENT METHOD.**　The use of installment accounting is also a permissible method. Under this method, the recognition of gain or income is deferred, and is recognized only as cash installment payments are received. This allows the taxpayer to pay the tax under the accrual method when the payments are to be strung out over a period of time. Installment sales accounting used to be elective at one time, but since the enactment of the Installment Sales Revision Act of 1980, the use of this method is mandated unless the taxpayer specifically elects out of it.

**CONSTRUCTION ACCOUNTING METHODS.**　For taxpayers in the construction industry, the "completed contract" method is available for the reporting of income. This method defers the recognition of income until such time as a construction job is essentially completed. It is interesting to note that the taxpayer may use "completed-contract" for tax purposes, while using "percentage-of-completion" for financial statement purposes. This latter method recognizes income on a ratable basis as the job progresses. Of course, either method may be used for both tax and accounting purposes.

The proper selection of an accounting method is a decision that will facilitate the planning for retention of funds in a business. We will not discuss the technicalities of changing a method of accounting which has been adopted and utilized in prior years. Suffice it to say that this is possible; when the need arises, some research is necessary to determine the then current requirements to institute such a change.

# CAPITALIZATION

Another decision that must be made at the inception of a corporation is the capitalization of the business. The original investment in the business, whether it be designated as *common stock*, *preferred stock*, *contributed capital*, or any combination of them, is deemed to be the permanent capitalization of the business, and may not be diminished by voluntary withdrawals. Loans, on the other hand, usually may be withdrawn from the business without the incurrence of a penalty (in the form of a tax on dividends), and without violating any state laws.

**USE OF LOANS.** From the investor's point of view, the use of loans to structure the capitalization of a business may be preferable to the use of stock. Furthermore, interest on the loans is deductible as a business expense, whereas dividends are not, and can only be paid with after-tax dollars. This freedom to take money out of the corporation and/or to get an interest deduction leads many to attempt to capitalize a business with as many "loans" as possible and with a minimum of capital stock. Such a situation gives rise to what is known as the "thin" capitalization problem. The IRS has long been aware of this problem, and has, on many occasions, challenged the taxpayer and contended that the alleged debt of the corporation is, in reality, an equity interest, and has attempted to deny to the stockholders the advantages of capitalizing by the use of debt.[6] If the IRS is sustained in its position, then the debt will be considered to be a form of stock, and any withdrawals of principal and interest will be considered to be dividends (to the extent of available earnings and profits). The question arises as to how much debt will be allowed as reasonable, but there is no definitive answer to this question. A frequently relied on rule of thumb is that debt will be considered to be reasonable if it does not exceed the capital of the corporation by three or four times. Too much reliance cannot be placed on such a ratio, however, because the courts have been inconsistent on this issue. In reality, it means that each corporation must decide for itself as to what the debt-equity ratio should be and, if challenged, to be prepared to argue its decision.

In 1969, Congress added Section 385 to the IRC. This section lists several factors that may be applied to determine whether a stockholder-corporation relationship (capital) or a debtor-creditor relationship (loan) exists. The Secretary of the Treasury was empowered to prepare regulations in this area. Because of the complexity of the problems, however, no final regulations have ever been put into effect. Several times, proposed regulations were slated to become final, but each time the proposed regulations were withdrawn before the effective date.

---

[6] The question may arise as to whether the IRS has the power to change the classification of debt to equity. The authority exists in the Code; Section 385 deals with this problem. Even in the absence of Section 385 the IRS would still be able to make the claim.

There is a whole area of problems in federal income taxation dealing with "substance over form." The consequences of a transaction should depend on the "substance" rather than the "form" of the transaction. In addition to "loans" being reclassified as "equity," the IRS has the authority to classify a "salary" as a "dividend," and to ignore so-called "sham" transactions. This authority also extends to areas other than those cited here.

As a result, the only guide available to the taxpayer is essentially the "rule of reason." The debt, if that is what it is, should be in proper legal form, calling for a legitimate rate of interest, with an indicated time of repayment. The decision to capitalize with the use of debt is one that should be given consideration. However, there must be an awareness of the problems related thereto.

**SECTION 1244.**   We cannot leave a discussion of the organization of a corporation without mentioning Section 1244. This is a relief section for stockholders of a corporation who may lose money on the sale of their corporate stock or on liquidation of the corporation. Normally, a sale or exchange of corporate stock triggers a capital gain or loss. If there is a gain, capital gain treatment is beneficial, but capital losses obviously are not as desirable as ordinary losses. Section 1244 converts what would otherwise be a capital loss into an ordinary loss (and fully deductible against other income). Section 1244 presently provides for this special treatment on the first $1 million of common stock issued by any corporation for property. This privilege is limited to individual taxpayers. The maximum loss deductible by an individual on a separate return is $50,000, and $100,000 on a joint return. Capital loss treatment applies to amounts in excess. This is a "no-lose" situation. If the disposition of the stock results in a gain, Section 1244 does not apply. If there is a loss, at least the severity of the loss can be partially mitigated by the tax savings resulting from an ordinary loss rather than a capital loss.

# MINIMIZING INCOME TAXES

Once the problems of capitalization have been resolved, attention can be directed to the major objective of the business, which is obviously that of maximizing profits and giving the investors an adequate return on investment, whether or not such a return is paid out in dividends or is retained in the business.

The minimization of income taxes obviously goes hand in hand with the maximization of income. Keeping income taxes down, however, generally means keeping taxable income down as well (at least for income tax purposes). It is here that an antithetical situation may exist. In order for a business to obtain financing (either long-term or short-term), the business has to present financial statements. Obviously, the better the financial statements are the easier it will be to obtain financing. Thus, we face a situation wherein the business would like to present the best possible picture for financial statement purposes, and yet would like to show as little income as possible for income tax purposes. Within reason, it is possible to do so, because the rules in accounting for financial statement purposes are different than those used for income tax purposes.

**GENERALLY ACCEPTED ACCOUNTING PRINCIPLES VERSUS THE INTERNAL REVENUE CODE.** In the presentation of financial statements, the business is required to follow generally accepted accounting principles (GAAP), whereas for income tax purposes, the rules of the IRC must be used. These are not necessarily synonymous in all areas. Thus, it is possible, for example, to use one method of depreciation for financial accounting purposes and another method for income tax purposes. Generally accepted accounting principles merely require the use of a proper method. They are silent as to what is permissible for tax purposes.

On the other hand, the IRC spells out the rules for accounting for depreciation and is not concerned about the method used for financial accounting purposes. Where such a situation exists, it is possible to use a method that will limit the amount of depreciation taken for statement purposes, and will maximize the amount to be taken for tax purposes, thereby reducing the income tax.[7]

**DEFERRED TAXES.** The company is required by GAAP to take into account the potential tax liability which is being deferred, and does require the inclusion of the deferred amount as an expense of the current period (under the "matching" concept of accrual accounting). It also requires the recognition of the deferred income tax liability on the balance sheet. The income tax applicable to the deferral can be shown as a separate item on the income statement, however, the deferred income tax liability will not be shown as a current liability (except for the portion that will reverse within the next year). Rather, the deferred income tax liability will be shown separately (generally after long-term liabilities) on the balance sheet. This treatment allows for a better working capital ratio. As a general rule, the individual who analyzes the financial statement will give little consideration to deferred income tax liability in making a decision.

In economic times such as at present, in an inflationary economy, the deferred income tax liability will merely increase over the years. Those items that will become a current liability will be replaced by other items (usually of greater dollar amount). In any event, the ability to defer income taxes, regardless of its effect (or lack of effect) on the income statement or the balance sheet, will help to improve the cash flow of the business.[8]

---

[7] As of January 1, 1981, the rules for depreciation for income tax purposes have been generally liberalized. We now have available the accelerated cost recovery system (ACRS) for assets acquired subsequent to December 31, 1980. This system allows for a rapid write-off of assets to a greater extent than formerly permissible. Included in the ACRS rules is permission to use shorter asset lives than used for book purposes. Prior to 1981, even if the methods used for book and tax purposes were different, the estimated useful lives had to be the same. This is no longer a requirement.

[8] The rules to be followed for the accounting treatment of income taxes are covered in Accounting Principles Board (APB) Opinion Number 11, which is still the definitive pronouncement in this area, and comprises an important segment of generally accepted accounting principles.

Depreciation accounting has been used as an example for reflecting differences between book and tax accounting. There are other areas where differences in accounting are permissible. Included in these is the accounting for long-term contracts mentioned earlier. There are two methods in this area. One is the "percentage-of-completion" (with its many variations), and the other is the "completed contract" method. It is permissible to use "percentage of completion" for book purposes (which, incidentally, is the method that bonding companies generally insist on), and to use the "completed contract" method for tax purposes.

**ACCOUNTING FOR INVENTORIES.**　There is one area, however, in which no deviation between book and tax accounting is allowed; this is in the accounting for inventories. An unequivocal statement can be made, which is that the inventories used for tax purposes must be identical with those used for book purposes. This is not because GAAP says so, but rather because the IRC takes such a position. Section 471 requires that inventories conform "as nearly as may be to the best accounting practice in the trade or business and as most clearly reflecting the income." It is this requirement which has created a major upheaval in the accounting for inventories by many businesses.

As has been noted, a major objective is to minimize the current income tax liability. The lower the ending inventory is, the smaller the current year's income and tax liability will be. The desire to reduce taxes has to be weighed against the desire to present the best financial statement possible. In the area of inventories, these two desires go in opposite directions. If income tax reduction wins out over financial statement presentation, then a way will have to be found to report inventories at the lowest amount possible.

**LAST-IN, FIRST-OUT METHOD.**　The above problem has led to the use of the last-in, first-out (LIFO) method in accounting for inventories. When accounting for inventories in a period of rising prices, the LIFO method will generally result in a lower dollar amount for the inventory. Under the LIFO method it is presumed that the most recent goods acquired or manufactured are the goods which are sold first. Presumably, the goods remaining on hand are those which have a lower cost, having been acquired or manufactured at an earlier time, when costs were less. As a result, the inventory value at the end of the year will be less than if the first-in, first-out (FIFO) approach is taken. The LIFO method can be used even if goods can be specifically identified. There are a number of different methods of costing inventories under LIFO. These are too technical in nature to be included herein, but are readily available in any technical tax treatise dealing with this problem.[9]

---

[9]For a good concise discussion of LIFO, for example, see Prentice-Hall, 1986 *Federal Tax Course*, paragraph 2606.

The businesses that can benefit most by utilization of the LIFO method are those where the value of the inventories comprises a large part of the assets, and are large in comparison to sales (where the gross profit percentage is relatively low), where there are fluctuations in the cost of goods included in inventory and in a manufacturing business, or where the production of goods covers a relatively long period of time.

To elect LIFO, Form 970 is required to be filed with the return for the first year in which LIFO is to be used. Once LIFO is adopted, the taxpayer must use this method for all subsequent periods unless permission is obtained from the IRS to change methods.

The foregoing demonstrates the power of the IRC to indirectly promulgate GAAP. Were it not for the prohibition on the part of the Code against a difference in method for the valuation of inventories, the use of the LIFO method as a generally accepted accounting principle would be severely restricted. As it stands, any taxpayer, regardless of the nature of the business, may elect LIFO.[10]

**RECONCILING BOOK VERSUS TAX ACCOUNTING.**    Now that we know that tax accounting does not necessarily have to follow the methods used for financial reporting, how do we reconcile the two approaches? Do we have to "keep two sets of books," as the layperson frequently states? Obviously, this is not the case. We merely have to reconcile the differences. This is done in the case of a corporation on page 4 of the corporate return in Schedule M-1. This schedule begins with income per the financial statement, and the differences in treatment of the various items for book and tax purposes are indicated in the schedule. The final figure is then the income that is reported on the face of the tax return.[11]

The corporate return and the partnership return call for the presentation of an opening and closing balance sheet. We cannot overemphasize the fact, sometimes not understood, that there is only one balance sheet on any given date, and that this is the one which is used for financial reporting purposes. There is no such thing as a tax balance sheet. The reconciliation schedule is used to tie in tax income to book income.

There is also another schedule on the last page of the corporate return (Schedule M-2) which will reconcile beginning and ending retained earnings. The term *retained earnings* is a financial accounting term. The tax term for this is *earnings and profits*. The two items are similar in concept, and indeed may

---

[10] See Regulation 1.472.

[11] Where the taxpayer is a partnership, the reconciliation between book and tax income will appear in a different manner on the tax return. This is because of the unique method of accounting for partnership income for tax purposes. Where the taxpayer is an individual, the tax return calls for no reconciliation between book and tax income.

even be the same, but they need not be. The tax treatment of items such as dividends is based upon *earnings and profits* and not on *retained earnings*. For example, accelerated depreciation reduces retained earnings, but only the straight-line portion is allowed for "earnings and profits," even though the accelerated amount was properly deductible in arriving at the income tax.

The period covered by any tax return cannot exceed one year. The 52-or 53-week return is not an exception, but rather is merely a modification, and is used for the sake of convenience. The fiscal year of an entity must end on the last day of a month (except in the final year). The end of the fiscal year for income taxation has to conform with the year that is used for book purposes. Generally, this will present no problems. In the case of partnerships and S corporations, which will be discussed later, however, the Code now mandates the use of a calendar year for new entities except in certain instances.

**STATE AND LOCAL TAXES.** All too frequently, attention is focused on the federal income tax and the effect of tax planning on state and local taxes is overlooked or given short shrift. The importance of planning, including local taxes, should not be overlooked. These taxes, which are based all or in part on income, have an effect on the ultimate federal tax. All such taxes are deductible in arriving at taxable income for federal income tax purposes, and consideration has to be given to them.

In recent years, local taxing authorties have tended to use income taxes to supply a greater proportion of revenue than at any time in the past. At the time of this writing, there is a constitutional battle going on between state authorities and multibased companies as to how far the states can go in taxing corporate income presumed to have been earned (at least in corporate eyes) outside of a particular state. The final results are not yet in, and the topic is merely mentioned herein in passing to alert the reader to a problem that may present the need for significant tax planning.

**CARRYBACKS AND CARRYFORWARDS.** Regardless of opinions to the contrary, the people who write the tax laws usually try to have the basic elements of fairness built into them. The major attempt in this direction is the availability to taxpayers of the net operating loss (NOL) carryback and carryforward.[12] Simply put, this provision of the tax law allows a loss incurred in one year to reduce the taxable income of another year or years.

A carryback of a currently incurred loss can result in the almost immediate refund of taxes paid in prior years. If the loss is not absorbed by the profits of prior years, it can be carried forward to future years and reduce taxes for such

---

[12] See IRC Section 172.

years. Under present rules, a net operating loss can be carried back three years and forward 15 years.

Prior to 1981, the carryforward was limited to seven years, and, at one time (prior to 1976), it was mandatory that losses be carried back before they could be carried forward. At present, the taxpayer has the option to elect not to carry back a loss, but rather to carry the loss forward. In essence, the taxpayer foregoes the right to an immediate refund, in favor of using the loss against future years' income only. The 15-year period is not extended, however. This election not to carry back must be made on a timely filed (including extensions) return for the year of the loss, and it is irrevocable.

Why would a taxpayer elect to forego an immediate refund? There are several reasons why this may be advisable. First, the utilization of an NOL against future high income years (it is hoped) will result in greater tax benefits than the offset of earlier low income year earnings. Second, there is the fear on the part of many tax practitioners (in the author's opinion, generally unfounded) that the carryback of an NOL may trigger an audit for the earlier years. Although this may have been true at one time, it is not necessarily so at present.

In any event, if the taxpayer decides to utilize the NOL against earlier years, the speediest way to claim the refund is to file Form 1139 for corporate taxpayers.[13] This is called "Corporate Application for Tentative Refund." If this form is filed, the Treasury Department will make every effort to issue a refund within a 60-day period, apparently on the assumption that there is a need for the funds on the part of the taxpayers who have sustained losses.

**INVESTMENT TAX CREDIT.**    In recent years, there have been other items that can also be carried back in addition to the NOL. Chief among these is the investment tax credit (ITC). This credit[14] can be carried back three years and forward 15 years. Unlike the NOL, however, the carryback provisions are not optional. So a situation may arise where a taxpayer may have both NOL and ITC carrybacks. Which takes precedence? It has been established that the NOL carryback takes precedence over any other carryback.[15]

---

[13] Form 1045 is used for noncorporate taxpayers.

[14] A credit is not the same as a deduction. Whereas a deduction reduces the taxable income, a credit is a dollar-for-dollar offset against the tax.

[15] This may give rise to a situation where an NOL carryback reduces the income of a prior year, and in that prior year the tax had already been reduced by the application of an ITC. In such a case the NOL nevertheless applies, and the ITC which had been used in that year would be available to be carried back to an earlier year's tax, or be carried forward and be utilized in future years. This can lead to confusion and complications, but no one ever said that the application of the tax laws was easy. Add to this other credits that may also be carried back [e.g., the Work Incentive Credit (WIN)], and the confusion mounts.

The ITC is a credit for qualified investment in eligible business property, and is an important consideration in business and tax planning. In reality, for property eligible for this credit, it is the same as receiving a cash discount on the purchase of an item. To add to the credit's attractiveness, eligibility for it is not limited to the amount of cash invested in an asset. The credit is measured by the total cost of the asset, which is the sum of the down payment and the stream of future payments comprising the cost of the asset.

**LIMITATIONS ON THE INVESTMENT TAX CREDIT.**    The ITC is currently limited to 100 percent of the first $25,000 of tax liability plus 85 percent of the excess over $25,000. It is allowed for the year the property is placed into service, and generally applies to depreciable tangible personal property. The property may be new or used, but only $125,000 of the cost of used property is eligible for the credit. No credit is allowed for ACRS property with a useful life of less than three year. For ACRS three-year property, the credit is 6 percent of the cost of the asset, and for five-year ACRS property, the credit is 10 percent.

If the credit exceeds the amount allowable for the current years, the excess may be carried back and forward as previously mentioned. Credits of prior years are used first and then current credits are used. If qualified property is prematurely disposed of, or otherwise ceases to be qualified property, all or part of the credit may be subject to recapture. If the full 10 percent credit is claimed, the adjusted basis of the property must be reduced by 50 percent of the credit. Alternatively, the basis reduction may be avoided by reducing the 10 percent credit to 8 percent. For three-year property, the reduction is from 6 percent to 4 percent. This election is made on a property-by-property basis.

The ITC normally does not apply to buildings or their structural components. There is an exception for qualified rehabilitation expenditures on certain commercial property and on certified historical structures. This is a specialized and limited area, however, and is not considered here.

When property is needed in a business, frequently a decision must be made as to whether to lease or buy. It is possible for a corporate lessee to get the ITC on agreement with the lessor. The rules are substantially more restrictive for noncorporate lessors and S corporations.

The foregoing is a relatively limited treatment of the ITC to be used by the accountant as a business advisor. It is recommended that a greater familiarization be made with the subject matter when an asset is to be acquired.

Other credits that exist in the law but are not covered herein include the targeted jobs credit and the research and development (R&D) credit, among others. The R&D credit is an interesting credit, which has an expiration date of January 1, 1986. The credit is 25 percent of "qualified research and experimental expenses." For businesses which have expenses of this nature, this credit bears examination.

# ACCOUNTING FOR LONG-TERM (FIXED) ASSETS

**EXPENSING OPTION.**    Even though the acquisitions for fixed assets generally must be capitalized and then systematically written off either through depreciation, depletion allowances, or through other amortization, as always, there are exceptions. The major exception is the provision which allows the taxpayer to deduct currently all or a portion of assets acquired. This provision has only been made available for years beginning after 1981. For 1982 and 1983, the maximum expensing of assets was $5000 in the year in which the asset was acquired. For 1984 and 1985, the total was increased to $7500, and for years beginning in 1986, there is a further increase to $10,000. This expensing is only allowed for assets acquired by purchase and for use in a trade or business. The property must be of such a nature that it would qualify for the ITC if it were not expensed.

There are other restrictions which limit the applicability of expensing. For example, acquiring the asset from related parties, or from other members of a controlled group, would negate using this option. Obviously, if the asset is expensed, it cannot also be depreciated, and the ITC is not available for such an asset.

The expense deduction can be allocated among more than one asset acquired during the year, but any unused deductions cannot be carried over or back to other years. Being forced to give up the ITC in essence means giving up a discount on the purchase price of the asset. Purists, of course, can argue otherwise, possibly using present value concepts, but in the author's experience the utilization of the expensing option has been relatively limited.

**SECTIONS 1231, 1245, AND 1250.**    The disposition of a fixed asset gives rise to the problem of recognizing gain or loss. There should be a familiarity with Sections 1231, 1245, and 1250, which deal with this problem. Section 1231 is a relief provision which, broadly speaking, states that if a depreciable asset is disposed of at a loss, the loss can be deducted as an ordinary loss. On the other hand, if there is a gain on the sale of the asset, the gain can be treated as a capital gain (subject to the provisions of Sections 1245 and 1250, which override Section 1231).

Section 1245 states that, notwithstanding the provisions of Section 1231, the gain on the disposition of personal property assets will be treated as an ordinary gain, to the extent of depreciation taken. Only when this depreciation has been "recaptured" as ordinary income will the excess amount of gain be considered a capital gain.

Section 1245 deals with personal property, whereas Section 1250 deals with real property. The Section 1250 recapture rules are more liberal, however, meaning that a lesser amount of the depreciation taken may be subject to ordinary income taxation. Under Section 1250, except for depreciation taken on an asset which is disposed of in the same year as acquired (in which case all depreciation is recaptured), the amount of recapture is limited only to the depreciation taken which was in excess of what straight-line depreciation would have been, had it been used for the entire period of ownership.

The rules in this area are complex, and are based on when the realty is acquired. It is sufficient to be aware that the depreciation recapture could be less than it would be if the asset is personalty, and when the problem arises, the computation can be made by reference to Form 4797. For realty subject to ACRS rules (for assets acquired subsequent to 1980), where accelerated rates were used, then there will be recapture. In that case, nonresidential realty will have all of the depreciation recaptured (i.e., taxed at ordinary income rates to the extent of all the depreciation taken, instead of being taxed at capital gain rates). There is a slightly more liberal rule for residential realty. Keeping these recapture rules in mind, and with the availability of net operating loss carryovers and carrybacks, it would seem advisable to select straight-line depreciation for real property assets acquired subsequent to 1980. Even if straight-line depreciation is used for nonresidential realty there will nevertheless be some recapture (See Section 291(a)(1) of the Code). This section applies only to corporations and not individuals, thus corporations have more recapture of depreciation under Section 1250 than do individuals.

**ACCELERATED COST RECOVERY SYSTEM DEPRECIATION.** As previously mentioned, the rules for the deduction of depreciation underwent a radical change for years beginning in 1981. The ACRS became effective in that year for assets acquired subsequent to December 31, 1980 and are covered in Section 168 of the Code. For assets acquired prior to January 1, 1981, the provisions of Section 167 still apply. The changes in depreciation allowances are a classic example of where the tax laws are used to further economic policy. ACRS was an attempt to stimulate capital investments by allowing such investments to be deducted over a shorter period of time than was formerly permissible. Gone are the days when the life of an asset, for depreciation purposes, had to have a reasonable relationship to its actual physical life expectancy. For assets acquired in 1981 or thereafter, shorter lives may be used for cost recovery. All assets used in a trade or business have been divided into four class lives. Personalty is divided into 3,5,10, and 15-year lives, and all realty is considered to have a 15-year existence. For personalty, all automobiles, trucks, R&D equipment, and other assets having an ADR life (to be discussed later) of four years or less are deemed to have a class life of three years. Most other tangible personalty, such as machinery and furniture, are deemed to have a life of five years. Some personalty, such as public utility property, amusement park property, and railroad tank cars, are deemed to have a useful life of 10 years. There is some public utility personal property that is deemed to have a class life of 15 years. Commercial and residential realty is generally deemed to have a class life of 18 years. Prior to March 16, 1984 the class life was 15 years. The latter life still applies to low-income housing buildings, however.

Personalty is allowed to be recovered using the 150 percent declining balance method. Commercial realty is allowed to be recovered using the 175 percent declining balance method, and residential realty can use 200 percent declining balance for low income housing and 175 percent for all other residential realty.

In order to simplify the calculations, tables are provided for the percentages to be used. These tables use the half-year convention for personal property but not for real property. Thus, it makes no difference in what month of the year that personal property is acquired; the half-year convention applies (which simply means that the asset is deemed to have been acquired at mid-point during the year).

For those businesses that prefer to use straight-line depreciation, the ACRS rules provide alternatives. Three-year class life assets may use 5 or 12 years as alternatives. Five-year class life assets may use 12 or 25 years. Other personalty may use 25 or 35 years (or even 45 years for some public utility property). Real property may use 35 or 45 years as alternative lives.

For assets acquired prior to 1981, the taxpayer had to select a useful life. The taxpayer's useful life estimate was often at variance with that of the government, and there were frequent disputes between taxpayer and the IRS as to the appropriate life. Over the years, the government tried to establish useful lives for assets in order to diminish these controversies. Furthermore, there is a requirement in Section 167 of the Code that assets should not be allowed to be depreciated below salvage value (whatever that may be). The taxpayer was allowed to ignore salvage value up to 10 percent of the basis of the asset where personalty was concerned.

Section 167 allows various methods of depreciation to be used. Included in these methods is straight-line depreciation, the declining balance method, sum of the years digits, and any other rational method (with some restrictions on the latter). There was a distinction made between new and used properties, and there were some additional restrictions placed on commercial realty. In addition, there was an additional first-year depreciation allowance (optional) on personalty.

**ASSET DEPRECIATION RANGE.** In 1971, the concept of asset depreciation range (ADR) was introduced. This allowed for the grouping of similar assets acquired in any year and depreciating them as a unit. A range of years was provided for each class of assets. If taxpayers used the lower range for an asset group, they would no longer have to worry about being challenged by the IRS as to useful life. In 1981, ADR was replaced by ACRS for assets acquired after 1980.

**TRADE-IN VERSUS SALE.**   When a fixed asset which has been capitalized has outlived its usefulness to the company, a decision has to be made whether or not to trade in the asset for another like kind one, or whether to sell the asset, obtain the proceeds, and then go out and buy the new replacement asset.

The need for this decision is most frequently encountered with company motor vehicles. A trade-in is a nontaxable exchange. The additional cost is added to the undepreciated basis of the asset, and depreciation continues on the total amount. The trade-in rules are mandatory, not optional.

If the value of the old asset is less than its adjusted basis (original cost minus accumulated depreciation), it may be advisable to sell the asset, recognize the loss (which would be a Section 1231 loss and therefore fully deductible), and acquire the new asset. One caveat should be noted in this connection, namely that the sale should be made to someone other than the one from whom the new asset is to be acquired. If the same party is involved both in the buying and the selling, the government could claim "substance" over "form," and recast the transaction into a trade-in, with the resultant elimination of the loss, and with probably a reduction in the amount of depreciation which can be taken currently.

On the other hand, if the asset to be disposed of will generate a gain on the sale (which will be taxed at ordinary income rates under the recapture rules), the transaction should most likely be structured as a trade-in. This will eliminate recognition of current gain.

The effect on the ITC under either a trade-in or a sale is the same. If there is any recapture of ITC, a trade-in will not eliminate such recapture. Rather, the ITC will be recaptured in part on the old asset, and a full ITC will be available on the new asset. One might think that the net effect will be the same in all cases, and usually this is true. However, in a year in which a company utilizes a net operating loss carryforward and eliminates the current year's tax, the ITC recapture on the asset disposed of will have to be paid nevertheless. It cannot be offset against the ITC on the new asset. That ITC will have to be carried back and then forward to a future year. This is because the NOL takes precedence over the ITC.

# ACCOUNTING FOR CURRENT ASSETS

Turning to another area, the company is sometimes faced with the problem of accounting for bad debts, and in what year to take such a bad debt deduction.

Of course, if the company is on a cash basis method of accounting, the question does not arise, because income is not recognized until payment is received. It is safe to say that any business which has been operating for some time will have bad debts. A bad debt is different from an adjustment in the terms of sale, or in the allowance of credits to the customer. Such items are merely price adjustments, and should not be treated as bad debts.

In the case of individuals there can be a business bad debt, or a nonbusiness bad debt. The distinction will not be discussed here, except to note that a nonbusiness bad debt is always treated as a short-term capital loss (with the limitations inherent therein in the ability to be offset against current income in its entirety). A business bad debt, on the other hand, is fully deductible against other income. A corporation's bad debts are always business bad debts.

**"RESERVE" METHOD FOR BAD DEBTS.** The deductibility of bad debts is allowed under either the so-called reserve method, or the direct charge-off method. The method used for income tax purposes must be the same one that is used for financial accounting purposes. Unlike other areas in taxation (such as accounting for depreciation), the Code does not permit alternate methods to be used for bad debts. Use of either method is allowed by GAAP, however, the "reserve" method (the term is an antiquated one, but is still used in taxation), is generally recognized as the method of choice. The concept of matching income and expenses would appear to make this preferable for financial reporting, because the year in which sales are incurred should be charged with the expenses attributable thereto.

Of course, it is usually impossible to determine with certainty the amount of the bad debt losses which will be incurred, so estimates have to be used; and this estimation process takes place for the reserve method. On the other hand, the direct charge-off method does not allow a deduction for bad debts until the debt is worthless, all or in part.[16]

Under the reserve method, a deduction is available in an earlier year, without waiting for proof positive that there is a bad debt. Furthermore, under this method there will always be an amount which has been written off in anticipation of future events, so that there is a tax deduction for something that has not yet occurred. In order that taxpayers do not abuse the bad debt allowance by taking excessive deductions, the IRS, on audit, may challenge the deduction as to the amount. What is a reasonable addition to the reserve account, each year, depends upon the taxpayer's individual circumstances.[17]

---

[16] A deduction is allowed for partially worthless business bad debts. This does allow for a deduction even if there is expectation of some payment. However, the amount taken as a bad debt deduction is subject to attack by the IRS as to the year of deduction. Was the amount written off really nonrecoverable in the year of the write-off?

[17] See Reg. 1.166-4(b)(1) for mention of the relevant factors to be considered.

**BLACK MOTOR COMPANY CASE.** Because of the subjective nature of the bad debt deduction, the IRS frequently uses a formula based on the *Black Motor Company*[18] case. This method uses a six-year moving average approach to come up with a reasonable addition to the reserve, and can limit an otherwise larger deduction to the reserve account in a year. The use of this formula is not binding on the taxpayer, however, and opposition to the Black Motor formula can be defended by the establishment of special circumstances which allow for a larger allowance in one particular year.

Unfortunately, the IRS is gifted with 20–20 hindsight, and if these special circumstances which were anticipated never arose, the deduction may be disallowed in part upon audit. The corporation and partnership tax returns require a schedule of bad debts to be included, which gives a history of receivable balances, sales on account, annual provision for bad debts, recoveries of bad debts, charges against the reserve account, and reserve balances at the end of each of the six most recent years. This gives the agent an indication of the possibility of getting an adjustment to income, and may be a factor to be considered in determining whether a return is to be audited.[19] If it is ever determined that a bad debt reserve is no longer required, and should be reduced, the company has to take the reduction in the balance into income. Such a situation is admittedly rare, but could occur when a company sells off its accounts receivable (to a bank, for instance).

If a decision has been made to use the direct charge-off method, and in a subsequent year, the company wants to use the reserve method, this can be done. Form 3115 is used to make the change. It is filed with the tax return for the year of the change, and a separate copy must be mailed to the IRS during the first nine months (acutally the first 270 days) of the year of the change.[20] In the year of change it is therefore possible to get a bad debt deduction under both methods. For those accounts determined to have become "bad" in the year of the write-off, the direct charge-off method is used. For other accounts still on the books as unpaid, a reserve can be set up.

## DISPOSITION OF ASSETS

The disposition of an asset at a gain (other than in a trade-in transaction) generates the recognition of income. Normally GAAP require that the entire

---

[18] *Black Motor Co.*, 41 BTA 300, affirmed by the 6th Circuit Court in 1942; see 125 F.2d 977.

[19] The IRS guards its audit criteria closely, so that no one outside the Service ever knows exactly what factors go into the audit–nonaudit decision. A statistical approach is used, known as *discriminant function* (DIF), to start. How much weight is given to each factor and what factors are involved are top secret. Even if the taxpayer's return fits the criteria, the agent involved may sometimes override the audit decision, and survey the return as "not worthy of audit."

[20] See Rev. Proc. 82-19 1982-1CB463.

amount of the gain be recognized in the year of sale, regardless of when the money is received.[21] However, for tax purposes, as has been mentioned, all or part of the gain can be deferred. The tax is related to the profit portion of each installment, so that no tax need be paid until the money flows in to the sellers.

**INSTALLMENT METHOD.** Until 1980, the election to use the installment method had to be made in a timely return filed for the year of the sale. There were other restrictions as well. For casual sales of personal property, and for sales of real property, the payments received on principal could not exceed 30 percent of the selling price in the year of sale. This restriction has now been removed. The installment sale method is deemed to be the method of choice unless the seller makes a timely election not to use it. A dealer must, however, continue to make an election to use the installment sales method.

The use of the installment method has no effect on the character of the gain, that is, capital or ordinary. If the character of the gain is both ordinary and long-term capital gain (which occurs when a depreciable asset is sold and the gain is subject to depreciation recapture), however, the use of the installment method mandates the recognition of the ordinary income first. It is only when recognition of all of the ordinary income has been completed that the capital gain portion is recognized. The gain on each installment is not broken up between ordinary and capital gain, as might be expected.

With the ease in now using the installment sales provision, why would anyone elect to opt out of using the method? It may be desirable to do so when a company has an unused capital loss carryover, which, unlike that of an individual, has a time limit to it. In such a case, it could be desirable to recognize the entire gain in the year of sale, and offset the unused capital loss which could otherwise lapse before it could be used against the installment received. Installment sales must be subject to interest on the unpaid principal amounts. If the agreement between the parties is silent as to interest, or if the rate of interest provided for is not adequate, then the government will restructure the entire transaction. It will use a higher interest rate, thereby lowering the selling price, regardless of the term of the contract, and while the gain will be less, the interest portion imputed will be greater, giving the seller more ordinary income.[22] The imputed interest rates will vary depending on whether the transaction took part after December 31, 1984 or not.

One more point should be noted in connection with installment sales. This occurs when property is sold subject to an obligation, such as a mortagage or where the seller assumes a mortgage, and the unpaid balance of the mortgage is greater than the book value of the asset sold. To the extent that the obligation

---

[21] See APB Opinion No. 10.

[22] See Code Section 483(b) and Regulations 1.483-1 and 1.483-2.

transferred to the purchaser is greater than the adjusted basis of the asset, the excess is treated as cash received in the year of sale, and is recognized as such. Furthermore, all subsequent payments on principal are 100 percent taxable when received. The character of the gain, ordinary or capital (or part each), remains unaffected.

**DETERMINING CAPITAL GAIN OR LOSS.**   Determining what is a capital gain (or loss), and what is not, is another problem. The law defines capital assets by exception. All assets are capital assets except those that the Code says are not. Included in noncapital assets are items which would be considered as inventory in the hands of the taxpayer (this includes real property held primarily for sale to customers), accounts and/or notes receivable acquired as a result of the sale of the inventory assets, or acquired for services rendered in the ordinary course of business, and depreciable property or real property used in the taxpayer's business. These are the major items (there are others) with which a business will have to deal.

Note that depreciable property, and real property used in a business, are not capital assets by definition. At first, this may seem to be at odds with the common concept of a capital asset. However, this exclusion does not work to the disadvantage of the taxpayer. That is because of Section 1231, which provides that gains on such assets shall be treated as capital gains, whereas losses on such assets can be deducted in full. This is a relief provision that gives the taxpayer the best of two worlds. However, Section 1231 is subject to the prior imposition of Sections 1245 (since 1962) and 1250 (since 1964). These sections require that, in the case of depreciable personal property (Section 1245), all of the gain to the extent of the depreciation previously taken shall be ordinary and in the case of real property (Section 1250), a part or all of the gain shall be ordinary.

**NETTING SECTION 1231 GAINS AND LOSSES.**   All Section 1231 gains and losses have to be netted for the year. One cannot apply Section 1231 and have a gain treated as a capital gain, and a loss treated as an ordinary loss. It is only if the Section 1231 gains exceed the Section 1231 losses for the year that the net amount will be treated as capital gain. If there is a net loss, it will be treated as an ordinary loss. When a company has both potential Section 1231 gains and losses, it might be wise to consider the timing of the sales of such items to avoid the netting effect. The loss should be taken, if possible, in a different fiscal year from the one in which the gain is taken.

A capital gain or capital loss is the same for a corporation as for an individual, or any other entity; it is the tax treatment that is different. Whereas individual capital gains and losses can be offset all or in part against the ordinary income and may not be carried back, the losses of a corporation cannot be used to offset ordinary income. They can only be carried back and can then offset only capital losses (if any) of the prior three years. If the losses cannot be utilized in a carryback, they may be carried forward for only five years, again only against capital gains. In the case of the individual, unused losses can be carried forward for such individual's lifetime. If the capital losses have not been utilized in that time, they are lost forever.

Long-term capital gains for corporations are not discounted as for individuals. When they occur, they are included like all other elements of income and are taxed accordingly. Whereas individuals have a net effective rate of 20 percent (subject, of course, to a possible alternative minimum tax), the corporation has a limit on capital gain taxation of 28 percent. If the alternative method is advantageous, the corporation can (and should) use an alternative tax method where long-term capital gains exist. Of course, if the corporation does not move into at least the 30 percent bracket, then it is pointless to use the alternative tax. The ordinary tax computation will obviously result in the lesser tax. Long-term capital gains in the hands of a corporation may also be subject to a minimum tax (calculated differently than for an individual) because they are a tax preference item.

Corporations have a maximum over-all tax rate of 46 percent except for corporations which have taxable income of more than $1 million. These have an additional 5 percent on the excess over $1 million limited to an additional tax of $20,250. Corporation rates are no longer substantially higher. Now the top rate is lower than that for individuals. However, there are other drawbacks inherent in the operation of a business in the corporate form. There are the controlled corporation problem, the problem of unreasonable accumulations of retained earnings, and the personal holding corporation trap.

**CONSOLIDATED RETURNS.**   Corporations may, under certain circumstances, file consolidated returns. Also, the filing of consolidated returns no longer subject the return to an additional 2 percent tax rate. Corporations that are members of an affiliated group are entitled to file consolidated returns. This allows the losses of one corporation to offset the profits of another corporation in the same affiliated group. Even though this may be permissible for federal purposes, care must be taken to see that the rules for state purposes are observed. In New York State, for example, notification must be given to the state within 30 days after the close of the fiscal year that a consolidated return will be filed. Other states may have their own rules and some may not permit consolidated returns.

Another advantage of the consolidated return is that gains and losses on intercompany transactions are eliminated. Also eliminated are the taxability of intercompany dividends. Whereas normally 85 percent of dividends from domestic corporations are excluded from taxable income, in the case of an affiliated group, the entire amount of the dividend is exempt.

In order for an affiliated group to exist, there must be the requisite percentage ownership. For financial statement purposes, it is sufficient for one company to prepare a consolidated financial statement as soon as the parent company has more than 50 percent ownership of one or more other companies. This is not so for federal tax purposes. The common parent must own at least 80 percent of each class of nonvoting common stock in at least one other "includible" corporation. Each remaining includible corporation must be 80 percent owned by one or more of the other includible corporations.[23]

Once a group elects to file a consolidated return, it must continue to do so for all subsequent years, unless permission is obtained from the IRS to change. Occasionally, when there is a major change in the law, permission may be granted to change the form of filing without prior approval. If a corporation is disposed of during a fiscal period, through the sale of stock, it could happen that the corporation disposed of is a subsidiary of more than one company during the year, and is a member of two different affiliated groups during the year. In such a situation, it is included within the affiliated group of each parent, for the period of time that it was a member of each group.

**CONTROLLED GROUP.**   All affiliated groups of corporations are part of a controlled group, but not all controlled groups are affiliated groups. As was mentioned previously, it is only affiliated groups that can file consolidated returns. The other types of controlled groups are the brother-sister type and the combined group. The latter may be a combination of a group of corporations, some of which are brother-sister, and some of which are affiliated. Those that are affiliated can, of course, file consolidated returns, but other corporations which are part of the controlled group (the brother-sister corporations) cannot be included in the consolidated return, even though they may all be owned by the same individual or group of individuals. Consolidated returns are permissible only when the common parent is a another corporation.

The concept of the controlled group (other than the affiliated group) came into the law in 1964. It was put in to stop a favorite tax-saving device, namely to organize as many corporations as necessary and to limit the tax for each corporation to the lowest tax bracket. Groups of individual corporations, with as many as 50 corporations all with a common ownership, were not uncommon. Much litigation resulted over the years, and the controlled group concept was put into the law to limit such disputes. At first, if a controlled group existed,

[23] See Code Sections 1501–1505 and the related regulations covering the consolidated return requirements.

then the lower rate(s) had to be apportioned among the various corporations in the group unless an additional penalty tax was paid for the privilege of filing returns without the apportionment.

Since 1975, the privilege of paying an additional penalty tax no longer exists so that the test is now purely a mechanical one. If two or more corporations are brother-sister, then each taxable tier of rates has to be apportioned among them, in any way that the group sees fit. However, the losses of one corporation cannot be used to offset the profits of another corporation in the group. Fortunately, the decision to apportion each tax tier is not irrevocable. It is possible to change the amounts as long as the statute of limitations is open on the returns. This could stand the taxpayer in good stead on audit. The reapportionment can be made even when the revenue agent's results are known.

**COMMON DATE FOR CONTROLLED GROUP.** Whereas in a consolidated return all of the corporations in the affiliated group have to have the same fiscal year, this is not a requirement of the brother-sister controlled group. The corporations involved can all have different fiscal years. One may well ask how the years are matched for apportionment purposes. All of the corporations will have a common date. Arbitrarily, December 31 has been selected for the date to be used for matching purposes. For example, if one corporation has a fiscal year that extends from February 1, 1984 to January 31, 1985, and another corporation in the group has a fiscal year that runs from September 1, 1984 to August 31, 1985, and a third corporation is a calendar year corporation, all will have a common December 31—namely, December 31, 1984. Therefore the apportionment has to be made for the foregoing years. It is immaterial that one corporation has only four months in 1984. It is the common December 31 that governs.

What constitutes a brother-sister controlled group is spelled out in Sections 1561 and 1563 of the Code. The rules have now been liberalized so that it is much easier to avoid the controlled group test. In *Vogel Fertilizer*,[24] the Supreme Court ruled that if some stockholders were not owners of a corporation, that corporation was not to be taken into consideration at all for the determination of a controlled group. This has necessitated the changing of the regulations on the part of the IRS. Specifically, the IRS threw out the existing regulations in this area.

**ACCUMULATED EARNINGS TAX.** In addition to the apportionment requirement, the controlled group rules impose another restriction on the member corporations. They are limited to one $250,000 amount for earnings and profits possibly being subjected to the "unreasonable" accumulation of earnings and

---

[24] See *Vogel Fertilizer Co.* 455 U.S. 16 (1982).

profits tax. This is the only tax for which no tax form exists, because no corporation will voluntarily admit to the "unreasonable" accumulation. The members of a controlled group are treated as one corporation, even though separate returns may be filed.

The accumulated earnings tax (commonly called a Section 531 penalty tax) is assessed at the rate of 27 1/2 percent on the first $100,000 of accumulated taxable income, and at 38 1/2 percent on amounts in excess of $100,000. The tax will not be assessed on amounts greater than the corporation's current taxable income, reduced by the income taxes attributable thereto, so there is no need to worry that the same earnings and profits will be taxed again and again. Nor will any tax be assessed on any amount that is being accumulated for the reasonable needs of the business.

What the reasonable needs of the business are is subjective in nature, and often depends on the skill of the taxpayer's representative (a term that the IRS likes to use for the accountant or lawyer handling the corporation audit). The reasonable needs of the business include such items as retention of funds for expansion purposes, purchasing another business, working capital needs, and for any other purpose that may be held to be reasonable. Purposes which are usually held to be "unreasonable" include the lending of funds for personal use by stockholders, investments in securities unrelated to the business, and the retention of funds for contingency claims that appear to be unrealistic.

The accumulated earnings tax will usually be asserted only against closely held corporations and not against publicly held ones. In a publicly held corporation, the theory seems to be that the independent boards of directors will not allow funds to be accumulated unreasonably, and will insist that excess funds be paid out to the shareholders in the form of dividends. This may be true with major corporations, but there are myriads of publicly held corporations in which the major portion of the outstanding stock is held by insiders. In such a situation, the publicly held corporation could be subject to the Section 531 tax, but again, the major thrust of this penalty tax is against the closely held corporation.

**PERSONAL HOLDING COMPANY TAX.**    Another trap that one should be aware of is the personal holding company (PHC) tax. Normally, an operating company, or one whose major source of income is from rentals, will not be exposed to this tax. The raison d'etre for this tax is to limit a corporation's use for the purpose of sheltering income that normally would be taxed to individuals. The tax has been around for many years, but with the lowering of the maximum tax rate for individuals from 70 percent (and at one time even higher) to 50 percent, the temptation to use a corporation as an "incorporated pocketbook" has diminished. Nevertheless, this tax is purely mechanical in its nature, unlike the accumulated (Section 531) earnings tax, and it is possible for a corporation under certain circumstances inadvertantly to become a personal holding company.

A PHC situation could occur, for example, when a company sells its assets on the installment basis, and does not liquidate immediately. During the time that the company is in a passive state, merely earning interest on the installment obligations, and also possibly getting some payments of principal on those obligations, the company could become a personal holding company. Motivation is of no concern here, only the nature of the income. If at any time during the last half of the taxable year more than 50 percent in value of the outstanding stock of a corporation is owned by five or fewer individuals, and at least 60 percent of the "adjusted ordinary gross income" is PHC income, the PHC tax could apply.[25] Any corporation that has nine or fewer stockholders (after giving effect to the attribution rules of Section 544 in the last six months of a year) will automatically pass the first test, so that this tax is applicable only to closely held corporations.

For the purposes of determining stock ownership, Section 544, referred to in the previous sentence, provides that:

1. Stock owned, directly or indirectly by or for a corporation, partnership, estate, or trust shall be considered as being owned proportionately by its shareholders, partners, or beneficiaries;

2. An individual shall be considered as owning the stock owned, directly or indirectly, by or for his or her family, or by or for his or her partner. Family, as used in this section, includes only brothers and sisters (whole or half-blood), spouse, ancestors, and lineal descendants;

3. If any person has an option to acquire stock, such stock shall be considered as owned by such person;

4. Outstanding securities convertible into stock are considered as outstanding stock, but only if including all such securities will make the company a personal holding company.

One area of concern for the PHC is the personal service contract. Included in PHC income are amounts received by a corporation, where it is to furnish personal services. Someone other than the corporation has the right to designate the individual who is required to perform such services and, at some time during the taxable year, 25 percent or more of the value of the outstanding stock is owned by or for that individual (again giving effect to the attribution rules).

[25] For the definition of "adjusted ordinary gross income" see Code Section 543(b)(2).

**AVOIDING TAX.**   All is not lost if a corporation does become a PHC. A deduction for dividends paid is allowed before the imposition of the PHC tax. So in the year that a corporation is a PHC, a sufficiently large dividend payout will avoid the tax. Incidentally, the PHC tax is 50 percent of undistributed PHC income. There may be some question on occasion as to whether or not a corporation is a PHC for a particular year. In such a case, the recommendation is to file Schedule 1120PH with the corporate return. This will limit the IRS to the normal three year period for the assessment of the PHC tax. Failure to attach Schedule PH extends the assessment time to six years.

One final statement in this area should be included. Even if a corporation is held to be liable for the PHC tax, and sufficient or timely dividends have not been made, the tax can still be avoided. Suppose on audit the IRS establishes that there is a PHC liability, the company can distribute a "deficiency" dividend. This will eliminate the PHC tax, but will not eliminate any interest or penalites on such a tax. These taxes will still have to be paid. The failure to attach Schedule PH to the corporate return will not only extend the statute of limitations, as previously mentioned, but will also allow for the imposition of a 25 percent penalty on the PHC tax. The "deficiency" dividend will negate the tax, but not the penalty.

One more item that should be mentioned before we leave the problems unique to C corporations is the repeal of the two and one-half month rule for years beginning after December 31, 1983. Prior thereto, corporations could accrue payments for compensation or other expenses that were payable to a more than 50 percent stockholder who is a cash basis taxpayer provided that such payments were made within the first two and one-half months of the ensuing year. This has now been eliminated. The effect of this change is that the expense cannot be deducted by the payor in a year earlier than the year in which payment is taken into account by the payee. However, a current deduction will still be permitted by an accrual basis taxpayer when dealing with an accrual basis payee. Incidentally, this rule also applies to S corporations, a discussion of which follows in the next section.

**THE S CORPORATION.**   Until now, all references to corporations have been to the C corporation. However, there exists (and has existed since 1958) another type of corporation known as the S corporation. Formerly, this type of corporation was commonly referred to as a Subchapter S Corporation, or sometimes as a "pseudo-corporation." The Subchapter S Revision Act of 1982, as its name indicates, revised the rules, and labels such a corporation merely as an "S" corporation.

**ELECTING S CORPORATION STATUS.** Electing S status is optional, and an election to be treated as an S corporation does not in any way detract from the legality of the corporation. The election to be treated as an S corporation only has significance as to federal income tax treatment. Many states do not recognize S status, and treat such corporations the same as any other corporation for tax purposes. For example, only within the past several years has New York State recognized the S corporation for tax purposes; California and New Jersey do not do so.

In an S corporation, the corporation income (with one exception) is not fixed at the corporate level. The income (or loss) is allocated to the shareholders, in proportion to the stock owned by them. Thus, an S corporation does not have a net operating loss deduction. The loss is passed on to the shareholders. This loss is then co-mingled with other elements of income to arrive at adjusted gross income of the individual shareholder.

**BENEFITS OF S CORPORATIONS.** When is S treatment advisable? This is a determination that must be made on a case-by-case basis. It is sometimes possible that in a corporation which has more than one shareholder, the interests of the various shareholders may not be the same. Some may desire S status, whereas others may not. In such a case, there must be a meeting of the minds, because the election to be treated as an S corporation must be unanimous on the part of all of the shareholders. Some situations that may make an election advisable are in the case of a start-up corporation where losses are anticipated for the first year or two; the avoidance of the double tax (once at the corporate level, and again when a dividend is paid); the pass-through of investment tax credits to the stockholders; and the possibility of passing through anticipated long-term capital gains to the stockholders directly, with the concomitant avoidance of a double tax.[26]

One beneficial area for an S election that is normally not mentioned in textbooks is in the case of a corporation which deducts expenses paid to its stockholder employees, and which could be challenged by the IRS on audit. The disallowance of some of these expenses could result in the imposition of a double tax. First, if the expenses are disallowed to the corporation, there will obviously be an additional tax to the corporation. Second, some or all of the expenses may be charged to the individual shareholder(s) as a constructive dividend, and another tax will be extracted from them. If, however, the cor-

---

[26] It is possible that some of the gains might be taxed to the corporation by virtue of Sections 1374 and 1375. Even so, the election may nevertheless result in a tax savings.

poration were an S corporation, there would be no tax at the corporate level. The foregoing could be a most important consideration in determining whether or not to utilize the S corporation election.

Using the S corporation does not impinge on the major nontax advantage of the corporate form, namely limited liability, and yet allows the income or losses to be taxed to the shareholders.

Assuming that a determination has been made to go the S route, how is this done, and who is eligible to do so (not everyone is)? The election is made by filing Form 2553, and all shareholders must consent to the election. The election must be made at any time during the year preceding the election year, or before the fifteenth day of the third month of the tax year of election. If an election is not made on time, it will be will be ineffective for the current tax year, and will only become effective for the following year. Once the election is made, it does not have to be renewed annually and remains in effect until voluntarily revoked or otherwise lost.[27]

**REQUIREMENTS FOR ELIGIBILITY.**    There are two types of requirements for eligibility for S corporation status. First, the requirements must be condsidered from the stockholder viewpoint. There cannot be more than 35 shareholders. Originally, in 1958, when the S corporation had its beginning, the maximum was 10, but this has been expanded to 35. Second, all of the shareholders must be individuals, estates, and certain types of trusts rather than corporations or partnerships.[28]

The corporate requirements state that the corporation must be a "domestic" corporation (this merely means that it is a corporation created under the laws of the United States or of any state thereof). It cannot be an ineligible corporation with any special tax status, meaning that an S corporation cannot be a corporation that owns 80 percent or more of the stock of an active subsidiary, nor can it be a domestic international sales corporation (DISC) or a former DISC. These are the major restrictions, although there are a few others of a relatively rare nature.

The S corporation can have only one class of stock outstanding. A major modification was made in the Subchapter S Revision Act of 1982 regarding the nature of the income allowed to be earned by an S corporation. Prior to this act, there were restrictions as to the amount of passive income that could be earned by an S corporation. Now the S election will terminate only if more than

---

[27]Section 1362(b)(3) imposes some other restrictions in certain special situations.

[28]Section 1361(b)(1)(B) outlines the types of trusts. They are essentially trusts which have their income passed through to individuals (such as a grantor trust). Thus the concept of the individual stockholder as the owner of the stock is not violated.

25 percent of the corporation's gross receipts is passive investment income for each of three consecutive taxable years, *and* the corporation has Subchapter C earnings and profits at the end of each of the three consecutive taxable years. Thus if a corporation was never a C corporation (being an S corporation from inception), or if it had a deficit in its earnings and profits account at the time it changed over from a C to an S corporation, the passive income test will not be used.

**EFFECT ON SHAREHOLDERS.** The adoption of S status affects the individual shareholders as follows:

1. The shareholder is taxed on his or her pro rata share of the corporation's taxable income, and if there is a loss at the corporate level, the loss passes through on a pro rata basis also.

2. Any item of income, loss, deduction, or credit whose separate treatment could affect any shareholder's tax liability, must be stated separately by the S corporation. This essentially follows the partnership rules. The major items so affected are capital and Section 1231 gains and losses (the distinction must be made for each kind of loss), and charitable contributions. The shareholders must also be notified as to ITCs which pass through, and preference items. There are other items that also require notification and separate treatment and which are outlined in Schedule K of Form 1120S.

The current rules provide that each shareholder reports income on a pro rata basis. If the stock ownership of the shareholder did not change during the entire year, there are no problems. If there was a change in ownership during the year, however, there must be an apportionment of the items, which is made on a daily basis. This is different from the pre-1983 rules where profits for the entire year were reported by the owner of the stock on the last day of the corporate year, but if there were losses, an apportionment between stockholders had to be made on a daily basis.

**IMPOSING TAX ON AN S CORPORATION.** Although an S corporation is generally considered to be a nontaxable entity, there can be a tax imposed in a number of instances, namely:

1. If there is excess passive investment income;
2. In the case of certain capital gains, if the S election has not been in effect for three years (and even then only sometimes);

3.　In the case of the minimum tax on certain long-term capital gains;

4.　The recapture of previously claimed ITCs when the corporation was not an S corporation

The foregoing certainly is not intended to be a complete exposition on the S corporation. It is merely intended to make the reader aware of some of the problems and advantages involved with such corporations. If there is an awareness that a potential problem may exist, or if there is uncertainty as to treatment, then additional expert help should be sought.

It should be noted that if S corporation treatment is elected, it is incumbent that records be kept for the basis of each shareholder's stock in the corporation. A shareholder's basis is increased by his or her share of income items allocated to the shareholder at the end of the year. The reverse is also true; a shareholder's basis must be reduced by losses or deductions which are passed through. Failure to adjust basis for income recognized would have an adverse affect on the shareholder on the disposition of stock, causing a greater amount of gain to be recognized (or a smaller loss) on disposition. The converse is also obviously true in the case of losses or deductions which are passed through. Distributions to shareholders reduce basis. This is logical since basis is increased by income items allocated to the shareholder, even if not distributed.

**TERMINATING S STATUS.**　Once a corporation has S status, it is, nevertheless, not necessarily forever. The election can be abrogated (either voluntarily or involuntarily) in three different ways. The election can be revoked voluntarily. Holders of more than 50 percent of the stock must consent. To be effective for the current year, the election must be made within the first two and one-half months of the year. If made later than that, the election will not be effective until the following year. The election will also terminate if the corporation ceases to meet S requirements (more than 35 shareholders, ineligible shareholders, second class of stock outstanding, acquisition of a subsidiary corporation, or special tax status). In such a situation, the election terminates immediately, and the tax year is divided into two (the S short year and the C short year). Two returns will be required for the one year, even though there is no requirement to formally close the books on termination. Income and expense allocations between the periods are required, because the tax treatment for each is different.

Once an election is terminated, the corporation is generally not eligible to make a new S election until there have been five intervening years as a C corporation. Special permission may be obtained from the IRS in certain cases where the election has been terminated inadvertently, or where an inequity may exist. Again, for greater details in this area some research is required.

# CORPORATE LIQUIDATIONS

We have previously considered the problems of organizing a business, selecting the form of organization, and the variuos tax problems relative to its operation (with emphasis on the corporate form). To complete the life cycle, we now move on to the problems involved in liquidating the corporation.

The formation of a corporation, as was mentioned earlier, normally will not trigger off any recognition of gain on the part of the stockholders, thanks to the operation of Section 351. The liquidation of a corporation is a different matter, however, the motivation for such liquidation may vary. Short of terminating the business, it may be desirable to change the format to that of an unincorporated entity, so as to avoid corporate taxation of income at the state level, or to permit losses to pass through to the shareholders directly, or to avoid double taxation (once at the corporate level, and again at the stockholder level, especially when there is an accumulated earnings problem). As we have seen, the selection of S status may solve some of these problems, but not all of them. For example, S status will not be available to a corporation where one or more of the shareholders is an ineligible entity, such as another corporation.

**Sections 331 and 336.** When a corporation is liquidated,[29] the general Sections 331 and 336 of the Code apply. However, there are other sections which may come into play, either by the election of such by the shareholders or by the operation of law. The principal sections referred to here are 333 and 337.

In an ordinary liquidation of a corporation under Section 331, the following results occur insofar as the shareholders are concerned. They get the assets of the corporation (cash or any other assets), and their gain or loss is measured by the difference between the fair market value (FMV) of the assets received, less the stockholders' basis for the stock. The gain or loss will usually be of a capital nature. There are exceptions, such as in the case of Section 1244 stock (previously mentioned) and for losses in the case of the stock of a small business investment company. In both cases, all or part of the loss may be an ordinary one.

As to the corporation, Section 336 states that normally no gain or loss will be recognized to it on the distribution of assets in complete liquidation. Unfortunately, again, there are exceptions. Gain will be recognized on a distribution

---

[29] Regulation 1.221-1(c) states that:

A liquidation may be completed prior to the actual dissolution of the liquidating corporation. However, legal dissolution of the corporation is not required. Nor will the mere retention of a nominal amount of assets for the sole purpose of preserving the corporation's legal status disqualify the transaction.

of LIFO inventory, on property subject to recapture of depreciation under Sections 1245 and 1250, and on installment sales gains not yet recognized because the principal payments have not yet been received. There are also a number of other instances where gain will be recognized, but they are relatively insignificant.

It may well be that a Section 331 liquidation is the proper procedure. However, what if a business is to be sold and there would be a gain on the sale? All too frequently, the purchasers would not want to buy the capital stock of the present shareholders, fearing to stand in their place. They may be reluctant to take on possible hidden liabilities of the corporation, or to face tax audits for years still open. Furthermore, the purchasers may very well want a step-up in basis for the assets that are being acquired. In the latter situation, the normal operation of Section 331 will give recognizable gain to the selling corporation, on sale of the assets, with the attendant payment of income taxes.

If the corporation is subsequently liquidated, there will be another tax at the stockholder level, as we have seen, measured by the difference between the FMV of the assets received less the adjusted basis of the stock in the hands of the shareholders. In addition, to further compound the situation, the liquidation of the corporation will trigger recognition of the gain to the corporation which may be contained in any installment obligation received as part of the purchase, and as yet uncollected. Taxes may have to be paid without adequate funds being available to pay them. In the past, such situations, gave rise to subterfuges on the part of the selling corporation and its shareholders. Attempts were made to keep negotiations secret, liquidate the corporation, and then sell the assets. This approach attempted to eliminate the corporate tax. (The stockholders would pay one tax on liquidation of the corporation, receive assets with a stepped-up basis, and then sell the assets at an amount equal to the stepped-up basis.) The government, if it recognized the existence of such a situation, would hold that the gain was that of the corporation, nevertheless, assert a tax at the corporate level, and another tax on the shareholders on liquidation. This was a classic example of "substance over form." Even though the corporation no longer existed, the tax effects remained the same. This doctrine was emphasized in a classic case, commonly known as the *Court Holding Company* case.[30]

**Section 337.**   In order to ameliorate this problem, Section 337 was enacted in 1954. This section (which, incidentally, is a mandatory one—it applies if the facts fit) provides that if a corporation is liquidated within one year from the date of adoption of a plan of liquidation, then no gain will be recognized to the corporation on the disposition of certain assets. The enactment of this section

---

[30]*Commissioner of Internal Revenue* vs. Court Holding Co., 324 U.S. 331 (1945).

had the effect of changing the results of *Court Holding Company.* The corporation can now openly engage in negotiations even prior to the adoption of a plan of liquidation. The normal procedure is to negotiate, come to an agreement, adopt a plan of liquidation, and then make the sale. It is even permissible just to enter into a contract for future sale, and adopt a plan of liquidation immediately prior to the actual sale.

Under Section 337, no gain on the sale of the assets will be recognized to the corporation (except for those situations mentioned in the following). Thus, there will be no corporate tax. The tax will be paid by the shareholders, and will be measured by the difference between the FMV of the assets received less the shareholders' basis in the stock. As far as the corporation is concerned, it is as if the gain bypassed the income statement, and was credited directly to retained earnings. Certainly, Section 337 did much to solve a nagging tax problem and is a device that every tax practitioner or advisor must be aware of.

As was previously stated, Section 337 is a mandatory section, so the failure to file the necessary notification with the IRS that a plan was adopted (Form 966) will not negate the plan. The section does require that all corporate assets are to be distributed in complete liquidation within the 12-month period commencing on the date the plan is adopted (except for those assets which may be retained to meet claims). It is not recommended that assets be retained to meet claims. A better approach would be to distribute sufficient assets to an escrow account or trustee for the former shareholders of the corporation, who will then make payments as required.

Section 337 has a number of restrictions, however. It will not apply to sales of merchandise inventory unless there is a bulk sale of "substantially all" of the inventory to one person in one transaction. Section 337 is also subordinate to Sections 1245 and 1250 dealing with the recapture of depreciation, and is also subordinate to Section 47(a) dealing with recapture of ITC. This means that income will have to be recognized by the corporation to the extent of the depreciation recapture, and that the corporation may have to give back some of the ITC previously taken. In addition, Section 337 applies also to assets sold at a loss. This means that the losses will not be recognized at the corporate level, and cannot be used or carried back to offset other elements of income.

Until the passage of the Installment Sales Revision Act of 1980, the pass-through of installment sales obligations triggered recognition of gain to the corporation as provided in Section 331, even though the obligation was acquired as part of a sale under Section 337. However, for obligations received after April 1, 1980 in a 337 transaction, this rule no longer applies. Now the shareholder may report the gain on the exchange of his or her stock as the installment obligations are collected, provided that they are the result of a sale of property which qualifies for non-recognition of gain to the corporation under Section 337.

In effect, the utilization of Section 337 in a corporate sale may be of inestimable benefit to the sellers.

But what if the shareholders want to continue operating the business, but not in the corporate form? Liquidation under Section 337 is of no use. Liquidation under Section 331 may trigger recognition of gain to the shareholders, where the property has appreciated in value, so that the FMV of the net assets is in excess of the basis of the stock in the hands of the shareholders. Is there an out under such a situation? Fortunately, the answer is "yes."

**One-Month Liquidation.**    The answer can be found in Section 333. This section is generally known as the "one-month liquidation section." Section 333, unlike Section 337, is an optional section; that is, the shareholders are free to adopt it at their own discretion. Once adopted, the benefits of Section 337 do not apply. The 333 election is an irrevocable one. It can be used to advantage, however, under certain circumstances, as mentioned earlier. It will allow the business to be operated in a noncorporate form, with (under certain circumstances) minimal tax consequences.

Because of its requirements and restrictions, Section 333 normally should not be adopted by corporations that have large "earnings and profits," the tax equivalent of "retained earnings." This is so because, to the extent of "earnings and profits," the shareholders (other than corporations) will have ordinary income, rather than capital gain, as under Section 331. Furthermore, the shareholders may have capital gain to the extent of cash and securities (acquired after 1953) distributed to them, if their proportionate share is greater than their proportionate share of "earnings and profits."

The benefits of Section 333 are available to "qualified electing shareholders" only. Shareholders are first divided into three categories:

1. Corporations which are shareholders, but that own more than 50 percent of the stock of the corporation. Such corporations are excluded from availing themselves of Section 333.

2. Corporate shareholders who own 50 percent or less of the corporation.

3. Noncorporate shareholders.

Only the members of 1 and 2 may qualify for Section 333, and then only if they file an election to do so and 80 percent or more of the voting power of the group elects to be governed by Section 333. Thus, it may very well be that 333 can apply to one group (3), for example, and not the other. Furthermore, the nonelecting members may elect not to have Section 333 apply to them. In such cases. The Section 331 rules will apply. Usually, however, this will not occur.

Electing shareholders under 333 are merely postponing recognition of the tax. The property is transferred out to them at a basis which is usually less than the FMV of the assets. If the property is disposed of at a later date, at a price higher than the basis, gain will be recognized at that time.

In a 333 liquidation the basis of property received (except for cash) is the same as the shareholder's basis for the stock surrendered, decreased by the cash received, and increased by gain recognized and liabilities assumed. This amount is allocated to the various assets (other than cash and marketable securities). The allocation of basis to the various assets is somewhat complex, but not overwhelmingly so, and will not be discussed here. The intention herein is to create an awareness of a tool that can be used when the situation is appropriate.

A word of caution is necessary in connection with Section 333. Inasmuch as it is an optional (unlike 337) device, strict adherence to the rules must be observed; otherwise the election will not be deemed to be valid. Basically, the rules are as follows:

1. A plan of liquidation must be adopted by the liquidating corporation.

2. Within 30 days after adoption, an election to have Section 333 apply must be filed on Form 964 with the IRS by the qualified electing shareholders.

3. A complete liquidation must take place within one calendar month. There can be no overlap of months, even though the period of liquidation is 30 days or less.

4. Each "qualified electing shareholder" must file, with the tax return for the year involved, a statement indicating that a 333 liquidation occurred and how gain realized was treated.

# CONCLUSION

In this chapter, we have explained some of the tax problems incurred in setting up a business, operating it, and liquidating it. The major thrust of this chapter has been concentrated on its applicability generally to the smaller business. That does not mean that the statements made herein do not apply to large corporations as well; they do. The Code, generally, does not make any distinctions as to size. However, the larger businesses frequently have tax personnel available to them on a full-time basis. It is the smaller businesses that need to be made more aware of the tax implications of their actions.

I am well aware of the areas not covered herein. The emphasis in the foregoing has been on the corporate form of operation, although many of the topics mentioned apply to other types of entities as well. Topics which have not been covered include the "at-risk" concept inherent in investments made by noncorporate investors, partial liquidations involving corporations, stock redemptions as distinguished from liquidations, collapsible corporations, corporate reorganizations, and other topics. I have tried to limit myself to those problems that arise most frequently, based on my own experience as a practicing accountant as well as an educator. The area of deferred compensation, pension, and profit-sharing plans has not been included herein, inasmuch as this topic is covered elsewhere in this book.

My purpose has been to give the reader an awareness of potential problem areas in taxation. Awareness of the existence of a potential problem is the major factor in successfully coping with the intricacies of taxation, and that is where your ability as a business advisor will be of value.

Knowing the solution is secondary. No one can be expected to know the answers to all tax problems offhand—expert advice can always be sought. In addition, answers are usually available when one does some research. Not being aware of the existence of a problem can lead to disaster. All those who are interested should become familiar with some of the myriad reference works available in taxation. Do not let the imposing look of the books intimidate you. Each time you use them, it becomes easier.

# CHAPTER 10

# BUSINESS INSURANCE

## Howard C. Alper

A client's or company's business insurance coverage certainly is not your primary responsibility. But all too often, a client's business insurance has areas of inadequate coverage, excess or duplicate coverage, and incorrect ratings and premiums. Your business experience and your intimate knowledge of a company's operations often enable you to understand its insurance needs better than management does.

Working with the company's insurance professionals, you can help them obtain better insurance protection, save them premium dollars, and possibly alert them to uninsured hazards that have the potential of wiping out the business.

You can perform this valuable service without getting involved technically. You need only know just enough of the fundamentals to recognize a weak insurance program.

This chapter will review more than three dozen insurable risks that a typical business is exposed to. The discussion will follow and be keyed to the checklist in Exhibit 10.1, which groups the risks into three major categories: property damage, income or cash flow loss, and legal liability.

Examples from actual cases will be used to help illustrate the kinds of oversights and errors that occur frequently.

## PROPERTY DAMAGE

We'll first consider the risks of loss, damage, or destruction of buildings, contents, equipment, and other owned property, which are covered in the first part of Exhibit 10.1.

This chapter is based on an article written for the October 1984 issue of *The Practical Accountant* and is reprinted with their permission.

# EXHIBIT 10.1  Analysis of Insurable Risks

Prepared for: _____Date: _____

This form will help a business analyze the risks of loss it is exposed to. It will help identify areas in which insurance is inadequate, excessive or improper. The information on this form should be discussed in detail with the company's management and/or insurance representatives.

| *Property Damage:* | *Current insurance* | *Optimum insurance* | *Self insurance* | *Insurance not applicable* |
|---|---|---|---|---|
| Loss, damage, or destruction of buildings, contents, equipment, or other owned property: | | | | |
| 1. Fire | | | | |
| 2. Extended coverage | | | | |
| 3. Vandalism and malicious mischief | | | | |
| 4. Sprinkler leakage | | | | |
| 5. Water damage, collapse | | | | |
| 6. Earthquake, flood | | | | |
| 7. War, nuclear damage, atomic reaction | | | | |
| 8. Boiler explosion | | | | |
| 9. Replacement costs | | | | |
| 10. Demolition of building | | | | |
| 11. Property in transit | | | | |
| 12. Property at other locations | | | | |
| 13. Plate glass | | | | |
| 14. Burglary of merchandise, supplies or equipment | | | | |
| 15. Damage to owned vehicles | | | | |
| Other: | | | | |

*Income or Cash Flow Loss:*

Loss, damage, or destruction of money, records, property, or other business assets which affect current or future cash flow or income:

| | | | | |
|---|---|---|---|---|
| 16. Business interruption | | | | |
| • Fire, extended coverage, vandalism and malicious mischief, sprinkler leakage | | | | |
| • Water damage, collapse | | | | |
| • Boiler | | | | |
| • Contingent operations | | | | |
| • Power failure | | | | |
| 17. Destruction of records | | | | |
| • Accounts receivable | | | | |
| • Valuable papers | | | | |
| 18. Criminal acts | | | | |
| • Holdup or theft of money | | | | |
| • Employee dishonesty | | | | |
| • Forgery | | | | |
| 19. Personnel | | | | |
| • Death of owner or key man | | | | |
| • Disability of owner or key men | | | | |
| • Group medical insurance | | | | |

284

| Income or Cash Flow Loss (Cont'd): | Current insurance | Optimum insurance | Self insurance | Insurance not applicable |
|---|---|---|---|---|
| • Pension and profit-sharing plans | | | | |
| Other: | | | | |
| *Legal Liability Claims:* | | | | |
| Liability to others for injury or damage to persons or property: 20. Operation of owned and non-owned vehicles | | | | |
| 21. General liability | | | | |
| 22. Products liability | | | | |
| 23. Contractual liability | | | | |
| 24. Personal injury claims | | | | |
| 25. Fire legal liability—subrogation | | | | |
| 26. Host liquor liability | | | | |
| 27. Umbrella liability | | | | |
| 28. Workers' compensation | | | | |
| 29. Employer's liability | | | | |
| 30. Property of others—bailee | | | | |
| 31. Property of others—storage | | | | |
| Other: | | | | |

Copyright: AuditRate

**1, 2, 3. Fire, extended coverage, and vandalism and malicious mischief.** A frequent error here is that coverage of equipment is based on *book* values. Insurance recovery is based on current replacement cost less physical depreciation (not tax depreciation). A professional appraisal is usually the best way to determine these values.

A second situation to watch for is the company with many types of property or several locations that has separate insurance limits for each location. It usually costs no more to have "blanket" coverage for *all* owned property at *all* locations—such as buildings, equipment, supplies, and stock. This eliminates the need to state specific amounts of coverage for separate buildings and contents that would limit recoveries, and also minimizes loss adjustment problems. In addition, coverage is for 100 percent of the total value at any location, rather than the usual 80 or 90 percent coinsurance. That's because the maximum the company will pay is the total amount of insurance on *all* property at *all* locations, rather than the amount scheduled for *one* type of property at any *one* location.

EXAMPLE:  A company carries separate insurance on a building (value $800,000) and on the contents of the building (value $300,000). Because of a 90 percent coinsurance requirement, it insures the building for $720,000 and the contents for $270,000. In the event of a partial damage to the building and a total loss to the contents, the insurance company would pay for the full partial damage to the building, but would pay only $270,000 (the face amount of the policy) for the contents loss. In other words, the policyholder would lose $30,000. With blanket insurance covering building and contents, without allocation by type of property, the insurance company would be obligated to pay the *full* $300,000 contents loss, as well as the building damage.

A third area of potential savings is the use of incorrect rates. Fire rates are not standard for all property—they are based on the hazard and can often be reduced by taking certain measures that reduce the risk.

EXAMPLE:    A plant had installed a fire door on the firewall between a hazardous section and the main plant. This reduction of fire hazard to the main area would have resulted in a significant premium reduction, but the insurance broker didn't know about the fire door. In addition, the company had a fire detection alarm system for many years, for which it did not receive credit. For these oversights, the company overpaid its annual premiums by 50 percent (nearly $3,000) for six years—$18,000 that couldn't be recovered.

4.  **Sprinkler leakage.**  Damage from sprinkler leakage is not covered by the standard property policy, unless specifically included. When a building is protected by a sprinkler system, separate coverage is needed to protect against damage caused by accidental discharge of water from the sprinkler system.

5.  **Water damage and collapse.**  This coverage is not always essential, but it should not be dismissed without weighing the potential benefits against the cost. It covers losses such as damage to stock from water leakage, and roof collapse from the weight of accumulated snow. It is often practical to cover these and other risks (such as burglary) in an "All-Risk Floater" as part of a package policy.

6.  **Earthquake and flood.**  Coverage for these hazards should be appropriate to the areas where the company is located. The federal government makes flood insurance available through its National Flood Insurance Program. Earthquake insurance is available through commercial insurers.

7.  **War, nuclear damage, and atomic reaction.**  Hopefully, these are risks that are unlikely to occur. However, if a company has a facility located near a nuclear power plant, the hazards must be carefully assessed and benefits must be compared with costs because such insurance coverage is very costly, if available at all.

8. **Boiler explosion.** The regular building and contents insurance policy does not cover damage caused by explosion of steam boilers. Separate boiler insurance is a frequent omission. Coverage should be the "broad" form rather than the "limited" form. The "limited" form covers only explosion, whereas the "broad" form covers many other types of loss, such as bulging, burning, cracking, and certain boiler malfunctions. In addition, it may be desirable to cover equipment other than boilers, such as pumps, motors, converters, transformers, refrigeration, and air conditioners, or turbines.

9. **Replacement cost.** A company's insurance coverage may adequately cover its present depreciated equipment but be thoroughly inadequate to cover today's much higher replacement costs—particularly if the insured property was purchased several years ago. Replacement cost coverage allows a business that suffered a loss to purchase new equipment without having to finance it from capital or from borrowings.

10. **Demolition of building.** If a building is partially destroyed, as from a fire, the city or municipality may not provide a rebuilding permit and the portion of the building not damaged by fire would have to be destroyed. Fire insurance does not pay for the undamaged portion of the building, which value would be lost by the enforcement of the municipal requirement to demolish the balance of the building. This loss must be covered separately by a special endorsement to the building policy.

11. **Property in transit.** When the value of goods in transit in any one vehicle is significant and not otherwise insured, coverage should be considered. However, the risk of damage to goods in transit is often small enough to be self-insured. (*Note:* The carrier is seldom liable for the full value.)

12. **Property at other locations.** When inventory is sent out for subprocessing (such as plating or machining), and the amount of inventory at any one location at any one time is significant, separate coverage may be needed. As with goods-in-transit, when the amount at other locations is nominal, the risk could be self-insured.

13. **Plate glass.** The standard building policy covers broken glass, but only when the breakage is caused by one of the perils insured under the policy, such as fire, windstorm, explosion, vehicle damage, and such. The standard building policy does not cover broken glass caused by vandalism or malicious mischief. If the cost to replace plate glass is substantial, which is often the case with storefront glass, separate in-

surance may be needed. (Plate glass is the thick, usually large glass panes used in store windows, not the thinner glass used in small conventional windows.)

14. **Burglary of merchandise, supplies, or equipment.** Many types of contents are susceptible to burglary loss. If burglary coverage is desired, separate insurance should be purchased. Many insurance companies offer "All-Risk" coverage on property insurance, which usually includes fire, extended coverage, vandalism, water damage, collapse, *and burglary.* An All-Risk rider is often no more expensive than burglary insurance.

15. **Damage to owned vehicles.** Two frequent areas for savings are to switch to a higher deductible and to change comprehensive coverage from actual cash value to a stated value.

In dealing with deductibles, you may find that it's not unusual for an insurance company to charge an $80 premium for reducing the collision deductible on a car from $200 to $100. This $100 additional insurance at an $80 cost would be an unwise purchase from the company's viewpoint, and should be avoided by placing the deductible at the highest level consistent with advantageous savings. If this factor is repeated many times on a fleet policy, the premium differential can be significant, and the amount of additional insurance purchased meaningless.

Changing coverage from actual cash value to stated value may reduce the premiums, without affecting the insurance recovery in the event of a claim.

## INCOME OR CASH FLOW LOSS

Thus far, we've confined our discussion to loss or damage to a company's business operating assets. But the result of a loss to such assets could be a reduction in the company's earning power and/or cash flow. The second part of Exhibit 10.1, covering business interruption insurance, deals with this problem. In addition, it also covers insurance against destruction or damage to records and valuable papers, and criminal acts. Finally, it covers insurance on personnel—life, medical, and such.

16. **Business Interruption.** Losses from interruption of a business can arise from property damage but must be covered separately. In determining the amount of business interruption insurance required, you should be aware of these significant differences in terminology between the insurance and the accounting professions:

**Cost of Goods Sold.**   Accountants will usually include direct labor in cost of goods sold, whereas insurance companies exclude direct labor.

**Ordinary Payroll.**   Accountants usually think of ordinary payroll as the full amount of normal payroll for the firm, whereas the insurance industry defines ordinary payroll as non-key personnel (usually hourly paid unskilled employees).

**Supplies.**   Only supplies that are consumed directly in the conversion of new stock into finished stock should be considered for insurance purposes.

Business interruption losses are calculated by estimating the amount of sales a business would have made had there been no destruction of facilities, deducting from that figure the costs not incurred (material cost, outside processing, non-continuing payroll, and other expenses) and adding the extra expenses to replace the facilities on a rush basis, or to continue sales on an increased cost basis, subject to certain limitations. However, it is important to note that the calculation of amount of insurance required bears little relationship to the way in which a loss payment is calculated.

The business interruption policy usually insures "gross earnings," which essentially are defined as: (1) net sales, (2) operating earnings less the cost of (3) material cost on merchandise sold, and (4) services purchased from outsiders (not employees) for resale. The insurance company requires that the amount of insurance be at least 50 percent of the gross earnings as defined above (some policies require higher coinsurance clauses).

Most business interruption policies are written for a stated amount, without any adjustment provision. Business interruption insurance can also be written on a reporting form basis. This is valuable if substantial changes are anticipated, or if it is difficult to estimate future sales. The problem of determining how much insurance to buy for future periods can be solved by adding either the "premium adjustment agreement" or "agreed amount endorsement" to the policy.

There are other forms of business interruption coverage such as "Loss of Earnings" or "Earnings" insurance, but these often do not provide as broad a coverage. Also, it is possible to exclude ordinary payroll, but the offsetting disadvantages (higher coinsurance and less coverage) usually are not beneficial to the client.

> a.   *Fire, extended coverage, vandalism and malicious mischief, and sprinkler leakage.* One way to reduce premium costs is to match the business interruption coverage not with the risk of loss but with the risk of lost income.

EXAMPLE: A manufacturing company covered its several buildings equally. By eliminating business interruption insurance on two high-rated buildings that accounted for only 10 percent of production and by increasing the coverage on the plant that produced 90 percent of the output but had a very low fire rate, it saved 17 percent in premiums.

    **b.**  *Water damage and collapse.* As in property insurance, the standard business interruption policy does not cover losses such as water damage and collapse. These can be added to the policy at a minimal cost. Again, it might be more practical to write the business interruption insurance on an "All-Risk" basis which covers more types of loss than the specified peril policy (i.e., fire, extended coverages, vandalism, water damage, collapse).

    **c.**  *Boiler.* Again, as with boiler explosion property insurance (item 8), the standard business interruption policy does not cover loss caused by explosion of steam boilers. Specific coverage can be provided by a separate business interruption rider to the boiler policy.

    **d.**  *Contingent operations.* When a business would be significantly and adversely affected by a fire or other insurable peril at either a customer's or a supplier's location, it should carry contingent operations insurance against this risk.

    **e.**  *Power failure.* It usually is best to self-insure against this risk, unless the power failure could damage a costly process or spoil inventory. Exhibit 10.2 gives "rules of thumb" to use in estimating the proper amount of business interruption and other insurance to carry.

**17.**  **Destruction of records.** Insurance coverage for the destruction of records usually takes two forms:

    **a.**  *Accounts receivable.* This insurance provides coverage where the business is unable to collect accounts receivables because of destruction of its records. Coverage includes the cost of reconstruction. When an outside service bureau is used to handle accounts receivable, it is unlikely that *both* sets of records would be destroyed (i.e., the records at the client's office and at the service bureau). For current invoices (before transmitting the information to the service bureau), risk can be eliminated by taking an extra copy of the invoices off the premises each day and storing them elsewhere.

    **b.**  *Valuable papers.* This insurance provides coverage for the cost of reconstructing and/or reproducing valuable records, including blue-

## EXHIBIT 10.2   Insurance Rules of Thumb for Accountants

### *AuditRate, Inc.*

**Howard C. Alper, CPCU, RM**
*President*

INSURANCE COST REDUCTION CONSULTANTS
*A Division of Alper Services, Inc*
60 West Superior Street
Chicago, Illinois 60610
312/944-2000

Insurance "Rules of Thumb" for Accountants

**Business Interruption**

| | |
|---|---|
| Sales = 100% | 100% |
| - Material CGS % | _____% |
| = Balance % | _____% |
| X Policy Coinsurance Requirement | _____% |
| = Required Ratio of Ins. to Sales | _____% |
| X Estimated Sales for next 12 months | $_____ |
| = Estimated Proper Ins. Amount | $_____ |

**Building and Equipment (Fire)**

$\dfrac{\text{Accumulated Depreciation}}{\text{Original Cost}} = $ _____% X 2 X Original Cost =   $_____

\+ Original Cost   $_____

= Estimated Proper Ins. Amt. (Replacement Cost)   $_____

**Umbrella Liability**

| | |
|---|---|
| Minimum Limit | $1,000,000 |
| + 20% of sales above $1,000,000 | _____ |
| = Tentative limit | $_____ |
| X Estimated Risk Factor for | |
| type of business | |
| (1=low, 2=moderate, 3=high) | _____ |
| = Estimated Proper Umbrella Limit | _____ |

Do Primary Underlying Liability policy limits **exactly** match Umbrella Liability policy requirements?

**Dishonesty Bond**

| | |
|---|---|
| 5% of first $1,000,000 sales | $_____ |
| + 1% of sales over 1,000,000 | _____ |
| + 10% of Y/E Accounts Receivable | _____ |
| + 20% of Y/E Cash (on hand & in bank) | _____ |
| = Tentative Proper Bond Limit | $_____ |
| X Estimated Risk Factor for | |
| type of business (inventory, cash, etc.) | |
| (1 = low, 2 = moderate, 3 = high) | _____ |
| = Estimated Proper Bond Limit | $_____ |

©7/84

291

prints, drawings, financial data, and any other type of records specifically insured. The intrinsic value of records and papers lost in a fire or other casualty is small compared to the value of the information, and the cost that would be incurred in reconstructing data. If the business could lose substantially due to destruction of valuable papers, copies of the pertinent data should be made and taken off premises. If this is not practical, insurance should be purchased.

18. **Criminal acts.** Theft of property is generally covered as part of burglary or all-risk coverage. Insurance coverage for loss from other criminal acts takes the following forms:

   **a.** *Holdups or theft of money.* Retail stores can have considerable amounts of cash on hand, and need a separate holdup policy. Theft of merchandise should be covered as part of contents insurance.

   **b.** *Employee dishonesty.* Many firms do not carry an Employee Dishonesty bond, even when they are exposed to substantial losses. A blanket bond covering all employees is usually the most desirable type of bond. However, some bonds may exclude all corporate officers. This may be acceptable when the business is small, and all officers are shareholders, but as the company grows, there could be a problem.

EXAMPLE:   Two years after it began, a successful corporation made its office manager an assistant vice president. Three years later, the office manager confessed to a $90,000 shortage. When the company filed a bond claim, it learned that the office manager was excluded because he was an officer.

One way to minimize the problem is to have a bond that excludes only those who are named individually, not by job title.

   **c.** *Forgery.* Depositor's forgery coverage protects the forgery or alteration of a company check when a bank is not liable. This coverage is very inexpensive.

EXAMPLE:   The bookkeeper drew a check, and left too much space between the dollar sign and the amount, and the beginning of the dollar line. An independent maintenance man added "2" and "Two Thousand" to the check, raising the amount from $143 to $2,143. The bank cleared the check, but was not liable due to the carelessness of the bookkeeper in completing the check. Forgery coverage would have made the employer whole.

**19. Personnel.** The success of many companies depends on a small group of owners or key persons. Protection against their deaths or disability is an insurable risk, not only so that the business can continue, but to preserve its value to the estate of the deceased or disabled principal. There are several different types of personal coverage:

**a.** *Death of a key person.* Every small business should have a buy-sell agreement among its principals so the business would be able to continue smoothly. Often, the agreement is funded with life insurance. With such an agreement, surviving owner-managers can avoid costly, time-consuming disputes with survivors, and the survivors would receive cash instead of stock in a closely-held corporation that could not easily be sold. This often is a primary element in the estate plan of an owner of a closely-held business.

**b.** *Disability of a key person.* Even when it is not permanent, the disability of a key person can be as devastating to the business as his or her death. Yet this coverage is frequently omitted. Disability insurance covers the very purpose of a business— to provide continued and comfortable income to its owners. Recently, special disability policies have been developed which will fund a buy-sell agreement, the same way that life insurance is used to fund such agreements. This is a separate form of insurance, and is usually low in premium cost.

**c.** *Group medical insurance.* The owners of a small business often are the primary beneficiaries of its group medical insurance, yet, many policies carry two significant limitations. An overall catastrophe limit—frequently $50,000— isn't enough when medical bills can easily run into six figures. And, an 80 percent coinsurance clause is acceptable on small claims, but should have a maximum—for example, $5000 of claims—so that out-of-pocket costs will be limited at a time of financial and emotional stress. It is also important to verify that the policy does not contain further unacceptable limitations, such as $100 per day room and board, or a surgery schedule only up to $1000.

**d.** *Pension and profit-sharing plans.* ERISA requires a bond on trustees for at least 10 percent of a plan's assets. The ERISA bond requirement can usually be added to the Employee Dishonesty policy without premium charge.

It may also be advantageous for a business to use a portion of the pension or profit sharing funds to purchase life insurance for employees.

## LEGAL LIABILITY CLAIMS

Businesses today are extremely vulnerable to many claims for legal liability for injury to people or damage to property. Insurance can cover the areas of greatest exposure.

20. **Owned and nonowned vehicles.** With owned vehicles, the primary problem is improper liability coverage. Maintaining insurance coverage on vehicles that have already been sold is one common error. But the more important omission is not insuring newly acquired vehicles. Medical payments coverage on trucks is superfluous because a company's drivers are already covered under workers' compensation. Elimination of such coverage can save hundreds of dollars a year.

Coverage for nonowned vehicles is important when employees use their own cars for any business purpose. Failure to provide "nonowned vehicle coverage" could result in a major uninsured claim. It is important to carry an adequate amount of liability insurance. Although it is difficult to determine exactly how much liability insurance is needed, most businesses should carry an "Umbrella Liability" policy (see item 27). The liability limits under vehicle policies should be the amount required by the umbrella liability policy, as the umbrella policy would cover limits *above* the vehicle liability policy limits. It is also important to automatically cover any vehicles which the client owns, acquires or uses during the policy year. This is done by adding the "Fleet Automatic" rider and is provided by insurance companies if requested.

21. **General liability.** Limits on a company's general operations insurance must be reviewed regularly to see if they must be increased to keep pace with the trend of liberal jury awards and court judgments. This is a vital area which often is overlooked although the added premium cost is small—usually under 10 percent more. Like the vehicle policy, the limits should be coordinated with the umbrella liability policy.

22. **Products liability.** Products liability insurance protects a business for any claims arising out of the product, once it has been distributed. In today's legal climate, product liability claims are relatively common, and most companies do carry such insurance. However, businesses often fail to allocate their premium calculation for products liability into categories producing the lowest premiums.

EXAMPLE: A manufacturing company whose service department generated 30 percent of its revenues was paying all its products liability premium based on the higher rating for the service department. By taking advantage of the substantially lower rating for its outright equipment sales, the company saved $14,000 (45 percent) of its annual premium.

Coverage also is available for products recall. Small firms can face this costly situation. For example, a manufacturer of precision parts for relays suffered a very substantial expense in replacing defective parts.

23. **Contractual liability.** Purchase orders from customers often contain contractual liability clauses not covered under regular products liability insurance. Products liability insurance covers only the "common law" exposure, whereas contractual liability imposes additional obligations— which can be covered with specific contractual liability coverage. This can be accomplished by adding a separate rider to the general liability policy. The cost for this endorsement is minor—usually 10 percent of the products liability premium.

24. **Personal injury.** A personal injury endorsement to the general liability policy is designed to protect against the remote, but potentially costly, possibility of a large court award in such situations as where an executive makes an innocent but misleading and damaging comment about someone, or where an employee forcibly evicts an obnoxious visitor. This rider usually costs 10 to 20 percent of the general liability premium.

25. **Fire legal liability—subrogation.** A business may cause a fire, which damages property of others. If the insurance company that insures the damaged property can prove the negligence, it can recover the claim payment from the business that caused the fire. Such liability exposure may not be covered in the general liability policy because that policy usually excludes property in the care, custody, or control of the insured.

EXAMPLE: The space that XYZ Manufacturing leased from ABC Corp. was destroyed by a fire that the fire department said started from a lighted cigarette that fell into a bin. ABC's insurance company paid ABC but then sued XYZ because of its employee's negligence.

26. **Host liquor liability.** Liability policies are not clear as to whether the company that serves or allows liquor on its premises, or even off the premises at company-sponsored events, would be covered for claims if an employee, or a member of the public, is injured as a result of the serving of liquor. Host liquor liability insurance protects the company from such claims.

EXAMPLE: Bottle Co. sponsors an annual Christmas party (and a summer outing) for employees, where liquor is served. Bruno drinks too much and while driving home he has an accident, and seriously injures three people in another car. If they sue the company, host liquor liability coverage will protect the company.

*Note*: A catch-all liability rider, known as a liability extension endorsement, provides coverage at nominal cost for about 10 different liability risks, including contractual, personal injury, fire legal, and host liquor liability.

27.  **Umbrella liability.**   Umbrella liability insurance is a broad excess liability policy, designed to provide two types of protection:

    (1)  Broader coverage than is available under the basic policies (i.e., general liability, products liability, vehicle fleet, or other liability policies).

    (2)  Higher limits than provided by the underlying policies mentioned. It is common for the underlying policies to have a $500,000 limit, and the umbrella policy to be written with limits of several million dollars.

The cost of Umbrella liability insurance varies significantly by type of business and size of operations, but is usually 20 to 40 percent of the primary liability policy premiums.

28.  **Workers' compensation.**   Workers' compensation coverage usually is standard—controlled by the state. However, businesses often are classified improperly, which can result in substantial premium overpayments.

EXAMPLE: A company that manufactured industrial filters was classified improperly in the iron and steel works category. With a nearly half million dollar factory payroll, it paid $48,000 in annual premiums instead of $26,000.

29.  **Employer's liability.**   Employer's liability is a section of workers' compansation policy that provides coverage when an employee sues under common law, rather than under the Workers' Compensation Act. Claims of this nature are very rare, but if they do occur, the $100,000 limit in the workers' compensation policy may not be enough. Excess coverage for such claims also can be included in an umbrella liability policy.

EXAMPLE: An injured employee sues under common law as he believes he can collect more than under the Workers' Compensation Act if he proves liability. (Under Workers' Compensation, the employee does not have to establish any negligence on the part of the employer.)

The Workers' Compensation Act would not come into effect, but the Employers' Liability section of the Workers' Compensation policy would. If the Employers' Liability limit is only $100,000, there would be no coverage for any recovery above the $100,000.

30. **Property of others—bailee.** If customers' goods are damaged in a fire and the company is legally liable, its contents fire insurance will provide coverage. However, if a loss is caused by an occurrence for which the company is not liable (e.g., an act of God), its contents insurance will not apply and either the customer or the company will have to bear the loss. Covering customers' goods with the company's property insurance usually is not wise because it often is very difficult to determine the value of customers' property and this could adversely affect the firm's property insurance claim. Unless the value of customers' property is small enough to self-insure, it can and should be covered under a "bailee" policy at a moderate cost.

31. **Property of others—storage.** A bailee policy may not cover the storage of customers' goods for extended periods of time. If this is needed, the bailee policy should be amended, or a separate storage policy obtained.

# CONTROL COSTS BY WATCHING AUDITS

As you know, workers' compensation, general liability and umbrella liability premiums are based on payroll or sales figures determined by annual audit by the insurance carrier. If errors occur during these audits, the client's premium may be overstated. Fortunately, by monitoring these audits, you have an opportunity to help your clients/company avoid such overcharges.

Here are some of the more common errors in the payroll and sales bases which are used to set the premiums:

**Payroll**

1. Make sure that employees are categorized properly. For example, including office personnel as plant workers will result in higher premiums.

2. Ascertain that "Excess" payroll is not counted. Overtime pay in excess of straight time and officers' payroll in excess of a stated weekly amount (which varies by state) need not be counted.

3. If sub-contractors are used, obtain evidence of their insurance coverage so their payrolls can be excluded. If not, the insurer can include payments to them in your client's payroll base.

4. Truck drivers' wages can be omitted from the payroll computation on liability policies. The offsetting disadvantage may be that they could be rated as drivers rather than plant employees under the workers' compensation policy, which frequently takes a higher rate. Be sure to explore this both ways.

Sales

1. Omit sales taxes.

2. Omit intercompany sales.

3. Omit sales of a type excluded by the policy, such as foreign sales or professional engineering services.

4. If sales are divided into two or more categories with different ratings, make sure that the allocation is proper.

## CONCLUSION

Insurance problems are not always solved by buying more insurance. By shifting coverage to where it is needed most and confirming that it is accurate, many companies can get better coverage at less cost. And, because brokers are paid by commissions, the analysis of insurance coverage should be at no cost to the company.

As the checklist indicates, selecting proper insurance coverage can be bewildering. To make an informed choice of which protection is needed, management must know what is available. Then a broker can analyze the risks and related costs and obtain the proper coverage.

If the owner and the insurance broker do not meet at least once a year to analyze the business' insurance needs, they can become outdated. This is where the accountant can be of added service to the client.

# CHAPTER 11

# MERGERS AND ACQUISITIONS

## Joseph M. Morris

The accountant will find that the many roles required in the environment of changing business entities present some of the most significant career challenges available. Great amounts of expertise and creativity are needed to perform the role of business advisor as companies acquire and merge with other business entities. Here, the accountant must be doubly alert, because one is dealing with real-life business decisions that can seriously impact an employer or client.

## WHY COMPANIES ACQUIRE OR MERGE

Mergers and acquisitions are a common and important aspect of modern business. A company may be motivated to acquire or combine with other business entities for various reasons, including the ones discussed in the following paragraphs.

Although the following comments cannot by any means be considered all-inclusive, they give a representative cross section of the kinds of goals and objectives that motivate companies to grow and diversify through combining with and acquiring other companies, in working toward such overall objectives as maximizing growth, return on investment, and protection of invested capital.

These motivations are often directly or indirectly part of the carrying out of a corporate plan, and are best managed when performed as stepping stones in fulfilling short-, medium-, and long-term goals.

Growth and expansion, and shifting of corporate emphasis, will often involve dealing with the question of whether to acquire an existing operation or to start a new business from nothing. New businesses or entry into new industries through start-up, always seem to involve numerous difficulties, including the discouragement of a long initial investment cycle where the new business absorbs large amounts of cash while revenues and gross profits are s till growing. A successful acquisition of an existing operation will enable the acquirer to bypass much of the initial start-up aggravation, and achieve its short- and medium-term goals sooner.

**FASTER GROWTH.** Mergers and acquisitions make it possible to achieve growth at a rate higher than that which is possible solely through internal means. Furthermore, by creating a larger organization through acquisition, economies of scale can be achieved more rapidly, particularly where operations similar to the company's existing businesses are acquired.

**VERTICAL INTEGRATION.** Companies may wish to expand operations into new activities where a company's existing resources and activities provide a base for successful performance, resulting in improvement in the efficiency of the overall organization. Important motivations for vertical integration are to achieve more stable outlet markets and greater profits through elimination of the "middle-person," and more cost efficient and stable sources of supply. Vertical integration is, for example, where a manufacturer selling on a wholesale basis acquires an existing retail distribution operation in the same industry, or acquires a company that supplies its raw materials.

**ACQUIRING MARKET SHARE.** Through acquiring other entities, an acquirer can strengthen its market share in geographic areas where the acquiring company already operates, or achieve instantaneous geographic expansion by acquiring operations in new locations. Acquisition of existing market share is often easier than starting up a new operation to compete with another entity that already has a share of the market.

**PORTFOLIO INVESTMENT.** Some companies function as holding companies, by acquiring entities in unrelated industries for the purpose of investment. Ownership of a controlling interest is considered more desirable by some than acquiring small percentages of ownership because of the ability to influence the policies and activities of an investee. This approach is used by certain larger conglomerates, where the parent company functions substantially as a holding company, and evaluates performance of subsidiary companies primarily from an investment analysis standpoint. The parent company may not be committed to any particular industry or industries, and may acquire and dispose of the controlling interests in other companies the way an investor manages a securities investment portfolio.

In recent years, however, manay of the aggressive conglomerates have found that the acquisition of unrelated businesses sometimes creates an inefficient, unwieldly organization, and many of these conglomerates have narrowed their field of operations by divesting some of the operations previously acquired.

**CHANGING INDUSTRIES.**   By acquiring companies in different industries, an acquirer can shift its emphasis to industries believed to have a better outlook for the future. Sometimes an acquisition program motivated for this reason will be combined with a divestiture program, thereby resulting in a redeployment of capital.

**DIVERSIFICATION FOR COUNTERCYCLICALITY.**   Diversification is sometimes achieved by acquiring entities in industries expected to produce results countercyclical to those of the acquirer's present activities. That is, when seasonal or economic conditions normally cause unfavorable results in one line of business, results in the countercyclical business will typically improve. This can produce a more consistent earnings stream for a consolidated entity, both within fiscal years in the case of seasonally countercyclical businesses, and from year to year in the case of combining businesses that are countercyclical based on longer-term economic trends.

**DIVERSIFICATION TO REDUCE RISK.**   Diversification into unrelated industries can reduce overall risks of the acquirer by limiting the potential total impact of negative economic trends important to individual industries.

# THE ACQUISITION PROCESS

The following sections present a discussion of the acquisition process. Although the accountant's involvement in the process can take many different shapes, an understanding of the overall process and proper administration of an acquisition are essential to carry out the role of advisor effectively.

The discussion is divided into the following sections:

The acquisition team

Overall acquisition strategy and criteria

Structuring acquisitions

Establishing price

Financing acquisitions

Formalizing the deal and due diligence

Consummation of the acquisition

After the merger or acquisition

**THE ACQUISITION TEAM.** The carrying out of a successful acquisition should utilize contributions from personnel in virtually every significant area of expertise within the acquirer organization, and usually will require assistance from outside specialists. There should be a single individual assigned responsibility as team leader to coordinate the work of all personnel involved, and to be sure that proper steps are taken in every area of importance. The leader may be someone with financial or legal orientation, but often will be someone in a general management line position, such as the acquirer's chief executive officer or executive vice president, or someone in a business development capacity. The person having overall responsibility should delegate to someone with a financial or legal orientation, responsibility for coordinating all items of an accounting, financial, and systems nature. This person might also be given responsibility to coordinate the legal side of the acquisition process, or to serve as the liaison between the financial and legal sides of the acquisition, as well as with marketing, production, and other areas.

**Required Expertise.** At a minimum, personnel having the required expertise and ability to perform in the following areas should be included on the acquisition team from the accounting, financial, and systems side:

1. Preacquisition review of the acquisition candidate
2. Accounting for the acquisition, and review of accounting principles and policies followed by the acquisition candidate
3. Accounting systems review and transition, and setting up initial reporting mechanisms for monthly operating results
4. Systems evaluation and transition from a data processing standpoint
5. Liaison for continuing matters requiring coordination with the seller's financial personnel
6. Tax aspects of the acquisition, including evaluating structure of the acquisition, evaluating possible exposure to past tax liabilities and transitional tax matters (new registrations, etc.), and planning procedures for future tax compliance

With respect to the legal area, specialized legal counsel should be available for matters dealing with the following areas:

1. Negotiation, contract preparation, and corporate structure
2. Legal compliance with regulatory laws applicable to acquisitions, such as Blue Sky laws and Federal Trade Commission regulations
3. Review of contractual and other legal commitments of the acquisition candidate
4. Securities and Exchange Commission and stock exchange requirements

Periodic meetings should be held with the people assigned responsibility in each of these areas. It is wise for the "core" of the team, which would include those individuals whose tasks overlap and require more coordination, to attend all general meetings and to hold specialized meetings involving other personnel. The results of all meetings, including action plans and timetables, should be recorded in written memoranda, but distribution may be restricted depending on the sensitivity and confidentiality of the subject matter.

**Outside Experts.**    Outside experts who may also be part of the acquisitions team include:

1. Outside appraisers
2. Outside attorneys
3. Certified Public Accountants
4. Financial and other types of merger and acquisition consultants

In some cases, these outside specialists may function as integral members of the team, in addition to peforming specific professional services as outsiders.

The actual discussions and negotiations surrounding an acquisition can be handled any number of ways, and by different types of personnel representing the buyer and seller organizations. Depending on the size of the respective organizations and magnitude of the transaction, there may be significant involvement from the highest managerial levels, or the responsibility may be delegated to middle management levels. Normally, one would expect that each side will have an individual assigned primary responsibility for handling the transaction. This individual will draw on the support of internal and external experts from many disciplines in evaluating the acquisition candidate, and developing and negotiating the terms of the acquisition. Lawyers will often handle the actual negotiations.

**OVERALL ACQUISITION STRATEGY AND CRITERIA.**    Acquisition strategies and procedures will vary widely from company to company. For some companies, an acquisition may be an isolated event. For others, acquisitions may be an integral part of the overall corporate plan, and on an ongoing basis significant resources may be allocated to developing strategies, identifying and evaluating acquisition candidates, and carrying out the acquisition process.

**Acquisition Guidelines.**    Some companies are so involved in acquisitions that they employ specialists in this area, and have organized acquisition guideline and screening criteria which are followed in identifying and evaluating acquisition candidates. Whether a company makes acquisitions frequently or infrequently, it is a good idea to compare each acquisition candidate with predetermined criteria which have been carefully developed based on a company's goals, capabilities, and style. The following are some general criteria that should be included in any organized acquisition guideline and screening program:

1.  Kinds of industries and company characteristics and size
2.  Size of markets and expected market growth
3.  Share of market held by the candidate
4.  Ease with which competitors can enter the market
5.  Stage of the technology—for example, still in the development stage or a mature technology
6.  Competitive advantages of the acquisition candidate's product or service
7.  Amount of investment required and anticipated return rates
8.  Existence of skilled in-place management

**Acquisition Resources.**    The process of searching for and identifying acquisition candidates can be multifaceted involving extensive use of internal and external resources. A search may consist of analysis of all companies in an industry with volume or assets in specified ranges of size, or using other criteria to develop the initial listing of companies to submit to the screening process. The Standard Industrial Classification (SIC) codes developed by the federal government can often be used as a source for identifying companies in a particular industry.

Outside sources, including commercial and investment bankers and business brokers can be asked for advice and assistance in identifying acquisition candidates. However, many large corporations will try to avoid using business brokers because of the large fees that may be involved. Of course, the acquirer would not be concerned where the seller has contracted with a business broker and agreed to pay any fees.

**Initiating Contacts.**   Acquisition discussions are sometimes initiated when a company desiring to be acquired establishes a contact with a potential acquirer, or is put into contact with a potential acquirer by a broker or another third party. Companies may wish to be acquired for such reasons as financial difficulties or a desire of major shareholders/officers to retire or sell at a good price, and may seek out potential acquirers. A divestiture of an individual line of business by a larger company might also be a reason for the initial contact between acquirer and seller.

In practice, a small percentage of acquisition investigations result in consummation of a business combination, because there will usually be one or more circumstances that will eliminate the candidate from consideration. Additionally, the parties may be unable to negotiate an agreeable transaction from the standpoint of purchase price, form of consideration, or for other reasons.

An acquiring company will want to acquire at the lowest price, and for that reason the most attractive acquisition candidates are often those whose potential value is greater than current fair market value, whether based on stock market prices or negotiable purchase price. An acquirer may believe that an acquisition candidate has been underutilizing its resources, and that with changes the acquirer has in mind, the operating results of the acquisition candidate can be improved. This sometimes works to the seller's advantage to create the impression that the seller, for whatever reason, has done an inferior job in managing the entity being sold, even though most of the fundamentals of a successful business are present.

**STRUCTURING ACQUISITIONS.**   In conducting negotiations, extending and accepting offers, and working out the terms of an acquisition, two fundamental issues are always present:

1.   The identification of what is to be purchased (e.g., which assets, stock, or business).

2.   The structure of the transaction and the form and amount of consideration to be paid, including treatment of liabilities of the entity to be acquired.

The acquirer and seller, in negotiating and developing the structure of an acquisition transaction may be influenced by many factors, including tax ramifications. Two primary forms of structuring acquisitions are for the acquirer to purchase: (1) assets, together with an associated business or (b) stock of a corporation that owns assets and operates an associated business.

**Asset Purchases.**   A major advantage to the acquirer commonly envisioned with a transaction structured as an asset purchase is the opportunity for the acquirer to eliminate uncertainty as to liabilities being assumed. In respect to the agreement with the seller, it may be that the acquirer assumes no liabilities, making the transaction "clean" from the acquirer's standpoint. Responsibility for unidentified claims from creditors related to prior transactions will usually remain with the seller. It has been said that "the acquirer always wants to purchase assets, and the seller always wants to sell stock." Although this may be an oversimplification, many people concur. There are pitfalls that should be taken into consideration by the acquirer in an asset purchase, however, including statutory responsibilities which impact an acquirer of assets in certain cases. The Bulk Transfer Act as included in Article 6 of the Uniform Commercial Code requires that notice of an intended sale of assets be given to the creditors of a business where the principal business of the seller is the sale of inventory from stock.

To be subject to the bulk transfer disclosure requirements, a major portion of the inventory must be sold. The transfer of a substantial portion of the fixed assets of a business is a bulk transfer for purposes of the Bulk Transfer Act only if in connection with a bulk transfer of inventory. There is no clear definition in Article 6 of what is precisely meant by a "major" portion of the inventory or a "substantial" portion of fixed assets.

The Bulk Transfer Act requires that for covered transactions, specific information about the assets being transferred and the debts of the seller be given to all creditors and claimants against the seller at least 10 days before the transfer or payment for the goods. This supposedly gives the creditor ample time to take any action considered necessary. If the required notices are not given, the acquirer may be exposed for claims with respect to the assets purchased. These are some of the general concerns of the Bulk Transfer Act; a more detailed legal treatment is beyond the scope of this book. The accountant should advise the purchaser to consult with legal counsel where this law seems to apply.

Other areas to consider are possible exposure for product liability where a consumer previously dealt with the business now operated by the acquirer, and possible exposure to unpaid taxes and workers' compensation claims associated with the acquired business. Again, legal counsel should be sought in these areas.

These types of liabilities would normally initially result in claims against the seller, but in the seller's inability to pay, they could lead to claims against the acquirer. This gives great importance to proper compliance with statutes, to the indemnifications normally requested from a seller with respect to liabilities, and also to the insurance coverages maintained by the seller and acquirer both before and after the acquisition.

Another perceived major advantage of an asset purchase is that the acquirer will achieve a stepped-up basis on the assets for tax purposes through allocation of the purchase price to the assets acquired. Although stepped-up basis can sometimes also be achieved after a stock purchase, the process of stepping up basis after a purchase of stock is somewhat more complex, often involving liquidation of the acquired corporation.

The tax aspects of a sale of assets often are not favorable to the seller, because this can result in a tax gain at the corporate level on the sale of the assets, followed by a tax of gain to the shareholders of a selling corporation on payment of dividends or liquidation of the selling corporation. Careful tax planning and proper tax elections by a selling corporation are required to avoid or minimize this double taxation.

**Stock Purchases.** Stock purchases are often structured as tax-free reorganizations, which have stringent requirements as to the forms of consideration that may be given (generally an exchange of stock of the acquirer for the stock of the acquired company). This has the obvious advantage to the seller of deferring any tax gains, and may often be an important point in negotiation to the seller. The tax disadvantage to the acquirer is that it is not as easy to obtain a stepped-up basis of the assets for tax purposes.

Whether the transaction is a tax-free exchange or a purchase of stock for cash or other consideration (resulting in a tax gain to the seller), the tax attributes of the acquired corporation in a stock purchase are normally carried forward into the consolidated tax return of the acquirer. This includes carrying forward the tax losses for offset against future taxable income. Restrictions exist, however, regarding the extent to which these losses can be offset against future income, based on the nature of the business of the acquired corporation before and after the acquisition, and on the percentages of ownership changes.

Some stock acquisitions are made through the use of tender offers, where an offer is made to the stockholders of another company to exchange cash or other consideration for their shares of the target company. "Friendly" tender offers involve cooperation between the acquirer and directors and management of the target company before the tender offer is made. In an "unfriendly" tender offer, directors and management of the target company may be opposed to the tender offer, and may fight to convince the stockholders not to convey their shares to the company extending the tender offer. Occasionally, several prospective acquirers will attempt to obtain control of the same company through competing tender offers.

**ESTABLISHING PRICE.** The potential acquirer may use traditional valuation techniques in developing estimates of purchase prices to propose in negotiation, and in estimating maximum purchase prices it might agree to. Five general valuation approaches used in estimating the value of an acquisition candidate (and the selling price to be asked for by the seller, for that matter) are discussed in the following sections.

**Discounted Cash Flow.** Because an acquisition is an investment decision, use of the discounted cash flow return on investment concept (DCF-ROI) is an important step for the potential acquirer to employ in evaluating most acquisitions. This approach is based on a fundamental concept that as a result of the acquisition of the new entity, two things will happen: (1) cash goes out for the purchase and (2) cash comes in from positive cash flow from operations. In performing a DCF-ROI evaluation, the cash outflows (presumably early in the cycle) are related to the cash inflows provided by the earnings of the acquired entity, plus a final cash inflow provided by the assumed sale of the entity at the end of the holding period (frequently referred to as residual value). In many cases the residual value will be assumed to be far in the future, and will have less impact on the results of the DCF-ROI computation than the positive cash flows expected for the years closer to the acquisition.

One way that the DCF-ROI concept can be used in forming an opinion as to the estimated value of an acquisition candidate is to determine the present value of the estimated future cash inflows which would be provided by the acquisition candidate, using an assumed rate. In theory, the present value obtained by using the minimum rate of return that the acquirer considers acceptable should produce a present value which is equal to the highest amount that the acquirer should be willing to pay for the acquisition candidate. Many alternative computations using different estimates of future cash inflows and different assumed discount rates, or required rates of return, can be made in analyzing the effects of potential future events and developing ranges of potential present values of the acquisition candidate.

Another use of the DCF-ROI approach is to determine the discount rate, or rate of return implicit in the relationship between the asking price for an acquisition candidate and the acquirer's estimate of future cash inflows, or even for future cash inflows projected by the seller. If this rate is below the rate of return required by the acquirer, then the acquirer might consider the asking price too high.

**Price/Earnings Multiples.** Simply stated, a price earnings multiple of an acquisition candidate is its purchase price divided by its net income after income taxes for a one-year period. The one-year period will normally be the current year, although another way to calculate is to take the present quarter's net income and annualize it. As can be noted for some publically traded securities, the price/earnings (P/E) ratio of an entity on a rapid earnings growth trend can become high (e.g., 40 times earnings) in that investors are paying a higher price in the belief that future earnings will be much greater.

Often P/E ratio statistics are available for major companies in a particular industry. Sometimes, recent purchase prices paid for similar businesses can be used for a guideline comparison by applying the P/E ratio implicit in the comparative business acquisitions to the earnings of the acquisition candidate to arrive at an estimate of comparative value. Businesses in the same industry, or with similar risk and reward characteristics, provide the best basis for comparison.

**Percentage of Gross.**  In some situations, particularly where much smaller businesses are involved, an acquirer may compare the possible purchase price with the gross sales of the entity, and express the purchase price as, for example, 50 percent of gross. Undeniably, a prudent acquirer will also look at the acquisition candidate's assets, and also examine the costs and expenses of the acquisition candidate to determine whether there is anything that would prevent the acquirer from realizing the normal profit margins expected in a particular industry.

**Value of Assets.**  Most acquisitions involve the purchase of net tangible assets with a premium arising from the ongoing value of the business as a going concern. Therefore the fair market value of the net tangible assets of an acquisition will in most cases be a useful item of information to the acquirer in establishing a minimum (and probably below-minimum) value for the acquisition candidate. If a seller cannot sell a business as a whole for at least the fair market value of the tangible assets, then the seller is usually better advised to liquidate the entity by selling the assets individually. The seller may not do this, however, because of the comparative difficulty of taking apart an ongoing business for individual sale of assets, or for tax reasons.

To the acquirer, the "bargain" purchase of assets bears some value in that if the acquisition turns sour from the standpoint of continued operations as a going concern, the assets can always be disposed of to recover a good percentage of the acquirer's investment.

**Market Value of Stock.**  Market value of recent transactions in stock of an acquisition candidate will give an overall indicated market value of the stockholders' equity of the acquisition candidate. This will be most determinable where public companies are involved, but may also be determinable in some cases for the shares of privately owned companies where such have recently changed hands.

The fair market value of an acquisition candidate's shares of stock will be of particular concern to an acquirer who is attempting a tender offer; normally a higher price than the present market will be offered to induce stockholders to sell. However, one should note that the acquirer, in arriving at the price to be offered in a tender offer, has probably evaluated the acquisition candidate's tangible asset value and future earnings and cash flow potential in comparison with the market value of stock, and the price that must be paid to make the tender offer successful.

**Establishing Price—Summary.**    Although quantitative evaluations such as the preceding can provide guidelines in developing a proposed purchase price, there are many other factors that affect purchase prices, and a purely mathematical approach to pricing an acquisition will rarely be the sole determinant. The accountant, in functioning as advisor, must be cognizant of the more subjective influences that can affect purchase prices. For example, market values of stock sometimes do not reflect the fair market value of a company's assets, so the market price of stock at some point may not be an adequate measure of the value of a company or its assets on a liquidation basis. The market value of shares of stock owned by many shareholders can take on a significantly higher value in the context of a single acquirer owning a majority of the shares and therefore controlling the acquired company.

In many acquisitions, the effects of the structuring of the transaction on future taxes can be an important negotiation point in determining the price. Furthermore, and perhaps most significant, the dynamics of negotiation, economic considerations, and other motivations of the acquirer and seller can affect a negotiated purchase price substantially.

An important procedure for the accountant to include in carrying out the advisory role is to evaluate carefully the pro forma projections of future operating results and the financial position assuming the acquisition is consummated. This information can be used to measure the ramifications of consummating an acquisition at various purchase prices, or consummating a transaction at all. The effects of a proposed acquisition on projected earnings per share may have a bearing on the total purchase price and form of consideration an acquirer can afford to offer. For example, where new shares of stock are issued to consummate a business combination, earnings per share of the acquiring company (or issuing company in the case of a pooling of interests) can decline if the increased earnings of the combined operation are not sufficient to offset the effect of the increased outstanding shares in the computation of earnings per share. This is why the market prices of public companies sometimes decline immediately after the announcement of the intent to acquire another company in exchange for newly issued common stock. The implications of any impact such as this should be carefully  evaluated.

**FINANCING ACQUISITIONS.**    Many major corporate acquisitions are carried out with the purchase price being paid in cash, or by an exchange of shares of stock. However, many smaller acquirers (and even some large corporations) will need to, or wish to, finance a portion of the purchase price. This may be in the form of the seller holding notes for a part of the purchase price on a short-, medium-, or long-term basis, or in the form of outside financing from banks or other lenders. Acquisitions will typically be easier to finance from outside sources where the company being acquired has a strong asset base that can be pledged as collateral.

**Asset-based Lenders.**  Banks and other asset-based lenders (including commercial finance companies) function solely as creditors of the acquirer. Often, the assets of the acquired entity will be pledged as collateral for funds borrowed from these senior lenders with the amount that may be borrowed limited to percentages of the different kinds of assets. The best interest rates from this group will be obtained from banks.

**Subordinated Lenders.**  Subordinated lenders, which include insurance companies and pension funds, take a subordinated position in liquidation to the senior lenders. Frequently, for this subordinated position, a lender will have some equity participation, either through the right to convert the debt instruments into common stock, or through a bargain purchase of stock at the time of lending funds pursuant to the subordinated debt instrument.

**Equity Participation.**  A third layer of funding for financing acquisitions involves those entities that provide funds on the basis of heavy equity participation. Although subordinated debt may also be involved, the entities which provide financing of this sort will normally receive significant equity positions in the acquired company. This form of financing would not have much applicability to major corporate acquisitions. The types of entities providing this kind of funding include venture capital firms and some insurance companies.

Many smaller acquisitions, particularly those made by individuals or small groups of investors, do not involve the complicated financing considerations implied by the dealings that would be required with the various types of lenders previously mentioned. In fact, in a typical smaller acquisition made by these types of acquirers, one might expect to see a down payment for a portion of the purchase price, perhaps a bank loan for working capital needs or a little more of the down payment, and the seller holding a term note over 5 to 10 years for over 50 percent of the purchase price at a favorable interest rate.

Although the accountant may advise an acquirer in the raising of funds for an acquisition or leveraged buyout, where the use of leverage plays a significant part in the character of the transaction, raising the funds normally is handled by other professionals, such as merger and acquisition consultants. The foregoing is provided to give the accountant an overview of some of the major considerations, and to point out the importance of financing in the acquisition process for some transactions.

## FORMALIZING THE DEAL AND DUE DILIGENCE

**Letters of Intent.**   At a point where the parties have arrived at an understanding that an acceptable transaction can be consummated, the parties may exchange a document referred to as a letter of intent. Letters of intent are used to define the major terms of the proposed transaction. They usually are not legally binding, but serve as a working document signed by both parties to ensure that their understandings are consistent, and to provide a guide for the preparation of the formal contracts. Some or all of the following items are typically covered in letters of intent:

1. The nature of the transaction, including the assets or stock to be sold and treatment of liabilities.
2. The form and amount of consideration and structure.
3. Definition of what procedures the acquirer and seller must carry out before the final determination to proceed with the transaction, including verification of assets, financial records, and examination of contracts and other legal documents.
4. A proposed timetable for carrying out the previously mentioned procedures, preparing the formal agreements and consummating the transaction.
5. A statement that although the letter of intent accurately sets forth the intent of the parties, it is not legally binding.

Also, either as part of a letter of intent or as the subject of a separate agreement, it is advisable for the parties to enter into a confidentiality agreement in which each party agrees to deep confidential any business information or trade secrets learned during the discussions of the possible acquisition.

**Due Diligence.**   Due diligence is a term used to refer to the process of reviewing and verifying information about the company being acquired, and is often carried out by accountants. It is perhaps the most important role of the accountant in functioning as advisor in a merger and acquisition situation. It often is carried out after the parties have arrived at a preliminary understanding that an acquisition is likely, and may even take place after a letter of intent has been exchanged.

Due diligence procedures may also be performed by other persons representing an acquirer's organization, such as lawyers or other specialists. The depth and intensity of due diligence procedures can vary from cursory inquiry and investigation of only the most general and obvious areas such as corporate documentation matters, to in-depth audit and verification of asset ownership, reviews or audits of financial records, and due diligence procedures that are less financial and legal in nature. For example, if a major item of value is an apparent technological development, due diligence procedures might include an evaluation of the technology by qualified scientists or experts, including developing an estimate of how defensible patents would be with respect to technology of the acquisition candidate.

The term *preacquisition reviews* has been used in this chapter to describe the due diligence procedures typically performed by accountants. This area is covered in detail later in a separate section.

**CONSUMMATION OF THE ACQUISITION.** Somewhere along the line, most acquisitions under investigation fail to materialize for one reason or another. For those that pass all the tests and survive the investigations, evaluations, and negotiations, the actual consummation can sometimes seem anticlimactic in relation to the excitement and uncertainty of all the events that lead up to the actual closing. Lawyers for either the purchaser or seller will prepare a draft of the pertinent contracts, and it is common for many details requiring further negotiation to arise as the formal contract is developed and agreed upon.

If all goes well, the day for closing will finally arrive. At a closing, various kinds of documents are executed by lawyers and officers of the buyer and seller.

**Closing Documents.** The following is a general list of major documents executed or provided at the closing of an acquisition transaction. Of course, the documents needed for any one transaction will depend on the nature of the specific transaction.

Stock purchases:

1. Stock purchase agreement
2. Opinion of counsel as to legality of transaction
3. Stock power conveying control of corporation
4. Promissory notes and security instruments
5. Resolutions of boards of directors
6. Assignments and required consents from third parties

Asset purchases:

1. Asset sale and purchase agreement
2. Opinion of counsel as to legality of the transaction
3. Bills of sale and deeds
4. Promissory notes, mortgages, and security instruments
5. Assignments and required consents from third parties

# THE ACCOUNTANT'S ADVISORY ROLE

Although the accountant can provide valuable advice and counsel through use of his or her business experience and familiarity with all the general topics that have already been discussed, there are two major areas where the accountant can make an especially important contribution. One area is in performing an effective preacquisition review, and the second involves providing advice and counsel in the sometimes difficult task of dealing with financial and organizational concerns in the postacquisition integration of the acquired or merged entity.

**PREACQUISITION REVIEWS.**  An accountant may be called on to perform specific procedures, or to investigate an acquisition candidate using general guidelines as to the conduct and types of matters to be investigated, with the accountant planning the specific procedures. Such assignments are frequently referred to as *preacquisition reviews.* Preacquisition reviews can be performed by accountants from an acquirer organization, by outside consultants, or outside CPAs in conjunction with an audit, review, or compilation of financial statements, as a separate special service.

A preacquisition review should enable accountants to comment on all significant accounting and business matters coming to their attention as a result of the procedures from their perspective as financial experts and businesspersons.

The following sections discuss different aspects of preacquisition reviews that are important to the accountant.

**GENERAL BUSINESS CONSIDERATIONS.**  An understanding of the industry environment in which the acquisition candidate operates is important for properly carrying out a preacquisition review. Where the acquisition candidate is engaged in more than one industry or line of business, each should be considered separately, if significant. The study should include analyzing the industries in which the principal customers and suppliers operate, and also identifying and analyzing the major competitors of the acquisition candidate. Recent and expected future trends in the availability and cost of key materials and services are important.

Trends and growth of the market with respect to the industry as a whole and the individual companies in the industry, and the potential of the acquisition candidate to maintain or increase market share in light of the indicated trends, can be important and indicative of the future potential of the acquisition candidate.

The relative financial, operational, and technological strengths of the companies in the industry should be compared, together with the relative acceptance and demand for each competitor's products or services.

The possibility of customers or suppliers further integrating their operations, thereby increasing competition, should be evaluated. This may depend to some degree on the complexity of the industry's technology, or the amount of investment required to enter the industry.

The potential for technological obsolescence through technological advances, creating a need to invest heavily in research and development, is an important consideration.

The company's activities and commitment to research and development activities should be noted, as well as the results of past efforts. In this area in particular, the accountant may not be qualified to evaluate the implications of research and development activities, but inquiries may provide additional information of interest to persons in the acquirer organization who are qualified to evaluate this area.

The overall stability and seasonal and cyclical aspects of the industry should be focused on, and also the extent to which government regulation may influence the business.

**ORGANIZATIONAL INFORMATION.**  The review of the organization of the acquisition candidate should include identifying key management personnel in each area of needed expertise, and reviewing the background and present responsibilities of each. The ages of management should be considered in light of anticipated needs to provide continuity of competent management after the acquisition. Where the successful management of the company is dependent on the abilities of one or a few individuals, that fact should be identified and carefully evaluated.

The compensation of management, in relation to compensation of officials at comparable levels of responsibility in the acquirer organization, should be noted and also any employment contracts that may have been entered into. Frequently, companies expecting to be acquired enter into employment contracts with key management, especially where members of management are also significant stockholders.

Review and discussion of organization charts and procedures manuals can provide extensive insight into the business and operations of the acquisition candidate, and identify areas where efficiency may be improved. This type of information can assist the acquirer in measuring the profit potential in the future through better utilization of resources, or the ability to reduce staff.

Major plants, assets, facilities, and productive capacity in relation to actual capacity utilized should be identified, together with remaining estimated useful lives of the assets and facilities.

Company records such as minutes of board meetings, articles of incorporation, corporate bylaws, stockholder agreements, and listings of all legal and corporate entities controlled by or affiliated with the acquisition candidate should be reviewed.

Employee benefit plans, particularly pension plans, should be carefully reviewed, including the funding status of pension funds. Review of this information can provide the acquirer with insight into important matters that should be negotiated in the terms of the purchase agreement in situations such as where the vested benefits under a pension plan exceed the balance of the pension fund assets. These possible "hidden" liabilities related to employee benefit plans can be of great concern.

The insurance program and policies of the acquisition candidate should be analyzed to determine major risks that are present, and adequacy of coverage. Any self-insurance practices should be particularly noted. Even though in the circumstances self-insurance may be a prudent decision, the potential for financial exposure from self-insured losses from events both before and after the acquisition should be focused on by the acquirer. The review of product liability insurance policies can point out a product line that might be more susceptible to liability claims than the acquirer may consider acceptable. The acquirer may also note possible reductions in premiums available by combining policies of the acquisition candidate with those of the acquirer.

**EVALUATING PURCHASE AGREEMENTS.**    Any preacquisition review should include a careful review of the purchase agreement to ensure that the procedures are planned with an understanding of all significant aspects of the proposed transaction. In addition, the review of the purchase contract will enable the accountant to make suggestions on how to improve the structure of the transaction, or to provide advice on implications of an accounting, business, or operational nature.

The accountant should carefully examine any sections that include terms dependent on accounting measurements. These types of terms can impact determination or adjustment of the purchase price, or representations made by the seller regarding the financial condition of the business being sold.

An area of particular concern for the accountant to focus on is the accounting basis on which the acquisition candidate's financial statements and data referred to in the purchase agreement are based. Frequently, "usual and customary accounting practices" will be mentioned and reference made to an attached set of financial statements. A typical passage from a purchase agreement will read "consistent with the company's usual and customary accounting practices used in preparing the attached financial statements in accordance with generally accepted accounting principles." A problem could develop in interpretation of the agreement at a later date if any of the accounting practices of the acquisition candidate are thought not to be compliance with generally accepted accounting principles, and the accountant should be alert for any problems that could result from interpretation of such a definition.

The possibility of a problem in this area will be reduced significantly if the financial statements have been audited and reported on by an outside CPA. Differences of opinion on matters of generally accepted accounting principles can exist, however, which cause one accountant to disagree with another about the preferability or correctness of accounting practices and principles used in preparing financial statements.

The following are some specific areas that the accountant should be particularly alert for in reviewing a purchase agreement:

1.  Guarantees of net realizable values of accounts receivable and inventories, where the purchase price will be adjusted depending on amounts realized.

2.  Provisions dealing with the assumption of liabilities which may be handled any number of ways in purchase agreements, ranging from the buyer indemnifying the seller completely from all past liabilities associated with the business, to the seller assuming all liabilities, whether or not they have been recorded in the balance sheet at the purchase date.

3.  The accountant should ensure that the acquirer understands the accounting and business ramifications of any contingencies that it will be assuming exposure for in the purchase agreement. The resolution of a preacquisition contingency can ordinarily be treated as an increase of the acquisition cost for accounting purposes in a purchase method acquisition, thereby avoiding an immediate reduction in reported earnings from an unfavorable resolution of a preacquisition contingency. However, the economic effect of a cash outlay which could be caused by an unfavorable contingency resolution should be discussed with the acquirer for consideration in negotiation.

4.  The seller may represent in the agreement that the net worth of the company being acquired is at least equal to a specified minimum amount. The existence of this type of provision normally requires ascertaining

that operating results and other factors between the date the agreement was drafted and the transaction date do not cause the net worth to decline below the minumum required amount.

5.  Provisions that would prevent pooling of interest treatment, if such is the intent of the parties, or any provisions that might cause a problem with the desired tax structure of the transaction.

6.  Terms that the accountant believes should be considered for legality such as possible antitrust violations.

7.  Covenants or representations which the accountant believes may not be accurate, or which either the acquirer or seller may have difficulty complying with.

8.  Contracts or obligations being assumed by the acquirer which may be unfavorable or which could be at other than current market rates.

9.  Terms regarding employee benefit and pension plans, and the disposition of existing pension and other employee benefit funds.

10. Maintenance of prior year's accounting and tax records and changeover of accounting and data processing systems.

**REVIEW OF PROPOSED TRANSACTION.**   A key area to be considered in reviewing a proposed acquisition is whether the terms of the transaction are consistent with the desired tax and accounting effects. In particular, the accountant or a tax specialist should ascertain that if a tax-free transaction is desired, none of the terms of the agreement would prevent the transaction from being tax-free. Similar considerations would result in confirming that pooling of interests accounting will be applicable, if the parties so desire.

It may be appropriate, in reviewing the proposed transaction, to review or prepare pro forma financial statements on a historical and projected basis to provide a clear, forward-looking view of the impact of the transaction. Part of the evaluation of a proposed acquisition should include evaluating the expected financial impact on reported earnings after the acquisition. With the pooling of interests method, pro forma combination of data of the previously separate companies will be a more simple process than where a purchase acquisition is involved. Projecting the future earnings impact of a purchase acquisition will often require estimating higher depreciation charges from the written-up value of acquired fixed assets and the amortization of goodwill.

Furthermore, the initial period after an acquisition may include in cost of sales a higher charge for acquired inventories stated at a higher than normal amount. In view of the normal expectations of an acquirer that its accountants will provide advice on the accounting aspects of an acquisition, it is important that the accountant anticipate the postacquisition financial reporting implications of a proposed acquisition and that he or she advise the acquirer accordingly.

Besides projected reported earnings, projected cash flow after the acquisition should be carefully reviewed. Often, an acquired operation can require supplemental working capital or other investments by the acquirer soon after the acquisition, and this should not come as a surprise.

Computation of pro forma financial ratios may provide additional insight into the economic effects of the proposed transaction.

**ACCOUNTING AND FINANCIAL CONSIDERATIONS.** The analysis and review of historical financial data should include identifying any unusual or nonrecurring items that distorted reported earnings. Inquiry should be made regarding any significant adjustments made at year-ends which may indicate the kinds of items that could cause distortion of current interim period data. Funds flows should be scrutinized carefully through reviewing the statements of changes in financial position and cash flow statements. Prior years' budget to actual comparisons should be reviewed. Balance sheets and components of financial position should be analyzed and related to the proposed purchase price where possible, on a historical and current cost replacement basis.

Forecasted and projected balance sheet and income statement data provided by the acquisition candidate should be reviewed and critically analyzed. A forecast refers to what is believed to be the most likely outcome based on the most probable future conditions, and may also include the effects of certain strategies planned by management. The assumptions on which the forecasted or projected data are based should be reviewed for reasonableness, and the accountant should consider to what degree the assumptions may be motivational or overly optimistic. Where major assumptions have a significant effect, ranges should be computed to indicate the effects of possible variations in the future outcomes that would be caused by different assumptions. Prior forecasts or projections should be compared with subsequent actual results to ascertain how accurate these have been in the past.

One should expect that a company trying to sell itself will present an optimistic impression of its future potential, and there is always a risk that projections and forecasts of future financial results provided by an acquisition candidate are unrealistic. This is particularly noticeable where an acquisition candidate is young in its growth cycle or is introducing a new technology. In a preacquisition review, the accountant should keep an open mind to recognize the potential of an acquisition candidate, but should be prepared to adopt a posture of professional skepticism should the circumstances require.

Historical, forecasted, and projected data should be analyzed on the basis of product lines, by facility, or any other breakdown that depicts results in separately identifiable segments. Firm order backlogs should be reviewed on this basis also, and compared with sales trends and firm order backlogs existing in prior periods to identify any trends that should be investigated further.

**AFTER THE MERGER OR ACQUISITION.**    Once an acquisition has been completed, the transition phase begins. Actually, the well-organized acquisition team will have begun to study the situation well in advance of the actual closing of the transaction, and already begun to make its plans for transitioning the systems of the entity being acquired.

Overall responsibility for coordinating the accounting and systems transition will usually rest with someone in the controller's department of the acquirer. This team leader, with the support of specialists in the accounting and data processing areas, should develop a priority list of the most critical areas to get under immediate control.

**Systems Evaluation.**    In all cases, the most critical area will be to ensure that systems will be in place to handle the ongoing processing of transactions with minimal slowing down or loss of control over the normal flow of business. These areas include payroll, billing and collection, and recording purchases and making disbursements. The situation will be much simplified if the acquired operation has its own freestanding data processing capability—in fact, business may continue without missing a step. Where the acquired operation has been a remote job entry site of a larger system with a central data processing organization, however, the transitional situation is more complex. In the extreme sense, one could picture the seller "pulling the plug" that connects the remote job entry site to the host computer, thereby bringing processing to a virtual stop. The accountant should immediately determine if this kind of situation exists.

Often, an arrangement must be made with the seller to continue to process transactions, and sometimes even general ledgers and other systems using the seller's data processing capabilities, until the acquirer can establish independent systems for the acquired operation, or integrate the acquired operation into its own systems. Sometimes, portions of some systems must be handled manually on a temporary basis until data processing capability can be increased.

**Procedures for Financial Reporting.**    After satisfying the need to continue processing business transactions, the accountant should ensure that procedures are set up for normal monthly and periodic operational and financial reporting. This will include establishing monthly closing schedules, procedures and formats for providing balance sheets, income statements, and other data to the new parent company for consolidation. In addition, procedures should be established for monthly commentary by management of the acquired entity on the operating performance. In this respect, it is a great service to general management for the accountant to ask general management personnel responsible for the entity what kind of information they would like to receive to monitor the performance of the acquired entity.

On the accounting side, someone should be assigned responsibility for handling the acquisition accounting and reviewing the internal controls, accounting policies, and practices of the acquired entity for compatibility with those of the acquirer, and ensuring that any required reclassifications or adjustments are made in consolidation with the parent.

The personnel aspects of the accounting and systems areas are of great importance in the transition of the acquired entity. In some cases, it will be wise to transfer one or more supervisory or management persons from the acquirer organization into the acquired entity. An alternative is to assign someone in the parent organization as liaison to the newly acquired entity to assist and provide consultation regarding the new owner's requirements and policies. This will give the acquired entity access to someone familiar with the acquirer's systems and procedures, and will also give the acquirer some comfort in having some of its own management personnel on site "minding the store."

**Personnel Considerations.**    The area of personnel matters and staffing will, as in all departments of the acquired company, be critical in the financial and systems areas. When an acquisition is in process, or has occurred, the obvious questions about possible organizational and personnel changes can cause employees great concern about job security. If not properly addressed, there could be losses of key employees, reducing the ability of the acquirer to carry forward the benefits of the existing work force of the acquired company.

In an acquisition environment, morale and productivity may decline, partly because of uncertainty about the future. Furthermore, there may even be negative feelings due to the prospect of new management control, because employees, having worked hard to gain recognition and credibility, may now have the task of proving themselves all over again to a new management group. Effective communication is usually the best way to address this situation.

Employees on all levels will have questions about the future operation of the acquired entity which are important to them, but which are sometimes difficult to answer. The staff of the acquired company will desire, and deserves, professional treatment in a trying, difficult time.

Despite its best efforts, an acquirer should be prepared to lose some employees from the acquired company because of concerns about new management and possible termination.

It is essential to understand the levels of professional expertise in each department. In the medium term, all key employees should be evaluated. A good starting point is review of individual personnel files to develop an understanding of the background, talents, and career progress of the individuals in the acquired company. Many failures in integrating acquisitions are caused by the acquirer not properly assessing the level of personnel skills and resources needed to continue operating and controlling the acquired company, and to integrate the acquired company into the acquirer's organization.

The important question will arise of whether to place managerial personnel from the acquirer organization in the lead roles in the accounting and systems departments of the acquired entity. Although some acquirers have specific policies in this area, based on the relative qualifications of the management staff in place, sometimes it is best to have existing management continue in the role. This is an important area and should be reviewed carefully.

**Accounting and Reporting.**    Starting the accounting and reporting process for an acquired entity involves a combination of technical and administrative considerations. It would be easy if the acquirer simply had to absorb the financial numbers as previously generated by the acquired entity, but this is rarely the case.

The accounting principles for business combinations, generally based on Accounting Principles Board Opinion No. 16, can be complex and tricky in implementation. In the real world, often more time is spent trying to assemble and comprehend the facts and circumstances related to an acquisition, and evaluating the accounts of an acquiree than time spent puzzling over the accounting rules. Therefore it is important that someone qualified in this area be assigned responsibility for handling the acquisition accounting.

*Recording the Opening Balance Sheet.*    The acquirer will need to book the acquisition into its balance sheet (in the sense of reporting the acquiree as a consoslidated subsidiary) for the month in which the acquisition occurred, and this is frequently done using estimates. At this point, the process of compiling and analyzing the information may have only begun. A special effort to finalize these estimates should be made for a year-end balance sheet, or when financial data are first released to the public such as at the end of a quarter.

These comments essentially relate to purchase method acquisitions. Where the transaction has been accounted for as a pooling, the accounts of the separate entities are combined, with much less in the way of transitional adjustment to the accounting records.

Following every acquisition, with every month that passes, an acquirer becomes aware of more and more information which provides greater clarity as to the correct opening balance sheet. The kinds of items that an acquirer may "discover" after an acquisition include:

1. Liabilities for items that relate to expenses properly allocable to prior periods. These should be recorded as liabilities in the opening balance sheet, unless the purchase agreement provides for recovery of such items from the seller.

2. Assets that do not have the value originally believed. This will include uncollectible receivables, obsolete or damaged inventories that must be written off or sold at a loss, or equipment or other fixed assets which do not have the usefulness or fair market value originally believed.

3. Extraordinary repairs and maintenance costs required to put machinery and equipment into normal operating condition.

4. Employee termination costs.

5. Rentals on facilities to be abandoned or otherwise not used.

Many of these items will fall under the category of resolution of preacquisition contingencies, for which adjustment to the opening balance sheet is required for an allocation period usually expected to last up to one year after the acquisition.

Although technically it would be acceptable to adjust the opening balance sheet continually as these preacquisition items become known and resolved, it is not desirable to have the estimated opening balance sheet changing every month for the first year of ownership. Consequently, the initial and subsequent estimates used become very important, and at some time the acquirer should freeze the estimates into a final opening balance sheet. Unless any significant adjustments are thereafter required, the acquirer should adopt a practical and sensible approach by running any smaller additional differences through post-acquisition profit and loss.

***Reporting Profit and Loss of the Acquiree.***   Frequently, in the initial months after an acquisition, there will not have been time to "push down" the opening balance sheet adjustments and the accounting practices of the acquirer into the records and the reporting cycle of the acquiree, and the results reported by the acquiree will be on the same basis as prior to the acquisition. These results must be adjusted for the acquisition accounting adjustments and accounting policy adjustments prior to consolidation with the parent.

The most apparent adjustments required to profit and loss on the basis of accounting previously used by the acquiree will be:

1. Providing goodwill amortization for goodwill to be included in the balance sheet at the acquisition date.

2. Adjusting depreciation expense for any revaluations to the carrying value of fixed assets and new estimated remaining useful lives as of the acquisition date.

3.  Reversing from reported postacquisition profit and loss any items that may have been included as assets or liabilities in the balance sheet at acquisition date by reason of acquisition accounting adjustment by the acquirer, where such items have been included as profit and loss items in the postacquisition income statement of the acquiree on a separate company historial basis.

4.  Adjustment of profit-and-loss items to conform to accounting policies of the acquirer, where such differ significantly from the policies previously used by the acquiree.

***Keeping the Books of an Acquired Company.***   The "push-down" method of accounting for acquisition accounting results in the acquisition accounting adjustments being reflected in the separate financial statements of the acquiree. For an acquirer's review of financial data regarding the acquiree, and for external financial presentation, this up-to-date recognition of the fair market values of the assets and liabilities will be meaningful.

However, the practical question will arise of whether the actual books and records of the acquiree should be maintained on this basis or whether they should be maintained on an historical basis, with adjustments made after closing the historical books. The decision should be made based on the degree to which historical data will be required in the future. Two reasons for this may exist:

1.  Tax returns of the separate legal entity, whether the entity is to file separate tax returns or to be included in the consolidated tax return of the acquirer, may have to be filed on an historical basis if a tax-free reorganization has occurred, or if the acquirer purchased the stock of the acquiree in a taxable transaction after which the basis of the acquiree's assets was not stepped up.

2.  The existence of minority interests will require continuing data to be accounted for on a historical basis for the percentage of minority interest outstanding.

In some circumstances, it will be appropriate for the acquisition accounting adjustments to be made by the accounting staff of the acquiree prior to submission to the acquirer for consolidation. Where the acquisition accounting adjustments involve sensitive information that the acquirer wishes to keep confidential, it may be best for the acquirer to receive the financial reports from the acquiree on a historical basis, and for the acquirer to make the acquisition accounting adjustments.

**Systems Transition.**   A project team consisting of accounting, data processing, and user department personnel should be formed for evaluating the degree and scope of transitional changes required, development of timetables, implementing procedures, and carrying out the transition of specific systems.

An organized approach should be used in developing an action plan for dealing with each individual system, using the following in order of priority:

1.  Ensure that ongoing business transactions can continue to be processed (payrolls, payables and disbursements, billing, and collections) so that the company can continue to function on a short-term basis.

2.  Ensure that adequate controls will be present and that data wll be properly summarized through transaction listings and general ledgers to enable monthly closings and operational reporting.

3.  Establish temporary procedures for screening all transactions over a specified dollar amount for review for proper cutoff and possible claim against the seller where the purchase agreement indicates that the seller is responsible for any unrecorded liabilities or any recorded assets that are determined to have lower value than reflected on the books. The incidence of claims for overvalued assets will commonly include uncollectible receivables and obsolete or damaged inventories or machinery and equipment.

4.  Develop plans for transition to the systems and procedures which will be used on a medium- and long-term basis.

The transition of individual operating and accounting systems after an acquisition can range from situations where most systems can be left essentially intact (as where an autonomous, freestanding corporation is acquired) to situations where substantial revamping, and modification, or replacement of systems is required. To the extent that existing systems can be left intact, the task of transition is much easier. The first step in dealing with this area should be to evaluate the degree of modification required for each system.

**Dealing with Host Computer.**   The most critical short-range planning situations will exist where the acquirer's transactions have been processed through remote job entry sites communicating with a host computer at a central location, which is not part of the acquired operation. It is unlikely that the seller will agree to continue processing the acquirer's transactions (essentially functioning as a service bureau) for any great length of time. Furthermore, this kind of an arrangement would not be advisable for the acquirer on a long-term basis.

Usually, it will be best to try to arrange this service bureau type relationship for some period of time to give the systems and staff support people adequate time to install and establish the acquirer's own hardware capability and establish the new systems. In some cases, however, the seller cannot or will not provide this service, and "pulls the plug" on the existing systems on the effective date of sale. When this happens, if an outside service bureau or the acquirer's own data processing capabilities cannot pick up the processing load immediately, some hastily designed and implemented manual systems and procedures will have to be put in place for the short term.

**Forms Evaluation.**   An immediate area of concern for all systems is to determine whether any new forms (e.g., invoices, purchase orders, checks) will have to be ordered because of changes in printed titles or legal terms. If so, this should be addressed immediately by compiling a comprehensive list of all forms used in each system and conducting an evaluation process. Outside printers and job shoppers usually require approximately one month in an expedite mode at a premium price to deliver preprinted forms. Normal turnaround time for new forms is even longer.

Major applications which will usually be of concern in transactions are:

1. Payroll
2. Purchasing and disbursements
3. Billing and accounts receivable
4. Fixed assets
5. Personnel data reporting
6. General ledger
7. Automated IRS reporting
8. Data and master file back-up systems

There may be other systems that are unique to an individual company which require transition. They should be prioritized, researched, and dealt with in the same manner as the aforementioned systems.

**Computer Systems Transition.**   Companies of all sizes rely to a great extent on computers and data processing to accomplish financial and operational reporting and processing of business transactions, through an in-house data center staffed by data processing professionals. Proper coordination and integration of the data processing function of an acquired company are an important part of administering the acquisition process and, as advisor, the accountant should be prepared to participate in evaluating and integrating the data processing function in an acquisition.

**_Computer Hardware._**  A well-organized inventory of computer hardware is very important. A comprehensive list of all equipment and related contracts should be prepared by equipment type, manufacturer or lessor, indicating location and serial number. All this information will be useful in the decision process of whether to utilize or dispose of the acquired computer hardware. The equipment list shsould include details on each of the following main categories:

1. Central processing units and related input and output equipment
2. Data entry devices
3. Interactive input/output devices (CRTs)

Communications capabilities between the equipment is another important point to note.

At the time of compiling the list of hardware, it is wise to review the hardware maintenance records to ensure that the hardware has been maintained in conformity with the manufacturer's recommended schedule.

As an alternative to owning or leasing computer hardware, service bureau processing is used in some companies. If the service bureau will not be used in the future, a transition plan will have to be developed.

**_Computer Software._**  Since the inception of computers it has become an established fact that no two programmers will write programming code to satisfy a business reporting need in the same way, even where the same computer language is used. This difference factor can be carried into the full scope of an existing system design, making evaluation of code and existing software of an acquired company somewhat involved.

The task of evaluating software of an acquired company should be based on establishing the quality of the code that was produced. This, besides leading to a conclusion on the continuing value of software, can tell an acquirer many things about the new staff.

If, as a result of the review, it is concluded that a data center has poorly written, poorly documented systems, new programs should be considered instead of maintenance of the existing programs.

Validation of a computerized business system means evaluating two distinct and separate qualities: (1) the degree to which the system supplies the user with what is needed and (2) the degree of smoothness with which the system processes.

Discussions should be held with the users to establish whether reports are being utilized and to determine whether any necessary information is not being provided. The latter can sometimes be identified by reviewing user manually prepared reports.

Most computer operations will have a process control log. This log, if properly maintained, will indicate system stops and any reruns that have taken place during system processing, providing an indication of systems that do not run smoothly.

Preparation of complete systems documentation is usually done at the time new systems are created. Unfortunately, original system design and original programs often do not remain intact, because requirements and computer systems designs change. Only in the most thorough of computer centers will timely updating of systems documentation faithfully occur.

If computer software of an acquired company is to be retained, it is important that systems documentation be compared with the actual applications.

# CHAPTER 12

# GOVERNMENT REGULATIONS

## Philip Kropatkin

## HERCULEAN TASK

Accountants, whether CPAs, managerial accountants, or internal auditors, face a herculean, if not impossible, advisory task in protecting their clients or employers from incurring regulatory violations. It is extremely difficult for the average practitioner to be aware of all the thousands of regulations in so many everyday situations—regulations that prescribe this; prescribe that; prohibit this; prohibit that. It is so easy to overlook material requirements, and so easy to go wrong!

Our society has become awkwardly entangled in its own administrative maze. Just sorting out what is legal, and what is prohibited (much less what is ethical or abusive) seems like an endless maze. And it can be so if one attempts to master it all. Our economic web has become so complex, so vulnerable to itself (with computer record keeping and data collection), and the environment around us so threatening, that we have attempted to ward off or control the important (sometimes only what we erroneously perceive as important) threats to our physical health and safety with whole libraries full of administrative prescriptions. These prescriptions (defenses) can be called government regulations. They are issued by all levels of government, right down to the smallest of municipalities. They can vary from rules of practice before the U.S. Supreme Court to ordinances issued by the local hometown.

Some background is in order. The "separation of power" doctrine is a relatively straightforward and well-known principle of our democratic government. Every student learns about this in his or her elementary civics classes. There are three branches—the legislative, judicial, and executive. They are conceptually cooperative, yet self-balancing (and self-policing). This federal system has counterparts at state, city, and county levels—in most respects. Seems relatively clean cut. Not so!

We have omitted the regulatory branch. The FCC, the ICC, the NLRB, the FPC, the CPSC, the FDA—and dozens of other alphabet agencies that operate under various acts of legislation. All for the most part are independent of the regular judicial, legislative, and executive branches. What is more, there are over 60 other agencies that issue major regulations in federal government. Many are only a part of separate cabinet-level departments, but they all have full regulatory functions of an independent nature within their own purview.

To further illustrate the overall concern and difficulty in easily dealing with this entire subject—in some sort of useful and practical manner—we must ask the reader to share with us a brief sampling (there are a great many more) of just the titles to some articles written over the past few years, by a number of very perceptive and concerned writers. These are drawn at random and are by no means complete or orderly. They may, however, be aptly listed (in any old fashion), because the subject itself is cumbersome and generally disorderly. It is merely intended to highlight and illustrate to the potential advisor what astute writers and editors think he or she is up against. Then, to just list a few: "Waist deep in Regulation," "Regulations Cost $2.6 Billion" (in only 48 sampled companies), "Who Runs the Government," "FTC Is Becoming the Consumers' Aggressive Crusader," "Regulations, Regulations, Regulations," "On Regulatory Reform," "Should the President Control the Regulators," "Regulations for Human Beings," "Expensive Rules," "Time for a Fourth Branch of Government," and so on.

# MAJOR REGULATORY AGENCIES

Let us take it one more step. We have compiled a highly condensed list of only the *major* regulatory agencies. It is interesting to note that almost half of them were set in motion after 1950. If we were also to add those regulations that affect most of our population, in one respect or another, emanating from sub-cabinet groups—like the giant Internal Revenue Service, Social Security Administration, Health Care Financing Administration (Medicare, Medicaid), Student Loan Offices, and such, it is easy to see that the last 25 years have been more than the equal of the previous 150 years in the impact and creation of regulatory influences. They obviously represent an enormous chore regarding general compliance with, or at least awareness of them by all businesspersons and their financial advisors.

## The Vast Regulatory Establishment

Year Created

| | |
|---|---|
| 1824 to 1900 | Army Corps of Engineers |
| | Patent and Trademark Offices |
| | Comptroller of the Currencies |
| | Bureau of Fisheries |
| | Interstate Commerce Commission |
| 1900 to 1930. | Antitrust Division |
| | Federal Reserve Board |
| | Federal Trade Commission |
| | Coast Guard |
| | Tariff Commission |
| | Commodity Exchange Authority |
| | Customs Service |
| 1930 to 1940. | Federal Power Commission |
| | Food and Drug Administration |
| | Federal Home Loan Bank Board |
| | Employment Standards Commission |
| | Federal Deposit Insurance Corporation |
| | Federal Communications Commission |
| | Securities and Exchange Commission |
| | National Labor Relations Board |
| | Federal Maritime Commission |
| | Consumer and Marketing Service |
| | Civil Aeronautics Board |
| | Atomic Energy Commission |
| | Federal Aviation Agency |
| 1950 to 1960. | U.S. Commission on Civil Rights |
| | Renegotiation Board |
| | Small Business Administration |
| 1960 to 1970. | Agricultural Stabilization and Conservation Service |
| | Equal Employment Opportunity Commission |
| | Federal Highway Administration |
| | Federal Railroad Administration |
| 1970 to 1980 and on. | Cost Accounting Standards Board |
| | Environmental Protection Agency |
| | National Credit Union Administration |

## The Vast Regulatory Establishment

Year Created

National Highway Traffic Safety
Administration
Farm Credit Administration
Bureau of Alcohol, Tobacco and
Firearms
Consumer Product Safety Commission
Drug Enforcement Agency
Federal Energy Administration
Mine Safety and Health Administration
Occupational Safety and Health
Administration
Council on Wage and Price Stability
Federal Election Commission
National Safety Board
Office of Consumer Affairs and
Regulatory Functions
Office of Surface Mining Reclamation

This, of course, does not include the enormous number of regulations that pertain to a particular industry or section of the population as a discrete grouping. If, for example, one is in or connected with the nursing home industry, there are shelves full of rules and regulations pertaining to safety requirements, health code standards, nursing service, food handling, cost reimbursement, billing procedures, and so on. Hospitals are in a similar situation. There are also dozens and dozens of specialized newsletters and industry magazines devoted to the intricacies and special requirements of each identifiable industry. Separate trade associations abound. One of their key objectives is to provide their constituencies with insider knowledge, current trends, and changes to all regulations, and their impact.

Where does this leave the financial advisor whose client/company may be in a variety of businesses, not in just one specialized area; or may be only tangentially involved in a certain industry?

# REGULATORY INFLUENCES

Let us, however, put the entire subject in another perspective. One might ask: What takes place *before* a rule or regulation becomes a requirement for private citizens, and businesses— and a *concern* for financial advisors to consider? Some of the bureaucratic answers are illustrated in Exhibit 12.1. It shows what a staggering variety of inputs, direct and indirect, are placed into motion by the major elements of our multileveled political structure. All of these have an impact on our "rulemakers" before any of the complicated administrative pieces are put into play.

Besides the various elements of Congress, we have the Office of Management and Budget, the General Accounting Office, The Treasury Department, The Office of Personnel Management, the whole professional organization network — all participate very strongly, and participate much like all the official "rulemakers." Let us not overlook the host of state and local entities that put their official multipronged oars into the same muddy waters all over the country.

Every small box in Exhibit 12.1 represents a wide sphere of regulatory influence. This is the best birds-eye view of the three branches (*outside* of the judiciary) that we could compile for an advisory service to financial advisors!

## ADVISORY ROLE

The regulatory agencies have an immense impact on many aspects of the society we live in, which is becoming more complex and diverse every day. Accountants and auditors, because of their specialized knowledge, broad training, and extensive exposure to many of our different business organizations and their internal mechanisms, are increasingly being called on for help by their clients/companies to review and assess their vulnerability to problems emanating from rules and prescriptions inherent in government regulations, and advise them accordingly.

The advisory role is not new. It can realistically be viewed as being only enlarged, and becoming increasingly important. Consider the way accountants and auditors have routinely reviewed their company's/client's insurance coverage (see Chapter 10). They ask the following questions: Is it sufficient, current, precise enough for the industry dangers? Is it documented sufficiently for proof of coverage, if the need arises? How about evidence of assets? What if the whole place burns down with everything in it — could the remaining records — wherever they are, sustain a satisfactory claim?

An accountant doesn't have to be an insurance expert to be a helpful and protective business advisor. It is usual (and expected) for accountants to assume this role. So should it be with some of the other vulnerable areas that are likely to affect the mainstream of the organizations served by these same accountants and auditors. They should be aware of the potential problem areas and warning signals emanating from the need for legal compliance with regulations, so that costly (and even dangerous) violations may be avoided, to the greatest extent practicable.

Private groups such as the Ralph Nader organization have constructed "cit-

Responsibilities and Players

| The U.S. Congress (Congressional Committee) | Federal Agencies | | | | Professional Organizations | State and Local Entities |
|---|---|---|---|---|---|---|
| | OMB | GAO | Treasury | Office of Personnel Management | | |
| Oversight | Policy direction | Audit standards | Circulars | Staffing | AICPA | State laws |
| Committee reports | Uniform principle | Guides | Cash advances | Qualifications | Audit standards (GAAS) | Standards |
| Hearings | Administrative procedures | Forum member | Letters of Credit | Grades | Industry guides | Accounting principles |
| Public laws | Forum member | Accounting principles | | Standards | Position statements | Chartered responsibility |
| | Circulars | Oversight responsibility | | | Publications | |
| | Publications | Special studies | | | Leadership role | |
| | | Rulings | | | FASB-Accounting principles (GAAP) | |
| | | Policy direction: | | | Others · Includes: NACUBO, COGR, AAU, C88P, JFMIP, IIA, MFOA, S&L auditors, AGA, State societies, Private interest groups, etc. | |
| | | Computer | | | | |
| | | Sampling | | | | |
| | | Publications | | | | |
| | | • | | | | |

Federal agencies

Generate — Disseminate — Monitor

Implementation of rules ⟷ Regulatory agents

Thousands of recipients

334

izens advisory manuals," but evidencing the difficulty of brevity in this entire area is the fact that it took over 900 pages to compile what is purported to be just a short, concise, starting reference document!

A few major areas with specific interest to a wide range of companies are described in the following pages, which illustrate the general problem (OSHA, Medicare, Medicaid, EPA, and the Federal Trade Commission). Although these summaries are useful in their own right, they are only relatively *short* summaries of the regulations.

# OCCUPATIONAL SAFETY AND HEALTH ADMINISTRATION

The OSHA program essentially entails seven basic elements:

Management leadership

Assignment of responsibility

Identification and control of hazards

Employee and supervisor training

Safety and health record keeping

First-aid and medical assistance.

Your client should do these things under these seven points:

### MANAGEMENT LEADERSHIP

Post the OSHA workplace poster, Job Safety and Health Protection, where all employees can see it. (This is an OSHA requirement.)

Meet with all employees to discuss job safety and health matters. Discuss your mutual responsibilities under the Act.

Show all employees a copy of the Act and a copy of the OSHA standards that apply to business. Tell them where these will be kept and where they may have access to them.

Write a "policy statement" and post this statement near the OSHA workplace poster so that everyone can see the concern.

Consider establishing a "Code of Safe Practices and Operating Procedures" to provide specific instructions for all employees.

Include job safety and health topics in future meetings or in conversations with employees.

Personally review all inspection and accident reports to ensure followup when needed.

Comment on good or bad safety records and provide accident prevention guidance on a routine basis.

Set a good example. Require that hard hats be worn by everyone in specific areas.

**ASSIGNMENT OF RESPONSIBILITY.**   In terms of management responsibility, the direct supervisors of your employees are usually your key personnel.

After you have set the basic policy for your company, you can delegate the details for carrying out your program to those same people to whom you delegate your operating and production details. If you have supervisors, group leaders, "straw bosses," or other key people, you can assign them specific responsibility for safety and health and hold them accountable for getting the job done.

A good rule of thumb is to assign safety and health responsibilities in the same manner that production responsibilities are assigned. Make it part of their jobs to operate safely.

To maintain a *safe and healthful workplace*, your client will need to do two things:

Identidy workplace hazards which exist now or could develop.

Install procedures to control these hazards and eliminate them if possible.

But where and how to start? How does a small business employer make this a reality in the smallest of workplaces?

To begin, you must remember that this activity will have to be keyed to their workplace, their materials, processes, employees, and production needs.

It is helpful to look on this activity as a two-stage process:

1.  Getting started and working up to a satisfactory level.

2.  Maintaining this activity at a satisfactory level over a period of time. (See the following suggested checklist.)

    a.  No employee is expected to undertake a job until he or she has received job instructions on how to do it properly and has been authorized to perform that job.

    b.  No employee should undertake a job that appears to be unsafe.

    c.  Mechanical safeguards must be kept in place.

    d.  Each employee should report all unsafe conditions encountered during work.

e.  Any injury or illness suffered by an employee, even a slight one, must be reported to you at once.

In addition to the previous items, any safety rules that are a condition of employment such as the use of safety shoes or eye protection should be explained clearly and then enforced.

The direct supervisors must know how to *train employees* in the proper way of doing their jobs. Encourage and consider providing training for these supervisors. (Many community colleges offer management training courses for little or no cost.)

There are some *specific Training requirements* in the OSHA standards that you must meet, such as those which pertain to first aid, powered industrial trucks (including forklifts), power presses, and welding. In general, they deal with situations where the use of untrained or improperly trained operators on skill machinery could cause hazardous situations to develop, not only for the operator, but possibly for nearby workers as well.

**INJURY/ILLNESS RECORDS.**    There are injury/illness record keeping requirements under OSHA that require a minimum of paperwork. These records will provide you with one measure for evaluating the success of your safety and health activities. Success would generally mean a lack of, or a reduced number of, employee injuries or illnesses during a calendar year.

There are five important steps required by the OSHA record keeping system:

1.  Obtain a report on every injury requiring medical treatment (other than first aid).

2.  Record each injury on OSHA Form No. 200 according to the instructions provided.

3.  Prepare a supplementary record of occupational injuries and illnesses for recordable cases either on OSHA Form No. 101 or workers' compensation reports giving the same information.

4.  Every year, prepare the annual summary (OSHA Form No. 200); post it no later than February 1, and keep it posted until March 1. (Is next to the OSHA workplace poster.) A good place to post it.

5.  Retain these records for at least five years.

During the year, periodically review the records to see where injuries are occurring. Look for any patterns or repeat situations. These records can help you to identify those high- risk areas to which you should direct your immediate attention.

Because the basic OSHA records include only injuries and illnesses, you might consider expanding your own system to include all incidents, including those where no injury or illness resulted, if you think such information would assist you in pinpointing unsafe conditions and/or procedures. Safety councils, insurance carriers, and others can assist you in instituting such a system.

# DOCUMENTATION OF YOUR ACTIVITIES

Essential records, including those legally required for workers' compensation, insurance audits, and government inspections must be maintained as long as the actual need exists.

**FIRST AID.**  You must ensure the ready availability of medical personnel for advice and consultation on matters of employee health. This does not mean that you must provide health care. But, if health problems develop in your workplace, you are expected to get medical help to treat them and their causes.

Most small businesses do not have an organized medical and first-aid system, nor are they expected to have one. But all businesses are required to have the following:

> In the absence of an infirmary, clinic, or hospital near your workplace that can be used for the emergency treatment of all injured employees, you as the employer must ensure that a person or persons be adequately trained and available to render first aid. Adequate first-aid supplies must be readily available for emergency use.

> Where the eyes or body of any employee may be exposed to injurious corrosive materials, suitable equipment for quick drenching or flushing of the eyes and body must be provided in the work area for immediate emergency use. Employees should be trained in using the equipment.

The following is a list of useful questions an employee of your client/company might want to ask.

## SELF-INSPECTION CHECKLISTS

### General

1. Is the required OSHA workplace poster displayed in our place of business as required where all employees are likely to see it?
2. Are we aware of the requirement to report all workplace fatalities and any

serious accidents (where five or more are hospitalized) to a federal or state OSHA office within 48 hours?

3. Are workplace injury and illness records being kept as required by OSHA?

4. Are we aware that the OSHA annual summary of workplace injuries and illnesses must be posted by February 1 and must remain posted until March 1?

5. Are we aware that employers with 10 or fewer employees are exempt from the OSHA record-keeping requirements unless they are part of an official BLS or state survey and have received specific instructions to keep records?

6. Have we demonstrated an active interest in safety and health matters by defining a policy for our business and communicating it to all employees?

7. Do we have a safety committee or group that allows participation of employees in safety and health activities?

8. Does the safety committee or group meet regularly and report, in writing, its activities?

9. Do we provide safety and health training for all employees requiring such training, and is it documented?

10. Is one person clearly in charge of safety and health activities?

11. Do our employees know what to do in emergencies?

12. Are emergency telephone numbers posted?

13. Do we have a procedure for handling employee complaints regarding safety and health?

## Workplace

### *Electrical Wiring, Fixtures, and Controls*

1. Are our workplace electricians familiar with the requirements of the National Electrical Code (NEC)?

2. Do we specify compliance with the NEC for all contract electrical work?

3. If we have electrical installations in hazardous dust or vapor areas, do they meet the NEC standards for hazardous locations?

4. Are all electrical cords strung so they do not hang on pipes, nails, hooks, and so on?

5. Is all conduit, BX cable, and such, properly attached to all supports and tightly connected to junction and outlet boxes?

6. Is there any evidence of fraying on any electrical cords?

7. Are rubber cords kept free of grease, oil, and chemicals?

8. Are metallic cable and conduit systems properly grounded?

9. Are portable electric tools and appliances grounded or double insulated?

10. Are all ground connections clean and tight?
11. Are fuses and circuit breakers the right type and size for the load on each circuit?
12. Are all fuses free of "jumping" with pennies or metal strips?
13. Do switches show evidence of overheating?
14. Are switches mounted in clean, tightly closed metal boxes?
15. Are all electrical switches marked to show their purpose?
16. Are motors clean and kept free of excessive grease and oil?
17. Are motors properly maintained and provided with adequate overcurrent protection?
18. Are bearings in good condition?
19. Are portable lights equipped with proper guards?
20. Are all lamps kept free of combustible material?
21. Is our electrical system checked periodically by someone competent in the NEC?

## Exits and Access

1. Are all exits visible and unobstructed?
2. Are all exits marked with a readily visible sign that is properly illuminated?
3. Are there sufficient exits to ensure prompt escape in case of emergency?
4. Are areas with limited occupancy posted and is access/egress controlled to persons specifically authorized to be in those areas?
5. Do we take special precautions to protect employees during construction and repair operations?

## Fire Protection

1. Are portable fire extinguishers provided in adequate number and type?
2. Are fire extinguishers inspected monthly for general condition and operability and noted on the inspection tag?
3. Are fire extinguishers recharged regularly and properly noted on the inspection tag?
4. Are fire extinguishers mounted in readily accessible locations?
5. If we have interior standpipes and valves, are these inspected regularly?
6. If we have a fire alarm system, is it tested at least annually?
7. Are plant employees periodically instructed in the use of extinguishers and fire protection procedures?

8. If we have outside private fire hydrants, were they flushed within the last year and placed on a regular maintenance schedule?

9. Are fire doors and shutters in good operating condition?

   Are they unobstructed and protected against obstruction?

10. Are fusible links in place?

11. Is our local fire department well acquainted with our plant, location, and specific hazards?

12. Automatic sprinkler:

    Are water control valves, air, and water pressures checked weekly?

    Are control valves locked open?

    Is maintenance of the system assigned to responsible persons or a sprinkler contractor?

    Are sprinkler heads protected by metal guards where exposed to mechanical damage?

    Is proper minimum clearance maintained around sprinkler heads?

### Housekeeping and General Work Environment

1. Is smoking permitted in designated "safe areas" only?

2. Are NO SMOKING signs prominently posted in areas containing combustibles and inflammables?

3. Are covered metal waste cans used for oily and paint-soaked waste? Are they emptied at least daily?

4. Are paint spray booths, dip tanks, and such, and their exhaust ducts cleaned regularly?

5. Are stand mats, platforms, or similar protection provided to protect employees from wet floors in wet processes?

6. Are waste receptacles provided, and are they emptied regularly?

7. Do our toilet facilities meet the requirements of applicable sanitary codes?

8. Are washing facilities provided?

9. Are all areas of our business adequately illuminated?

10. Are floor load capacities posted in second floors, lofts, storage areas, and such?

11. Are floor openings provided with toe boards and railings or a floor hole cover?

12. Are stairways in good condition with standard railings provided for every flight having four or more risers?

13. Are portable wood ladders and metal ladders adequate for their purposes, in good condition, and provided with secure footing?

14. If we have fixed ladders, are they adequate, and are they in good condition and equipped with side rails or cages or special safety climbing devices, if required?

15. Loading docks: Are dockplates kept in serviceable condition and secured to prevent slipping? Do we have means to prevent car or truck movement when dock plates are in place?

### Machines and Equipment

1. Are all machines or operations that expose operators or other employees to rotating parts, pinch points, flying chips, particles, or sparks adequately guarded?

2. Are mechanical power transmission belts and pinch points guarded?

3. Is exposed power shafting less than 7 feet from the floor guarded?

4. Are hand tools and other equipment regularly inspected for safe condition?

5. Is compressed air used for cleaning reduced to less than 30 psi?

6. Are power saws and similar equipment provided with safety guards?

7. Are grinding wheel tool rests set to within 1/8 inch or less of the wheel?

8. Is there any system for inspecting small hand tools for burred ends, cracked handles, and such?

9. Are compressed gas cylinders examined regularly for obvious signs of defects, deep rusting, or leakage?

10. Is care used in handling and storing cylinders and valves to prevent damage?

11. Are all air receivers periodically examined, including the safety valves?

12. Are safety valves tested regularly and frequently?

13. Is there sufficient clearance from stoves, furnaces, and such, for stock, woodwork, or other combustible materials?

14. Is there clearance of at least 4 feet in front of heating equipment involving open flames such as gas radiant heaters, and fronts of firing doors of stoves, furnaces, and so on?

15. Are all oil- and gas-fired devices equipped with flame failure controls that will prevent flow of fuel if pilots or main burners are not working?

16. Is there at least a 2-inch clearance between chimney brickwork and all woodwork or other combustible materials?

17. Welding or flame cutting operations: Are only authorized, trained personnel permitted to use such equipment?

   Have operators been given a copy of operating instructions and asked to follow them?

Are welding gas cylinders stored so they are not subjected to damage?

Are valve protection caps in place on all cylinders not connected for use?

Are all combustible materials near the operator covered with protective shields or otherwise protected?

Is a fire extinguisher provided at the welding site?

Do operators have the proper protective clothing and equipment?

## Materials

1. Are approved safety cans or other acceptable containers used for handling and dispensing inflammable liquids?

2. Are all inflammable liquids that are kept inside buildings stored in proper storage containers or cabinets?

3. Do we meet OSHA standards for all spray painting or dip tank operations using combustible liquids?

4. Are oxidizing chemicals stored in areas separate from all organic material except shipping bags?

5. Do we have an enforced NO SMOKING rule in areas for storage and use of hazardous materials?

6. Are NO SMOKING signs posted where needed?

7. Is ventilation equipment provided for removal of air contaminants from operations such as production grinding, buffing, spray painting, and/or vapor degreasing, and is it operating properly?

8. Are protective measures in effect for operations involved with x-rays or other radiation?

9. Lift truck operations: Are only trained personnel allowed to operate forklift trucks? Is overhead protection provided on high lift rider trucks?

10. Toxic materials:

    Are all materials used in our plant checked for toxic qualities?

    Have appropriate control procedures such as ventilation systems, enclosed operations, safety handling practices, proper personal protective equipment (e.g., respirators, glasses or goggles, gloves, etc.) been instituted for toxic materials?

## Employee Protection

1. Is there a hospital, clinic, or infirmary for medical care near our business?

2. If medical and first-aid facilities are not nearby, do we have one or more employees trained in first aid?

3. Are our first-aid supplies adequate for the type of potential injuries in our workplace?

4. Are there quick water flush facilities available where employees are exposed to corrosive materials?

5. Are hard hats provided and worn where any danger of falling objects exists?

6. Are protective goggles or glasses provided and worn where there is any danger of flying particles or splashing of corrosive materials?

7. Are protective gloves, aprons, shields, or other means provided for protection from sharp, hot, or corrosive materials?

8. Are approved respirators provided for regular or emergency use where needed?

9. Is all protective equipment maintained in a sanitary condition and readily available for use?

10. Where special equipment is needed for electrical workers, is it available?

11. When lunches are eaten on the premises, are they eaten in areas where there is no exposure to toxic materials, and not in toilet facility areas?

12. Is protection against the effects of occupational noise exposure provided when the sound levels exceed the OSHA noise standard?

## ADDITIONAL SELF-INSPECTION HINTS AND AREAS OF CONCERN

1. *Processing, receiving, shipping and storage*—equipment, job planning, layout, heights, floor loads, projection of materials, materials-handling, and storage methods.

2. *Building and grounds conditions*—floors, walls, ceilings, exits, stairs, walkways, ramps, platforms, driveways, and aisles.

3. *Housekeeping program*—waste disposal, tools, objects, materials, leakage and spillage, cleaning methods, schedules, work areas, remote areas, and storage areas.

4. *Electricity*—equipment, switches, breakers, fuses, switchboxes, junctions, special fixtures, circuits, insulation, extensions, tools, motors, grounding, and NEC compliance.

5. *Lighting*—type, intensity, controls, conditions, diffusion, location, glare and shadow control.

6. *Heating and ventilating*—Type, effectiveness, temperature, humidity, controls, natural and artificial ventilation, and exhausting.

7. *Machinery*—Points of operation, flywheels, gears, shafts, pulleys, key ways, belts, couplings, sprockets, chains, frames, controls, lighting for tools and

equipment, brakes, exhausting, feeding, oiling, adjusting, maintenance, lock out, grounding, work space, location, and purchasing standards.

8. *Personnel*— Training, experience, methods of checking machines before use, type clothing, personal protective equipment, use of guards, tool storage, work practices, method of cleaning, oiling, or adjusting machinery.

9. *Hand and power tools*— Purchasing standards, inspection, storage, repair, types, maintenance, grounding, use, and handling.

10. *Chemicals*— Storage, handling, transportation, spills, disposals, amounts used, toxicity or other harmful effects, warning signs, supervision, training, protective clothing, and equipment.

11. *Fire prevention*— Extinguishers, alarms, sprinklers, smoking rules, exits, personnel assigned, separation of flammable materials and dangerous operations, explosive-proof fixtures in hazardous locations, and waste disposal.

12. *Maintenance*— Regularity, effectiveness, training of personnel, materials and equipment used, records maintained, method of locking out machinery, and general methods.

13. *Personal protective equipment*— Type, size, maintenance, repair, storage, assignment of responsibility, purchasing methods, standards observed, training in care and use, rules of use, and method of assignment.

# MEDICARE-MEDICAID

There are almost 50 million aged, disabled, or poor beneficiaries entitled to Medicare and/or Medicaid coverage in this country. The Health Care Financing Administration (HCFA), a major agency in the Department of Health and Human Services, administers these programs. A brief but detailed outline of the major features of the Medicare provisions follow. Accountants and auditors are certain to be posed questions of coverage and reimbursement by their clients/company during the course of an average year.

In short, there are two programs of health insurance protection: Hospital insurance—Part A, which covers hospitalization and related care, and Medical insurance—Part B, which covers physicians' care and certain medical and other health services.

Who can qualify? For Part A—Hospital Insurance, people age 65 and older and entitled to monthly Social Security (SS) benefits, or railroad retirement (RR) annuity, or over 65 and a U.S. resident or a U.S. citizen (or alien lawfully admitted for permanent residence with five years continuous residence).

Additionally, coverage is provided to people any age with end-stage renal disease (ESRD) requiring transplant or dialysis and either: (a) SS beneficiary or

RR annuitant, (b) fully or currently insured (railroad work may count), or (c) spouse or dependent child of (a) or (b).

As for Part B—Medical Insurance, people entitled to Part A or people age 65 and older and a U.S. resident and citizen (or alien lawfully admitted for permanent residence with five years continuous residence) are eligible. Most eligible people have automatic enrollment in Part B unless they specifically decline.

Part A—Hospital Insurance provides three major services:

1. Inpatient hospital care includes:
   a. Up to 90 days per benefit period (renewable in subsequent benefit periods) plus 60 days lifetime reserve (nonrenewable) in a participating hospital (and under limited conditions, in a nonparticipating U.S. hospital or a foreign hospital).
   b. Psychiatric hospital care (190 days lifetime with special reduction for first benefit period), semiprivate room and board, operating room, special care units, recovery room, drugs, medical supplies, and appliances furnished by the hospital, laboratory tests, x-ray, and radiological services, rehabilitation services, and medical social services.
   c. Emergency services can also be covered in nonparticipating hospitals under certain conditions.
   d. Foreign services emergency and nonemergency inpatient care in Canada and Mexico may be covered under limited conditions.

Part A—Hospital Insurance excludes: Services not resonable and necessary for diagnosis or treatment of illness or injury, personal comfort items (such as television and telephones), private duty nurses, physicians' services which may be covered under Part B, private room (unless medically necessary).

2. Extended care includes:
   a. Up to 100 inpatient days in a participating skilled nursing facility (SNF) per benefit period. This includes semiprivate room and board, regular nursing services, drugs, medical supplies, and appliances furnished by the SNF, therapy (physical, occupational, speech), and medical social services.
   b. Admission to the SNF must follow within 14 days, a qualifying hospital stay of at least three consecutive days (the 14-day requirement may be extended under certain conditions).

**3.** Home health services are covered only if the beneficiary is:

    **a.** Confined to home, under care of physician, under written home health plan established by physician within 14 days after discharge from hospital or SNF; needs intermittent or part-time skilled nursing care or physical or speech therapy for condition for which inpatient hospital or extended care services were received; is provided services within year following most recent discharge from three-day hospital or covered SNF stay, whichever is later. It also includes:

    **b.** Up to 100 visits from a participating home health agency (HHA) after start of one benefit period and before start of next, part-time nursing care, therapy (physical, occupational, speech), part-time services of home health aides, medical supplies and appliances furnished by the HHA, and medical social services.

Part B—Medical Insurance includes:

Physicians' services (and services and supplies furnished incident to a physician's professional service), outpatient hospital services: incident to physicians' services, diagnostic and therapeutic services provided by a participating hospital; diagnostic tests: x-ray, clinical lab tests, other diagnostic tests; therapy: x-ray, radium, radioactive isotope, and limited chiropractic services.

Certified rural health clinics (RHC) may furnish the following services: physician services, physician assistant services, nurse practitioner services, nurse midwife services, part-time visiting nurse services to homebound patients in areas with a shortage of home health services, services and supplies incident to the services of physicians, physician assistants, nurse practitioners, and nurse midwives.

Other medical items and services furnished are: surgical dressings, splints, casts, other devices used for reduction of fractures and dislocations. Durable medical equipment for use in patient's home (rental or purchase), including home dialysis equipment and supplies are also authorized.

Other services include: End-stage renal disease facility care by approved suppliers of maintenance dialysis services, certain ambulance services, prosthetic devices replacing all or part of an internal body organ (including prosthetic eyeglasses and contact lenses which replace the lens of the eye removed during cataract surgery), braces for arm, leg, back, neck, artificial arms, legs, eyes, and home health services—up to 100 visits in a calendar year, in addition to Part A visits (same requirements as Part A except prior hospitalization not required).

It also includes outpatient physical therapy and speech pathology by a participating hospital, SNF, HHA, or approved clinic, rehabilitation agency or public health agency, coverage of services of independently practicing physical therapists (up to $100 of incurred expenses per calendar year).

Part B—Medical Insurance excludes:

Items and services not reasonable and necessary for diagnosis or treatment of illness or injury, routine physical checkups, hearing aids, eyeglasses, and examinations for fitting or changing them (exception: see prosthetic devices above) and refractive services, and immunizations (except where immediate risk of infection), cosmetic surgery;

Care treatment, filling, removal, or replacement of teeth, routine and certain other foot care, orthopedic shoes (unless built into leg braces) and other supportive devices for the feet;

Prescription drugs (except when not self-administered and cost included in administering physician's bill).

There are some general exclusions from coverage. No payment can be made under either the hospital or medical insurance programs for certain items and services that are excluded under the Medicare law. These are items or services:

For which the beneficiary has no legal obligation to pay and for which no other person has a legal obligation to provide or pay for, which are paid for by governmental entities—federal, state, or local—which are required as a result of war, for which charges are imposed by an immediate relative of the beneficiary or a member of his/her household, or for which payment has been made or can reasonably be expected to be made under a workers' compensation law.

These are the general costs:

Part A—Hospital Insurance: No monthly premium for insured beneficiaries, and available with premium for uninsureds.

Inpatient hospital care program pays reasonable costs after:

Inpatient hospital deductible per benefit period which amount determined each year by the Secretary of HHS, approximates the national average cost of a one-day hospital stay, and changes effective for benefit periods beginning on or after January 1.

The coinsurance from 61st through 90th day equals 1/4 of inpatient hospital deductible, and the coinsurance during lifetime reserve equals 1/2 of inpatient hospital deductible.

Blood deductible is the first 3 pints (or equivalent units of packed red blood cells) per benefit period (beneficiary has the option to replace this blood).

For extended care, there is coinsurance from 21st through 100th day which equals 1/8 of inpatient hospital deductible.

There is no deductible or coinsurance for home health services.

As for Part B—Medical Insurance, the program pays 80 percent of reasonable charges (80 percent of reasonable costs when a provider—hospital, SNF, or HHA—furnishes the services) after:

Annual deductible (amounts applied to the deductible must be the reasonable charges), coinsurance—20 percent of reasonable charges, and blood deductible—first 3 pints (or equivalent units of packed red blood cells) in a calendar year (beneficiary has the option to replace this blood).

Exceptions:

For inpatient services of pathologists and radiologists—no deductible or coinsurance. For Part B home health services—deductible applies but not coinsurance. For outpatient physician treatment of mental illness—only 62n percent of reasonable charges may be allowed for benefit computation; after subtraction of any unmet deductible, the benefit is 80 percent of this adjusted amount.

Part A—Hospital Insurance:

Provider performs a service for a Medicare beneficiary.

Service is reviewed by a PSRO or an institutional utilization review committee for medical necessity and appropriateness.

Provider files a claim; claim is processed and paid for by the intermediary (or ODR) if certified to be medically necessary and appropriate and if all other coverage provisions are met.

Provider receives payment; beneficiary receives "Medicare Hospital, Extended Care, and Home Health Benefits Record," an explanation of payments made;

Provider has agreed not to charge Medicare beneficiary for covered items and services, but can bill for deductible, coinsurance, and noncovered items and services (for certain noncovered items and services, waiver of liability provisions may apply).

There are two methods of filing:

Assignment Method:

Must be agreed to by both the beneficiary and the physician or supplier

Physician or supplier files claim

Payment is made by the carrier directly to the physician or supplier

Beneficiary receives "Explanation of Medicare Benefits" (EOMB)

Physician or supplier agrees to accept reasonable charge as full charge

Physician or supplier can bill the patient for no more than the unmet deductible, coinsurance, and for noncovered items and services

For certain noncovered items and services, waiver of liability provision may apply

Nonassignment Method:

Beneficiary sends HCFA-1490 directly to the carrier with itemized bill (or with Part II of HCFA-1490 completed by physician)

Beneficiary receives EOMB and payment directly

Medicare payment to beneficiary is based on reasonable charge but physician or supplier is not restricted to reasonable charge

Waiver of liability provision does not apply to nonassignment method

When a provider (hospital, SNF, or HHA) furnishes Part B services, the provider always submits the claim.

Payment made by carrier except when a provider (hospital, NF, or HHA) furnishes Part B services; payment is then made by the intermediary in the same manner as outlined under Part A.

A person denied Medicare benefits or in disagreement with the amount of benefits payable may appeal the decision on their claim as follows:

In Part A—Hospital Insurance, issues involving benefits payable under Part A follow:

Reconsideration—use HCFA-2649 with 60 days for filing

Hearing—use HA-501 U6 with 60 days for filing; disputed amount must be $100 or more

Appeals Council Review—use HA-520 U6 with 60 days for filing

Judicial Review—60 days for filing; disputed amount must be $1000 or more

With regard to Part B—Medical Insurance, issues involving benefits payable under Part B follow:

Review—use HCFA-1964 with 6 months for filing

Hearing—use HCFA-1965 with 6 months for filing; disputed amount must be $100 or more

No judicial review is provided.

For issues involving Medicare entitlement or enrollment:

Reconsideration—use SSA-561 U2 with 60 days for filing

Hearing—use HA-501 U5 with 60 days for filing

Appeals Council Review—use HA-520 U6 with 60 days for filing

Judicial Review—60 days for filing

The Social Security Office serves as a focal point for interrelationships between the beneficiary and the organizations that administer and operate the Medicare program. The Social Security Office may assist in any of the following ways:

Establish entitlement to Hospital Insurance—Part A

Enrollment for Medical Insurance—Part B

Explain benefits available under Part A and Part B

Assist beneficiaries in claiming Part A and Part B benefits

Assist in filing claims for hospital emergency services

Assist direct-dealing providers in filing for Part A and Part B benefits (see ODR)

Obtain correct H1 claim numbers for providers, intermediaries, carriers, and others

Assist other components in resolving problems related to Part A and Part B claims

Explain benefits paid to or on behalf of beneficiaries (beneficiaries are encouraged to call carriers directly on claims-related matters)

Explain appeal rights and assist claimants in filing appeals

Assist beneficiaries with name or address changes

Assist beneficiaries in obtaining correct Medicare cards, and replacement of lost or stolen cards

Assist beneficiaries in forwarding premiums

Receive and refer complaints of violations of Title VI of the Civil Rights Act

Assist in maintaining the integrity of the Medicare program by identifying potential waste and program abuse

Promote public awareness of Medicare protection through public information programs.

The following is an excerpt from a news release (June 18, 1984) which ends this portion of regulation change just to illustrate the nature of the regulatory thickets that make each major regulatory area a difficult arena for accountants and auditors to be satisfactorily equipped to offer practical (and current) advice.

## HHS News Release

The Department of Health and Human Services today announced that 1985 Medicare payments to hospitals are projected to increase by 6 percent. This increase results from the new rates incorporated in a notice of proposed rulemaking which will be sent to the Federal Register later this week.

The projected payments for 1985 represent the lowest rate of increase since the Medicare program began in 1965. Although the increase in actual payments would still be higher than the projected increase in the 1985 consumer price index, this represents a great reduction in the double-digit increase of the late 1970s.

The 1985 6 percent projected increase in payments represents proof that the reimbursement formula mandated by Congress under TEFRA together with the budget neutrality provisions in the 1983 Social Security Amendments have started to succeed in bringing Medicare health payments under control while preserving the high quality of care which the Medicare beneficiary deserves.

As part of the Social Security Amendments of 1983, "prospective payment" is a new method for reimbursing Medicare hospitals. It establishes set rates for 468 Diagnosis-Related Groups or DRG'—such as cataract, hip replacement, heart attack and other major procedures. Since October 1983, Medicare prospective payments have been based on standardized rates keyed to the patients' diagnoses rather than the previous open-ended cost based system, which was a dominant contributor to health care inflation. This new system is being phased in over three years. It provides that, of the total reimbursement to hospitals treating Medicare patients in FY 1985, half will come from the federal rate and half derives from the recent experience of individual hospitals. Each year, the secretary of HHS must announce revisions of these payment rates.

By using the formulae mandated by the Tax Equity and Fiscal Responsibility Act of 1982 (TEFRA) and adhering to the budget neutrality provisions in the 1983 Social Security Amendments, the 1985 DRG published rates will increase 5.6 percent over the 1984 published rates. The average payment per case to Medicare hospitals will actually rise to 6 percent over what was projected for FY 1984 under the prospective payment system because of other changes in the regulations and the phasing of hospital accounting years.

The prospective payment system requires that estimates be made regarding the intensity of Medicare admissions. In calculating budget neutrality for FY 1984, estimates were used in the base computations. With the 1985 rates HHS is revising these estimates to reflect the mix of cases actually reported in the prospective payment system. An adjustment in each of the DRG weights was required in order to reflect the more complete coding of diagnoses by the hospitals.

The proposed regulations provide for special treatment for rural hospitals which qualify as referral centers and special accommodations for hospitals which have been negatively impacted by geographic designation.

# ENVIRONMENTAL PROTECTION AGENCY

The U.S. Environmental Protection Agency (EPA) was created by Presidential directive in 1970 to consolidate the major environmental activities of the federal government into a single agency.

Throughout the 1970s and continuing into the 1980s, Congress has passed new environmental laws and amended existing ones in a sustained effort to reduce the harmful effects of pollution on human health and the environment.

The EPA was formally established as an independent agency in the Executive Branch on December 2, 1970.

EPA was formed from 15 components of five Executive departments and independent agencies. Air pollution control, solid waste management, radiation, and the drinking water program were transferred from the Department of Health, Education, and Welfare (now the Department of Health and Human Services). The federal water pollution control program was taken from the Department of Interior. From the Department of Agriculture the EPA acquired authority to register pesticides and to regulate their use, and from the Food and Drug Administration responsibility to set tolerance levels for pesticides in food. It also assumed part of a pesticide research program in the Department of the Interior. EPA was assigned some responsibility for setting environmental radiation protection standards from the old Atomic Energy Commission and absorbed the duties of the Federal Radiation Council.

The enactment of major new environmental laws and important amendments to older laws in the 1970s greatly expanded the agency's responsibilities. It now administers eight comprehensive environmental protection laws. These concern water, air, waste, pesticides, toxic substances, radiation, and related research and development.

As for *water*, the EPA has the dual responsibility of reducing the pollution of waterways and maintaining safe drinking water. The Clean Water Act of 1972, as amended in 1977 and 1981, and the Marine Protection, Research, and Sanctuaries Act of 1972 provide the basic authority for water pollution control programs now being carried out by federal, state, and local agencies. Major provisions of the Act are:

**Municipal Pollution Control.**  A program for the construction or modification of sewage treatment systems under federal grants. Through EPA, the federal government currently funds 75 to 85 percent of sewage project costs. In fiscal year 1985, by which time major projects were underway, the federal share of construction grants dropped to 55 percent.

**Regional Planning.**  A process for selecting the most effective and economical wastewater treatment facilities for a contiguous area. Independent, but adjacent, metropolitan areas in a region join in planning and building treatment facilities to meet needs established under state water quality management plans, including projections of population shifts.

**Effluent Limitations.**  A system for defining the amount and kinds of pollutants that can be discharged into the nation's waters. Limitations apply both to municipal and industrial sources of water pollution.

**Water Quality Standards.**  Standards for surface waters established by EPA according to the use of the water—for agriculture, industry, recreation, or drinking. Standards cover factors such as water temperature, oxygen content, microbiological count, toxic pollutants, and others.

**Wastewater Discharge Permits.**  A system for registering and controlling the discharge of waste into public waterways and of ensuring that discharges conform to effluent limitations. All municipal sewage treatment systems and businesses that discharge waste must have a permit to do so. Permits are issued by states or EPA.

**Dredge and Fill Permits.**  A system to regulate dredging, filling of wetlands, or dumping of dredged material that affects navigable waters. Permits are granted by the Corps of Engineers, subject to EPA approval. The Marine Protection, Research, and Sanctuaries Act authorizes EPA to regulate ocean dumping by designating dumping areas, issuing permits, and assessing penalties for unauthorized dumping.

Concerning drinking water, the Safe Drinking Water Act of 1974, amended in 1977, EPA sets national standards to protect drinking water. Assisted in part with federal funds, states bear primary responsibility for enforcing the standards. The EPA Office of Water administers the Act.

Twentieth-century methods of drinking water treatment—particularly chlorination—have been remarkably effective in eliminating major epidemics of water-borne disease in the United States. However, outbreaks still occur with unnecessary frequency. The Center for Disease Control reported about 80 outbreaks in 1980 involving 20,000 confirmed cases of water-borne illness.

In recent years there has also been increasing concern about contamination from chemicals such as nitrate, fluoride, arsenic, and lead and from various organic chemicals and pesticides. All of these substances have found their way into drinking water in certain locations from time to time.

To deal with these problems under the Safe Drinking Water Act, EPA issues regulations that set national drinking water standards, and assists states financially in carrying out the regulations.

EPA also has issued rules to protect underground sources of drinking water (aquifers) from contamination by various injection practices. Called the underground injection control program, this effort is part of broad EPA response to potential sources of drinking water contamination.

The Safe Drinking Water Act of 1974 grants EPA the authority to regulate public drinking water supplies. Major provisions are:

*Drinking water regulations* established by EPA to protect health and welfare.

*State enforcement* of drinking water standards established by EPA. The EPA can assume that responsibility if a state fails to enforce the standards.

*Protection of underground water supplies* against contamination by underground injection of wastes and other materials.

The EPA Office of Air, Noise and Radiation is given responsibility for federal actions to reduce air pollution under the Clean Air Act of 1970 as amended in 1977.

Under the Clean Air Act, state and local governments must ensure that air quality complies with primary and secondary standards. The EPA plays an important role in this by setting nationwide emissions standards for a variety of air pollution sources, essentially enforcing the limits set by Congress in the Act.

The EPA also establishes nationwide emissions standards for hazardous air pollutants. Emissions limits are in effect for asbestos, beryllium, mercury, and vinyl chloride, and standards for others have been proposed.

Because controls required by law relate primarily to new pollution sources, they are generally not sufficient to bring air quality up to primary and secondary standards. States therefore must draw up State Implementation Plans, with additional ways to achieve the standards such as controls on older sources of pollution and measures to reduce motor traffic. These plans are subject to EPA approval. If a state fails to develop an acceptable plan, EPA is required to assume this function.

The Clean Air Act, as amended in 1970 and 1977, provides the basic legal authority for the nation's air pollution control programs. Major provisions:

National ambient air quality standards for specific air pollutants to protect public health and welfare. Standards have been set for sulfur dioxide, particulates, oxides of nitrogen, carbon monoxide, hydrocarbons, ozone, and lead.

State implementation plans stipulating steps that will be taken to achieve satisfactory air quality. The EPA must review the plans and, if necessary, require revisions or substitute its own plan.

New source performance standards for new, or modified, stationary sources of air pollution. Emission limitations are established for specific types of sources such as power plants and cement plants.

Hazardous air pollutants national standards limiting emissions of such substances as asbestos, beryllium, mercury, vinyl chloride, and benzene from both new and old stationary sources.

Prevention of significant deterioration of air quality in areas that have pristine or good to moderate air quality. Subject to EPA approval, states identify areas of good, moderate, and poor air quality (Class I, Class II, and Class III). Class I, which includes national parks and wilderness areas, permits no additional air pollution. The Class II designation allows additional pollution up to prescribed limits, and Class III areas must conform to general national standards.

Automobile emission controls to achieve a 90 percent reduction in carbon monoxide and hydrocarbon emissions (based on 1970 emission levels).

Waste in most countries represents a monstrous problem. Residential and commercial sources generate solid waste at the rate of some 132 million metric tons per year, enough to fill the New Orleans Superdome from floor to ceiling twice a day every day. Industrial waste is more than double that amount, totaling 350 million metric tons a year.

Disposing of wastes, including those considered hazardous, is a costly business, requiring measures to protect the environment. Uncontrolled waste sites present environmental risks, requiring action to prevent degradation of water, soil, and air.

Control and eradication of solid waste problems is the responsibility of the EPA Office of Solid Waste and Emergency Response. This Office implements two federal environmental laws: the Resource Conservation and Recovery Act (RCRA), whch regulates current and future waste practices; and the Comprehensive Environmental Response, Compensation, and Liability Act (CERCLA), commonly called Superfund, which cleans up old waste sites.

RCRA provides federal guidance and support to states to develop environmentally sound methods of solid waste disposal. This legislation deals with both municipal and hazardous waste. To improve solid waste disposal practices, EPA encourages states to develop solid waste plans. The Agency has provided technical assistance for these efforts.

The RCRA requires states to develop and implement municipal waste disposal plans as part of their solid waste plan. To set the stage for establishment of environmentally sound disposal practices, states have been asked to inventory all existing municipal waste disposal sites and determine whether they are environmentally sound. Federal technical assistance has been provided through EPA for these efforts. The EPA has also assisted states in programs for recovery and reuse of valuable materials from municipal waste, such as glass, plastic, silver, and aluminum, and in utilization of the energy potential of waste.

Under RCRA, EPA ensures proper disposal of hazardous wastes, such as toxic substances, caustics, pesticides, and inflammable, corrosive, and explosive materials. The EPA estimates that in 1980 approximately 41 million metric tons of hazardous wastes were generated in the United States.

To carry out RCRA's provisions for dealing with hazardous wastes, EPA has developed a national hazardous waste management system to monitor the movement of hazardous wastes from production to disposal. Under the system, hazardous waste generators must identify the wastes they create and report the means of on-site treatment, storage, or disposal. Transportation of wastes to off-site facilities is regulated and tracked.

All treatment, storage, and disposal sites must have permits to operate, and their design must be adequate to prevent the waste from moving through the soil and reaching water sources. Active land disposal sites are monitored constantly for groundwater contamination. Closed sites are to be properly capped, and groundwater monitoring must continue for an extended period. The owner or operator of a facility is required to demonstrate financial responsibility for damage occurring during active operations and to set aside funds for monitoring and maintenance after the site is closed.

As for pesticides, these are defined as chemical or biological substances used to control pests on farms, homes, hospitals, commercial and governmental establishments. As herbicides, these products control weeds, unwanted brush and trees, and serve as defoliants to stimulate plant maturity so mechanical harvesting can be used more effectively. Pesticides are used to retard growth of fungi in asphalt, paint, and plastics, and to destroy harmful bacteria.

The benefits of pesticides are evident: Greater quantities of food; reduced loss of food in storage, and control of disease carriers have significantly improved health throughout the world and contribute to the quality of life. In 1981 consumers spent over $6.5 billion on approximately 1.2 billion pounds of pesticides. Agriculture accounts for 71 percent of their use, home gardening and lawns for 7 percent, and industry, commerce, and government for 22 percent.

To retain these advantages and address the potential adverse effects, Congress passed the Federal Insecticide, Fungicide and Rodenticide Act (FIFRA) in 1947. This bill was amended in 1972 and its responsibilities were passed from the U.S. Department of Agriculture to EPA. Additional amendments were made in 1975, 1978, and 1980.

Under this statute, EPA is required to review pesticide products and determine whether they can be used without causing unreasonable risks to human health or the environment. This process must take into account economic, social, and environmental costs and benefits.

Registration is a license or premarket clearance which EPA provides, based on a scientific review of a wide variety of health and safety data submitted by the manufacturer of the pesticide product. This process includes the approval of the product label which outlines the directions and precautions for use. The EPA classifies all pesticides for general or restricted use. Restricted use products may be applied only by or under the supervision of a certified applicator. Certification is designed to insure that users of restricted use products are properly qualified to handle these products safely. Certification programs for applicators are administered by EPA-approved state training programs.

Another function of registration is the establishment of tolerance levels—the amount of pesticide residue that may safely remain on food and feed crops after harvesting.

Toxic substances is another problem area and include a number of manufactured chemicals, as well as naturally occurring heavy metals such as mercury, cadmium, and lead which are mined and released into the environment.

Today, nearly 60,000 chemicals are in use in the United States and approximately 800 new chemical substances are proposed each year for manufacture.

In 1976, Congress passed the Toxic Substances Control Act (TSCA), which was intended to prevent unreasonable risks of injury to health or the environment associated with the manufacture, processing, distribution in commerce, use, or disposal of new or existing chemical substances.

Chemicals used exclusively in pesticides, food, food additives, drugs, and cosmetics are exempted from the Act. Also exempted are nuclear materials, tobacco, firearms, and ammunition. All of these are regulated under other laws.

Implementing TSCA is the responsibility of the EPA Office of Toxic Substances. Programs now exist under the Act to require companies to submit information on all new chemicals before they are manufactured. Also, EPA must gather available information about the toxicity of particular chemicals and the extent to which people and the environment are exposed to them. The Agency must also bring about industry testing where existing data are inadequate, assess whether particular chemicals cause unreasonable risks to humans or the environment, institute appropriate control actions, or refer such action to another federal agency.

Instituting a mandatory program for schools to inspect their buildings for asbestos-containing materials, and hiring retired engineers in all 10 EPA regional offices to help states and local districts in this inspection effort, and advise on appropriate containment or removal techniques where warranted.

The EPA coordinates and consults with other federal agencies involved in toxic chemical regulation, including: the Occupational Safety and Health Administration (in the Department of Labor), the Food and Drug Administration (Department of Health and Human Services), the Consumer Product Safety Commission, and the Food Safety and Quality Service (Department of Agriculture).

The EPA also works very closely with the 24-nation Organization for Economic Cooperation and Development to develop chemical testing guidelines and good laboratory practices. The agency places a high priority on these activities because of benefits both for international chemical trade and for more effective health and environmental protection. The EPA cooperates in a number of other international forums aimed at exchanging information and building mutual understanding on chemical safety issues, including those sponsored by the United Nations Environment Program and the World Health Organization.

TSCA was signed into law by President Ford On October 12, 1976. On signing the Act, the President stated, "[TSCA] is a strong bill and focuses on the most critical environmental problems not covered by existing legislation, while not overburdening either the regulatory agency, the regulated industry, or the American people."

Major provisions include:

Reporting and record keeping by industry to enable EPA to gather information on the manufacture, processing, use, and disposal of chemical substances, by-products produced, and estimates of the number of people exposed in the workplace.

Testing by manufacturers if a chemical substance is suspected of presenting an unreasonable risk of injury to health or the environment and there are insufficient data to evaluate its toxicity, cancer-causing potential, potential for birth defects, or other characteristics.

Screening of new chemicals through premanufacture notification to EPA at least 90 days before a company produces a new chemical substance, or intends to use an existing chemical in a significantly new way.

Regulation of chemical substances allowing EPA to prohibit or limit the manufacture, processing, distribution, use, or disposal of a chemical substance that presents an unreasonable risk of injury to health or the environment.

**Radiation.**   A number of federal agencies, among them EPA, are responsible for protecting the public from unnecessary radiation exposure. The EPA radiation authorities include portions of the Atomic Energy Act of 1954, the Public Health Service Act of 1962, the Safe Drinking Water Act of 1974, the Clean Air Act Amendments of 1977, and the Uranium Mill Tailings Radiation Control Act of 1978. The agency's major regulatory responsibilities are the setting of generally applicable environmental standards and the development of federal radiation guidelines. Additionally, the agency has a general responsibility for environmental radiation monitoring.

The EPA responsibilities for setting standards to protect the general public from environmental exposure to radiation have included limiting releases from nuclear power plants, from the processing of uranium, and from radionuclides in drinking water. EPA, in cooperation with the Food and Drug Administration, has developed guidance to other federal agencies on the use of x-rays in medicine. The agency is currently developing standards for disposal of high- and low-level radioactive wastes, and for the control of hazards at active and inactive uranium mill tailing sites. Also under development are nuclear accident protective action guidelines, clean-up guidelines for areas contaminated by plutonium, guidance for occupational exposure to radiation, and guidance limiting environmental exposure to nonionizing radiation from radio broadcast sources.

Finally, EPA carries out several projects to monitor radiation in the environment. The EPA maintains a monitoring network of 67 sampling stations and measures environmental radiation levels. This network is particularly important in detecting radioactive environmental contamination resulting from above-ground nuclear weapons tests conducted by foreign nations. The EPA also monitors drinking water supplies and other media to estimate radiation exposure to the public from both ionizing and nonionizing radiation.

**Research and Development.**   The Office of Research and Development directs the EPA research program to provide the information that EPA program officials require. About 70 percent of the ORD research program is in direct support of environmental problems of immediate concern to the Agency, the other 30 percent being longer-term by design in order to provide a strong basis for addresing future regulatory needs.

The ultimate goal of the EPA research is to support the development of environmental standards and regulations that protect human health and the environment from pollutant damage.

An example is included next, merely to illustrate how regulatory information may be obtained. This is a listing of the regional offices and laboratory facilities of EPA; all regulatory agencies have one. Check with their Public Information Office as a starter.

# FEDERAL TRADE COMMISSION

The Federal Trade Commission (FTC), created in 1914, was intended to be an antitrust enforcement agency and information clearinghouse. It was to serve business by issuing rules protecting against violators of unfair methods of competition and deceptive practices affecting commerce. These generally come under the heading of consumer protection programs.

Enforces equal credit opportunities

Monitors fair credit reporting

Oversees truth in lending and electronic fund transfer acts

Watches marketing and deceptive sales practices and warranty items

Food and drug and energy, cigarette, and other advertising is also monitored

Enforces consumer protection rules in many industries—mail orders, book and record clubs, franchises, labels, hobbies, auto repairs, funeral industry, and so on.

To enlarge on this, somewhat, for illustrative purposes, the Commission consists of three main bureaus: The Bureau of Consumer Protection, the Bureau of Competition, and the Bureau of Economics.

The Bureau of Consumer Protection tries to keep the marketplace free from unfair, deceptive, and fraudulent practices so that consumers can make intelligent buying decisions. Also, the FTC enforces a variety of consumer protection laws enacted by Congress, as well as trade regulation rules passed by the Commissions to protect consumers from industrywide violations.

The Bureau has these major objectives:

1. To eliminate private and public restrictions that cause unnecessarily high prices and limit the range of goods and services available to consumers.
2. To reduce consumer exposure to illegal sales techniques.
3. To encourage sellers to provide consumers with accurate and relevant information so they can compare competing brands. If the marketplace is competitive, consumers get a fairer deal.

The bureau also focuses on advertising practices, credit practices, service-industry practices, marketing practices, and consumer business education:

**Advertising.** If the Commission feels a company is making a false or deceptive claim that the average consumer would not be able to evaluate adequately, without buying the product, the Commission may seek to remove the advertisement or require some other appropriate remedy. In addition, the Commission encourages truthful advertising by doctors, lawyers, dentists, and other professionals.

**Credit.** The Commission enforces the Fair Credit Reporting Act. Credit reporting agencies wield enormous power over consumers' ability to obtain credit. The Act contains safeguards to prevent abuses and puts consumers on a more even footing with the credit agencies. Other credit acts enforced by the Commissions include the Equal Credit Opportunity Act, which prevents discrimination and harassment in the credit area, and the Truth-in-Lending Act, which protects consumers who are obtaining loans.

**Service industry.** In order for consumers to make an adequate evaluation of such services as gemstone investment sales, oil and gas lotteries, eye care and other health care services, they need truthful information. When necessary, the Commission requires a company or an entire industry to provide essential information for the consumer and to stop any dissemination of false or deceptive information.

**Marketing practices.** Deceptive product claims, fraudulent marketing techniques, warranty misrepresentations, and other similar practices may harm consumers and prevent them from choosing the goods and services they desire. The Divison of Marketing Practices monitors and investigates possible law violations in these areas.

The Bureau of Competition, the FTC's antitrust arm, is responsible for investigating and prosecuting "unfair methods of competition." It also shares authority with the Justice Department, to stop actions that "lessen competition or tend to create a monopoly." Such activity by a business might include price-fixing, other types of collusion between "competitors," or coercion such as boycotts by competitors.

The antitrust laws can be enforced by the FTC, the Justice Department, and private parties. There are two major differences between FTC and Justice Department enforcement:

1. The FTC can seek civil remedies, including cease-and-desist orders, injunction, and fines (civil penalties), whereas the Justice Department can bring both criminal and civil charges.

2. The FTC has its own administrative hearing procedure, and files suit in federal court only when necessary to obtain temporary orders barring

likely violations of the antitrust laws or to compel compliance with a previous Commission order. The Justice Department always files suit in federal courts.

The FTC seeks to ensure that all its actions are based on sound economic principles. To achieve this, the Bureau of Economics provides economic support to the agency's antitrust and consumer-protection activities, advises the Commissions about the impact of government regulation on competition and gathers and analyzes financial information on American businesses.

The bureau performs these main functions:

**Economic advice.** The bureau provides guidance with support to the agency's antitrust and consumer protection activities. In the antitrust area, economists offer advice on the economic merits of potential antitrust actions. If an enforcement action is initiated, economists work to integrate economic analysis into the proceeding and to devise remedies to improve consumer well-being.

Economists provide estimates of the benefits and costs of potential Commission actions in the consumer protection area as well. The data are evaluated not only for their immediate impact, but also for long-run effects on price, product variety, consumer harm, and the effects of FTC intervention.

**Data collection.** The bureau collects, analyzes, and publishes information about the nation's business firms. Recent studies have focused on such diverse topics as the benefits and costs of international trade restrictions, the impact of conspiracies to maintain prices, and the effects of state laws prohibiting advertising by professionals.

**Study effects of government regulation.** Commission economists also focus on the competitive impact of government regulation. Using expertise derived from FTC studies of industries and trade practices, economists help to evaluate the benefits and costs of regulatory actions.

The public can obtain copies of all public documents from the FTC Public Reference Branch, Room 130, 6th Street and Pennsylvania Avenue N.W., Washington, DC 20580. The phone number is 202-523-3598; TTY 202-523-3638.

The premise underlying the Commissions's public affairs program is the public's right to know what the FTC is doing. The Office of Public Affairs informs the public about the Commission's law enforcement actions, speeches, and testimony through the news releases and close contact with national, local, and trade press.

The Office of Public Affairs also coordinates an outreach program to inform people, through their local media, about a variety of consumer issues the Commission follows. These include tips about joining health spas, creatively financing home mortgages, and buying used cars.

In 1980, Congress passed the Sherman Antitrust Act, which prohibits any "combination or conspiracy in restraint of trade." Following its passage, however, public concern about the growing power of big business continued because of a general feeling that the Sherman Act, as interpreted by the courts, was not strong enough to "bust the trusts." As a result, Congress passed the Federal Trade Commission Act of 1914, creating the Commission and authorizing it to prevent and prosecute "unfair methods of competition in commerce."

A second law passed in 1914, the Clayton Act, also was designed to strengthen the Sherman Act. Its provisions, which were more specific than those of the FTC Act, prohibited certain kinds of mergers and other actions that "lessen competition or tend to create a monopoly." The new FTC and the Justice Department were given joint authority to enforce the Clayton Act.

Congress passed the Robinson-Patman Act in 1936. The Act was intended to help small businesses compete with large corporations by prohibiting unjustified price discrimination by manufacturers and suppliers in sales to competing customers.

Although the purpose of these new laws was to protect and promote competition, Congress gave the FTC a more direct order to protect consumers in 1983, when it passed the Wheeler-Lea Amendment to the FTC Act. This amendment included a broad prohibition against "unfair and deceptive acts," even if the practices in question did not hurt competition or tend to create a monopoly.

In 1975, Congress passed the Magnuson-Moss Act, which enabled the Commission to adopt trade regulation rules. These rules set standards that define "unfair or deceptive acts or practices" in a particular industry, forbid or require certain actions. Trade regulation rules have the force of law. Violations are considered violations of the FTC Act and are enforceable in federal court.

The FTC Improvements Act of 1980 imposed limitations on the Commission's activity in a number of areas such as regulating advertising products for children.

Over the years, the FTC has been given other additional authority by Congress. Among these laws are the Truth-in-Lending Act, which requires that stores, banks, and credit card companies disclose all credit terms before an account is opened or a loan made, and the Equal Credit Opportunity Act, which provides that a consumer cannot be denied credit because of his or her age, sex, marital status, race, religion, or national origin.

In 1977, "Government in the Sunshine Act" made government meetings as open as possible. However, Commission meetings that deal with ongoing or proposed law enforcement investigations are closed to the public.

Many of the Commission's meetings are open and the FTC publishes a weekly calendar of its hearings, meetings, and other activities. To be put on the mailing list for this bulletin, contact the FTC Office of Public Affairs.

If you want an FTC report, a copy of a trade regulation rule, a pamphlet explaining your rights under a law enforced by the Commission, or other information, write, call, or visit the FTC Public Reference Branch, Room 130, 6th Street and Pennsylvania Avenue N.W., Washington, DC 20580 (202-523-3598; TTY 202-523-3638).

This office also offers copies of FTC rules, statutes, reports, decisions, and news releases. If you are not sure whether the FTC has what you are looking for, you might start by consulting a free booklet called *Federal Trade Commission: List of Publications.*

You also might be interested in receiving the Consumer Information Center's free catalog of consumer publications (many of which will be sent to you free). Write: Consumer Information Center, Pueblo, Colorado 81009.

## WHAT ABOUT THE FUTURE?

Every single day, chemists are churning out new chemicals and drugs and other products that enter our everyday routines. Each day we are, as a not unexpected offshoot of this proliferation of new and sometimes scientifically uncertain products, learning about new hazards. Practices heretofore considered to be innocuous for many years, such as pouring waste into unused and secluded open areas, are becoming worrisome techniques because they seep into the underground water supply. These practices are now considered as possible abuses and under the purview of some regulatory agency.

Literally, whole libraries are filled with the specifics relating to all the separate industries or the different factors affecting conditions of work or play.

Here is just one small example how government regulations evolve. A professional boxer recently lost most of his sight through injuries sustained in a fight. It was claimed that this fight should never have been allowed to take place. The public, reflecting current concern, is now pushing for a *new* regulation making it a felony (a pretty stiff regulatory provision) for a trainer, manager, or physician *knowingly* to allow a boxer, who is vulnerable to serious injury of this type, to engage in a boxing event.

It is easy to see how a legislator reacts to this pressure. The public itself has clamored for most of the regulations now on the books. *They* wanted fair labor standards, equal rights for minorities, dangerous chemicals curbed, better dissemination of knowledge about hazardous working conditions in factories — or hazardous conditions in nursing homes or hospitals.

In the face of all this, what then can the average accountant or auditor do in a general mode? Obviously, to be conversant and somewhat expert on the entire range of needed information is not realistic; but knowing where and how to get basic information is. One somewhat positive note to this subject is that most of the literature emanating from these regulatory agencies emphasizes the fact that they will prosecute *willful* and *repeated* offenders (emphasis provided). It follows then that the entirely innocent offender will be given more lenient consideration for infractions. Therefore it must also follow that decent and good citizen and corporate behavior will always be helpful in keeping companies free of regulatory pursuers.

Practitioners should take the same general tack that appears similarly sensible in dealing with generally accepted accounting principles that, almost all agree, tend to overload (and intimidate) many. They should know and master *the general, and material,* aspects of the major regulations that have a direct effect on their clients' operations. They should know how (and when) to get specific information as the need arises! Otherwise, the task is impossible.

Let's conclude this chapter by offering some practical suggestions on how to get specific information from any of the bureaucratic agencies when the need is perceived.

First, it's important to know that, for the most part, inquiring telephone calls are a waste of time. At best you will reach some polite respondee with a modest amount of information. The best method is to put your request for a ruling, or for clarification of a special, or general, point in writing and send it directly to your state representative. Or better yet, to your Senator's office. If you can make your request very specific, so that a pinpointed answer is unavoidable, so much the better.

Second, don't be hesitant about using this resource. They are very responsive to these inquiries! They will invariably forward your request to the appropriate agency. And they will do it with a cover letter that goes directly to the head person. Agencies in their turn are also very responsive to "Congressionals." In fact most departments set a very short time limit, internally, for getting answers to members of Congress.

Third, when you get the response it will usually have the "official action officer" designated. A letter normally will be sent from a fairly high government official, which often reads like this: "The Secretary has asked me to respond to your inquiry of (such and such a date) concerning (the specific subject). This is the rule (regulation or set of pertinent facts) that governs your questions."

Fourth, now you can direct subsequent follow-up requests to a discrete subsection of a particular agency. You can even call the particular respondee who has signed the answer for the Secretary and get useful answers with a high degree of authenticity.

In conclusion, let's sum up by saying that government regulations are, even to the localized expert, an awesome and cumbersome area. To the novice, or only partly conversant, they represent a difficult task, which can only be made workable by learning how to tune into the right network. This can be a trade association, a specialty group, or your local member of Congress. It is not productive to try to master them yourself.

## Regional Offices and Laboratory Facilities of EPA

**EPA Region 1**
Lester Sutton
JFK Federal Bldg.
Boston, MA 02203
Connecticut, Maine,
Massachusetts, New Hampshire,
Rhode Island, Vermont
617-223-7210

**EPA Region 2**
Jacqueline Schafer
26 Federal Plaza
New York, NY 10007
New Jersey, New York, Puerto
Rico, Virgin Islands
212-264-2525

**EPA Region 3**
Peter Bibko
6th and Walnut Streets
Philadelphia, PA 19106
Delaware, Maryland,
Pennsylvania, Virginia, West
Virginia, District of Columbia
215-597-9814

**EPA Region 4**
Charles Jeter
345 Courtland Street NE
Atlanta, GA 30308
Alabama, Georgia, Florida,
Mississippi, North Carolina,
South Carolina, Tennessee,
Kentucky
404-881-4727

**EPA Region 5**
Val Adamkus
230 S. Dearborn
Chicago, IL 60604
Illinois, Indiana, Ohio, Michigan,
Wisconsin, Minnesota
312-353-2000

**EPA Region 6**
Dick Whittington
1201 Elm Street
Dallas, TX 75270
Arkansas, Louisiana, Oklahoma,
Texas, New Mexico
214-767-2600

## Regional Offices and Laboratory Facilities of EPA

**EPA Region 7**
324 East 11th Street
Kansas City, MO 64106
Iowa, Kansas, Missouri,
Nebraska
816-374-5493

**EPA Region 8**
Steve Durham
1860 Lincoln Street
Denver, CO 80295
Colorado, Utah, Wyoming,
Montana, North Dakota,
South Dakota
303-837-3895

**EPA Region 9**
Sonia Crow
215 Fremont Street
San Francisco, CA 94105
Arizona, California, Nevada,
Hawaii, Guam, American Samoa,
Trust Territories of the Pacific
415-556-2320

**EPA Region 10**
John Spencer
1200 Sixth Avenue
Seattle, WA 98101
Alaska, Idaho, Oregon,
Washington
206-442-1220

Environmental Monitoring and
  Support Laboratory
Cincinnati, OH 45268
(513) 684-7301

Environmental Monitoring Systems
  Laboratory
P.O. Box 15027
Las Vegas, NV 89114
(702) 798-2100

Environmental Monitoring Systems
  Laboratory
Research Triangle Park, NC 27711
(919) 541-2106

Environmental Research Laboratory
College Station Road
Athens, GA 30605
(404) 546-3134

Environmental Research Laboratory
200 SW 35th Street
Corvallis, OR 97330
(503) 757-4601

Environmental Research Laboratory
6201 Congdon Boulevard
Duluth, MN 55804
(218) 727-6692

Environmental Research Laboratory
Sabine Island
Gulf Breeze, FL 32561
(904) 932-5311

Environmental Research Laboratory
South Ferry Road
Narragansett, RI 02882
(401) 789-1071

Environmental Sciences Research
  Laboratory
Research Triangle Park, NC 27711
(919) 541-2191

## Regional Offices and Laboratory Facilities of EPA

Health Effects Research Laboratory
Research Triangle Park, NC 27711
(919) 541-2281

Industrial Environmental Research
Laboratory
Cincinnati, OH 45268
(513) 684-4402

Industrial Environmental Research
Laboratory
Research Triangle Park, NC 27711
(919) 541-2821

Municipal Environmental Research
Laboratory
Cincinnati, OH 45268
(513) 684-7951

Robert S. Kerr Environmental
Research Laboratory
P.O. Box 1198
(S. Craddock & Kerr Road)
Ada, OK 74820
(405) 332-8800

# PART 3

# Managing the Human Element

# CHAPTER 13

# EMPLOYEE AND EXECUTIVE BENEFITS

## Raymond J. Beninato

## THE NEED FOR PENSION AND PROFIT SHARING PLANS

The main purpose of qualified plans is to defer income. This need has become intensified in the 1980s because of the high rate of inflation and the desire to maintain high living standards. The goal of accumulating real wealth is accomplished by both the tax deductibility of pension contributions and the tax-free accumulation of those funds. Exhibit 13.1 shows the appreciation potential of an annual $2000 lump sum investment. There are a number of reasons to start a retirement program. First and foremost is the ability to accumulate wealth.

An individual in the 50-percent tax bracket can easily accumulate wealth through a qualified retirement plan. With taxes taken into consideration, an employee in the 50-percent bracket would have only half as much to save and would pay taxes on the accumulating interest. Using the example above, the individual would only save $1000 a year. With an effective compounding rate of 5 percent, the total will be $60,235 at the end of 30 years.

A significant reason for instituting a qualified plan is to retain key employees. Many qualified plans are established to discourage employees from leaving.

It is helpful to become familiar with other retirement plans within your client's/company's industry. This knowledge will be beneficial when developing a plan that will be both appreciated by the employees and compatible with industry and/or local standards. Another important reason for considering qualified plans would be to forestall unionization.

Pension plans are a good public relations tool. They show that the employer has a concern for the employee's welfare. One has only to look at the computer firms in Silicon Valley to see that employees appreciate this paternalistic concern

EXHIBIT 13.1.  $2,000 Annual Lump Sum Investment Value

|  | Total Contributions | 8% | 10% |
|---|---|---|---|
| Year 5 | 10,000 | 12,672 | 12,432 |
| Year 10 | 20,000 | 31,920 | 35,062 |
| Year 20 | 40,000 | 98,846 | 126,004 |
| Year 30 | 60,000 | 244,692 | 361,886 |

for their welfare. The desire to provide retirement security for employees may also increase employee morale and productivity, thereby increasing profits for the firm. Many arguments center around which is the best plan for improving productivity and the bottom line. This is most easily accomplished by instituting a profit sharing plan where the employees' productivity will be shown directly on the bottom line and result in larger contributions into their own individual accounts.

Another important reason to consider deferring income has been the awareness of the economic problems of the aging. Since 1950 the average life expectancy has increased significantly. A child born today will live approximately 76 and 1/3 years.

In addition to increased longevity, most people need at least the same amount of income, not less, to maintain their standard of living, especially because of inflation. Inflation has also hampered many individuals from saving sufficient funds for their retirement, and therefore they have turned increasingly to their corporations for added employee benefits. Deferred compensation, in lieu of salary increases, is a good way for individuals to save money in light of confiscatory tax rates. Union demands for pensions, and the need for comparability between union and nonunion employees, has sparked an increase in the establishment of pension plans. Finally, because of high taxes, especially in a closely-held corporation, it has been necessary to shelter corporate profits from taxes.

# TYPES OF PLANS

**DEFINED BENEFIT.**  A defined benefit plan is a program where the retirement benefit is fixed by formula and changes only to reflect increasing compensation. Unlike a defined contribution plan where the deposit is fixed as a percentage of payroll, the benefit floats on whatever the contribution will buy at retirement. Amounts contributed to a defined benefit plan may be higher than under money purchase or profit sharing plans. Three approaches for defined benefit plans are: flat benefit, fixed benefit, and unit benefit. A fixed benefit pension plan is the most common. It is based on a formula requiring only a minimum number of years of credited service for participation. Typically, this plan is based on a straight percentage of final average pay or the final five years average of pay using a specified percentage. A person earning $80,000, using a 50-percent formula, would retire on $40,000 a year.

A fixed benefit plan is a fixed amount pension plan. It is a benefit-oriented plan in which a stated dollar benefit will be paid for all employees regardless of years of service or salary histories; it is based on a bracket basis. This is almost exclusively seen with union pension plans. An example of how bracket works is shown in the following example: Employees who have a yearly average pay of $500 to $700 a month would get a flat benefit of $250 a month, whereas those who have an average salary of $751 or more might get $500 a month. The pension benefit is determined by the income bracket of a retiring individual.

A unit benefit pension plan provides a fixed benefit determined by a formula that has two factors: one is the years of service or years of plan membership and the second is a percentage of salary. The formula involved for unit benefit could work as follows. An employee might be credited with 2 percent of final compensation or the average of the final five years' compensation for every year the employee is a plan member or credited with a year of service. Based on this formula, someone who has 25 years of service would receive a pension benefit of 50 percent of final pay or the average of their last five years. Another formula is a flat dollar amount per year of service. For example, a flat benefit of $100 per month times the number of years of service. Someone who has worked 20 years would be entitled to a benefit of $2000 (20 years $\times$ $100). One advantage of a defined benefit plan is that the employee knows what the benefit will be at retirement.

When instituting a plan for a closely held corporation, where the owner employee happens to be an older employee, the defined benefit plan allows substantial contributions to be made for the benefit of older employees in light of the short time available to accumulate benefits. Another advantage of defined benefit plans is the ability to reward higher-paid employees and keep a control on the cost of the plan through integration with social security.

A corporation may prefer a defined benefit plan because it can shelter greater amounts of income than under normal pension plans. Under a defined benefit plan, the dividends, excess interest, or excess earnings help offset the annual contribution to the plan. This helps the cost-conscious employer to keep a lid on the cost. If there is life insurance in the pension plan, the cost of normal life insurance premiums and any ratings are deductible. Finally, there is a psychological benefit because the benefits under a defined benefit plan are promised benefits.

There are some disadvantages to the defined benefit plan. The greatest would be poor cost control because there is little direct relationship between profits and the cost of the plan. The cost of the plan will fluctuate for a variety of reasons, including investment earnings, mortality, termination of employment, and salary increases. Salary increases would raise the cost of the plan. Another disadvantage is additional employer contributions in the event of poor investment performance. These plans require an enrolled actuary. They are also subject to the minimum funding standards, the Pension Benefit Guaranty Corporation and its contingent employer liability. No contributions are allowed beyond the normal retirement date.

**HYBRID PLANS.**   A hybrid plan (IRC Section 414(k)) is a defined benefit plan that provides benefits based in part on separate accounts for employees. These plans are called "hybrid plans" because they have characteristics of both the defined benefit plans and defined contribution plans. A major distinction is that the funding formula itself is based on a defined benefit calculation that must be determined actuarially. After the initial contribution is determined, all monies are placed into separate employee accounts and the value of these accounts grows based on their investment performance. There is additional employer liability if these funds do not reach the determined level needed to realize the defined benefit initially stated and funded. In an era of high investment yields, a hybrid plan can be very attractive because the actuarial calculation used to determine the contribution is based on an assumed interest of 5 or 6 percent as prescribed by the IRS. With interest rates of 10, 11, and 12 percent, the excess interest would stay in the employee's account and give each employee a larger benefit than was initially being funded.

The "target plan" is a type of hybrid plan. It favors older employees, allowing substantial contributions because of the short accumulation period until retirement. The employer's cost in the target plan does not fluctuate because of investment performance. Older employees receive larger allocation of the employer's contribution than younger employees with the same salary. An important fact to note is that there is no benefit limitations, because the benefit will be based on the value of the participants account at retirement. This value is a function of contribution size and timing, length of participation, and investment results. The participant's total account is payable either at retirement or at death. After the initial contribution is calculated, enrolled actuary calculations are not required nor are Pension Benefit Guaranty Corporation guaranties required. The plan is simple to understand and administer, and the employee, not the employer, assumes investment risks.

The disadvantages are that the benefits are only estimated and are not guaranteed. No contributions are allowed beyond the normal retirement date. The plan is subject to all of the ERISA contribution limits, participation, and vesting requirements.

**DEFINED CONTRIBUTION PLANS.** A defined contribution is one in which the contributions are defined and the benefit is not guaranteed. The benefit will be whatever the contributions can buy at retirement. The total value of the participant's account will depend entirely on the size and timing of contributions, the length of service, and investment performance. The employer has flexibility in the level of contributions, and a contribution is determined as a percentage of the payroll or accumulated earnings and profits.

**PROFIT SHARING.** A profit sharing plan is a contribution-oriented plan in which employer contributions can be made only from accumulated earnings or profits. The employer has maximum flexibility as to the size of contributions to be made under this plan, and in a year without profits no contribution need be made. The maximum employer contribution is limited to 25 percent of covered payroll, not to exceed $30,000 per participant. The only IRS requirement is that contributions be "substantial and recurring." A profit sharing plan may have different formulas based on the level of contributions and a definition of what constitutes profits. A profit sharing plan promises no specific benefit to an employee except the value of the account at retirement or at a specified event (e.g., death, disability, or termination of employment).

The plan participant's account value is a function of contribution size, length of participation, and investment results. An advantage of a profit sharing plan is the direct relationship between contributions and profits. Therefore, it serves as an excellent employee incentive device because, if there are no profits, there are no contributions. Profit sharing plans promote loyalty to the employer. This loyalty is rewarded because employees who remain with the firm are entitled to share in the reallocation of forfeitures from members of the plan who terminate employment early.

Another advantage of a profit sharing plan is that it does not favor older employees, it treats all employees alike. The contributions are the same for all employees earning the same compensation. A business with a great number of older employees will have lower contributions to a profit sharing plan than to a defined benefit plan. Another advantage is that employees may continue contributions after the normal retirement date. Profit sharing plans are easy to understand and administer because they are directly related to profits. There is no actuarial cost and no Pension Benefit Guaranty Corporation premiums are required.

The disadvantages of a profit sharing plan are twofold. It does not benefit older employees who may have had prior service with the employer, and it will penalize older employees who have the same salary as younger employees. In addition, older employees have no way of determining their retirement benefits. The uncertainty of contributions, and the fact the contributions are contingent on profits, makes the addition of life insurance in a profit sharing plan speculative at best because there may be years when no contributions are made under the plan.

**MONEY PURCHASE.** Defined contribution (money purchase) plans are similar to profit sharing plans. They are contribution oriented and promise no specific retirement benefit to employees. A money purchase plan obligates the employer to a specific level of contributions. These contributions are fixed and the provisions of the plan are subject to IRS minimum funding requirements. Forfeitures from defined contribution (money purchase) pension plans must be applied to reduce employer contributions. In a profit sharing plan, the forfeitures are normally applied to the remaining participants accounts. The IRS requirements as to participation and vesting are the same in the case of profit sharing or defined contribution plan.

Most of the advantages and disadvantages of defined contribution plans apply to profit sharing plans. The major difference is the defined contribution plan requires contributions each year.

# 401(k) PLANS

A 401(k) plan can be designed using only employee contributions (salary reduction), a combination of employee and employer contributions, or only employer contributions. Employer-only contributions can be in the form of cash or on a deferred basis.

There was concern in Congress that 401(k) plans would benefit only the higher paid employees. To correct this problem, Congress enacted certain nondiscriminatory tests (section 401(k)(3)(A)(i)(ii)) that must be met in order for the plan to qualify elective contributions as employer contributions.

Two nondiscrimination tests are: (1) the average deferral percentage of the highest paid one-third may not be more than 1½ times the deferral percentage of all other employees; or (2) the average deferral percentage of the highest paid one-third cannot be more than 3 percentage points.

The sum of the deferral percentage of the highest paid one-third and the deferral percentage of all other employees cannot be more than 2½ times the deferral percentage of all other employees.

401(k) plans are subject to the same rules as profit sharing plans for vesting and eligibility. This qualification enables the corporation to receive a tax deduction as a business expense. Many companies with current qualified profit sharing plans may consider 401(k) plans instead, because they produce larger deductions for the higher paid employees.

Employees can elect to defer employer contributions or receive them in cash.

The employee receives no taxable income on corporate contributions made or on the deferred salary. All employee contributions are forfeitable and immediately vested.

Under a 401(k) plan, employees can borrow money for a financial hardship. Many professionals consider the purchase of a home, college expenses, or extraordinary medical expenses to be examples of financial hardships.

A distinct advantage of a 401(k) plan is that participants who are in the plan five or more years are eligible for the tax-favored 10-year forward averaging method, which provides significant tax savings. Employees covered under a 401(k) plan may still maintain an IRA.

After 1983, amounts deferred under a 401(k) plan are subject to payroll and Social Security taxes. The employer will still recognize savings on unemployment insurance and workers' compensation. The disadvantage under a 401(k) plan is the uncertainty of contributions for the top one-third of payroll. The top one-third of payroll's contributions is determined by what the bottom two-thirds of payroll contributes.

The following chart illustrates acceptable contribution formulas:

### 401(k) Contribution Formula

| If the lower 2/3 group contributes: | Then the higher 1/3 group may contribute: |
| --- | --- |
| Under 2% of pay | 2 1/2 times the rate of the lower group |
| 2–6% of pay | 3% of pay more than the lower group |
| Over 6% of pay | 1 1/2 times the rate of the lower group |

# IRA

Initially, individual retirement plans were provided to help employees who are not covered under a pension plan to set up their own individual plan. ERISA gave the authorization for IRAs and set the original contribution limits and requirements. The Economic Recovery Act (ERTA) in 1981 liberalized the eligibility requirements. Employees covered under corporate or individual pension plans may also make contributions to their own individual retirement plans. In addition, ERTA raised the maximum annual contribution for one person from $1500 to $2000. The contribution formula is 100 percent of compensation or $2000, whichever is less. There is a nonworking spouse IRA where up to $250 can be contributed. This brings the total for a family with a nonworking spouse up to $2250. Any eligible individual under age 70½ can participate.

Prior to age 59½ no distribution may be made from an IRA without penalty, except in the event of death or disability. Distributions that are made before age 59½ are subject to a 10 percent nondeductible excise tax. Distributions must begin in the year a participant reaches age 70½.

IRA retirement benefits are taxed as ordinary income when received. Death benefits paid under an IRA will be income taxed at ordinary rate when received but can be sheltered from estate taxes. The Tax Reform Act of 1976 provides that substantially equal periodic payments be received over a beneficiary's life. The Economic Recovery Tax Act of 1981 increased the estate and gift tax credit and provides for unlimited marital deductions. If the beneficiary is a spouse, there will no longer be estate taxes imposed. Excess contributions to an IRA are subject to a nondeductible 6 percent excise tax. This tax is imposed each year the excess remains in the IRA. The excise tax is not imposed if the excess is refunded to a participant before the tax filing date. A premature distribution is included in a participant's gross income and a penalty tax equal to 10 percent of the distribution is imposed. An individual must start distributions by age 70 either by taking a lifetime annuity or a joint and survivor annuity, or by setting up a withdrawal system that will not extend beyond life expectancy.

The minimum life expectancy distribution can be recalculated annually for the new life expectancy of the participant and the participant's spouse under section 401(a)(9)(D). This gives significant flexibility of distributions and will provide an increasing benefit for a number of years. This annual recalculation of benefits is not allowed for a nonspouse beneficiary.

# EMPLOYEE STOCK OWNERSHIP PLANS

The first tax-exempt stock bonus plans were regulated under the Revenue Act of 1921. It was not until the 1970s and the passage of ERISA that these plans were rediscovered.

An employee stock ownership plan (ESOP) must qualify under Section 401(a) of the Internal Revenue Code. Section 407(d)(6) of ERISA and Section 4975(e)(7) of the IRC define an ESOP as a stock bonus plan or a combination of stock bonus plan and money purchase plan, designed primarily to invest in employer's stock. An ESOP is permitted to borrow money. Under Section 406(a)(1)(B) of ERISA and Section 4975(c)(1)(B) IRC lending of money is prohibited, whereas Section 408(b)(3) of ERISA and Section 4975(d)(3)(C) provide exceptions in the case of ESOPs. An ESOP is used as a technique of corporate financing for an employee retirement plan, an employee incentive plan, or an executive compensation plan.

One great advantage of an ESOP is its flexibility in meeting more than just one goal. An ESOP may be used by a public or private company and can create markets for stock. In the event that an ESOP borrows money, there must be a binding commitment by the employer to make future payments to the ESOP in amounts necessary to repay the loan. Normally, if an ESOP borrows money, the portion that will be required to pay back the loan will include a defined contribution formula subject to the minimum funding standards of Code Section 4112. The balance of any corporate contribution could be in the same manner as a profit sharing plan with discretionary employer contribution. The plan may be integrated with social security. Depending on the formula used, either the money purchase plan or profit sharing, the forfeiture requirements of either plan will prevail. In the case of a profit sharing plan, the reallocation of forfeitures will be distributed to the remaining participants. In the event of forfeitures under the defined contribution formula, the forfeitures must be applied or must reduce the employer contributions.

The purpose of a stock bonus plan under Revenue Ruling 69-65 is to give the employee participants an interest in the ownership and performance of the employer's business. This is a major distinction from most other pension and profit sharing plans. Because the employees receive an ownership interest, an ESOP differs greatly from other pension plans in the areas of fiduciary responsibilities and investment practices. One of the main purposes of an ESOP is to use credit to acquire employers' stock for the participants' benefit. It was because of these reasons that an ESOP was granted an exemption for borrowing and for investing primarily in the employer's own stock.

As mentioned previously, an ESOP is an ideal vehicle for corporate financing. The corporation establishes an ESOP and qualifies it under Section 401(a) and Section 4975(e)(7). The ESOP must meet the Code requirements as to nondiscrimination and the benefits must be in relationship to relevant compensation. A corporation arranges for the ESOP to borrow a stated sum of money, for instance $500,000, which the corporation guarantees to repay to the ESOP. The corporation then issues shares of stock with a market value of $500,000. This $500,000 worth of stock is held in escrow and is released to the ESOP as the corporation makes payments to it to release this stock. The ESOP then uses this money to retire the loan from the bank or other lending institution. The corporation in effect is able to float a loan and make the required payments on a tax-deductible basis instead of with after-tax dollars. This happens because the corporation is making a contribution to a qualified pension plan. It receives a deduction for this contribution and the ESOP then retires the bank note. An ESOP is the only qualified plan that can borrow money, and receive loans and other extensions of credit, from a party in interest (such as a major stockholder or the employer).

Participants of ESOPs are taxed generally in the same method as other qualified plan participants. A special distinction must be made under a lump sum distribution that qualifies under the Internal Revenue Code. The participant is taxed to the extent of the cost basis of the stock to the ESOP trust. Employer's stock attributed to the employer contribution is tax-free to the recipient to the extent of any unrealized appreciation in the stock. This would be the excess of current value over the cost basis to the ESOP. Employer stock attributed to an employee's contributions is a tax-free distribution to the participant, including any unrealized value in the stock. The employee, on a subsequent sale of stock, will be taxed on the unrealized appreciation in the stock as a long-term capital gain, regardless of how long the stock is held by the participant. If the gain is greater than the unrealized appreciation at the time it is distributed to the participant, the excess is treated as either a short-term or long-term capital gain, depending on the participant's holding period. This is a great tax advantage for participants in an ESOP, because they only have to report as income from a distribution, the ESOP's cost basis. This cost basis can use the extremely favorable 10-year forwarding average technique. In addition, the unrealized appreciation is not taxed to the participant until his or her subsequent sale.

The sale of stock would be subject to long-term capital gains, unless the gain is greater than the value at which the employee received the stock. If the value of the stock is greater at the time of sale than at the time the participant received the stock, the difference is subject to tax. The tax rate (capital gain/ordinary income) would depend on the holding period.

An ESOP can be a source of income to the employee because any cash dividends on the employer's stock can be paid directly to the plan participants. This would provide the employees with additional income which would be taxed. An ESOP provides great motivation to employees because they are given shares of stock in their participating accounts in the ESOP plan. Unlike a profit sharing plan where the contributions are invested in different areas, most of the contributions in an ESOP are required to be in an employer's stock. An employee can directly influence the value of his or her account, because the greater the corporate profit, normally the greater the price per share of the stock. In this way the participant's efforts can be rewarded directly through work productivity. In addition, the employee receives the added tax benefits of any normal pension plan and the special long-term capital gain treatment associated with an ESOP.

The corporation has an additional financing vehicle. It can raise capital on a tax-deductible basis by issuing stock to an ESOP and by incurring bank financing. Insurance can be purchased under an ESOP as with any other qualified plan, but no more than 25 percent of the contribution can go toward insurance.

Term insurance should be discouraged because there is no economic benefit, only a death benefit. An ESOP can also be used as an estate planning tool, thus creating a market for stock in a closely held corporation providing liquidity for a Section 303 stock redemption. An ESOP can be used to provide an in-house market for closely held corporations and thus eliminate one of the needs for a company to go public.

An ESOP does have certain disadvantages. It involves greater administrative expense than other qualified plans. In certain situations the different security laws may come into play and a stock may have to be registered. Many employees may not like the uncertainty associated with an ESOP plan. Retirement benefits are directly linked to the employer's stock values. The corporation may not like the fact that in a leveraged ESOP, stock purchased with borrowed funds must be held in escrow, and can never revert to the employer, even if the trust is terminated.

For an ESOP to receive IRS approval, the plan must be for the exclusive benefit of the employees. The employer must prove that the plan is more than a corporate financing tool. A leveraged ESOP limits an employer's tax deduction to the current market value of stock. In the event the stock appreciates greatly, the employer's deduction is limited to the predetermined amount necessary to liquidate the bank borrowing.

# DEFINED BENEFITS PLANS: COVERAGE AND CONTRIBUTIONS

One factor for determining pension eligibility is based on length of service. An employee must be given credit for each year of service that the employee has worked at least 1000 hours. This 1000 hours of service is determined over a 12-month period which could cover either the calendar year, plan year, or an employment year. Determining service sometimes is more complex than it appears. If the employee does not have 1000 hours of service, he or she may still be considered eligible. There are a number of tests an employer must use to determine eligibility. One test is counting the actual hours worked. This method is administratively difficult because of the record keeping required. In determining the hours worked, only regular or actual hours worked, including overtime but excluding nonworking hours such as vacations and holidays, are credited to the total hours worked. You can also use regular hours worked, excluding overtime. Finally, you can use the earnings method. This is where employees' earning hours are related to actual earnings received.

There are certain equivalencies when using some of the above-mentioned methods. If you use the hours-worked method, an employee will be credited with one year of service for only 870 hours instead of the commonly used 1000 hours of service. In addition, the employee will be credited with a break in service if he or she has worked 435 hours instead of the commonly used 501 hours. Under the regular hours worked, and the earnings method, a year of service must be given if the employee has worked 750 hours; a break in service must be credited if the employee has only 375 hours. If using the earnings method, hourly rated employees only need 870 hours to get a year of service and 435 hours to receive credit for a break in service. Under the earnings method, other employees (salaried) will receive a year of service for 750 hours and a break in service for 375 hours.

There are other methods in determining a year of service. The computed number of hours method gives credit for different time periods involved, as long as an employee is credited with at least 1 hour of service. The credit that must be given under different various computed methods is as follows:

> 1 day - 10 hours of credit
> 1 week - 45 hours of credit
> $1/2$ month - 95 hours of credit
> 1 month - 190 hours of credit

**ELIGIBILITY REQUIREMENTS.**    The Internal Revenue Code has a very broad requirement for eligibility under a qualified retirement plan. Eligibility requirements are those conditions that must be met before an employee can be included in a retirement plan. The code includes these requirements to encourage widespread participation and to prevent discrimination in favor of the "prohibited group." "Prohibited group" refers to officers, stockholders, or other highly compensated employees. Eligibility requirements may either defer an employee's entrance into a retirement plan or permanently bar the employee from participation in a retirement plan. An employee might be permanently excluded from a retirement plan if he or she is a member of an ineligible group (job classification), such as hourly paid employees. Another reason an employee might be permanently denied entrance into a pension plan would be a maximum age limit, as in the case of a defined benefit plan. An employee might be deferred to a later date to enter a retirement plan because of a minimum age and/or length of service requirements. Union employees may be excluded if either a union pension plan exists or if one has been the subject of a collective bargaining agreement.

For a plan to qualify, and the employer to receive its tax deduction, the plan must meet one of two percentage coverage requirements. The first states that at least 70 percent of all employees must be covered, excluding those who have insufficient service or do not meet the minimum age requirement. The second percentage test refers to contributory plans. It states that 70 percent of the employees must be eligible and at least 80 percent of all eligible employees must actively participate. A contributory plan will qualify if only 56 percent of the employees participate. In addition to these percentage requirements there is another requirement that must be met if a plan is to be deemed nondiscriminatory. If a corporation is deemed to be a part of a controlled group of corporations, in accordance with IRC Section 1563(a), all employees are to be treated as if they were members of the same corporation. This does not mean that a plan can't be somewhat selective, but it does have to meet the nondiscriminatory tests. A plan may seem to be discriminatory and yet still qualify under the Internal Revenue Code. The Internal Revenue Service may approve a plan even if it excludes different classifications of employees, as long as it does not discriminate in favor of the "prohibited group."

**DETERMINATION OF EARNINGS.**    Earnings have a direct relationship with the cost of providing benefits under a qualified plan. In the case of a defined benefit plan, normally the benefit formula is a percentage of pay (highest, last five years, final). For a defined contribution plan the benefit formula is a percentage of earnings that is contributed for each employee. Generally, only basic compensation is considered under a qualified retirement plan. This is done so that there can not be discrimination in favor of a "prohibited group." Social security under certain plans is taken into account when determining either benefits or contributions. Under certain defined benefit plans, only earnings in excess of the social security base are credited in the plan. Under certain defined contribution plans, the greater contribution will be made for earnings over social security taxable base then for earnings under this amount. In both cases, when social security benefits are taken into account, the plan becomes an integrated qualified plan. Later in this chapter there are tables in Exhibit 13.1 describing the social security integration rules and limits.

The Retirement Equity Act of 1984 liberalized the maximum participation age an employer could incorporate into the plan design. The maximum participation age is 21 (lowered from 25) and the maximum vesting is 18 (lowered from 22). The plans of certain tax-exempt educational organizations decreased the maximum participation age from 30 to 26.

**CONTRIBUTION MAXIMUMS.**    Under a defined benefit plan, the largest benefit that can be funded is a straight-life annuity for the lesser of either 100 percent of pay or $90,000. The 100 percent of compensation refers to the average of the highest three consecutive calendar years of compensation. The $90,000 limit will be adjusted annually after 1986 and will be subject to regulations from the Secretary of the Treasury. There will be actuarial adjustments if the benefit is payable in other than a straight-life annuity or a joint and survivor annuity on the life of the participant and spouse. The earliest retirement age is age 62 under which an employee can be credited with the full $90,000 limit. If benefits start before age 62, then the $90,000 limit must be reduced to an actuarial equivalent of $90,000 at age 62 (IRC 415(b)(2)(C)). The reduced benefit does not have to be lower than a $75,000 benefit at age 55. Below age 55 the benefit never has to be less than the actuarial equivalent of $75,000 payable at age 55. If benefits are delayed until after age 65, the $90,000 limit can be increased by an actuarial equivalent. There is a $10,000 benefit that can be provided without the salary limitation or different adjustments for postretirement benefits if the participant has only been covered by the defined benefit plan of the employer (IRC Section 415(b)(4)). Finally, if an employee has less than 10 years of service, all these benefits can be reduced in proportion to the actual years of service as a percentage of 10 years.

**DEFINED CONTRIBUTION LIMITS.**    The maximum contribution under a defined contribution plan is 25 percent of compensation with a maximum limit of $30,000 per participant. This limit will be adjusted after 1986 in accordance with the Secretary of the Treasury. Taken into account as limits to an employee's account are any employer contributions, employee contributions in excess of 6 percent, and forfeitures.

**TWO OR MORE PLANS.**    The total benefits in contributions of combined plans cannot be more than 140 percent of the limitations applicable to one plan if the percentage of compensation limits apply, or more than 125 percent if the dollar limits apply. For full understanding of the combined limits, you must examine IRC Section 415(e). Section 415(e) determines a defined benefit plan fraction to be used for each year. The numerator of the defined benefit plan fraction is the projected annual benefit, assuming the participant keeps working at the present rate of pay until normal retirement age. The denominator is the lesser of 1.25 percent times the dollar limit applicable for the year ($90,000 or adjusted amount after 1986) or 1.4 times the participant's average compensation for the three highest years. For the defined contribution plan fraction, the numerator is the sum of the current year and all prior years of the allocations to the participant's account that are subject to the limits under Section 415 (employer contributions, employee contributions over 6 percent, and forfeitures). The denominator is the same for the current year and each prior year of the participant's service with the employer (regardless of whether the plan was in existence during those years) of the lesser of 1.25 times the dollar limit applicable to the year ($30,000 for 1983, 1984, and 1985, other amounts for prior and later years) or 1.4 times 25 percent of pay for each such year. The sum of the defined benefit plan fraction and the defined contribution plan fraction may not exceed 1.0 in any year. Special transition rules modify these calculations.

**TOP-HEAVY PLANS.**   A new definition called "top-heavy" was brought to us by ERTA. A plan is top-heavy when the value of accrued benefits for key employees (IRC Section 416(i) defines key employees) and their beneficiaries exceeds 60 percent of the accrued value to all employees and their beneficiaries. Normally, under a closely held corporation, the goal is to make the plans top-heavy; therefore, most of the contribution and benefits are geared toward the majority stockholders who are always the key employees.

Top-heavy plans must provide either minimum benefits or contributions for all participants who are not considered key employees. A defined benefit plan that is determined to be top-heavy must have a minimum benefit either equal to 20 percent of average compensation or at least 2 percent of average compensation multiplied by the participant's years of service. You can exclude years when the plan was not top-heavy, and you can exclude all years before 1984.

Generally, average compensation is based on the five highest consecutive years. Under a defined contribution plan, a minimum of 3 percent of the employee's compensation must be contributed or must be the same percentage at which contributions are made for key employees. There is a $200,000 compensation limit which the plan cannot exceed; this is also subject to Section 415 concerning cost-of-living adjustments. In the event that the plan is top-heavy and has both a defined benefit and a defined contribution plan, the 125 percent limit on contributions must be reduced to 100 percent. This reduction will not apply where the value of accrued benefits for key employees does not exceed 90 percent of the value for all employees.

# SOCIAL SECURITY INTEGRATION

Three approaches can be used to integrate plans with social security: offset plan (deduct social security benefits), excess plan (exclude for benefit calculation that portion of the participant's salary subject to social security taxes), step rate plan (divide contribution to the plan by using lower contributions on the participant's salary subject to social security than on amounts above the social security limit).

A plan today can reduce benefits payable by 83 1/3 percent of an employee's primary insurance amount under social security at the time the employee retires. Typically, 50 percent is the maximum offset used today and it applies to long-service employees only. The dollar amount offset is determined at retirement. Social security increases received after an employee retires cannot reduce the pension benefit.

There are three types of excess plans:

1. Flat benefit excess plan
2. Unit benefit excess plan
3. Defined contribution excess plan

The step-rate plan (supplemental benefit formula) provides contributions or benefits with a lower rate of contributions or benefits credit for compensation below the integration level than for compensation above this level. The IRS treats a step-rate benefit formula plan as two separate plans. The first part of the formula must provide a uniform rate of benefits or contributions to all compensation. This rate is the one used for compensation below the integration level. The IRS views the excess portion as a second plan. The difference between the two rates must meet IRS regulations.

Revenue Rulings 71-446 and 78-92 give a further understanding of how social security integration can be used in plan design.

The integration level may not exceed an employee's "covered compensation" when the excess plan is used. Covered compensation as defined by Revenue Ruling 71-446 is "the amount of compensation with respect to which old-age and survivors insurance benefits would be provided for him under the Social Security Act computed as though, for each year until he reaches age 65, his annual compensation is at least equal to the taxable wage base." The covered compensation of an employee is determined by the calendar year in which he reaches age 65; the later the year, the greater the average annual compensation.

Exhibit 13.2 is based on the 1984 taxable wage base. Both of the tables are permitted by the IRS and are recalculated annually to show increases in the taxable wage base.

# NONQUALIFIED DEFERRED COMPENSATION PLANS

A nonqualified deferred compensation plan is normally nothing more than a promise from a firm to pay benefits to an employee under specific circumstances. Benefits are payable at retirement, and may include preretirement disability benefits, preretirement death benefits, and postretirement death benefits.

A deferred compensation plan can be set up in many different ways. The two most popular are salary reduction basis and corporate pay-all basis. With a salary reduction basis the employee is fully vested in the amount that is deferred (by means of salary reduction) and is currently taxed on the vested benefits. The second most popular plan is for the corporation to make informal contributions and promise future benefits. When the corporation is making these

## EXHIBIT 13.2. Social Security Integration Levels

| 1984 Table I | | 1984 Table II | |
|---|---|---|---|
| Calendar Year of Retirement | Monthly Covered Compensation | Calendar Year of Retirement | Monthly Covered Compensation |
| 1984 | $1050 | 1984 | $1070 |
| 1985 | 1150 | 1985 | 1150 |
| 1986 | 1200 | 1986 | 1224 |
| 1987 | 1300 | 1987 | 1293 |
| 1988 | 1350 | 1988 | 1357 |
| 1989 | 1400 | 1989 | 1417 |
| 1990 | 1450 | 1990 | 1473 |
| 1991 | 1550 | 1991 | 1525 |
| 1992 | 1550 | 1992 | 1574 |
| 1993 | 1600 | 1993 | 1621 |
| 1994 | 1650 | 1994 | 1664 |
| 1995 | 1750 | 1995 | 1743 |
| 1996 | 1800 | 1996 | 1821 |
| 1997 | 1900 | 1997 | 1900 |
| 1998 | 2000 | 1998 | 1979 |
| 1999 | 2050 | 1999 | 2057 |
| 2000 | 2150 | 2000 | 2136 |
| 2001 | 2200 | 2001 | 2214 |
| 2002 | 2300 | 2002 | 2289 |
| 2003 | 2350 | 2003 | 2363 |
| 2004 | 2450 | 2004 | 2434 |
| 2005 | 2500 | 2005 | 2506 |
| 2006 | 2600 | 2006 | 2579 |
| 2007 | 2650 | 2007 | 2649 |
| 2008 | 2700 | 2008 | 2717 |
| 2009 | 2800 | 2009 | 2781 |
| 2010 | 2850 | 2010 | 2840 |
| 2011 | 2900 | 2011 | 2896 |
| 2012 | 2950 | 2012 | 2950 |
| 2013 | 3000 | 2013 | 3001 |
| 2014 | 3050 | 2014 | 3049 |
| 2015 | 3100 | 2015 | 3084 |
| 2016 | 3100 | 2016 | 3112 |
| 2017 | 3150 | 2017 | 3132 |
| 2018 | 3150 | 2018 | 3145 |
| 2019 or later | 3150 | 2019 or later | 3150 |

promises, it may provide gradual vesting or no vesting at all. Future benefits might be tied solely to the employee working for the corporation until the normal retirement date, with the employee losing all benefits if he or she leaves employment early.

## EMPLOYER ADVANTAGES AND DISADVANTAGES

1. A deferred compensation plan can be critical in keeping key employees.

2. The benefits can be selective as to who receives them and how much they receive.

3. Amounts contributed to a deferred compensation plan are considered to be a general corporate asset. Therefore there is no effect on the bottom line.

4. The corporation has the right to set up difficult criteria for obtaining benefits. When the corporation chooses normal retirement age as a criterion for receiving benefits under a deferred compensation plan, it places the employee in "golden handcuffs."

5. The corporation has a great deal of flexibility because it is not required to make annual contributions to the plan.

6. The corporation can transfer benefits from one employee to another in the event a key employee terminates employment.

7. Under a nonqualified deferred compensation plan the employer contributions are not tax deductible. The corporation receives the deductions when the benefits are paid to the employee.

## EMPLOYEE ADVANTAGES AND DISADVANTAGES

1. The employee receives additional retirement benefits.

2. The plan normally gives the employee preretirement death and disability benefits and postretirement death benefits.

3. The fringe benefits provided under a deferred compensation plan free the employee from having to pay for these benefits personally on an after-tax basis.

4. The plan has a direct tie-in with employment, and retirement benefits normally are not payable until the retirement date.

5. Most plans do not have a vesting schedule, and therefore employees have no vesting or nonforfeiture rights in any benefits that might be accruing.

6. The greatest danger to the employee might be that these promises are

unsecured. In the event of bankruptcy, the employee would only be a general creditor of the employer and in fact may be defeated by other creditors.

**HOW A DEFERRED COMPENSATION PLAN WORKS.** As mentioned previously, under a deferred compensation plan benefits are payable at retirement and there usually are preretirement death and disability benefits as well as postretirement death benefits.

Here is a typical example of a deferred compensation plan:

A 45-year-old employee is promised a retirement benefit of $20,000 a year for 10 years, starting at age 65. These benefits will be paid either to the employee or to a designated beneficiary in the event of the employee's death. In addition, the plan may also promise to pay the employee $20,000 for 10 years in the event the employee is disabled before normal retirement. There are many variations of deferred compensation plans. One of the greatest benefits of deferred compensation is that it can be tailor-made for each individual.

**FUNDING NONQUALIFIED DEFERRED COMPENSATION PLANS.** Although many deferred compensation plans are unfunded, it is prudent for the firm to make contributions to the plan. Funds for a deferred compensation plan can be invested in a wide variety of vehicles. Common stock, mutual funds, and other equity vehicles are excellent investments for deferred compensation funds. All funds are considered general corporate assets, and dividends declared through common stock and mutual funds owned by a corporation receive the 85 percent dividend exclusion allowance.

Life insurance is an inexpensive method to fund preretirement death benefits. Universal life is ideally suited for deferred compensation plans because the corporation receives current interest rates on the cash value buildup. The cash value can be used to fund the promised retirement benefits as well as guarantee the funds necessary in the event of an untimely death.

The split-dollar method of deferred compensation is a concept where the corporation enters into an arrangement with its executive to provide preretirement death benefits to the employee's beneficiary. This is accomplished through the purchase of life insurance protection. Under a split-dollar funding agreement the employer owns the plan. The employee's beneficiary receives the death benefit tax free. If the beneficiary is the spouse, it would also be subject to the unrestricted marital estate tax deduction.

The corporation benefits in the event of an early death by receiving all premiums paid into the plan. The corporation's only expense would be loss of interest on the money in the event of an early employee death. When the employee retires or terminates employment, the entire policy reverts back to the corporation.

There is a potential problem in using the split-dollar method if the employee is the controlling stockholder. The death benefit might be subject to federal and estate taxes under Revenue Ruling 82-145.

## WHERE DEFERRED COMPENSATION PLANS APPLY

1. Where there is no retirement plan
2. Where there is a plan where there are low pension benefits for key employees
3. Where TEFRA has reduced the executive's pension benefits
4. Where the cost of providing "adequate" retirement benefits for key employees would be prohibitive because of the current pension regulations
5. Where it is impossible to target benefits for key employees only
6. Where there is inadequate or nonexistent pre- and postretirement life insurance protection

The reasons mentioned above have led to the popularity of nonqualified deferred compensation plans. All of these aspects are taken into consideration when a deferred compensation plan is developed. Deferred compensation's use as a "golden handcuff" is an appealing reason for employers to install deferred compensation plans. A deferred compensation plan links the employee directly to the employer with substantial risks of losing all benefits if the employee changes employment.

**ERISA AND INTERNAL REVENUE REQUIREMENTS FOR NONQUALIFIED DEFERRED COMPENSATION PLANS.** The reasons nonqualified deferred compensation plans are only informally funded is because of ERISA requirements and IRS restrictions. Revenue Ruling 60-31 is the basis on which an employee is not currently taxed on an employer's unsecured promise to pay benefits. If the plan is formally funded and the employee is vested, then the employee is subject to current taxation on the amounts deferred (IRC Section 501(c)(3) constructive receipt). If the employee is not subject to a substantial risk of forfeiture, then the employee must pay current income taxes (IRC Section 83).

Unfunded or informally funded deferred compensation plans are exempt from ERISA requirements except that Part 1 (reporting and disclosure) and Part V (administration and enforcement) must be filed. The reporting and disclosure requirements are met by filing a statement with the Department of Labor. The ERISA requirement, Part V, can be met with a claims procedure form. If the plan is fully funded, it would create current tax problems for the employee and subject the employee to restrictive regulations.

# MAJOR IMPACT OF LEGISLATION SINCE ERISA

**EFFECTS OF ERISA.** ERISA gave us more disclosure rules and regulations than in the past. It changed the way a plan must meet minimum eligibility requirements. One purpose of ERISA is to make plans more nondiscriminatory in coverge or eligibility. Also ERISA gave us IRC Sections 414(b) and 414(c), defining what a controlled group is and requiring treating these employees as if employed by a single employer. ERISA introduced more liberal rules for minimum participation and vesting. Code 415 limited the maximum benefits and contributions that employers can fund. Code Section 1563(a) determines whether a corporation is a controlled group and what constitutes common control. These rules also apply to partnerships, sole proprietors, and unincorporated businesses. ERISA required new reporting and fiduciary requirements as well as plan termination insurance guarantees. In addition, ERISA introduced new fiduciary duties in areas of prohibited transactions and parties in interest.

In the area of disclosure, employees must now receive Summary Plan Descriptions. These disclosure requirements include pension and profit sharing plans, ESOPS, welfare plans, and also include group life insurance, surgical, medical, dental, vision-care benefits, and accidental death and disability benefits. The disclosure requirements demand that employees are entitled to a statement of accrued benefits, and when such benefits are or will be vested. New plan participants must be provided with the basis on which payments and distributions from the plan are to be made. Finally, a summary annual report must be given to each employee covered under the plan.

ERISA introduced the individual retirement account. The original limits were 15 percent of income with a maximum of $1500. The early IRAs made no provision for nonworking spouses and excluded those covered under other qualified retirement plans. ERISA also made Keogh plans more stringent, only a bank or other IRS preapproved institution could be a trustee. It made contributions for covered employees with three years of service nonforfeitable, and stated that there was no minimum age requirement. Profit sharing Keogh plans had to maintain a definite contribution formula. This was in contrast to other qualified profit sharing plans which could determine the formula on a year-by-year basis. Premature withdrawals, by an owner/employee, were prohibited under Keogh plans. If an owner/employee did withdraw for reasons other than death or disability, the amount withdrawn was subject to a 10 percent penalty excise tax. The owner/employee was also disqualified for five years from starting another Keogh plan. TEFRA eliminated most of the distinctions between Keogh's and other qualified plans.

**THE TAX ACT OF 1976.** The Tax Act of 1976 introduced IRAs for non-working spouses. IRAs were still restricted to those not covered by a qualified plan. The limit in 1976 was increased from $1500 to $1750. The IRA could be set with $1500 going toward the working spouse and $250 to the nonworking spouse, or it could be split evenly.

**THE TAX ACT OF 1978.** The Tax Act of 1978 prevented the IRS from adopting proposed regulations which would have disallowed tax deferral for salary reduction plans. In addition, Section 401(k) was defined and given detailed nondiscriminatory rules.

The Tax Act of 1978 introduced the Simplified Employee Pension which reduced the detailed administrative work normally involved in a qualified plan. A SEP's contribution is based on straight percentage of payroll for all covered employees. In effect it is an expanded IRA plan with the maximum contribution of $7500 per participant.

**ECONOMIC RECOVERY TAX ACT OF 1981.** The Economic Recovery Tax Act of 1981 (ERTA) has many far-reaching provisions. The Act opened up individual retirement accounts for everyone, regardless of whether they are covered under other qualified plans. It also increased the limits for Simplified Employee Pensions, increasing the maximum to 15 percent of compensation, up to $15,000 per participant.

Under ERTA, a divorced spouse is allowed a deduction for contributions toward a spousal IRA, establishment by an individual's former spouse, at least five years before the divorce, provided that the former spouse made contributions in three of those five years. ERTA allowed for deductible employee contributions to a qualified pension plan. Participants are eligible to make voluntary deductible contributions, if the plan provisions permit, and can also establish an IRA. The IRA limits were increased to $2000 per working individual. The nonworking spouse account was limited to $250. Keogh plan limits were increased by ERTA on the amount of includible compensation from $100,000 to $200,000.

Also ERTA liberalized the deductions available to leveraged ESOPS. For tax years beginning after 1981, 15 percent may be contributed to a profit sharing or stock bonus plan and an additional 25 percent toward a money purchase plan. In addition, ERTA provides a 25 percent deduction limitation for contributions used for paying load principle and also permits unlimited additional deductions for interest payments.

ERTA introduced the unlimited marital deduction and increased the unified credit available for estates. In 1986 the credit increases to $155,800 and in 1987 the credit increases to $192,800. The 1987 act credit represents the equivalent of $600,000 in assets that can be transferred to an estate tax-free. Also ERTA introduced unlimited marital gifts. In the past there was a $100,000 limit before gift taxes were imposed; now there is no restriction on marital gifts. Under ERTA the annual gift tax exclusion was raised from $3000 to $10,000.

Also ERTA eliminated the three-year rule, in contemplation of death, for gifts. However, the three-year limitation still applies to gifts of life insurance and gifts of a retained interest. ERTA was also the act that legislated a freeze covering the taxation of fringe benefits by the IRS.

**THE TAX EQUITY FISCAL RESPONSIBILITY ACT (1982).** TEFRA established parity between corporate qualified plans and Keogh plans in the areas of benefits and contributions. New termination (top-heavy plans) was introduced, bringing with it increased vesting and minimum contributions.

A defined benefit plan is top-heavy if the present value of the accrued benefits for key employees under the plan exceeds 60 percent of the value of accrued benefits for all participants under the plan. In a defined contribution plan the 60 percent test refers to the account balances of key employees and all plan participants (IRC Code 415 and 416).

A key employee is defined as either an officer of the firm, or one of the 10 largest owner/employees of the business. A participant will also be considered a key employee if the participant is a 5 percent owner or if the participant is a 1 percent owner with a compensation level of $150,000.

A top-heavy defined benefit plan must vest a participant either fully at the end of three years or 20 percent vesting after two years, increasing 20 percent a year to 100 percent after six years. There are special accrual rules that require a defined benefit plan to contribute at least 2 percent a year minimum benefit accrual, not to exceed 20 percent at the end of 10 years. In addition, under a defined contribution plan there is a minimum contribution of 3 percent of pay.

TEFRA limited benefits and contributions. The new benefit levels are 100 percent of pay up to $90,000 for a defined benefit plan. Defined contribution plans are limited to contributions of 25 percent of compensation to a maximum of $30,000. These limits are subject to cost-of-living increases as of 1986. TEFRA reduced the aggregate limits for multiple plan employers from 1.4 to 1.25 (IRC Section 416(h)). Also TEFRA introduced the $100,000 estate tax exclusion for death benefits under a qualified plan. IRAs and Keogh plans both qualified for this $100,000 exclusion. The Retirement Equity Act rescinded this exclusion.

Not only did TEFRA give us parity in benefits but also parity in regulations. Key employees or participants in a top-heavy plan must begin to receive distributions in the year they obtain age 70. The premature distribution regulation for Keogh plans was repealed by TEFRA, but TEFRA broadened the concept to include all qualified plans. Key employees of a qualified plan are still subject to a 10 percent penalty excise tax if they receive distributions before age 59¼. This excise tax is waived in a case of death or disability. All plans must be amended to provide that, if a key employee dies before his or her entire interest has been distributed, the balance must be distributed to the employee's beneficiary within a five-year period.

**THE RETIREMENT EQUITY ACT OF 1984.** The Retirement Equity Act of 1984 (REA) liberalized the maximum participation and vesting ages. The maximum participation age effective after December 31, 1984 will be age 21 for defined benefit plans (pre-REA was age 25). This provision is not retroactive, but all plans must be amended and conform to the new regulation in 1985. The maximum vesting age for defined contribution plans is age 18 (pre-REA was age 22). The maximum vesting age applies in the case of a participant who has at least one hour of service under the plan on or after the first day of the first plan year to which the amendments made by the act apply.

Years of service must be taken into account after a break in service for nonvested participants unless the number of one-year breaks in service equals or exceeds five consecutive one-year breaks in service. If the participant has four consecutive one-year breaks in service, the plan cannot disallow the years of service prior to the break in service. The years of service are not required to be taken into account under the new rules if there is a subsequent break in service. Maternity and paternity leave are not treated as a break in service for participation or vesting if the absence is due to childbirth, pregnancy, adoption of a child, or the care of a child immediately following birth or adoption. The employee must be credited with sufficient hours of service to prevent a break in service while on maternity and paternity leave. The hours of service (not more than 501) must be credited either in the year the absence occurs or the following year. This provision is coupled with the new break in service rules for nonvested employees.

REA revises the area of joint and survivor benefit requirements. Retirement plans must automatically provide survivor benefits to a surviving spouse of the retiree or the surviving spouse of a vested participant who dies prematurely. If a participant elects out of a joint and survivor annuity or preretirement survivor annuity coverage, spousal consent is required.

Plan administrators under REA are required to notify a plan participant that the plan distribution will not be taxed currently if the distribution is transferred either to another qualified plan or an IRA. The administrator must notify the participant that the transfer must be made within 60 days of the receipt in order to qualify for the tax-free rollover. If there are a series of distributions that constitute a lump sum distribution, the 60-day period does not begin until the last distribution is made. The administrator must also notify the plan participant that 10-year income averaging and/or capital gain provisions are available. This rule is effective for distributions made after December 31, 1984. The IRS will provide preapproved notices that plan administrators may use to satisfy this new requirement. The penalties for failure to give the notices will be $10 for each failure up to $5000 for each calender year.

**DEFICIT REDUCTION ACT OF 1984.**   The Deficit Reduction Act of 1984 (DEFRA) as of December 31, 1984 repealed the $100,000 estate tax exclusion for death benefits under a qualified plan. The law changed the definition of a key employee. A key employee is (a) an officer who earns 150 percent of the 415(c)(1) limits, (b) an employee who owns a 5 percent interest; or (c) an owner-employer who owns 1 percent and earns over $150,000. IRA contribution must now be made by April 15, even if the taxpayer receives an extension. The distributions from qualified plans at retirement can be recalculated annually for the life expectancy then attained.

# HOW TO DETERMINE WHETHER A BUSINESS NEEDS A RETIREMENT PLAN

The initial step in determining whether a business needs a retirement plan is to examine the employer's objectives. Often this will occur when an employer has a tax problem. In other cases a retirement plan may be suggested by the accountant, comptroller, employees, or a pension salesperson. Data gathering is the next step. The employer's entire fringe benefits package should be examined to make sure that there will be no duplication of benefits and wasted resources. The size of the organization is a factor in determining the type of plan. Other needs that should be examined together with the size are the type of business and whether it is closely held or publicly traded. A closely-held business may be on the verge of the accumulated earnings tax (IRC Section 531). An employer in this situation will set up a pension plan to reduce its exposure to Section 531 and receive as large a deduction as possible.

One or more interviews will be necessary with the employer to review the types of plans and benefits available. Other areas to be considered are:

1. Who is to be included?
2. What compensation (basic salary, bonuses, commissions, etc.) is to be used to determine contribution level?
3. Are there union, hourly, or commission-only employees?

4. Are there any other retirement plans (formal or informal) in place?

5. Are there any key people the employer wants to favor?

6. What is the composition of the employee census (age and salary)?

At this time a determination should be made whether the plan should be integrated with social security. The next step is to determine the benefit formula and contribution structure. Also to be considered is whether ancillary benefits (preretirement death and disability coverages) will be included.

**DETERMINING CASH FLOW REQUIREMENTS.** A retirement plan that proves to be too costly for the employer would be a complete disaster. Along with the employer not realizing corporate and personal objectives, employee morale could be destroyed. The employer will feel that inadequate data were gathered or that a poor plan was designed. As a result the employer will lose confidence in the plan's proponents.

The financial data that should be gathered are balance sheets and profit and loss statements for the last three years. Balance sheets are important because they will provide an idea of the employer's growth history and the cash the business has available for funding retirement plans. The balance sheet will also indicate if there might be a potential accumulated earnings problem (IRC Section 531).

The combination of the balance sheets and the profit and loss statements will give a better indication of the type of plan that should be suggested. These statements indicate the direction the company is going and its ability to fund future benefits. Firms that are chronically short of cash need a plan that offers the maximum contribution flexibility. Firms in this situation might be advised to set up a profit sharing plan or nonqualified plan. A cash-rich firm with a very strong balance sheet would be well advised to seek a plan that would maximize the tax shelter advantages in a qualified retirement plan.

An extensive financial profile will indicate whether the business is prepared to make contributions in years when there are little or no profits. The information gathered in the financial profile will indicate the level of contribution that the business is willing to undertake and can fund comfortably. It is only when these elements are known that a cost objective and a benefit structure can be implemented.

**FUTURE BUSINESS CIRCUMSTANCES.** When analyzing cash flow requirements and the ability of the employer to fund benefits, the accountant must be consulted. The accountant knows the business's needs for growth, expansion, and modernization. These needs will affect the availability of future funds for retirement plans.

It is important to examine the industry the firm is in. Many different industries are experiencing changes in profitability. This consideration must be given weight when determining future cash flow. As mentioned previously, it will dictate the type of retirement plan that should be installed.

When analyzing the cash flow requirements, discussions with the business owners, officers, and accountants are necessary to determine other cash needs. Specific needs may include:

1. Liquidity for estate taxes in a closely-held business
2. Mergers and acquisitions
3. Pending lawsuits

**TAX AND FISCAL IMPLICATIONS.** One important fiscal implication of the retirement plan is: Who is going to bear the risk of inflation or poor investment results? In the case of a defined benefit plan the employer bears these risks. Under a defined contribution program the employee bears the risk of inflation or poor investment.

Employers with diversified operations must take into consideration the cost and profit margins in their various divisions. Competitive needs and geographical differences are other elements to consider. The employer must decide whether different plans are to be offered to different operations or if the same plan should be offered to all employees. Defined plans for different divisions might inhibit the free transferability of employees from one division to another.

Since ERISA, employers also have to worry about the cost of plan termination. Under a defined benefit plan, if the employer terminates the plan and it is not fully funded, the employer is obligated to make up the difference. The plan could take up to 30 percent of the net worth of the business. This would have a negative impact on the firm's credit rating and also its ability to raise capital.

Social Security plays a very important role in plan design. Employers integrate their pension plans with Social Security to take advantage of their mandated Social Security contributions. Employers are given credit for Social Security taxes in determining their pension contribution. Social Security provides a much higher income replacement ratio for the lower paid employees than for the higher paid employees. If Social Security was not taken into consideration, many lower paid employees would be penalized and retire at a much lower ratio.

The type of plan an employer chooses will have a direct impact on the bottom line. Defined benefit plans must be funded even in years when there are no profits with money coming out of retained earnings. Profit sharing and defined contribution plans must come out of profits. Pension plan contributions reduce the funds available for future business growth, dividends, and acquisitions. A publicly traded firm will show reduced profits which would have an impact on the price per share. The employer must examine the proposed plan to distinguish between the ultimate real cost and the estimated annual cost. An employer might establish specific objectives for actuarial liabilities assumed under the plan and specific objectives for annual accruals. The employer must also establish a budgeting pattern to follow. The employer may desire a level cost, or a plan where the accrual levels are small in the beginning, rising over a number of years. The employer should analyze different funding methods available for the plan because these decisions will influence the type of plan and also whether or not employee contributions are desirable. If the employer needs contribution flexibility, this will have an influence on the actuarial funding methods and assumptions and could lead the employer to adopt a profit sharing plan.

If an employer wishes a limited commitment to the plan, this might dictate a choice of a career pay formula for a defined benefit plan or a choice of an integrated defined contribution plan. The need for a cost-efficient plan is an obvious goal. The employer must examine all benefit plans to avoid duplication of benefits and also fund the plan in the most efficient manner. Different benefits each have a primary focus: for example, group life with providing death benefits, salary continuation to provide disability benefits, and retirement plans to provide retirement benefits.

# ROLE OF THE ACCOUNTANT AND ATTORNEY

The accountant will review the plan with an eye toward the tax and fiscal implications for the employer. The accountant, the tax expert, will help budget pension contributions to optimize tax planning. The accountant will also give long-term projections of what capital will be necessary to fund expansion, salaries, and other business obligations.

**DECIDING ON ADOPTION PROCEDURES.**  Most of the factors involved in the installation and administration of a retirement program are interconnected and the timing of certain events is important. Several parties are usually involved in the installation and administration of a retirement plan. The efforts of these parties (accountant, attorney, actuary, and financial advisor) must all be coordinated with complete and open communication among all parties. The law is so complex that caution should be exercised to insure that the plan is installed and meets all the legal requirements. The procedure must clarify who is responsible for the plan administration, the preparation of legal documents, and the filing of different annual forms necessary for government compliance. There is also the administrative task of record keeping and of determining what payments should be made to and from the plan each year. Once these matters are resolved, then the plan can be installed.

**HOW TO INSTALL A PROGRAM.**    The actuary, accountant, attorney, and financial advisor each have different roles. It is the actuary's responsibility to formulate the different factors that determine the cost of the plan (in a defined benefit plan: mortality, interest rate, and turnover assumptions). The accountant's role is to oversee that the costs are acceptable with the employer's ability to fund the pension plan. The accountants must determine that the business has enough taxable income to take advantage of the tax deduction. The attorney prepares the legal documents necessary for the plan installation. These documents include either a trust agreement or the plan instrument (prototype), authorizing resolutions and enrollment forms. The pension trust dictates most of the requirements of the plan. Reviewing this information will minimize the conflicts between the plan provisions and the objectives of the employer. The financial advisor's role is to advise the employer about available investment vehicles that meet the interest rate assumption of the plan and maximize the return on investments.

**GETTING IRS APPROVAL.**    Most retirement plans are sold because contributions are tax deductible and the growth on these contributions is tax free. Most employers will request a ruling from the IRS on the acceptability of the retirement plan and related trust. This is normally done before the plan is put into operation. To receive an advance ruling, the employer or someone authorized to represent him or her (attorney, certified public accountant, or pension plan consultant) submits the necessary forms to the local district office of the IRS. Included in these forms are: copies of the plan, the trust agreement and insurance contracts (if any), the assumption used in determining the plan cost, and other data to prove that there is no discrimination in favor of officers, stockholders, or key employees. In addition, form 5300 is needed for defined benefit plans, form 5301 for defined contribution plans, form 5303 for a collectively bargained plan, form 5307 for an employee who adopts a master or prototype plan, or form 5309 for an employer stock ownership plan. The ruling that is received is in the form of a determination letter.

The IRS will issue a favorable determination letter if it finds the plan and other documents acceptable. The IRS determination letter will state that the employer contributions are deductible from gross income under the plan. This deduction is subject to verification on the employer's tax return. If the IRS rules that the plan is unsatisfactory, the employer is given an opportunity to discuss the questionable features of the plan. Sometimes the employer can convince the IRS to accept the plan as is, otherwise the employer might have to agree to certain modifications before the IRS will issue a favorable ruling. If the IRS and the employer do not reach an agreement, either the employer or the IRS can request a review by an appeals officer of the IRS. If the employer does not get satisfaction from the appeals officer, the only recourse is the courts. Rarely will an employer put a retirement plan in operation if the IRS rejects it. If a nonapproved plan is installed, a contribution might be disallowed upon an audit. At that time the employer would have to resort to the courts.

A favorable determination letter does not mean that the employer has a free hand in the future. Future changes must be cleared with the IRS because this might effect the qualified status of the plan. The fact that an employer receives a favorable determination letter does not mean that the deduction claimed in each tax return is justifiable. There is no guarantee that the plan will be allowed upon audit. A plan may be disallowed, although initially receiving a favorable determination, if it discriminates in practice. It must be remembered that a pension plan must be continually reviewed to make sure it meets current IRS and Department of Labor regulations.

**INSTALLATION COSTS.**    Factors that influence installation costs are the size of the plan, the funding method used, and the personnel responsible for administering the plan. All pension plans have certain cost factors in common relating to the maintenance of basic records, asset management, government compliance, the payment of benefits, and the determination of contributions. Installation costs for pension plans include actuarial, legal, administrative, and investment expenses. The total cost of the plan is a combination of administrative expenses and the plan contribution requirements. Expenses will depend on the type of administration and the funding methods used. Insurance companies include a loading expense in individual and group pension plan contracts. The expense charge is greater with an individual policy plan than under group pension contracts. Administrative expenses include fees charged for filing the many forms necessary for government compliance.

# ADMINISTRATIVE REQUIREMENTS

**GOVERNMENT COMPLIANCE.**    Annual reports are required by ERISA as well as reports under certain circumstances. For plans with 100 or more participants, form 5500 must be completed. Smaller plans must complete Form 5500C or 5500R (two out of every three years). In a case of an HR10 plan, Form 5500K must be filed. Government plans must submit Form 5500G. These 5500 series forms must be filed with the IRS within seven months after the end of the plan year unless an extension is filed. Copies of these forms must be also submitted to the Department of Labor. Information found on the 5500 form includes: identifying information, a balance sheet, a statement of income and expenses, statistics on participants, and other information about the plan. The form discloses compensation paid from the plan to employees who rendered services to the plan; for Forms 5500-C or 5500-K there is an attachment that discloses this information. Special schedules must be attached if the plan has any prohibited transactions; or for plans with more than 100 participants, you must include a schedule of all assets, schedules of any loans or leases in default, and a schedule of all transactions exceeding 3 percent of plan assets.

A qualified public accountant must be retained for plans with 100 or more participants. The accountant must certify that the plan meets the generally accepted accounting principles concerning the financial statements and supporting schedules. ERISA states who is acceptable as an independent qualified public accountant. An audited financial statement is not required for plans with less than 100 participants.

If insurance companies provide benefits, schedule A must be attached to the 5500 series. The information on Schedule A discloses premiums paid, commissions, benefits paid, the number of persons covered, administrative expenses, dividends paid, and other information. This information must be sent to the plan administrator by the respective insurance companies within 120 days after the close of the plan year.

Plans subject to ERISA funding requirements must submit an annual actuarial statement (Schedule B). This form is completed by an enrolled actuary and attached to the 5500 series. Schedule B shows that the funding requirements have been satisfied. The schedule also gives the most recent actuarial valuation, and states the actuarial assumptions. The actuarial assumptions used to compute plan cost must be reasonable expectations and anticipated experience. The accountant relies on the actuary's assumptions when reviewing the plan.

Form PBGC-1 must be filed with the Public Benefit Guaranty Corporation within seven months after the beginning of the plan year for plans covered by plan benefits insurance. The annual premium payment must be forwarded at the time the PBGC-1 is sent. Certain events trigger the necessity of filing additional forms. Form 5310 must be filed when a plan is terminating or when a merger, consolidation, or transfer of plan or liabilities is involved. The plan administrator must file form 5310 with the IRS at least 30 days before the event. When terminating a defined benefit plan, an actuarial statement must be included indicating that ERISA rules under IRC Section 6058(b) are met. The IRS will issue a determination letter concerning the plan qualification at this point. If applicable, the PBGC must be notified of termination at least 10 days before the termination, unless it was the PBGC that initiated the termination.

The PBGC or an appointed trustee will administer the terminated plan. The plan administrator must report: the amount of benefits payable to each participant, the amount of benefits that are insured under the PBGC, the actuarial present value as of the termination date, the actuarial assumptions used in calculating the actuarial liability, and the fair market value of plan assets.

**NOTICE TO EMPLOYEES.**    A retirement plan must be communicated to all eligible employees who have the right to become a member prior to its approval for submission to the IRS. Distributing the summary plan description to the employees will satisfy this requirement. Employers may post or distribute brief announcements with limited information concerning the retirement plan to satisfy this requirement.

ERISA dictates that an employer must provide each plan participant with a summary plan description. This description must be in plain, understandable language. Any participant can request and must be given a copy of the complete plan and other related documents. The summary plan description is available to every plan participant at the time the employee becomes a member of the plan or when the booklet is changed. Many employers use the summary plan decription as a public relations tool to reinforce to their employees the value of staying with the firm until retirement.

**DEVELOPMENT OF CONTRIBUTIONS.**    The actuary will set the mortality, turnover, and interest rates used on deposits for a defined benefit plan. The benefit that is determined in advance normally will be a percentage of salary. Employer contributions for social security may be taken into account (an integrated plan). The goal of the defined benefit plan is to have a certain amount of money for each employee at retirement so that the promised benefit will be funded at that time. The actuary will determine the anticipated annuity rates and interest rates at which the deposits will grow. This will give the employer a level contribution for the plan. This will change as the employee mix changes, as employees enter the plan, leave the plan, die, and retire.

In a defined contribution plan interest earned is credited to the allocated participants account. If better than average investment results are obtained, the benefits go directly to the employees. If plan participants leave before they are fully vested, any unallocated reserves are directed to the remaining plan participants. In case of a defined benefit plan any investment growth over the actuarially determined interest rate is used to lower the cost of the plan to the employer.

If benefits are provided through group deferred annuity contracts or through individual life insurance annuity contracts, the contributions will take the form of a premium or, in a case of annuity contracts, a payment purchase is related to the benefits formula. An employer's contribution is determined by the price charged by the insurance company for the benefits purchased. The contribution paid to an insurance company can be made directly or through a trustee. Other plan costs include fees that are charged by the insurance company, pension consultant, or others who are involved in the annual filings with the IRS and any actuarial expense the plan incurs.

**COST.** The ultimate cost of a pension plan is never known until the last employee retires. The true cost of the pension plan is the benefits paid plus expenses minus investment earnings. A plan that provides for a greater initial outlay may end up with lower ultimate contributions because of greater investment earnings. This may appeal to some employers who are seeking to stabilize or reduce future costs whereas others may shun this method because there may be less capital to work with in the business now than in the future.

**ACTUARIAL FACTORS.** Actuaries are able to give an educated estimate of the ultimate cost of a plan with a reasonable degree of accuracy and arrive at estimated plan contributions. An actuary determines the mortality rate for both active employees and retirees. In most cases the actuary will use the same mortality table for this purpose. A number of mortality tables are available, including the 1951 group annuity table and the 1971 group annuity mortality table. Many pension plan consultants and actuaries are divided as to whether to include a mortality table for smaller plans. Many feel that the employer does not have significant representation to allow the law of averages to work. The higher the mortality table used the more the cost of a plan will be reduced unless a preretirement death benefit is included. When a preretirement death benefit is included, this benefit should be insured to keep the plan's cost level.

The turnover rate is another factor actuaries consider when estimating the cost of a retirement plan. The turnover rate varies from industry to industry and with economic conditions. The ages of the employees are also examined, because turnover rates are higher for younger employees than for older ones. Length of service is examined because long-term employees are less likely to change employers.

Actuaries must consider whether there is an early retirement option and the rate at which this option might be used. Many firms have an early retirement option to keep the promotional channels open for younger employees.

Other cost factors include lump sum distribution if available under the plan. This would increase the cost of the plan because money would have to be made available in lump sums instead of under the annuity purchase options available. Another area to examine is the effect of having a social security offset provision using an early retirement option. Other factors that must be considered are ancillary plan benefits. Providing benefits for these events will increase plan cost and must be provided for in any calculation. Another important cost consideration to examine is compensation increases. This will have an impact on plans because salary increases will increase the cost of providing a benefit linked to compensation. If projected plan costs omit salary increase assumptions, there is the potential for substantially understating liabilities, resulting in an underfunded plan. This problem can be avoided by using a formula that states a flat dollar benefit or one based on a percentage of career pay. Corporations that have a strict budget should avoid plans with automatic increases in benefits.

An important factor to consider is the vesting schedule that is chosen. In defined benefit plans, if an employee leaves, either a lump sum distribution of the employee's vested benefit may be given or benefits may be held until retirement. For smaller plans it is advisable to make a lump sum distribution to a terminated employee rather than trying to maintain records for 10, 20, 30 or 40 years into the future. The employee's benefits that are not vested will help reduce future plan cost or be reallocated to the remaining employees.

As stated previously, the ultimate cost of a pension plan is the benefits paid plus expenses minus interest. For defined benefit plans, the higher the investment earnings, the lower the future cost of the plan and the lower the ultimate cost of the plan. All other things being equal, the greater the interest income the lower will be the projected cost of the plan. Interest rate assumptions are influenced by the funding vehicles used, the size of the fund and the investment policy. Historic, current, and long-term rates of return are also considered when making the assumptions.

**VALUATION.**   Many pension funds invest in common stocks. This creates difficulty in crediting an annual interest rate and raises the problem of how to allocate unrealized capital gains or losses. The decade of the 1960s saw explosive growth in common stock values. In contrast, the 1970s was a decade of plummeting market values while the 1980s is an era of volatile market swings.

It is required by ERISA that the value of a defined benefit plan's assets be determined by any reasonable actuarial method that takes into account fair market value. The Accounting Principles Board, Opinion No. 8, takes the position that unrealized capital gains and losses must be recognized in accounting for pension plan costs. The ERISA requirement is that pension plan gains or losses must be funded or amortized by level annual payments over no more than 15 years.

If the current market valuation method is used, the pension fund will experience wide swings in value. In times of relatively high corporate profits the value of stock market portfolios normally will be high also. This is a period when the employer is financially able to make larger contributions because of higher profits but is prevented from doing so because of the high market value of the plan's assets. Conversely, the opposite is true. During most periods of low corporate earnings the portfolio will have a low value. This situation would require higher contributions (because of low asset value) at a time when the employer may not be financially able to make its required contribution.

Three methods are used to recognize the gains or losses on equities: immediate, averaging, and percentage. The immediate method recognizes gains and losses on an annual basis. The averaging method uses the average market value over a certain number of years (e.g., a five-year period). The percentage method uses a fixed percentage of market value (e.g., 80 percent).

**FUNDING INSTRUMENTS.**    The ultimate cost of a plan does not differ with the funding instrument chosen. The funding instrument will determine the amount of flexibility the employer will have over the pension contribution, timing, and flexibility. The insured, split funded, and trust fund plan all have advantages and disadvantages. The type of plan chosen (not funding instruments) determines who must bear the investment risk. Under a defined benefit plan the benefits are guaranteed at retirement. The full investment risk is borne by the employer. The higher the investment return the lower the contributions to the plan. Under defined contribution and profit sharing plans the investment risk is borne by the plan participant. The employer is committed to making defined contributions to the plan, but no benefit is guaranteed. Employers feel a greater fiduciary responsibility under a defined contribution plan, and therefore many will take a more conservative investment future.

**FULLY INSURED.**    Since the advent of ERISA fully insured plans have received renewed interest. This is largely due to the increased burdens ERISA mandates. A fully insured plan's greatest advantage is its guarantees. The cost level can never exceed the premiums paid for the plan. Insured plans have undergone rapid changes over the last 10 years and now offer many investment alternatives. Insurance companies now offer current interest rates on their annuity products, much like banks' certificates of deposit. These new products have enabled fully insured plans to be more competitive with trust plans. Small employers (those with 15 employees or less) select fully insured plans because of the simplicity in setting up the plan, record keeping, and administration. Many full insured plans are installed for closely-held businesses. These plans enable the business owner to maximize preretirement death benefits (through life insurance) which aids in estate planning.

A fully insured plan has little funding flexibility and limits investment options. With a fully insured plan all investments are chosen by the insurance company with no direct control by the employer. Cash values in insurance contracts are taxable and only the pure insurance proceeds are received tax free. The small employer enjoys more cost control when providing benefits through a fully insured plan.

A fully insured plan can also be funded group products (Group Immediate Guarantee Contracts, Group Permanent Contracts, and Group Deposit Administration Contracts). Funding a fully insured plan through group funding vehicles gives an employer more flexibility than individual policies. Survivor benefits and disability benefits are available. Group products give the employer a wider range of retirement dates as well as different levels of death benefits. Larger employers have more investment options with group products. Larger employers are more likely to use group funded plans than individual plans.

A disadvantage of funding a retirement plan with group contracts is in the area of experience rating. If the insurance company rates the plan on the employer's experience only, and not on a pooled basis, the employer assumes the experience risk which could be positive or negative. Poor experience results in higher costs because premiums are not fixed.

**SPLIT-FUNDED PLANS.** The split-funded plan is extremely popular because it offers the best of both worlds. The employer has a degree of guarantees through insurance contracts, without giving up investment control over the side fund. The split-funded plan is most prevalent for those companies with 50 employees or less. The employer's contributions are split (not necessarily evenly) between insurance premiums and a side fund.

The greatest number of pension plans are split funded or combination plan pension programs. This allows the employer to offer preretirement death benefits through the use of insurance policies (either group or individual). The death benefits can either be related to earnings or a multiple of the participant's monthly pension benefit.

The employer has flexibility in investing the side fund money. The trustee can invest the side fund monies in any permissible vehicle (common stocks, mutual funds, bonds, money markets, etc.). The side fund permits a great deal of flexibility in choosing actuarial cost methods and assumptions. In addition, the retirement plan may recoup some of its contributions in the event of a death before retirement because the plan can be structured in such a way that the employee's beneficiary would receive only the insurance benefits payable by the insurance company. This could reduce the cost of the retirement plan.

**TRUST FUND PLANS.** Trust fund plans offer the maximum investment control and options. Trust fund plans are used by larger employers where no preretirement death benefits are offered. Larger companies believe they can achieve superior investment results. If investment earnings increase 1 percent, the plan cost decreases by 10 percent. Trust fund plans are limited only by federal regulations and state security laws. The employer can invest directly equities and other investments that the trust allows. A trust fund plan lacks guarantees; the investment risk and other risks are borne solely by the employer.

**PROTOTYPE PLANS.** The prototype plan was originally developed for HR10 plans. Many smaller corporations use the master or prototype plans because they have IRS approval and are easy to administer. These plans are offered by insurance companies, banks, trade associations, and mutual funds. Prototype plans are prepackaged and offer limited plan provision options.

# INVESTMENT STRATEGY AND VEHICLES

Most larger plans have a detailed investment strategy to aid the trustee in making investment decisions. The strategy may prohibit certain investments outright or be in more general terms. The more specific the instructions the easier it will be to measure investment results.

The IRS and ERISA mandate that retirement plan assets be segregated from other assets. There is statutory relief from this provision for insurance companies. Another important requirement of ERISA is the prudent man standard. ERISA states that the assets of a qualified pension plan must be handled "with the care, skill, prudence and diligence under the circumstances then prevailing, that a prudent man acting in a like capacity and familiar with such matters would use in conducting an enterprise of like character and with like aims" (ERISA Section 404(a)(1)(b)). In addition, investment strategy will also be based on the prevailing Department of Labor, IRS, Securities and Banking laws, and other federal and state regulations. The elements of an investment policy will contain risk and reward ratios and different rate of return objectives. Another factor to consider in an investment strategy is the liquidity requirements. The liquidity requirements will be dictated for each individual plan depending on the participants' ages and the amounts of monies that will be needed at retirement.

If there are many older employees, more liquidity will be required because retirement benefits must be paid in a shorter period of time. Diversification is another element of an investment strategy. This helps the plan to achieve stable results instead of investing in only one instrument. Until recently most pension portfolios were passive in nature; the strategy was buy and hold. Today this strategy does not seem to meet current economic realities. A more active stance must be taken because of the continually volatile markets and wide swings in interest rates and stock portfolios.

An important decision to make in investment strategy concerns who will manage the funds. Many larger pension plans use in-house management. This rule is not hard and fast. There are as many in-house managed plans as there are plans managed by outside professionals. A large number of plan sponsors have been disappointed by outside management, because frequently they are unable even to match the Dow Jones average. Along with investment strategies, there are a number of ideas about the selection and diversification of assets. There are probably as many investment strategies as there are pension plans. The next big step in determining an investment strategy would be allocation of assets.

Pension plans can invest in many different investments. The range spans from common stocks, bonds, and certificates of deposits to real estate, foreign securities, options, and so forth. The discussion here will center on the investment alternatives.

**COMMON STOCKS.**  Common stocks have been a mainstay in most pension portfolios over the last quarter of a century. This is because common stocks have historically offered a higher rate of return than fixed income securities, and up until the 1970s were viewed as a hedge against inflation. The decade of the 1970s saw stocks on a roller-coaster ride downward as inflation surged ahead. This caused many plan sponsors to reexamine the place of common stocks in their pension portfolios. Many plan sponsors still believe that in the long run common stocks will outperform most other investments.

**DEBT INSTRUMENTS.**  Debt instruments comprise short-term, intermediate, and long-term debt instruments. Long-term bonds offer the opportunity to lock in high rates of interest over the long term, especially if the call or refunding features are not exercised in volatile markets. When interest rates are down, the recall provisions give plan managers cash instead of the anticipated long-term return.

The intermediate bonds, those with a four- to 10-year life, appeal to pension plan managers because they are less volatile in price and still are locking in historically high rates of return. Inflation has remained at low levels since 1982, whereas the yields on intermediate debt instruments have reached historic high levels. A new concept in the intermediate bond market has been the issuance of zero coupon bonds. This eliminates the need to reinvest interest income from bonds and locks in favorable interest rates. These bonds are issued at a substantial discount with the full denomination price being paid at maturity.

Most corporate and government debt is publicly traded and therefore very marketable. Some plans purchase privately placed securities either through investment pools of insurance companies or banks. These privately placed debt instruments will carry a higher interest rate because they are less marketable.

Many pension plans acquire debt issued by the federal government or its agencies because it is virtually risk free. There is no risk of default and the securities are highly liquid. In addition, pension plans can also hold foreign bonds issued by foreign governments or business concerns. This will subject the pension plan assets to a degree of currency risk if the debt itself is not denominated in dollars but in foreign currency. Two popular foreign debt instruments are Eurobonds and Yankee bonds. Pension plans earn a higher rate of return on these foreign bonds and achieve a greater degree of diversification. Many pension plan administrators purchase short-term debt because they are uncertain of long-term interest rates and believe these instruments are better than leaving the plan assets idle.

**SHORT-TERM INSTRUMENTS.**    There are many short-term debt instruments, the most popular being U.S. Treasury bills which generally mature in 90 days to six months. Treasury bills are quoted on a discounted basis. They provide no interest payments but at maturity pay the par value.

Another popular debt instrument is a Ginnie May (GNMA). Ginnie May's are government backed mortgages. The advantage of investing in a Ginnie May is the superior return and the fact that capital is not locked up for a long period of time. A Ginnie May will return interest and principal monthly to the investor. The only drawback is that when interest rates decline, the mortgagors renegotiate the mortgages at lower interest rates and in turn pay off the original mortgages. This leaves the investor with more cash on hand when rates are lower and does not guarantee the interest rates for long periods of time.

There are a variety of short-term debt instruments that can be purchased from banks. The most popular is a certificate of deposit which can be issued in a negotiable or nonnegotiable form. Certificates of deposit are negotiable in amounts larger than $100,000. One advantage of having certificates of deposit is that they are fully insured by the FDIC for amounts up to $100,000. Certificate of deposits can also be purchased from European banks. These will yield a slightly higher return than domestic certificates of deposit because there are different reserve requirements and different risk perceptions. The plan could also buy a certificate of deposit in foreign currency with the risk of currency fluctuation.

An instrument currently out of favor with many pension plans is a repurchase agreement (REPO). A repurchase agreement involves an investor and a security dealer. The pension plan acquires ownership of a debt obligation and the seller (a securities dealer) agrees at that time to repurchase the debt at an agreed-on time and price. The yield is determined by the length of time the debt is held and the price. A number of security dealers have gone bankrupt and, because of this, the area of REPOs, as they are commonly called, is now in the courts.

Another popular investment for pension plans is commercial paper. Commercial paper is a short-term unsecured debt of a corporation. Many creditworthy firms use this instead of more expensive bank loans. Commercial paper is sold at a higher rate than the T-bills but normally lower than the prime rates of banks. Commercial paper maturities range from 30 to 270 days. Commercial paper is rated for its credit quality either by Moody's or Standard and Poor's. Many pension plans have investments in commercial paper because of the short-term holding period. This is usually preferable to leaving the money in other short-term investments. The yield will be higher than money markets and the investments themselves are marketable. There is minimal risk of loss because of the creditworthiness of the corporations issuing the commercial paper.

**OPTIONS AND FUTURES.**   The options and futures markets are for the very sophisticated and large pension fund, because this is a highly speculative area. An option is the right to buy and sell a security at a specified price during a stated period. The right to buy is a call option. A call option is purchased when the fund managers believe that the price of the security will rise; a put is the opposite. To exercise options a trustee must have authorization. In a pension fund where a large portion of the fund is invested in equities, the use of puts and calls will reduce the volatility of earnings of the fund. Trading options can protect against falling prices, earn income, or hedge in a rising market.

The futures market was developed to serve commodities. Its original purpose was to guarantee farmers a fixed price and to relieve them of the risk of wild price fluctuations. The use of the futures market has been expanded to trade in U.S. Treasury bonds, GNMA securities, T-bills, commercial paper, and even the Dow Jones average. Because of their speculative nature they are used only by the most sophisticated pension plans.

**REAL ESTATE INVESTMENTS.**   Real estate investments offer the chance for appreciation and annual income in the form of rental income. Real estate has shown exceptional growth through the 1970s and into the 1980s. There is no guarantee this superior return will continue, but at present, many pension plan managers have invested a portion of their funds in real estate. This has been accomplished through either direct purchase or the pooling of assets through limited partnerships or real estate pools managed by banks, life insurance companies, and trust companies.

Most real estate investments made by pension funds are concentrated in commercial properties: office buildings, industrial parks, and shopping centers. A small percentage of pension plan assets is invested in real estate mortgages. The real estate mortgages are limited to commercial properties. Although there has been a growing need to channel funds into residential mortgages, most pension plan funds have resisted this because of the problems associated with individual home ownership. Most pension plans do not want to be involved in the originating and servicing of individual mortgages. This would entail a great deal of work involving many loans at low dollar values.

**LEASED PROPERTY.**   Another investment that pension plan managers make is in equipment. These assets are purchased and leased out either to a commercial or industrial user. The assets being leased range from computers, aircraft, oil rigs, railroad rolling stock, and barges. Approval by the IRS is needed to engage in leasing; otherwise it might subject the plan to taxation for unrelated business income.

**OIL AND GAS.**    A small portion of pension plan assets are in the oil and gas area. These investments could take the form of equipment leasing, drilling for new oil, or oil income funds. The most prevalent area is in the oil income funds. These funds generate a substantial cash flow. Some of these oil investments were highly leveraged and showed superior results until the early 1980s, when the price of oil started to tumble. What seemed like a great investment only months before became a nightmare. One of the leaders in this field is Damson Oil. Damson does not use leverage and therefore is not subject to high interest rates on borrowing and subsequent reduction in income because of this fact. All investments in gas income funds are subject to volatile prices of oil.

**SEPARATE ACCOUNTS.**    Today life insurance companies compete with banks, trust companies, and mutual funds for pension plan assets. In the 1960s insurance companies established separate accounts for plan assets; before this time only the general account of the insurers was available. The general account limited the plan's investment opportunities and earned only the insurer's portfolio rate of return (this rate is a composite rate of return without regard for the timing of cash flows or the rate of return that these specific cash flows are earning).

Most insurers initially established only one separate account to invest in common stocks. Today each insurer has a number of separate accounts tailored to meet certain objectives. The separate accounts cover many types of investment vehicles: real estate mortgages, real estate equity, oil and gas, money market, common stock, publicly traded bonds, and direct placement bonds, to name a few.

**NONTRADITIONAL INVESTMENTS.**    Various pension plan assets have been invested to promote certain economic, social, or political goals. Sometimes this is in conflict with the traditional objective of trying to achieve the highest return. The groups that normally make these types of investments have been church organizations, state and local governments, and labor unions.

Various church groups have opposed investing their pension funds in companies doing business in South Africa or in products that they deem offensive— for example, liquor or tobacco. The AFL-CIO has favored investing their pension funds in ways to enhance the union and to maintain or create jobs for their membership. Labor unions sometimes take the posture that pension assets are actually deferred wages, owned by the plan participants, and should be invested in ways that will promote their own interests.

By far the most well-known example of a nontraditional investment is the labor unions' investment in Big Mac Bonds in the mid-1970s to save New York City from bankruptcy. At that time these bonds were of questionable investment grade. Many states have modified and changed laws so that labor unions can invest locally in ways to create jobs or help rebuild the inner city. This is by no means an all-inclusive list of investments that is open to pension funds. The plan sponsor must have competent advice and use reasonable assumptions before deciding on the type of funding agency to be used. After these steps have been taken, an investment strategy and the actual investments must be made. As Will Rogers said, "he's not so concerned with the return of the investment." These are important words, in the decade of the 1980s, where there have been volatile shifts in stock prices and interest rates.

**KEEPING THE PROGRAM CURRENT.**   A plan administrator is responsible for the reporting and disclosure requirements under ERISA. If there is no designated plan administrator, the plan sponsor serves as plan administrator. The plan administrator has full jurisdiction over all phases of a plan's operation. The area of benefit certification is very important because the plan administrator will interpret the provisions of the plan and will determine the amounts of all claims and benefits. If there is a dispute, the plan administrator will give a written explanation as to how the benefits, or lack of benefits, were determined. If there is a disagreement, the plan administrator will hold a hearing. The administrator's decision is final unless challenged by a court or arbitration. The actual payment of benefits is frequently handled by the trustee or insurance company, with the authorization coming from the plan administrator. To keep the plan current and to ensure that the retirement benefits are available for the participants, periodic contributions to the plan must be made. Employer contributions may be specified in the plan document as to timing and size. If this is not specified in the trust document, contributions are to be made during the tax year. If the plan is contributory, the employer will remit these contributions on a monthly basis. Pension contributions may also be made to insurance companies to fund group deferred annuities or other insurance contracts. The contribution, in premiums, will be paid either directly to the insurance company or through the trustee.

To keep the plan current you must keep up to date with the ever-changing regulations. It is a good idea to hold biannual meetings with the providers of outside services to stay current with the laws and to gauge their impact on the plan participants and the contributions necessary to keep the plan within the minimum funding standards.

# CHAPTER 14

# PERSONAL FINANCIAL PLANNING

## Patricia S. Miller and George S. Miller

## INTRODUCTION

Financial planning is a service which is expanding in scope and responsibility, to a degree that a "new" type of expert, the financial planner, has evolved. Although financial planners may serve either businesses or individuals—and in smaller businesses the two are often intertwined—it is the latter area on which we will concentrate in this chapter.

Personal financial planning requires knowledge of many subjects, including cash management, insurance, estate planning, individual taxes, and investments. As with other subjects covered in this book, it is expected that accountants will merely serve as advisors, and leave specific decisions in the hands of insurance agents, investment advisors, and attorneys who are experts in their respective fields. Although public accountants are becoming increasingly adept at financial planning, management accountants and internal auditors often possess the requisite skills to provide similar service if called upon by their companies.

Two new certificate programs have emerged in recent years—the certified financial planner (CFP) and the chartered financial consultant (CFC). Normally, those who sell investments, tax shelters, or insurance are most likely to undertake the comprehensive educational program to earn either certificate. Relatively few accountants, however, undertake a separate program to classify themselves as either CFPs or CFCs.

Undeniably, financial planning is emerging as a specialized service to aid individuals in planning for the future. The variety and number of firms and individuals offering financial planning services are indications of both the need and marketability of this service. Financial planning is now being offered by insurance companies, brokerage firms, banks, accounting firms, and independent planners.

Professional associations are attempting to standardize and improve the profession, which is evolving. Additionally, many professional planners are accessing sophisticated computer software programs in order to help analyze a client's needs and later, to generate a plan or alternate plans which can then be adjusted by the financial planner based on the individual's financial personality.

## FINANCIAL PERSONALITY

The basis of any individual financial plan should include up-to-date quantitative information about the individual *and* an assessment of personal information which will be used to refine the plan to that individual's circumstances.

**PERSONAL INFORMATION.**  In order to prepare a personal financial plan, the accountant will need the following types of data:

Age of individual and, consequently, the expected remaining years of earnings and life

Current expectation of job security

Marital status and the age and earnings of the spouse

Other sources of income—dividends, interest, rents, royalties, and so on

Dependents and their respective ages

Educational plans of children

Plans for major expenditures

Borrowings and other significant financial obligations

Marketable securities and other investments owned

Property holdings—principal residence, vacation home

Other major assets

Anticipated inheritances

Retirement provisions currently in place; company retirement plans, social security, personal retirement plans, and investments

Anticipated changes to this personal data

Assessing this, and other personal information, is essential in order to arrive at a financial planning recommendation aimed at helping an individual achieve his or her goal.

**QUANTITATIVE INFORMATION.** The accountant is particularly qualified to help the client develop this information. Normally, this would involve preparation of both a personal income statement and a balance sheet. The balance sheet prepared for personal financial statements differs from financial statements of businesses in that it reflects the individual's (or couple's) net worth at market value. In other words, it presents assets at their current values and liabilities at their estimated current amounts.

Equally important is the preparation of a cash flow statement. This is especially important when there is a seasonal pattern either to cash receipts or cash disbursements. For example, an individual may receive income from gainful employment monthly, from dividends quarterly, from bonds quarterly or semiannually, from publishing royalties semiannually or annually, from rents monthly, and so forth. On the disbursements side, the mortgage will be paid monthly, insurance premiums annually or in installments, interest expense on loans monthly, college tuition and associated expenses twice a year, an individual retirement account (IRA) annually, summer camp once a year, and normal home improvements and vacations as scheduled. Then, it is advisable to plan for major expenditures such as the purchase of an automobile or boat, extended overseas vacation, home furnishings, or a wedding.

The cash flow analysis will not only enable the financial planner to help the individual maximally invest idle funds or minimize interest expense on borrowed funds, it will also help the individual to budget for financial needs.

# FINANCIAL PLANNING GOALS

Once the planner understands the client's financial personality, then the planner must investigate that client's financial goals. In other words, what does the client want to do with his or her money?

Every individual has specific identified financial needs. However, these needs usually fall into one or more of the following categories:

Basic life-style expenditures

Financing education expenses and other support of children

Financing a major purchase (house, trip, boat)

Accumulating wealth

Planning for retirement

It is important for the planner to know the individual's goals and, before deriving any plan, the individual should, with the planner's assistance, prioritize, qualify, and quantify these goals. The financial planner can then begin to analyze the individual's priorities for financial planning.

**FINANCIAL PLANNING PRIORITIES.** There are many financial planning priorities which should be closely examined by the individual and the financial planner. The most typical priorities follow.

**Asset Protection.** Look at the individual's balance sheet and examine each asset separately to assure that it is adequately protected. Among other items, examine insurance policies that might apply, including disability insurance. (Insurance, as part of the overall financial plan, is discussed later in this chapter.)

It is also important to protect assets against the ravages of inflation. Real estate and common stocks are considered excellent hedges against inflation, whereas cash balances, receivables, and many fixed assets are among the worst.

**Tax Reduction.** This is, consistently, one area in which a client will consult with his or her accountant. Unfortunately, it is an area of financial planning that is not stable; in fact, at this writing, the federal government is currently proposing major income tax revisions. However, these key areas should help in determining strategies that might be beneficial in reducing income taxes:

Tax sheltered investments—real estate, oil and gas, equipment leasing, and so on

Retirement plans—employee pension and profit-sharing plans, individual retirement accounts (IRAs), Keogh plans

Municipal bonds

Tax-deferred annuities

Sale and purchase of personal residence (gain on sales is nontaxable if cost of new residence purchased is more than basis of old residence sold)

Like-kind nontaxable exchanges

Income shifting to lower-bracket taxpayers (gifting, establishing trusts, interest-free loans)

Deductions—trade or business expenses, employee expenses, medical, interest, charitable, casualty, and theft

Exemptions

Tax credits

**Estate Cost Reductions.** This priority cannot be considered or recommended without the advice of a qualified tax expert. Two examples of the considerations for this priority are trusts and joint tenancy. (Estate planning is discussed in greater detail later in this chapter.)

**Capital Accumulation.** Accumulating capital most likely will be achieved through planning, budgeting, income-producing work, and investing.

**Capital Preservation.** This priority is growing in importance as a result of a sociological occurrence—people are living longer! Consequently, the traditional revenue sources may be severely inadequate. Therefore, individuals should be advised to plan, save, and invest for their golden years.

Once the financial planner has analyzed his or her client's financial personality, financial planning goals, and financial planning priorities, these data can be used to propose a basic financial plan for that individual.

# INVESTMENTS

In preparing a financial plan, four principal areas of strategy should be considered: investments, insurance, estate planning, and personal taxes.

The composition of an investment portfolio is based on the client information that the financial planner begins to assemble from the point at which the initial financial personality is derived and, later, analyzed. During the financial planning process, the financial planner will help the individual determine his or her needs and goals, establish a time frame for the overall plan and, most important, work with the individual in order to gauge his or her comfort level at varying degrees of risk. The risk level of various investments can be generally categorized as follows:

| Risk Level | Type of Investments |
|---|---|
| Foundation investments (virtually no risk) | Annuities, certificates of deposit, treasury bills, and money market funds |
| Conservative investments (relatively small risk; investments known to appreciate/depreciate relatively little in value) | Municipal bonds, blue-chip stocks, and income-oriented real estate |

| | |
|---|---|
| Aggressive investments: (high risk-reward potential) | Growth stocks, precious metals, options, futures, and commodities |
| Speculative investments (very high risk; generally made with money the individual is willing to lose) | New issue stocks, uncovered options, and penny stocks |

With respect to an individual's needs and goals, the financial planner should recommend investments on the basis of the investment objectives which the particular individual, with the planner's help, has been able to isolate. Some objectives are:

**Principal Security.** The individual cannot risk the principal, in whole or in part.

**Inflation Hedging.** The individual needs a return that will keep up with the rate of inflation (in other words, the most important objective is to maintain purchasing power).

**Current Income.** The individual needs investment income to cover current expenses and cannot risk the principal.

**Future Appreciation.** The individual wants to add to his or her capital in order to meet future expenditures or retirement.

**Liquidity.** The individual needs to know that an investment can be easily liquidated, without penalty, in order to meet emergency requirements or to take advantage of other investment opportunities.

**Investment Management Ability.** The individual either manages the investments directly or utilizes the services of a third party to manage investments. If the individual decides to manage his or her own investments, it might be necessary to choose investments that require little ongoing involvement and/or judgment (savings accounts, savings certificates, and bonds held to maturity).

## TAX SHELTER INVESTMENTS

Accountants, as centers of influence, are constantly deluged by sponsors' offerings of tax shelter investments. The accountant should consider working closely with several tax shelter sponsors, in order to maintain a good working relationship with firms which consistently offer quality programs and also have ample product from which to choose.

**SYNDICATOR FEES.**   There have been certain criticisms about the fees charged by syndicators. On close scrutiny they are, in effect, not excessive. Anyone who has bought a house is prepared to pay 15 percent or so above the selling price in points, closing costs, and other miscellaneous expenses. For the investor there are no unexpected or unbudgeted costs in syndicated offerings. Fees include those for legal and accounting, verification, marketing and selling commissions, as well as the cost of due diligence. Typically, 15 to 20 percent of the investment goes to the costs of doing business.

A question worth asking about any program is whether or not the investment itself makes sense and to pass on the validity of the investment, primarily, not the fee structure.

**PRIVATE PLACEMENTS.**   Although the most common form of tax sheltered investment is the limited partnership, there are two forms—private placements and public programs. Both are regulated by the Securities and Exchange Commission (SEC) and offerings are governed by state laws where sold and offered.

Private placements refer to programs offered by an offering memorandum to qualified investors. These are usually Regulation D offerings which require that the investor meets suitability requirements regarding net worth or gross annual income (usually over a million-dollar net worth or a gross annual income of $200,000). Typically these programs are specified properties, involve a high degree of risk, and are highly leveraged. They require a substantial investment over a staged pay-in period, usually five to seven years. The offering memorandum, by law, must provide full disclosure of risk, financial data, and so on.

Private placements often sell out rapidly. It is important to evaluate quickly and take decisive action. In order to subscribe to private placements, the investor must provide detailed financial information, including a personal income statement and balance sheet.

Public offerings, by contrast, are sold to the public by prospectus. Typically, public programs require no financial statements but do require a completed subscription agreement. Investments are small and are sold in affordable units; therefore suitability guidelines are less stringent, and there is much less risk. Additionally, only one lump sum payment is required. (Private placements require annual payments.) Investments may be specified properties or a blind pool. Like the private placements, public offerings are regulated by the SEC. They must be "blue skyed"; that is, they must comply with state laws where offered before sale is permitted.

**SELECTING A SHELTER.**    There are many factors to consider in evaluating an offering:

| *Public Program* | versus | *Private Program* |
| --- | --- | --- |
| Lower net worth suitability; open to many subscribers | | Higher suitability requirements |
| Lower leverage programs, single payment, no further obligations, write-offs typically less than 1/1 | | Usually high-leveraged, staged payments over several years, high write-offs |
| Investment typically $5000, additional multiples of $1000 can be added, pool of properties or specified properties. | | Large financial obligation, specified program/properties, higher risk-reward, investor ability to assume ongoing commitment |

**INVESTMENT OBJECTIVES.**    It is important to match the needs and goals of the individual to the objectives stated in the offering. The four investment benefits which can be achieved in varying degrees in limited partnership offerings are:

Capital appreciation

Cash flow

Safety

Write-offs/tax benefits

Highly leveraged investments may offer high write-offs, with little or no cash flow, for example. Income programs offer high cash flow and safety with low tax write-offs, if any. It is virtually impossible to have all four goals in the same program. Therefore, to quantify the specific objectives, priorities should be allocated on a percentage basis in order to determine which benefit is most appropriate and where compromises can be made to achieve goals.

# TYPES OF TAX SHELTERS

The principal forms of tax shelter are real estate, oil and gas, and equipment leasing, whereas others are designed to take advantage of special credits (research and development tax shelters), investment tax credit, rapid depreciation, or other amortization write-offs (master recordings) or deferrals of income. Agriculture is another specialized tax shelter which combines many of the above tax advantages plus the use of the cash basis of accounting, although the cash basis is becoming increasingly more restricted.

The following is a more detailed description of three of the most common forms of tax shelters.

**OIL AND GAS TAX SHELTERS.** Demand for oil and gas remains high and available supplies are dwindling. Prices, which remained relatively stable for almost 20 years, have risen sharply and the decontrol of oil prices and phased decontrol of natural gas prices since 1978 have created a positive environment for these investments.

Industry statistics indicate only one of seven "wildcat wells" drilled to explore for new oil or gas "fields" is successful; only one out of 60 or 70 is a significant commercial success. Once a field is discovered, risk drops and returns become more predictable. About 70 percent of all "development wells," those drilled adjacent to existing producing wells, are successful.

For many years, oil and gas joint ventures were the key tax shelter tools for the very wealthy. In the late 1960s, however, publicly registered programs appeared in significant numbers and in unit sizes small enough to bring them within the reach of many investors. Approximately one million small investors have purchased interests in oil and gas programs with minimum investments of $5000 and $10,000.

In most oil and gas limited partnerships, the sponsor is an operating company that explores for and produces oil and gas. The sponsor supplies the expertise and, sometimes, a significant capital contribution. In return, the sponsor is compensated by some combination of expense reimbursement, management fees, or partnership income in excess of the sponsor's share of the costs. The share of the gross income is called an "overriding royalty"; the share of net income is called "net profits interest"; and the share of profit after the investors recover costs is called a "reversionary interest" or "working interest after payout."

Although there are a variety of oil and gas partnerships, the field is not nearly as diverse as real estate. Most oil and gas programs today are "multiple property blind pools." That is, sponsors attempt to invest in as many attractive wells as possible that meet the program's investment and risk criteria, but specific drilling sites aren't disclosed.

There are three basic approaches to drilling risk in oil and gas programs: high risk, potentially high return "wildcat programs," which only drill wells exploring for new fields; lower risk, lower return "development programs," which only drill adjacent to existing producing wells; and "balanced programs," which drill a mixture of wildcat wells and development wells.

Most oil and gas programs offer first year deductions equal to 60 to 90 percent of the amount invested. Assuming drilling success, income from the program is partially sheltered by the depletion allowance. Depletion, with respect to oil or gas property, may in many cases permit investors to deduct as much as 50 percent of net income from the property. Typically, however, about 25 percent will be recovered tax free. This means—because the investor's share comes from partnership net income—as much as 50 cents of every dollar received may be tax free, as long as the partnership's properties produce.

Depending on drilling success, the type of wells, leverage, and other factors, investors may begin collecting depletion-sheltered income within a year, or they may have to wait up to five years if pipeline or gas plant construction is necessary. Generally, the higher the risk, the longer the wait and the greater the return. Once cash flow begins, investors can collect it until the wells deplete—up to 20 years or longer in some cases. Alternatively, the partnership may allow the investor to "cash in" as soon as the value has been established, exchanging the partnership interest for cash or stock.

The major risk in oil and gas is that "dry holes" will be drilled. The risk that a single wildcat well will be dry is tremendous; even development wells involve risk. However, partnership diversification among many wells softens the overall risk factor.

**EQUIPMENT LEASING TAX SHELTERS.** As a method of financing capital assets for industry, leasing has grown tremendously in recent years. Frequently leased capital assets include computers, airplanes, railroad rolling stock, ships, barges, pollution control equipment, and industrial machinery. Several tax advantages are available for investors in this area: accelerated methods of depreciation for recovering the cost of equipment (150 percent declining balance for 1981 to 1984, 175 percent in 1985, and 200 percent in 1986); the new five-year depreciation period; and the interest deductions generated by loans.

Leasing of equipment came into existence in the late 1940s and by the mid-1960s was in full bloom. The rebirth of the Investment Tax Credit in 1971 gave further stimulus to equipment leasing so that today there are a number of leasing companies in existence as well as many banks that have entered the marketplace as lessors.

Two recent developments have radically changed the equipment leasing industry. The rules in the 1981 Economic Recovery Tax Act pertaining to equipment leasing changed dramatically. These rules provide very specific—and very attractive—terms for *corporate* investors. Individual investors should feel the impact of these rules significantly, too, because the rules allow for more rapid depreciation and lower taxation on cash distributions.

The second development, less dramatic although still significant, is the trend toward "operating" equipment leasing transactions, rather than net lease transactions. In an operating arrangement, the investor purchases an asset (e.g., an oil drilling rig suitable for offshore drilling) and hires a manager to find users for it.

The major advantage of operating transactions is the tax credit available to the investor. The major disadvantage is the significantly increased economic risk; there is no lessee guaranteeing to rent the equipment for an extended period.

In most equipment partnerships, the sponsor is a company that specializes in financing equipment lease transactions—ranging from large, national lessors to small, local equipment brokers that own little, if any, equipment.

Sponsors usually invest very little cash in their programs. They contribute their expertise in locating and arranging equipment leases and maintaining an ongoing relationship with the lessees. Their compensation is derived from a combination of initial fees, continuing management fees, and a share of the residual value of the equipment (value after the expiration of the original lease).

Most equipment leasing programs invest in a number of leases with several lessees. In "net lease" programs, the partnership purchases the equipment and then leases it under a "hell or high water" lease, which obligates the lessee to pay the rent, maintenance, and other costs related to the equipment under all circumstances.

The total partnership investment in an equipment program is usually a percentage (10 to 25 percent) of the cost of the equipment. The balance of the purchase price is provided by lending institutions. Prior to the Tax Reform Act of 1976, these borrowings were frequently without recourse to the partnership or to any partner. Under the new rules, however, it is common for investors to assume personal liability for a portion of the borrowing. Therefore it is important that the lessees have a top credit rating and be unconditionally obligated to pay the rent due with respect to equipment.

In operating equipment programs, the sponsor or operator will acquire equipment and then use it or lease it on a short-term basis on the best terms available.

Frequently, investors in operating equipment transactions agree to pay their share of all the money borrowed, but without the assurance of a net lease. Therefore these operating equipment programs contain a much higher degree of risk than other similar programs.

Equipment leasing tax objectives are summarized in one word—*deferral*. Deferral is a means of postponing a tax liability until a later, more convenient time. Here's how the deferral works: In years when tax liability is high, investors participate in an equipment leasing program. A large amount of depreciation is deducted in the first year, and the investor receives the investment tax credit as well as a deduction for front-end expenses and interest on the borrowings. After the first three to four years, the lease will begin generating taxable income; depreciation and interest will be exhausted, although there may not be any cash income to the investor because of debt service payments due on the borrowings. By the time this happens, however, the investor usually has had the use of the considerable tax savings for a significant period of time.

When the lease ends, the partnership usually will own the equipment free from all debts. Depending on the value of the equipment, some or all of the profit generated will be recaptured and taxed as ordinary income. This created a tremendous problem under the old laws, but under the new laws, the maximum tax is 50 percent rather than 70 percent and, therefore, more investors can benefit.

The biggest risk in equipment leasing is the possibility that the lessee will default on lease payments, because the worst possible situation is for the equipment to sit idle. To reduce this risk, programs include leases with major corporations with superior credit ratings.

Equipment leasing is an investment involving a medium amount of risk. If properly handled, it can offer significant deductions in the early years as well as some tax shelter for income. Most transactions are for periods between five and 10 years and can be used to defer tax liability.

Operating equipment leasing, a slightly different arrangement, is a higher risk investment offering significant deductions, investment tax credits, and the potential for significant medium-term profits.

**REAL ESTATE TAX SHELTERS.**   Many investors, including the largest public and private pension funds, choose real estate when first diversifying beyond stocks and bonds.

This country's population is still growing rapidly. For instance, in 1979, the U.S. population was recorded at 221,582,000. The estimate for the 1984 population was 231,925,000. These figures alone spell a healthy climate for the real estate field, especially in view of the low level of new construction. But other factors should also contribute. Cities are growing once again. Leisure and retirement time have been increasing. Urban renewal projets have been benefiting under the new tax laws, and the available supply of land is shrinking.

The field is vast; any real estate investment could involve several cycles of development, operation, demolition, and redevelopment. There are investments that involve holding land, or constructing and operating apartments, condominiums, office buildings, warehouses, shopping centers, mobile home parks, and recreational facilities—to name a few.

The sponsors of most real estate programs are generally real estate developers or real estate brokers. Some sponsors also have subsidiaries that manage properties, place mortgages, rent furniture, and so forth. Sponsors usually invest very little cash in their programs. Instead, they contribute the expertise needed to invest in properties which meet the partnership objectives. The sponsors and their affiliates usually receive compensation from some combination of brokerage commissions, property acquisition fees, property management fees, reimbursements of specified expenses, and a share of revenues or profits from the partnership's operation of the properties.

Although programs vary greatly, all have common characteristics. Any differences usually relate to the types of properties purchased or developed. For example, you may select among single-property programs or those that invest in exact properties selected for investment, or the program may involve an unspecified "blind pool," granting the sponsor authority to select any properties meeting partnership objectives. Some programs—generally larger ones—invest in both specified and unspecified properties.

Generally, public and private real estate programs concentrate in five areas: new, improved real estate; existing improved real estate; government-assisted housing; raw land; and rehabilitated buildings.

Because of new, attractive benefits in the 1981 Act applying to rehabilitation projects, programs involving older industrial and commercial buildings, as well as certified historical structures, should increase. The Act provides investment tax credits ranging from 15 to 25 percent and a depreciation period of 15 years.

New, improved real estate partnerships may appeal to investors who are risk and deduction oriented. They build on raw land, replace existing buildings, or purchase newly constructed "first owner" properties. They generally use leverage, management fees, interest, and depreciation to generate deductions. The goal is investment recovery through tax savings within four to seven years. Because of leverage, and the construction period, there is usually little or no cash flow for the first several years.

Although residential and nonresidential property can be depreciated identically (with the exception of low-income housing), residential property investment could provide an important advantage if the partnership elects accelerated depreciation. When the residential property is sold, the gain taxed at ordinary income rates (recaptured) will be only the amount of accelerated depreciation in excess of what could have been depreciated on a straight-line basis.

On the other hand, if nonresidential property is sold, the entire amount already depreciated will be recaptured, not just the accelerated portion. As a result, a real cost is not associated with accelerated depreciation for nonresidential property, and many programs depreciate commercial real estate using only the straight-line method.

New property creates a higher risk investment. It offers high deductions, high leverage, and a potential for rapid investment recovery and capital gain. Many of the first year deductions come from construction and start-up costs (although the IRS has successfully attacked some front-end expenses). Accelerated depreciation is another source of first year deductions, although, as mentioned previously, the investor may have to recapture some or all of the depreciation.

If any investor needs tax-sheltered income at a lower risk, existing improved properties may be the right vehicle. Partnerships in these properties use lower leverage while owning more predictable investment. From a tax standpoint, existing property has been made more attractive because the new Act eliminated the distinction between new and used real estate for purposes of depreciation methods.

The combination of moderate leverage and a 15-year depreciation period means moderate first-year write-offs and some sheltered cash flow. In summary, low-risk, moderate deductions, sheltered cash flow, and moderate capital gain possibilities characterize investments in existing properties.

The most favorable depreciation rates are offered to investors in government-assisted housing programs. These also receive large tax deductions and come in a wide variety of opportunities. Most offer annual deductions for up to 20 years.

Federal and state-assisted housing typically involves construction or rehabilitation of properties for low-income, middle-income, or elderly tenants. Each involves some form of government assistance such as rent subsidies or loan guarantees.

Although rehabilitation involves greater economic risk, "rehab deals" offer large deductions in the early years and, therefore, are often attractive to investors interested in high-risk, high-reward situations. Also, up to $40,000 may be spent rehabilitating an apartment and the cost may be written off over only five years.

Raw land programs try to buy unimproved or underdeveloped property (forest, farmland, marsh, etc.) near urban centers and hold it (after several years) for sale to developers or land speculators at a profit that may well be taxed at favored capital gain rates. Most of the annual expenses of carrying land are deductible, but these are usually small relative to total investment; land is not depreciable. Because this investment stresses very long-term capital gain and minimal tax shelter, few public programs invest exclusively in raw land.

Programs featuring rehabilitation of commercial buildings offer a number of attractive features, including investment tax credits of 15 percent for 30-year-old buildings, 20 percent for 40-year-old buildings, and 25 percent for certified historic structures. To qualify for these credits, however, the program must involve a substantial amount of rehabilitation. Depreciation is limited to the straight-line method, although the rehabilitation expenditures may be written off in five years and the remainder of the cost may be depreciated over the remaining 15-year period. Rehabilitation programs also feature excellent first year tax benefits, moderate deductions in later years, and long-term capital gain potential. On the negative side, substantial risks are usually associated with rehabilitation projects, possibly including cost overruns and the location's loss of economic viability in the future. It is most important, therefore, to be sure you are dealing with an experienced developer.

Real estate tax objectives vary greatly with the type of program chosen; each type offers different deductions, income shelter, and capital gain potential.

First year deductions are usually greatest in government-assisted housing programs and to-be-constructed private placement net lease transactions. Income shelter is leverage-sensitive; cash flow in highly leveraged programs normally goes to retiring debt rather than into your pocket. Income shelter is usually highest from partnerships that purchase existing residential or commercial real estate on a low-leverage or unleveraged basis.

Real estate investors have a wide range of possibilities. They may hold on to a partnership interest, collecting the available tax benefits and income for several years. Or, in some partnerships, they may wait for two or three years (or possibly longer) until a value for their interest is established, then sell, hoping for capital gain.

Although real estate investments may be less risky than some other shelters, definite risk is involved. Profitability depends on leverage, interest rates, percentage of occupancy, and so on. The key factor, however, is management. The sponsor must have the ability to conduct successful operations before the partnership can succeed.

On balance, real estate programs offer some very attractive benefits for investors informed of the possible pitfalls. Investors can receive a moderate amount of first year deductions, leverage-sensitive cash flow, comparatively low risk, and the possibility of capital gains (subject, in some cases, to recapture). In this instance, the waning need for insurance would not represent a sharp drop-off as in the case of the individual having financially independent children and, at the same time, no need to provide ready funds.

## INSURANCE

In gathering information for the individual's financial personality, the financial planner has accumulated personal information about the person's dependents. The planner has also helped the individual prioritize, qualify, and quantify his or her goals. On the basis of this data, the financial planner can help the individual assess needs for insurance coverage and the amount of insurance related to those needs. Primarily, the financial planner will focus the analysis on life insurance, property and casualty insurance, and disability insurance.

**LIFE INSURANCE.**   Life insurance should be used to provide income and/or capital for dependents in the event of the death of the individual. Requirements for life insurance change over one's life cycle. Principally, in the event that the individual has no dependents, the requirements for life insurance are minimal. If the individual has children and/or a home mortgage, the requirement should be greater until, at the time when the children are older and financially independent, the need for life insurance is less important. One deviation from this pattern might be for the individual who requires the availability of insurance benefits at death in order to provide the readily available funds needed to settle the estate.

There are two principal types of life insurance, namely term insurance and insurance combined with a "savings" program.

*Term insurance* protects a person for a limited time. At the end of the term, the coverage stops and the policy has no remaining value. This insurance is associated with the lowest possible premium and, therefore, an individual can elect coverage at a very high benefit rate while still restricting cash outlay. Term insurance policies may include provision for renewal or conversion; obviously, there is a cost associated with this option.

*Insurance combined with a "savings" program* provides for a fixed face amount of insurance, but the premium is applied to the life insurance protection and to a low interest savings account. Typically, as the savings account accumulates value, the amount of the actual insurance benefit decreases. With this type of insurance, the individual may withdraw the cash value of the policy at the time that he or she stops paying premiums but, of course, the insurance coverage is then terminated. Alternatively, the individual may borrow against cash value. The insurance coverage is reduced by the amount borrowed until the loan is repaid. Generally, the amount of interest associated with loans against cash value is less than the rate charged by a bank for a loan of equal amount.

The cash value can also be used to convert the contract to paid-up life insurance for a lesser amount, to have the original face amount continued as term insurance for a reduced period, or to provide for a minimum deposit plan that allows part of the dividend to be taken as additional term insurance instead of cash.

The insurance industry is becoming more competitive and, as a result, there have been new products introduced by members of this industry which, temporarily, have given these companies an advantage. Certain of these new product entries may be attractive to individuals. Two of the more prominent newer products are:

Universal life insurance, which, similar to a tax-deferred annuity, includes a tax-deferred cash value fund. Expense charges and the term insurance premium are deducted from the cash value fund. In addition to a high return, the plan provides for purchase of term insurance with untaxed earnings. If investment earnings decline, however, the insured may have to remit additional premiums or surrender the policy.

Variable whole life insurance provides that the return on the cash value and the amount of the death benefit are dependent on certain investment performances, usually resulting from money market funds or a common stock fund.

An individual may choose to work with an insurance advisor who may also be an insurance agent. The accountant should recognize that this dual role may present a conflict of interest for the advisor/agent. However, there are also insurance consultants who do not function as agents.

**PROPERTY AND CASUALTY INSURANCE.**    This should be considered for all applicable assets in the individual's balance sheet. In this respect, the accountant should determine whether the amount of coverage is realistic from the standpoint of replacing the asset in whole or in part if it is damaged or destroyed. Furthermore, the amounts of coverage available to protect the individual in the event of third party injury should be analyzed, especially in light of the egregious settlements which have accompanied bodily injury litigation in recent years.

The liability coverage is equally applicable to homeowner's policies and auto insurance. On homeowner's insurance, the coverage will usually provide protection against falls, mishaps, or other accidents suffered by third parties due to negligence of the homeowner. On auto insurance, the coverage provides protection against bodily injury or other extenuating damage resulting from an accident in which the insured was at fault.

Finally, the accountant should discuss disability insurance coverage as part of the individual's overall financial planning. Many individuals who have financially protected themselves against premature death by purchasing life insurance coverage have not protected themselves against loss of income caused by disability. No one can guarantee that he or she will not become unable to perform normal income-generating work activities.

Physical disability can be caused by sickness or accident. The advisor should make sure that insureds protect themselves against this very real financial peril. The amount of replacement income coverage needed can be determined by subtracting social security disability benefits from the monthly income that is desired. Insurance companies will not allow your combined disability income to exceed your normal income. Generally, disability income policies that start paying benefits after three or more months of disability are more economical than those that pay immediately. The basic idea behind this insurance is to protect the insured against a long period of disability.

**Use of Deductibles.**    One very economical means of reducing premiums is to raise the deductible limits. There is a significant difference in premium when raising the deductible on a homeowner's auto or health policy from $100 to $500, or even to $200 for that matter. The important point is to provide coverage against losses that the individual is not able to bear without financial strain, while keeping the premiums at an affordable level.

# ESTATE PLANNING

For purposes of this discussion on estate planning, assume that one of your client's goals is to maximize his or her estate. Estate distribution takes into account an individual's gross estate—that is, all assets to which the individual has title or legal ownership rights. State laws may affect the status of certain assets, especially assets that are "marital" property. Therefore the individual should be advised of his or her state's regulations with respect to marital property. (Not all states consider marital property to be synonomous with community property.)

**PROPERTY OWNERSHIP.**    There are two legal conventions which relate to the ownership of property and, because the goal of estate planning for this chapter assumes "maximization" of the estate's value, it is important to recognize these conventions.

**Community Property.**    If state laws recognize community property, then each spouse is determined to be an owner of one-half of any community property. In community property states, this one-half ownership determination extends beyond physical assets and includes salaries, wages, or other income derived from performing a service. Community property is, however, limited to those assets and income acquired by either spouse during the marriage period. It is possible to be married and living in a community property state and, yet, keep separate property. This separate property determination requires careful documentation and accounts. The benefits of choosing community versus separate property should be determined based on each individual's circumstances.

**Noncommunity Property.**   States that have no community property statutes do recognize joint property ownership. Joint property ownership allows the individual to achieve the same ownership treatment as do community property statutes (one-half ownership of assets to each spouse). There are three principal forms of joint property ownership:

**Joint Tenancy.**   This is co-ownership by husband and wife or by any other persons related or unrelated. Joint tenancy may apply to real estate or other property (stocks and bonds). Each share of property held under joint tenancy may be sold by the co-owner without permission of the other co-owner. Upon the death of one co-owner, his or her share of the property automatically passes to the other surviving co-owner.

**Tenancy by the Entirety.**   This is joint ownership by a husband and wife only. In many states this type of ownership is limited to real estate. Disposition of one spouse's share requires the permission of the other spouse. When one spouse dies, the entire property passes to the surviving spouse.

**Tenancy in Common.**   This is ownership of real or personal property by two or more persons, any one of whom may dispose of his or her share without permission of the other(s). When a co-owner dies, that person's share passes to his or her heirs or beneficiaries.

**ESTATE TAXES.**   The federal government imposes an estate tax which is payable by the estate; most state governments impose an inheritance tax which is assessed against the receiver of an inheritance. The state inheritance tax rate is determined based on the amount of the inheritance and the relationship between the deceased and the heir. Federal estate taxes and federal gift taxes are combined under a single tax rate table. Federal estate taxes are imposed on a decedent's taxable estate, and federal gift taxes are imposed on income bestowed as a gift and made during the lifetime of the individual making the gift.

The gross estate is determined by starting with the net worth prior to death. This includes the current value of liquid assets other than cash value of life insurance (because the insurance proceeds will be included in the gross estate), investment assets other than retirement funds, and all personal assets (home, automobiles, furnishings, etc.) less total liabilities. To this is added the value of the insurance owned on the individual and spouse's life plus other estate assets such as retirement plans.

The taxable estate is then determined by subtracting the following deductions from the gross estate: funeral expenses, administrative expenses of the estate, the marital deduction (which is equal to the amount left by the decedent to the surviving spouse, in whose estate it is taxable), and the charitable deductions for all amounts left to charitable, religious, scientific, literary, and educational organizations.

There is also a unified credit for estate and gift taxes, which will be $192,800 in 1987 and subsequent years. This in effect grants an exemption of $600,000 to the estate, which means that no estate tax will be paid on the first $600,000 of the taxable estate.

**ESTATE PLANNING STRATEGIES.**    There are several basic strategies in estate planning:

**Marital Deduction.**    Under this strategy, money or property that is transferred from one spouse to another is not subject to federal gift or estate taxes, providing certain conditions are met. These transfers may take place during the life of the spouses or at the death of either spouse. Transfers made during the lifetime of the spouses are advantageous in equalizing the estates of both spouses, thus minimizing the combined tax of both estates.

**Lifetime Gifts.**    There is an annual exclusion of a maximum of $10,000 to any one person, which may be given as a gift without gift tax consequences. The total of gifts given under the annual exclusion is not limited so long as any one person receives no more than $10,000. In addition, each spouse can be a donor, in effect enabling gifts of $20,000 each year to each donee from a married couple.

**Charitable Deductions.**    Such transfers reduce an individual's gross estate. These deductions may include property that has greatly increased in value since acquisition.

**Life Insurance.**    Benefits are treated on the basis of the ownership of the contract and/or the method under which premiums are paid (separate or community accounts). If an individual owns the contract and premiums are paid out of a separate account, then the death benefits are includable in the estate; if an individual owns the contract and premiums are paid out of a community account, one-half of the benefits paid are includable in the estate. If the individual's spouse is the beneficiary of any benefits includable in the estate, the benefits qualify for a marital deduction.

Insurance death benefits can be excluded from the gross estate if the contract is owned by someone other than the insured. However, the insured forfeits his or her rights to all powers over the policy and its benefits. This means that the insured cannot change beneficiaries, surrender or cancel the policy, borrow the cash value, and so on. Additionally, if the individual is assigning an already existing policy with cash value, there may be gift tax consequences.

**Retirement Plans.**   These may be a substantial portion of an estate. Whether an employee's retirement plan or an individual's retirement plan, the plan should be analyzed to determine whether benefits will be included in the gross estate and, if so, the potential amount of benefits which will be included. Under certain circumstances, the marital deduction will not apply to retirement plan benefits included in an estate.

**ESTATE DOCUMENTS.**   If the individual has a spouse and/or children, then he or she should have a will. Without a will, a probate court will determine who should be the guardian of the children and how the actual estate should be disposed.

For individuals of moderate wealth, a simple will should be sufficient. This will may contain specific bequests, bequests of personal and household effects (called tangible personal property), bequests of remaining assets, and appointment of a guardian for minor children.

If, at a later date, the individual elects to change an existing will, a completely new will can be prepared; however, the new will should specifically revoke all prior wills. To effect additions to an existing will, a simple codicil may be added to the already existing will.

Wills should be reviewed every few years in order to be sure that they serve the then existing situations. There is a common substitute for a will, the revocable living trust, which may offer certain nontaxable advantages.

**REVOCABLE LIVING TRUSTS.**   Under this arrangement, the estate owner, during his or her lifetime, transfers assets to a trust, reserving all the beneficial rights in the trust. On the death of the estate owner, the trust becomes irrevocable and the assets are administered and distributed in accordance with the provisions of the trust.

The assets of a living trust are controlled by the owner and the income of the trust is income of that person and consequently subject to income tax. On death, the value of the trusts assets is added to the estate owner's gross estate and is subject to federal estate tax.

# SUMMARY

In this chapter we have focused on the ever-growing area of personal financial planning. We discussed certificate programs for advisors, means of detailing the client's financial personality, goals and priorities of financial planning, various types of investment vehicles, tax shelters, insurance and estate planning, each of which is important to the accountant who wishes to be an advisor in this area.

# CHAPTER 15

# TRAINING AND OTHER AREAS FOR ADVISORY SERVICES

## William K. Grollman

## INTRODUCTION

Up to this point, we have analyzed many areas in which accountants commonly function as business advisors. Of course, there are many other areas in which accountants can serve a similar role. The purpose of this chapter is to provide a framework for the accountant to use in identifying and communicating problems, and then to describe briefly other areas not covered previously.

Accountants are becoming increasingly involved in training their client/employer. We will conclude this chapter by placing particular emphasis on that educational function which covers subjects previously discussed in this book.

## IDENTIFYING PROBLEMS

There are logical techniques that accountants can use to help identify problems in the client's/employer's activities. The identification of problems will either result from observation, inquiry, and analysis by the accountant or from a specific request by the client/employer.

The accountant/business advisor may be requested to conduct a preliminary survey, and then make a final recommendation and assist in the implementation of the recommendation after an appropriate expert completes the in-depth study. The following general areas will illustrate where the accountant may encounter problems and why.

**ORGANIZATION.**   Some businesses, at first, operate effectively without any formal organizational structure. In this early stage a person or a small group can usually effectively supervise all functions. This informal organization works well because the person or group is aware of all aspects of the business. As the business grows and expands, however, the accountant/business advisor should watch for the breakdown of the informal organization. At that time, it may become necessary to establish a more formal organization to communicate policies, operating procedures, and duties within the company and to define lines of responsibility and authority.

**GOALS AND OBJECTIVES.**   Many businesses start without explicitly stated goals and objectives. Those that are guided by set, formal goals and objectives are better able to monitor, measure, and assess their progress along the way. The mere setting of goals and objectives stimulates thinking about realistic operating methods.

A "mission" statement in which the company outlines its guiding principles, reasons for existence, and management philosophy, sets the atmosphere and circumstances in which the company intends to operate. This statement can set the tone for strategic planning in many areas that can be crucial to the organization's success or failure.

**SOURCES AND ADEQUACY OF CAPITAL.**   A frequent cause of business failure is the lack of capital. A strong program to provide adequate capital is a primary element in providing for business continuity. Adequate capital is needed for both the short and long term, as well as appropriate relationships to provide continuing sources of capital. Chapter 4, "Financing the Business," addresses the accountant's role as an advisor in this area.

**MARKETING.**   Marketing is defined as the product planning, pricing, promotion, distribution, and servicing of goods and services needed and desired by consumers. It includes all the activities that companies perform in order to sell what they want to sell, where they want to sell it, when they want to sell it, how they want to sell it and on their own terms.

A company may not have a formal marketing plan. Competition may make a better product or sell an equally good product at a lower price. Consumers' tastes change rapidly. Population shifts and other demographic factors can change markets drastically. Production must be coordinated with sales. These factors require a formal marketing plan in order for the business to survive and grow.

**PRODUCTS AND SERVICES.**   This area is related to marketing but is more limited in scope. The problems the accountant/business advisor should seek to identify in this area are: Does the company regularly monitor its product lines (products or services) to verify that it is meeting the needs of its customers? Relying on a single product or service can be risky, because of technological (buggy whips) obsolescence, environmental (asbestos) considerations, and political (oil embargo) factors. There must be a commitment to research and development. Failure to have a marketable product or service will result in obsolete inventories, lost customers, or, at worst, business failure.

**PRODUCTION.**   When a business is started, one person or a small group may control all aspects of the manufacturing process on an informal basis and the company may operate effectively without any formal production control system. But, as the business grows, or as more items are added to the product line, the informal system often breaks down, resulting in unbalanced production, production delays due to lack of raw materials or components, and defective products.

An effective production control system provides for coordination of output with anticipated sales, thus minimizing the investment in finished goods inventories. This involves coordinating raw materials and purchased components with anticipated production, for both quantities and timing of delivery, with the objective of minimizing these inventories. It also means scheduling production to minimize costly overtime premium and/or excessive down-time, and controlling and minimizing scrap. (In turn, these factors will facilitate the effective use of plant and equipment.)

**HUMAN RESOURCES.**   All businesses rely on people. Their success or failure depends on their personnel. People make the decisions that control the destiny of any business. There must be an awareness for the proper human resources because a few key people can have a significant influence and impact on the entire operation.

**MANAGEMENT INFORMATION AND CONTROLS.**   As a business expands beyond the point where informally kept information can adequately assure the making of informed decisions, it is advisable to restructure the manner of disseminating information to assure that the necessary information is available to those individuals who need it. A management information system is vital to a business in order to maximize effectiveness. A formal information system will enable an organization to provide information that will enhance management decision making.

The following are some clues to look for when the accountant/business advisor is attempting to identify problems:

**Planning**

No budgets

No cash requirements forecast

No plan for management succession

**Shortages of Capital**

Slow receivables collections

Late payment of bills

Excessive interest costs

**Low Employee Morale**

High turnover

Excessive out-time

Recruiting difficulties

**Unsatisfactory Profit**

Below industry averages

Poor return on investment

Excessive costs

**Chronic Late Shipment**

Order cancellations

Partially completed orders

Widespread "rush" shipping charges

**Regular Production Delays**

Production bottlenecks

Shortage of materials

Excessive equipment down-time

**Low Inventory Turnover**

Below industry averages

Extensive writedowns

Obsolete inventory

**Poor Management**

Late

Incomplete

Inaccurate

Not going to right people

**Loss of Market Share**

Product

Population

Area

**Overburdened Executives and Managers**

Health problems

Family problems

Unused vacation time

**Increased Selling Expense**

Travel and entertainment

Advertising

Sales promotion

**Excessive Scrap or Promotion Rework**

Visually apparent

Material and labor yield tests

Extensive spoilage

**Pricing of Guesstimate**

Low gross margins

Lack of accurate cost information

Erratic pricing policies

**Unorganized or Confused Work Flows**

Lack of position descriptions

Nobody responsible

Unclear lines of reporting

**Large Paperwork Backlog**

Visually apparent

Lack of timely billing

Overworked clerical staff

# COMMUNICATE PROBLEMS TO CLIENT/EMPLOYER

Once the accountant/business advisor identifies problems, it is important that he or she communicate ideas and suggestions for solving the problems to the client/employer so that they can realize as soon as possible any potential benefits to be derived. The client/employer may approve the suggestions for immediate implementation and thereby expedite the benefits.

The final report is one method of accomplishing this communication and usually is a summary of information that has been communicated at various times during the course of identifying the problems, together with the accountant's recommendations.

The most difficult part of communications is listening. In order to communicate well, you must be a good listener. You must listen in order to find out where the client/employer is coming from—the past, the present, or the future. Is the client/employer defensive or aggressive; open or closed-minded? Does he or she have one of the following emotional needs: greed, fear, pride, guilt, anger, or acceptance? Accountants/business advisors need to provide in their communications, enthusiasm, confidence, hope, and obvious concern.

In communicating problems, the accountant should restate the problem; show how he or she can solve it; give assurances that it is acceptable to have help and identify, again, the need.

# INVENTORIES

The acquisition and management of inventories is critically important to most businesses. It often represents the largest use of corporate funds and consequently has a significant impact on current and future profitability. Inventory management is an area that offers the accountant considerable opportunity to provide valuable assistance and advice to clients/employers. Effective inventory management and control includes the following activities: purchase order control, receiving, materials control, security, production reporting, inventory costs control, and general controls.

**PURCHASING.**   Effective purchasing includes buying the right items, obtaining sufficient sources of supply, buying at competitive prices, obtaining items of acceptable quality, and acquiring inventory and/or materials on time in order to reduce backlogs. If the accountant sees evidence of inefficient purchasing— high costs, late deliveries, poor shipping and handling, and such—it may be advisable to recommend competitive bidding for new jobs where appropriate. Other suggestions are: using multiple sources of supply, clarifying specifications on purchase orders, using wholesale buying services where efficient and economical, and grouping purchases through effective planning. Negotiation may also be useful, particularly with high dollar-value items or in situations where numerous factors influence the price such as overall quantity, size of order, delivery terms, delivery dates, and so on.

**INVENTORY CONTROL.** Inventory control goes hand in hand with purchasing. Once the company has determined the kind and quality of material it needs, the approximate quantities needed, and expected usage rates, there will be other major decisions concerning how much should be purchased and delivered at any one time. Inventory control has the objective of optimizing the balance between items purchased, used, and stored for future use. The following elements are common to most organizations:[1]

1.  **Stocks on Hand.** The maximum amount of an item which is desirable to be carried in inventory, or the amount needed for any production, is a combination of the amount already on hand and the amount which is procured and added to stocks already held.

2.  **Time and Extent of Probable Use.** This is based on the production data which provides information as to the time the item is to be used, the amount to be used, and the stability of that use.

3.  **Storage Costs.** This is the carrying cost of the item up until the time of use. This can include a space cost for the storage, labor, security devices, utilities and insurance as well as the time value of the money tied up in inventory.

4.  **Obsolescence.** In making decisions on the quantity of an item to be purchased, the possibility of changes in production plans and developments from research which may render the material obsolete should be given due consideration.

5.  **Handling Charges.** Factors which may or may not make it economical to purchase in large quantities items which may need to be stored at a distance from the production facility need to be considered.

6.  **Transportation Charges.** Transportation cost considerations include carload versus less-than-carload rates, and allowances by suppliers on shipments of certain volumes.

7.  **Cost of Buying.** This factor is particularly important in the purchase

[1] Wilbur B. England, *Modern Procurement Management* (Richard D. Irwin, Inc., Homewood, Ill., 1970), pp. 406–407.

of items of small value. Buying costs include labor, travel and lodging for out-of-town trips, cost of buying services or agents, and such.

8. **Quantity Price Differentials.** Many or perhaps most items will be offered at a quantity discount for large volume orders.

9. **Market Conditions and Price Trends.** Conditions will continually be shifting in both the market (industry and company factors) as well as the economy (degree of inflation and level of interest rates).

10. **Time Required for Delivery.** The degree of urgency in the timing of shipments can also have a great impact on transportation charges, as "rush" shipments will bear a premium charge.

11. **Financial Resources of the Buyer.** The amount of money available to the purchaser as well as the interest costs associated with it are crucial variables.

12. **Opportunity Cost of the Investment in Inventory.** If the investment is not made in the inventory, what other opportunities are available to the company (i.e., what are the sacrifices made by the company in order to invest in the inventory?).

Each of the preceding elements can influence the most economical quantity to buy and the quantity to be stored on premises. Balance is the key objective, because too much or too little of any item may result in unnecessarily high operating costs and an overall detriment to the company. There is also another item not included in the above list—the cost of being out of stock. The possible loss in customer confidence, the firm's reputation, or even wholesale defections to other suppliers may be the most critical factor of all. An out-of-stock situation for more than two or three days may be totally unacceptable to the organization.

**INVENTORY CONTROL METHODS.** *Economic order quantity* (EOQ) systems are commonly referred to as maximum-minimum methods. Mathematical formulas exist to determine the most economical quantity to order at any given time. Such systems balance the time necessary to receive inventory orders, the cost of placing each order, and the carrying charges of storing inventories, as well as taking into account the rate of obsolescence, price fluctuations, and available quantity discounts. Once the standard quantity is determined, the reorder point is determined and implemented. This is the point at which the placing of an order will give sufficient time to receive the item, so that the stock-on-hand will be reduced to the bare minimum if the maximum order time occurs.

A second, less sophisticated method of inventory control involves the *manufacture of goods to order* rather than for stock. Under this method, items are purchased when a specific order is received or contract is negotiated. Even when goods are manufactured to order, however, manufacturers may take advantage of unusually attractive purchasing terms to buy items in anticipation of future orders.

*Forward buying of materials* is yet another method that may be used, but it is more speculative in nature. As with other commodities, the buyer hedges against future market conditions by placing an order to receive goods at a future date with a price fixed in today's terms. Depending of the price paid, the buyer is in essence gambling that the price of the materials will rise or fall in the future, and is therefore locking in the current price.

*Material requirements planning (MRP)* is an important inventory control tool that has enjoyed widespread popularity in manufacturing companies in recent years. The objectives of material requirements planning are similar to those of other inventory planning systems in that MRP attempts to order sufficient quantities of materials to fulfill the company's production plan while minimizing the investment in inventories. However, it differs from other inventory control systems in that it anticipates future demand rather than relying on historical data.

Three major elements enter into material requirements planning: a master production schedule for all products, normally on a weekly basis; a bill of materials which details the exact parts and materials necessary to produce each item of inventory; and an inventory record file which contains the information on perpetual inventory status of every item in inventory, including quantity on hand and quantity on order, as well as the expected receiving date for arriving shipments and necessary lead time for future orders. The quantity of materials to be ordered each week is then determined by the computer, using the information from the master production schedule, bill of materials, and inventory record file. As with other systems, it is critical that accurate information be fed into the computer. However, it is useful to note that the information base that is needed for MRP is useful in an overall management information system for the organization.

Japanese firms have carried the concept of *just-in-time purchasing* systems to the extreme. The objective is for materials to arrive just in time to be used in the manufacturing process. Optimally, a manufacturer using a just-in-time system would maintain no raw material inventories at all. Obviously, under such a system, shipments from suppliers must be received daily or even twice a day. Obviously, for this system to succeed, the manufacturer must have an extremely high turnover of finished goods. In addition, it is critical under this system that vendors are highly reliable in securing adequate quantities, acceptable quality, and reliable prices. Also, because the system is so highly dependent upon precise production forecasts, it will not be applicable to companies that cannot forecast their demand with this degree of accuracy.

**MAKE OR BUY.**  A company will often purchase manufactured parts on the outside that enter into its own production process; however, the company may be able to manufacture some of these parts itself. A multitude of questions, in addition to cost, may then enter the decision-making process, as the company decides whether to make or buy the part. Some of these questions are: Can the parts be manufactured by unused capacity or will additional capital investment be necessary? Is it desirable to have additional sources of supply? Will it help the company to maintain a stable work force during slow periods? Will the quality be comparable for parts made by the company or purchased from the outside?

**INTERNAL CONTROL AND SECURITY.**  Internal control and security starts at the point at which inventories are received. Internal control includes comparing purchase orders, shipping reports, receiving reports and actual goods to make sure that all inventories ordered are in fact received or accounted for. Physical control at the manufacturing plant or warehouse includes physical security to protect against misappropriation, spoilage or, where possible, obsolescence. Security continues through the entire production process as materials are converted into inventories with the aid of labor and overhead.

Inventory cost control requires an effective cost accounting system to record costs of production accurately. Although design and implementation of such systems is a normal function of management accountants, external auditors often participate in the process as well, particularly for those companies lacking extensive internal accounting expertise.

**PRODUCTION.**  The accountant should also be alert to observing inefficient or obsolete production processes. Technological advances have increased almost exponentially in recent years, and it may be possible for clients/employers to more efficiently and effectively manufacture inventories through investment in new technology. The fixed cost of investing in new plant and equipment may be more than offset by savings in labor, materials usage, production time, and energy usage.

**PRICING.**  In smaller companies, accountants may be significant advisors in helping to determine pricing policies or even specific prices. Accountants are particularly valuable resources in this area, because they are responsible for establishing cost accounting systems which provide the data on which many pricing decisions are made. They are in an excellent position to determine relevant costs to use in deciding, for example, on aggressive pricing decisions to stimulate sales. In this context, accountants are particularly valuable in determining levels at which incremental revenues will exceed incremental costs.

Accountants can help to determine specific prices that will yield desired profit margins, and evaluate the potential effect of pricing decisions on sales volume and profits. The most common method for making decisions in this area is cost-volume-profit (CVP) analysis which is highlighted by the break-even chart. Accountants can also help determine product-pricing formulas given the goals and objectives of management.

# MARKETING ADMINISTRATION

From a cost perspective, accountants are in an advantageous position to evaluate the cost-effectiveness of various marketing strategies, however difficult this may be. Given appropriate data, accountants may attempt to evaluate the effectiveness of various advertising and sales promotion campaigns, determine the suitability of commission sales incentives, help establish or evaluate bonus compensation plans, help determine the overall advertising budget, or evaluate the adequacy of various marketing costs such as travel, room and board, and entertainment expenses. In all of these areas, the accountant's primary role is related directly or indirectly to financial measurements.

# ECONOMIC AND GENERAL BUSINESS CONDITIONS

The accountant is often seen as an astute business observer, possessing a wealth of knowledge to help analyze and interpret general economic and business conditions. For example, the knowledgeable accountant is expected to keep abreast of inflationary or disinflationary pressures as evidenced by general economic indicators. Accordingly, the accountant will be aware of upturns or downturns in the economy; recessionary influences; economic stimuli such as new housing starts, production backlogs, pent-up consumer demand, and inventory levels; relative strength of the dollar; aggregate money supply; fluctuations in foreign exchange markets and restrictions, and so on.

Of particular interest to most clients/employers are the current and expected trends of interest rates, because they have a potential to significantly increase or decrease a company's profitability or its ability to raise adequate capital. The accountant will often be asked for his or her opinion on the future direction of the economy or on the expected structure of interest rates. Although the accountant may make an informed decision, he or she should state clearly that this is in fact personal opinion not based on in-depth specialized expertise in this area.

In addition to general economic conditions, the accountant should be knowledgeable with respect to general business conditions. Through a regular reading program of selected daily, weekly, and monthly periodicals, as well as regular reading of economic services such as those published by banks, the accountant can stay informed at a level sufficient to speak knowledgeably with clients/employers. Of particular interest to most organizations is a working knowledge of special factors impacting the industry in which the organization operates. Supply and demand for the company's product, relative strength or weakness of competitors, direct or indirect competition from abroad, adequate labor supply such as in skilled areas, recruiting trends in the industry, and the impact of technological advances on the industry are a partial list of items relevant to the organization. Industry statistics, such as those published by Robert Morris and Standard and Poor, are other sources of data which the accountant can access.

# MANAGEMENT ACCOUNTING FUNCTIONS

For smaller organizations that do not have adequate in-house management accounting expertise, the external auditor will often help with management accounting functions. Included here are design and administration of a cost accounting system, assistance in preparing and evaluating operating and capital budgets, establishing and administrating management information systems, conducting operational audits, and setting up a responsibility accounting system to measure the effectiveness of each department.

Of course, the accountant's independence may come into question when designing systems that will be audited at a later date. However, the same consideration will come into play if an accountant participates in management decision making as opposed to helping to determine decision criteria for management to use in making their own decisions. Consequently, it is important that the accountant's role be limited to performing feasibility studies, designing and recommending systems, and assisting in implementation rather than making actual management decisions.

# SOUNDING BOARD

There is no greater measure of confidence that an employer or client can show the accountant than to call on him or her as a trusted overall advisor. The accountant, whether internal or external to the organization, may be thought of as having a great deal of expertise and sound judgment. Consequently, when management needs to make strategic decisions, it is often logical to consult the accountant(s).

There is virtually no limit to the areas in which accountants can serve as a general sounding board. For instance, management may be contemplating opening a new plant. It therefore wants to determine whether an additional shift at the existing plant may be more desirable or less desirable than opening a new plant with a large new capital investment. Or, it may be considering expanding into a new market that it has not previously served. For example, a publisher that has previously sold exclusively to colleges and universities may be considering entering the secondary school market or even the retail home market.

Accountants may also be asked to help identify and evaluate various candidates for mergers and/or acquisitions. In addition to helping to identify and select candidates, the accountant can perform many other functions in connection with mergers and acquisitions (see Chapter 11 on this subject).

Managerial succession is another area in which accountants may be called on for advice. Management may wish the external auditor to give an opinion on the suitability of various candidates for key managerial positions.

The list of areas in which accountants can serve as advisors is virtually unlimited. For example, accountants may be asked to evaluate the possibility of closing a factory, leasing a corporate airplane, entering a foreign market, establishing a new incentive bonus system, modernizing a production process, establishing a new pension plan, deciding on a salary compensation system, negotiating a new contract with the union, establishing a new health plan or other fringe benefits, or deciding how to lay out an office for maximum efficiency. The range in areas in which accountants will be asked for advice will be based upon the esteem in which the accountant is held and the other internal capabilities that the company possesses outside of the accounting functions. The accountant who is an effective business advisor will be able to respond appropriately and decisively. However, it is important for the accountant to indicate to management the limits on his or her degree of expertise in the area, and for external auditors to scrupulously maintain their independence.

# TRAINING

**BACKGROUND AND ORIENTATION.**  Accountants and auditors, by nature of their formal education and work experience, have a unique perspective that can prove to be of great help in training their clients or own organizations. By most standards, accountants and auditors—whether external auditors, internal auditors, or management accountants—are among the best educated of professional groups. In their university curriculum, they study all areas of accounting and auditing, plus a wide range of other business subjects, including computers, quantitative analysis, and taxation. Their curriculum includes corporate finance and investments, economics, and marketing, and there are usually elective courses in other business fields such as real estate and insurance. This obviously does not imply that accountants are experts in all of these areas, but it does mean that they have the background necessary to understand the basic concepts in each of these areas.

Of equal importance, accountants have a decided need to stay current in their field. Professional pronouncements are issued regularly in accounting and auditing, tax laws continuously change, computers and software are still in the evolutionary stages, and audit tools—specific audit software packages, sampling techniques, and risk analysis theories—are also undergoing rapid change. Faced by all these changes, accountants must continually educate themselves on a sink-or-swim basis. Accountants stay current by regularly reading professional pronouncements, new tax laws, business periodicals, and current news. Additionally, whether by choice or formal regulation, they undergo one of the most rigorous continuing professional education (CPE) programs of any professional group. Most CPAs, for example, regularly receive 40 hours of CPE annually.

Each of our basic groups—external auditors, internal auditors, and management accountants—has considerable access to and respect within the organizations they serve. The independent certified public accountant is often considered to be an outside expert, a continual source of knowledge to the client organization. The internal auditor, either in a separate internal role or when assisting the outside auditor, needs to know the latest auditing techniques, accounting and auditing pronouncements, and the most efficient, effective systems when performing an operational audit. The management accountant also needs to know the latest accounting pronouncements, have a basic knowledge of tax laws, understand the latest budgeting and cost accounting techniques, and understand accounting systems and controls.

Each group is held in high regard by the organization for their knowledge and technical expertise. Because of this, accountants and auditors are a prime source for training members of their own/client organizations. This training may take the form of on-the-job training or be part of a formal continuing professional education program. External auditing firms, particularly the larger firms that have extensive human resources and other training resources, are often called upon to train other accountants and auditors in client organizations.

**SUBJECT AREAS.**  Most of the subjects covered in this book represent potential areas for accountants to train their clients/own organization. However, the full range of subjects extends beyond those detailed here. Basically, they can be divided into five convenient categories: professional pronouncements, legislation, managerial accounting and systems, product knowledge, and other business advisory areas.

**Professional Pronouncements.**    As stated previously, accountants and auditors have to keep pace with the latest professional pronouncements in their field. This includes pronouncements issued on accounting subjects by the Financial Accounting Standards Board, auditing standards issued by the Auditing Standards Board, reporting requirements for publicly held companies issued by the SEC, Industry Audit and Accounting Guides issued by the American Institute of Certified Public Accountants, governmental standards issued by the Governmental Auditing Standards Board, and cost accounting standards promulgated by the Cost Accounting Standard Board. Depending on the primary area of their work, accountants and auditors will need to know in considerable detail about the pronouncements issued by one or more of the above groups. They are then in a unique position to train others in their own organization or client companies.

**Legislation.**    One thing is certain—the tax laws will continually change. In recent years alone, we have seen sweeping tax Acts passed by Congress, including the Tax Reform Act of 1976, Economic Recovery Tax Act of 1981, Tax Equity and Fiscal Responsibility Act of 1982, and the Tax Reform Act of 1984. Each of these, as well as other changes enacted by the federal legislature, has posed immense changes in areas such as depreciation, investment credit policies and procedures, pensions and profit-sharing plans, real estate, lease financing, executive perks, and so on. As these changes have occurred, and as sure as they will occur in the future, accountants and auditors are in an excellent position to train others who rely on their advice.

**Managerial Accounting and Systems.**    The topics included in this category are all-encompassing, including such areas as responsibility accounting, conventional budgeting, capital budgeting, internal control systems, and cost accounting systems involving job order costs, process costs, and/or standard costs. This does not even include the other areas of managerial decision making such as make versus buy, escapable versus inescapable cost, lease versus purchase, breakeven (cost-volume-profit) analysis, and others. Accountants are not only in a position to assist their own companies/clients in making the correct decisions, but also in briefing corporate managers/executives with the appropriate knowledge to aid them in making their own decisions.

**Product Knowledge.**    Increasingly, accountants are being called on to aid others in complex areas of product knowledge. For example, consider the banking industry. The range of product knowledge needed by bankers today is very large and constantly expanding. The area of mortgage financing, once a fairly straightforward subject, has recently changed drastically through such new types of financing as variable rate mortgages, home equity financing (second mortgages), and other techniques fueled by the twin specters of high inflation and rapidly fluctuating interest rates.

The area of foreign exchange, and in particular the complex area of swaps, is another topic to be considered. Internal auditors, for instance, need detailed knowledge of these areas in order to do their own work. This may then put them in an excellent position to train others in their own organizations.

**TRAINING METHODS AND TECHNIQUES.**    Many observers have tried to distinguish between the terms *training* and *education*. In fact, some have taken an entirely different viewpoint and called the area *professional development*. An individual who felt that the term *training* was condescending once said, "You train animals but you educate people." These distinctions have always seemed specious to this author, who has spent the better part of the last 20 years working in all areas of education at the professional, corporate, and university levels. The important concept is that one never stops learning and that education is a lifelong process. The means by which accountants and auditors can aid in this process are numerous.

**On-the-Job Training.**    Accountants and auditors are continually working with and/or exposed to others in their own organization. This provides a particular opportunity to educate fellow employees with on-the-job training. The extent to which this exists will, of course, depend on the size of the organization. For example, the accountant may be called on to explain applications of an electronic spread sheet software package that has recently been purchased. Or, the accountant may be asked to help interpret financial statements issued by the company itself or by competitors. Or, the accountants may be asked to help evaluate the terms of a proposed leasing arrangement or the financing terms of a proposed merger. In all of these areas, accountants may be able to provide on-the-job training as well as expertise in solving the problems.

**Meetings with Executives.**    Depending on the size of the organization, accountants or internal auditors may be asked to hold briefings when new pronouncements, legislation, or other noteworthy business events occur. Or, they may provide a regularly monthly briefing. The external auditor has a similar opportunity to provide this service whenever professional pronouncements, tax changes, new business practices, or other financial developments occur. These executive briefings, often held at the initiative of the accountant, are also excellent practice development opportunities. Failure to provide such briefings may provide an opening for other accountants to fill the void.

**Client Newsletters and Other Publications.**   Many accounting firms, and certainly not just the largest firms in today's environment, publish newsletters which they regularly send to their clients. These are intended to keep clients abreast of the latest trends and techniques. Particularly common are extensive analyses of the latest tax law changes, or year-end tax planning opportunities, as well as detailed analyses of new accounting and/or auditing pronouncements. So common are such newsletters and related publications today, that failure to provide these will often place a particular firm at an extreme competitive disadvantage.

**Group Seminars.**   When new tax changes or other significant events occur, many firms will choose to schedule public seminars in which all clients and other friends of the firm are invited to attend. These events are often provided free of charge to clients, and at a considerable cost to the accounting firms that provide them. In return, the firms expect to be able to provide more detailed advice to clients on a fee basis in the areas being discussed. Such seminars are an excellent opportunity for clients to keep abreast of important new events.

**Formal Continuing Professional Education Programs.**   This area provides opportunities for all major areas of accountants and auditors—whether in public accounting, management accounting, or internal auditing. Today, the largest public accounting firms, and many smaller ones as well, provide seminars to clients. They may consist of programs tailored specifically to a client's own needs, such as an educational program on an oil and gas accounting pronouncement for a client/company in the petroleum industry. Or, a new tax act may be analyzed specifically in terms of how it affects a particular company's business. Details for such seminars conducted by external auditors are often arranged between the accounting firm and the client on a regular fee basis as with any other engagement. Internal accountants and auditors are in a similar position to provide educational programs to others in their organizations when major events occur.

**Public Seminars.**   Public accounting firms are increasingly scheduling public seminars, which both clients and nonclients are invited to attend. Such seminars are normally priced at the full retail value in line with rates charged by other professional organizations that conduct seminars as part of their regular business. Of course, clients comprise a significant portion of the audience who attend these programs. Nonclients who attend represent a potential area of business expansion for the public accounting firms.

## SUMMARY

In this chapter we have described a methodology which accountants can use to help identify and communicate problems to clients/employers. The model is valuable in determining areas in which accountants can serve as business advisors. We have discussed briefly many of the areas not previously covered in greater depth in other chapters in this book. Two such areas are inventories—purchasing, inventory control, make or buy, internal control and security, production and pricing—and training, in which the accountant can help to educate clients/ employers in areas that accountants have particular expertise.

# INDEX